BISON
BOOKS

Digging Up Butch and Sundance

REVISED EDITION

Anne Meadows

University of Nebraska Press
Lincoln and London

⊖ The paper in this book meets the minimum requirements of American
National Standard for Information Sciences—Permanence of Paper for Printed
Library Materials, ANSI Z39.48-1984.

First Bison Books printing: 1996
Most recent printing indicated by the last digit below:
10 9   8   7   6   5   4   3   2   1

Library of Congress Cataloging-in-Publication Data
Meadows, Anne, 1948–
Digging up Butch and Sundance / Anne Meadows.
p. cm.
Includes bibliographical references and index.
ISBN 0-8032-8225-7 (pbk.: alk. paper)
1. Cassidy, Butch, b. 1866 2. Sundance Kid. 3. Outlaws—West (U.S.)
4. Outlaws—South America. 5. South America—Description and travel.
6. Adventure and adventurers—South America. I. Title.
F595.C362M42   1996
364.1′55′0922—dc20
96-11934   CIP

For Dan, Muth, and Lawren

CONTENTS

	Introduction	ix
1.	Cholila	1
2.	Hooked on History	18
3.	*Gringos* in Patagonia	38
4.	*Bandoleros* on the Run	63
5.	Nowhere to Hide	87
6.	Life After Death	105
7.	The Road to San Vicente	130
8.	The Aramayo Papers	154
9.	Chilean Hopscotch	172
10.	Old-Timers and *Ancianos*	200
11.	The Dead Cow	221
12.	The Man in the *Casa Rodante*	245
13.	The Boneyard	275
14.	Next of Kin	301
15.	Dust to Dust	331
	Some Sources	362
	Acknowledgments	365
	Index	373

INTRODUCTION

THE villagers shoo their children out of the cemetery in case the sacrifice fails to appease the spirits we are about to set loose in this barren bowl 14,370 feet up in the Bolivian Andes. Standing amid the jumble of tombstones and tin crosses, the mayor of San Vicente mumbles a few words in Spanish, and lesser officials pray in Quechua to the earth goddess Pachamama. Ribboned wreaths of plastic flowers flap and rattle in the icy wind. Forensic anthropologist Clyde Snow lays a long cigar on top of a crumbling concrete grave marker, and the rest of us add offerings—cigarettes, *coca* leaves, dashes of cane alcohol. A pickax bites into the hard soil. Three crones huddling on nearby tombs pull their shawls snug and prophesy disaster. The ritual completed, the children stream back into the cemetery to watch our international band of gravediggers try to solve one of the last great mysteries of the North American West: What really happened to Butch Cassidy and the Sundance Kid?

Did they die in a shootout with half the Bolivian army, as the characters played by Paul Newman and Robert Redford did at the end of the 1969 hit movie *Butch Cassidy and the Sundance Kid*? Or did they survive and return to the United States, as many researchers have claimed? The film was based on a true story, but how true was it?

Butch and Sundance were real people, although the names we know them by were not the ones they were born with. Butch led an outlaw band—known variously as the Wild Bunch, the Hole-in-the-Wall Gang, and the Train Robbers' Syndicate—that roamed the Rocky Mountain West in the late 1800s and early 1900s. The celluloid version of Sundance was a composite of the real Sundance and a man named Elzy Lay, who was Butch's best friend in the early days.

The outlaws perfected a formula of thoroughly casing prospective holdup sites, scouting the best escape routes, and stashing food and fresh horses at strategic places for fast getaways. Butch's meticulous planning allowed them to hit targets on the very days when substantial amounts of cash were on hand. The robberies planned by other members of the gang were not always successful, but between 1889 and 1901

Butch and his pals made off with some $200,000—the equivalent of $2.5 million today. The bandits' professionalism won them respect even from their enemies. In 1924, an official at the Pinkerton Detective Agency wrote that members of the Wild Bunch had committed "few murders in comparison to their great number of bold crimes. Their code must have been higher than [that of] the low class of criminal today, who kills on sight and gets away with motors."

Butch and Sundance's companion in exile was Etta Place, a tall, slender, Victorian enigma: She could ride and shoot as well as Annie Oakley in the morning and throw a tea party worthy of Emily Post in the afternoon. The Pinkerton detectives who dogged the Wild Bunch for years never found out who Etta really was, where she came from, or what happened to her. Her surname is an alias, acquired when she traveled as the wife of Harry A. Place, a name used by Sundance in South America. Her first name is also in doubt. The Pinkertons called her Ethel, Ethal, Eva, and Rita, before settling on Etta for their WANTED circulars. A detective's tracing of her signature from a hotel register shows that she went by Ethel, which may or may not have been her real name. Researchers have devoted a staggering amount of time to tracking down this most elusive member of the Wild Bunch, and several women have been posthumously nominated for the position. She has been portrayed as a teacher or a prostitute or both. But as the years slide by, Etta Place's true identity slips further and further beyond our ken.

Thanks to Butch and Sundance's roguish wit, polished to a modern sheen by screenwriter William Goldman, movie audiences fell in love with them. If a few western-history buffs disputed the film's accuracy, who was listening? Not I. What did it matter? Not much. A good story is a good story. As often happens, however, Hollywood skipped an interesting chapter: Instead of simply moving their criminal enterprise from the United States to Bolivia, the bandits and their winsome moll went to Argentina and tried to go straight before blazing the new outlaw trail that eventually led them to Bolivia.

When my husband, Dan Buck, and I learned that the trio had ranched for several years in northern Patagonia, one of our favorite places, we wanted to know more. Thinking that it might be fun to visit the bandits' homestead, we took a book about Butch Cassidy with us on vacation to Argentina in the mid-1980s. The South American section of the book was brief, because little was known of the outlaws' lives there, but one chapter included the text of a letter Butch had written to the mother-in-law of his friend Elzy Lay, who was in prison at the time.

Cholila, [Territory of] Chubut
Argentine Republic, S.Am.
August 10, 1902

Mrs. Davis
Ashley, Utah

My dear friend,

    I suppose you have thought long before this that I had forgotten you (or was dead) but my dear friend I am still alive, and when I think of my Old friends you are always the first to come to my mind. It will probably surprise you to hear from me away down in this country, but U.S. was too small for me. The last two years I was there, I was restless. I wanted to see more of the world. I had seen all of the U.S. that I thought was good, and a few months after I sent A——— over to see you, and get the Photo of the rope jumping of which I have got here and often look at and wish I could see the originals, and I think I could liven some of the characters up a little, for Maudie looks very sad to me. Another of my uncles died and left $30,000, Thirty Thousand, to our little family of 3 [a reference to the Winnemucca, Nevada, bank robbery committed by Butch, Sundance, and Will Carver in 1900], so I took my $10,000 and started to see a little more of the world. I visited the best Cities and best parts of the countrys [*sic*] of South A. till I got here, and this part of the country looked so good that I located, and I think for good, for I like the place better every day. I have 300 cattle, 1500 sheep, and 28 good Saddle horses, 2 men to do my work, also good 4-room house, wearhouse [*sic*], stable, chicken house and some chickens. The only thing lacking is a cook, for I am still living in Single Cussedness and I sometimes feel very lonely, for I am alone all day [Sundance and Etta were away at the time], and my neighbors don't amount to anything, besides, the only language spoken in this country is Spanish, and I don't speak it well enough yet to converse on the latest scandals so dear to the hearts of all nations, and without which conversations are very stale, but the country is first class. The only industry at present is stock raising (that is in this part) and it can't be beat for that purpose, for I have never seen a finer grass country, and lots of it hundreds and hundreds of miles that is unsettled and comparatively unknown, and where I am it is a good agricultural country. All kind of small grain and vegetables grow without Irrigation, but I am at the foot of the Andes Mountains, and all the land east of here is prairie and Deserts, very good for stock, but for farming it would have to be irrigated, but there is plenty of good land along the Mountains for all the people that will be here for the next hundred years, for I am a long way from Civilization. It is 16 hundred miles to Buenos Aires, the Capital of the Argentine, and over 400 miles to the nearest Rail Road or Sea Port in the Argentine Republic, but only about 150 miles to the Pacific Coast [of] Chile, but to get there we have to cross the mountains, which was thought impossible till last summer, when it was found that the Chilean Gov. had cut a road almost across, so that next summer we will be able to go to Port Mont, Chile, in about 4 days, where it use to take 2 months around the old trail, and it will be a great benefit to us for Chile is our Beef market and we can get our cattle there in $\frac{1}{10}$ the time and have them fat. And we can also get supplies in Chile for one third what they cost here. The climate here is a great deal milder than Ashley Valley. The summers are beautiful, never as warm as there. And grass knee high everywhere and lots of good cold mountain water, but the winters are very wet and disagreeable, for it rains most of the time, but sometimes we have lots of snow, but it don't last long, for it never gets cold enough to freeze much. I have never seen Ice one inch thick.

The rest of the letter is missing, perhaps discarded because of an incriminating signature. Enough survived, however, to lure us to Cholila. There, we found not only the ranch but also the mystery, and what had begun as a lark turned into a quest that has dragged us across two continents and more than a century back in time along the hazy boundary between history and folklore, in search of the truth behind the legend.

1 · CHOLILA

A DOG begins barking as we wade through the daisies and tall grass toward a cluster of wooden shacks aglow with afternoon sun in a stand of willows beside the Blanco River. To the west, granite peaks jut from the green foothills of the Patagonian Andes. A pair of roan horses edges away from us and nuzzles the fence by the gravel highway. As we approach the weathered buildings, the barking darkens into a growl.

"*Buenas tardes,*" Dan shouts.

I grab his hand, as if that would make a difference to any self-respecting canine, and we pass through a gate in the vine-tangled picket fence. Before us stands a log cabin straight out of nineteenth-century Wyoming.

"*¡Hola!*" I call, knocking on the front door. No answer, but the growl changes pitch.

We try the door, peer through the dirty windows, circle the cabin. "Nice doggie," I say from time to time. The beast does not show itself. Must be tied up somewhere—probably chewing through the rope at this very moment.

A wild-boar skin hangs like a coat of arms on the adjacent shed, which sags with age, its door permanently ajar. As we draw near, the growling ceases. Dan peers cautiously inside and chuckles. I squeeze past him into the low room. Light filters through chinks in the walls and dapples the set of leather saddlebags hanging from the rafters. Beneath a bench, a white sheepdog cowers.

A pickup truck clatters across the field and lurches to a stop by the picket fence. Out jumps a silver-haired man wearing blue jeans and a black beret. "*Buenas tardes,*" he yells. Introducing himself as Miguel Calderón, the owner of the Welsh teahouse where we stopped earlier for directions, he shakes Dan's hand and kisses mine. "You are looking for the *bandoleros,* no?"

"Right," says Dan. "Butch Cassidy and the Sundance Kid."

"Was there not a woman, as well?"

A feminist man in deepest Latin America!

He winks at Dan. "The woman was a beauty, no?"

Oh well.

"Etta Place," says Dan, "Sundance's girlfriend. Was this their house?"

"*Sí, sí,*" he says. "You can tell by the windows."

The windows? Surely we misunderstood him. This cabin has perfectly ordinary four-pane double-hung windows.

Don Miguel strides over and thumps the nearest window frame. "They are foreign, these windows. And the construction." He pats one of the hand-hewn cypress logs and brushes loose plaster from the chink above it. "We don't make houses like this. If we use wood at all, we use planks. Around here, we mostly use bricks or stones or concrete."

The cabin's current inhabitant, Don Miguel tells us, is a *gaucho* named Aladín Sepúlveda, who spends most of his time in the hills with his sheep. "It's just as well you didn't find him at home. Aladín is not particularly sociable, and it is said that he sometimes shoots at people who come poking around. Not that I believe everything I hear."

In the morning, over a breakfast of *café con leche* and homemade bread with rose-hip jam in a small inn on the shore of nearby Mosquito Lake, we meet Aladín Sepúlveda's niece Melania, who has recently married and is visiting Cholila for the first time in a decade. An effervescent blonde with sunburned cheeks, she has come from Buenos Aires to introduce her husband, Carlos, to her family, and she insists that we come along to meet Uncle Aladín.

Thus we find ourselves once more at the log cabin; this time the occupant is home. Standing in his front yard, wearing a white shirt and baggy brown *bombachas*, Aladín Sepúlveda looks every centimeter the working *gaucho*. Tucked beneath his red-and-green woven belt is the Argentine equivalent of the Swiss Army knife: the ubiquitous *facón*, whose single blade is more than enough for carving meat, picking teeth, or skewering nosy tourists.

Don Aladín was born in the cabin in 1923 and has lived here most of his life. His father, Rómulo Sepúlveda, came over the Andes from Chile to Cholila in the late 1800s at the age of seventeen, worked for Armando Duarte, sired fifteen children, and died in the 1950s. Don Aladín isn't sure how his family wound up at the cabin and doesn't know much about the North American bandits, although he vaguely recalls hearing stories about their having killed people. He has no idea what became of them. And clearly has no interest in the subject.

If he is displeased at our intrusion, however, he is helpless in the face of his niece's insistent cheerfulness. Like a frisky collie, Melania herds us around the grounds. Along the way, she names all the vegetables in the garden and points out the unusual aspects of the cabin's construction: "The windows go up and down instead of in and out!"

She pauses in a patch of lavender and Queen Anne's lace beside a wooden table laden with empty hard-cider bottles. "Boots Cassidy built a room underground in case he needed to hide from the police. Or maybe he kept his gold down there. I'm not sure. Anyway, nobody knew about it until one day when my mother was playing in the yard with her brothers and sisters, and she suddenly fell through the ground into the secret chamber." Melania's eyes widen. "The bandits didn't leave much of anything in it, but Mama still has an old strongbox she found there, and they had a telephone down there, too. It was the first phone in the valley. They used it to communicate with their lookout in the brick building two hundred meters down the road."

"On this side of the road?" Dan is taking notes.

"*Sí, sí.* It is a machine shop now. Señor Daher owns it. That's where Boots Cassidy died after the police shot him." Opening the back door, she calls to her uncle: "You don't mind if we look around inside, do you?"

Don Aladín's white brows knit above his rheumy eyes, but Melania and Carlos are already through the door, and our curiosity outweighs our sense of propriety. We step into a dark kitchen with a rotting wooden floor and a cast-iron stove, which Melania says belonged to the North Americans. To the rear is a cluttered bedroom. I take a quick peek, but my conscience checks me, and I move on into the living room. Above the scarred wainscoting, patches of faded wallpaper hang by little more than inertia; the paste has long since lost its hold on the wooden walls. Some of the wallpaper has been replaced with old newspapers, which have also begun to peel. What wallpaper remains is several layers thick. The bottom layer—the one the bandits must have installed—is a burgundy-and-gold brocade. Melania tears off a piece and hands it to me. Mercifully, her uncle is outside playing with his dog and doesn't notice. No wonder he shoots at tourists.

Against the south wall is an unmade bed with clothing piled on it. Stirrups hang from a rafter in the middle of the room, which is lit by a bare bulb. "In Boots Cassidy's day," chirps Melania, "they had brass lamps imported from the United States."

"Probably packed a Sears catalog along with their revolvers," says Dan.

Doors leading to two additional rooms are closed, and one is padlocked. Carlos starts to open the other door, but Dan says, "That's all right."

These shabby quarters are hard to reconcile with reports of how the place looked when Butch, Sundance, and Etta lived here. According to Primo Capraro, an Italian immigrant who passed through Cholila in 1904 and spent a night with them:

> The house was simply furnished and exhibited a certain pains-taking tidiness, a geometric arrangement of things, pictures with cane frames, wallpaper made of clippings from North American magazines, and many beautiful weapons and lassos braided from horsehair. The men were tall, slender, laconic, and nervous, with intense gazes. The lady, who was reading, was well-dressed. I had a friendly dinner with them, and as I couldn't offer them any gratuity, I made them a detailed sketch of a bungalow. I figured the necessary quantity of bricks, window panes, ironwork, nails, bolts, metal sheets, and even the projected number of windows, doors, tables, beds, ward-robes, chairs, etc. We agreed that in the event that they under-took the project, I would come down to Cholila with workers I would recruit in Bariloche. The trio lived near Mr. Perry, also a North American.
>
> Later, I learned that they were famous robbers of trains and banks in North America as well as in Argentina. They re-solved to go straight, but hanging over them was a reward of $10,000 a head, and someone informed on them to the North American authorities. They found out about it and ... pro-ceeded on to Chile and Peru, where it seems a military patrol killed them after they had attempted to rob a land shipment of gold ingots from a mine in Peru. Those who knew them well said that they were expert shooters capable of hitting a coin in the air.

Once we have finished snooping around the cabin, Melania and Carlos take us to a neighboring *estancia* to meet Raúl Cea, whose father—a miller named Manuel José Cea—was a teenager during the bandits' time in Cholila and knew them well. As we approach the hulking wooden mill, which dates back to 1909, Don Raúl's wife—a handsome, broad-shouldered woman in a turtleneck sweater, black skirt, and open-toed shoes—comes out to greet us.

"I can't help you, but Raúl would know about the *bandoleros*," says Doña Yolanda, brushing her thick hair away from her face. Her deep-set eyes, thin lips, and hollow cheeks are unspoiled by makeup. "If you want to wait for him, he should be back soon."

5

In the meantime, she fills Melania in on the local gossip, and Carlos—brand-new husband that he is—listens intently to their conversation, while Dan and I try to lure a kitten out from under the mill. The kitten is tempted, but just as he pokes a tentative paw out through a hole in the foundation, a chicken struts by and flaps its wings. The kitten hisses, leaps back into the darkness, and is seen no more.

The sputter of a Renault engine announces the arrival of Raúl Cea, a tall man with light-grey hair and dark triangular eyebrows. Moving easily, gracefully, he walks up the path to meet us. While his wife feeds the chickens, he takes us on a tour of the mill, with its three-story-high array of gigantic gears and wheels and pulleys and other moving parts, all of which look capable of inflicting serious bodily injury on anyone who happens to fall into the works. Dan and Carlos listen raptly to his explanation of how the contraption works, but I don't hear a word. I'm too busy watching my step.

Although the machinery still functions, the mill shut down years ago, and the Ceas now live in town. They use this place as a weekend home in good weather. Once the tour has ended, Doña Yolanda invites us into the modernized living quarters for cold drinks. Don Raúl is an amateur artist, and the dining room is his gallery; sketches of family members, alongside tango legend Carlos Gardel and *gaucho* icon Martín Fierro, decorate the walls. We sit around the table and sip 7UP as Don Raúl's gravelly voice takes us back to the early 1900s.

"My father knew his next-door neighbors as Santiago Ryan and Harry and Anna Marie Place. Señora Place had a dog—a spaniel, I think—that went with her everywhere. She was devoted to it. She danced with the governor at a local party, but Ryan was more gregarious than his companions, perhaps because his Spanish was better. He also loved to read and frequently borrowed books from English-speaking neighbors. At that time, you see, many foreigners— French, Basque, Italian, Welsh, and especially Chilean immigrants—lived in the area."

Don Raúl leans back in his chair and scrapes a hangnail across the stubble on his jaw. "The Places and Señor Ryan were people accustomed to living well, very cultured. They had a washstand with a fine pitcher and basin, which was unusual around here, and she put drops of perfume in the water. They set the table with a certain etiquette— napkins, china plates. Their windows went up and down."

The windows again.

6

"There was never a single fact that gave them away as bad men. They were very good neighbors. Nobody was ever mad at them."

Doña Yolanda refills our glasses, and we settle back to hear more of the stories Pedro Cea passed on to his son. "At first, the local *gauchos* thought the North Americans were too refined for ranch work. In those days, they didn't have fences and the cattle were all mixed together. The *gauchos* chortled at the prospect of watching the *gringos* try to separate their cattle from the herd, but they proved to be very good cowboys, handy with lassos, and the *gauchos* came away from the roundup with a new opinion."

The reason Butch and his companions left Cholila, says Don Raúl, is that someone recognized them. "Juan Comodoro Perry had a brother in Texas. The version told around here is that Perry corresponded with his brother and learned that Ryan was a wanted man. When they departed, they hid out near Lake Cholila and the Tigre River for about a year. I found their camp high in the *cordillera,* forty miles away. Their foreman, Alejandro Villagrán, a very concientious man, brought them food. He had to take different trails and use a birdcall to contact them. He never saw them; they would leave notes to communicate."

When the bandits left the area for good, they gave their furniture to Villagrán, who later left Sundance and Etta's bed and nightstand to Manuel José Cea. When he died, the pieces passed to his son. "It's a good bed—somewhat lumpy, but still usable, after all these years. The nightstand is porcelain with a metal frame. It was imported, but the bowl and pitcher that came with it were locally made."

The cabin was abandoned until 1914 or 1915, when Rómulo Sepúlveda moved into it. The last thing Pedro Cea heard about the bandits was that they had robbed a train in Nicaragua. Don Raúl knows nothing about their deaths.

"Then Butch Cassidy didn't die in Daher's machine shop?" asks Dan.

"No. That building came much later, in the 1930s or 1940s. They didn't die around here. In fact, when word reached Cholila that they had held up some banks, nobody believed it at first. They had never shown any sign of being criminals. That is what interests me. Cassidy was a gentleman bandit, not an ordinary delinquent. I have read that he came from a good Mormon family, and I want to know, how did he become an outlaw? What happened in his early life that led him down that path?"

Good questions.

Don Raúl gives us a copy of an article from an Argentine magazine in which Italian author Hugo Pratt writes that two *gringo* bandits killed on December 9, 1911, in Río Pico, a town 120 miles south of Cholila, are often mistaken for Butch and Sundance but were actually a couple of thugs named Robert Evans and William Wilson. According to Pratt, accomplices of Butch and Sundance deliberately misidentified one of the slain *gringos* as Sundance to free him from persecution. In fact, the article continues, Butch Cassidy and the Sundance Kid were "killed and resuscitated various times in various sites. Their tombs are found in Argentina, Bolivia, Chile, and Uruguay. All the crosses without names." Moreover, "they say that Cassidy returned to Argentina with a false name and lived out his last years as a prosperous rancher someplace in Chubut or Santa Cruz. The Sundance Kid disappeared forever. Someone said he worked as an actor in Buffalo Bill's Circus; others that he was buried in one of those much-disputed tombs."

Pratt is the creator of the cartoon-noir character Corto Maltese, an "adventurer, sailor, world traveler, witness and participant in a time of sweeping change: the first thirty years of this century." In Pratt's book *Tango,* Butch Cassidy comes out of his Patagonian refuge to save his chum Corto Maltese from corrupt policemen, wealthy landowners, and a Polish-Argentine prostitution ring.

One day at Cholila's Hue-Telén restaurant, three teenagers approach our table after overhearing our speculations about the bandits' departure from Cholila. "You should speak to Florencia Perry Gérez," says one youth. "She's the daughter of Juan Comodoro Perry, who was a sheriff in the United States and also in Argentina. He got into a confrontation with Cassidy, and afterward the *bandoleros* left the valley."

One of Doña Florencia's relatives, Señora Blanca de Gérez, lived near Butch, Sundance, and Etta and wrote about them before her death in the 1970s: "They were not good mixers, but whatever they did was correct. They often slept in our house. Ryan [Butch] was more sociable than Place [Sundance] and joined in the festivities of the settlement. On the first visit of Governor Lezana, Place played the samba on his guitar and Ryan danced with the daughter of Don Ventura Solís. No one suspected they were criminals."

I would rather move on, but Dan is eager to talk to someone who may actually have known the bandits, so we set off to visit Doña

Florencia. Although the directions are simple, they entail passing through several gates, which I must open and close. Unlike a rigid North American gate, which swings on hinges and latches with a simple mechanism, the Patagonian gate is made of flexible wires attached at intervals to wooden uprights and is fastened by twisting and looping some of the wire around the fence post and securing it, like a tourniquet, with a stick of wood. I can open the gates, but closing them is another matter. Each fastener is a unique puzzle, and I lack sufficient strength to pull the wires tight enough to slip the loops over the fence posts. After cutting my hands several times and straining every muscle in my arms and back, I have had enough sleuthing for the day.

"You drive," says Dan. "I'll handle the gates." His arms are equal to the task, but mechanical reasoning is not his forte, so we leave a series of bedraggled gates behind us as we bump through the fields toward the Perry homestead. At last, we arrive at Doña Florencia's house and mount the steps to her wide front porch. Newspapers cover the windows, and not a soul is stirring, not even a dog. We knock at the door several times, but no one answers. In the end, we must turn around and once again do battle with the gates, which someone has thoughtfully tidied up after our first trip through them. When we regain the highway with nothing to show for our trouble, I'd like to throttle Dan, but my hands are too sore.

We fare better with a visit to Simón Daher, a Lebanese immigrant's son, who owns the cabin built by Butch and Sundance and currently occupied by Aladín Sepúlveda. Don Simón is chopping wood by a shed behind his brick home, which sits about a quarter of a mile south of the cabin. "The *norteamericanos*, they didn't build the house right away," he says. "At first, they lived in a camp in the hills above there, but their campsite is difficult to reach. You must go on horseback or take a truck in the dry season." About the machine shop, the building where Melania said Butch had died, Don Simón says, "I don't know why people always want to connect that building with him. They say it was his store or that he died there. Preposterous! It wasn't built until 1944, so it couldn't have had anything to do with the *bandoleros*."

He takes us indoors to meet his wife, Griselda Irene Bonansea de Daher, who turns out to be a great-granddaughter of Juan Comodoro Perry. As John Perry, he had been the first sheriff of Crockett County, Texas, serving from 1891 to 1894. For an annual salary of $300, his duties included keeping the peace, collecting taxes, and overseeing the waterworks, which comprised a windmill, a tank, and a horse trough. After ranching in west Texas for several years and deciding that the United States was too crowded, Perry sold his cattle and moved to South America, where free grazing land was available.

His wife, Bertie, described life in Cholila in a letter to the *Ozona Kicker*, the local paper back in Crockett County: "We have a nice home, our house is two story 10 rooms, and have it well furnished, it's in the center of the farm. I have geese, ducks, turkeys, fine chickens and two dogs." She wrote that "after you live here 3 or 4 years you become a little contented," but that the region was "lonely until you become use to these heathens." Having heard that a friend of a friend was thinking of moving to Argentina, Mrs. Perry offered this advice: Unless all the people in [North America] have lost their minds and going crazy right they had better stay with Uncle Sam's side of the world. But if tired, here is the place to rest. No excitement whatever. To come, start from [New York], that is if you can leave there, for it is like leaving the world when you leave there for here." She recommended landing at the Welsh settlement of Puerto Madryn and taking the monthly mail hack from nearby Trelew to the town of Esquel, about thirty miles south of Cholila. "This hack man charges as long as he can hold his breath. $120 a trip and your own food along the road at stores. . . . You meet no one out for his health in Argentina. In Trelew and Esquel you will find English people but they had rather die than talk it." Only one doctor lived anywhere near Cholila, she wrote, so medical care was dispensed by Indian women. "All medicines are weeds and barks off trees, but it cures just the same." Mrs. Perry observed that hats in Buenos Aires cost five times what they cost in Texas. "So a woman costs money here. But never since I came have I bought one hat yet. No place to go, no one to see but Indians, what is the use to dress up. I have a pair of shoes I bought in Galveston I put on every few months, I take care of those, for when they are gone I can find no more Yankee shoes here."

In another letter, Mrs. Perry wrote that they had word of some Texans living in the region and went to visit them, only to find that they were outlaws Sheriff Perry had known back home. Doña Griselda says that after her great-grandfather became a *comisario*, the government asked him to investigate some North Americans, but she isn't certain when it happened or who his targets were. Checking would be difficult, because his letters burned in a fire.

The Perrys weren't the bandits' only English-speaking neighbors.

10

Their best pal was Daniel Gibbon, a Welsh immigrant who had settled in Esquel in the 1890s. Though not an outlaw, he served as the middle man for a gun shipment and lied to the police on occasion. His son Mansel ran with Evans and Wilson and, according to judicial records, once doctored a wound for Sundance. Butch, a frequent guest at Daniel Gibbon's home, wrote to him on February 29, 1904.

> Dear friend,
>
> I have been laid up with a bad dose of the *Town Disease* and I don't know when I will be able to ride, but as soon as I am able I will be down. And I will want to buy some Rams, so please keep your ears open for we don't know where to look for them. If you hear of any one that wants to sell please tell them about us. I have not been to Ñorquinco yet, so don't know what we will do there.
>
> Kindest Regards to your Wife & Family.
>> Yours Most Truly,
>> J. P. Ryan
>
> Look out for my horse.
> P.S. Place starts for the Lake tomorrow to Buy Bulls.

We've never heard of the "Town Disease," but we have a pretty good idea what it is: "Town pump" and "town bike" are slang for prostitute, and "dose" has been used to describe venereal ailments since the 1850s. Apparently, Butch had been "on the town" once too often—in the days before penicillin. I can just see him choking down a potion of weeds and bark prescribed by the local *curandera*.

Another friend was John Gardiner. As a sickly seventeen-year-old, he had left Scotland to live with a pair of uncles who bred stock near La Plata. His health restored, he set off to see the country, and wound up on a sheep ranch near Cholila, where he met three North Americans who introduced themselves as James Ryan and Mr. and Mrs. Harry Place. By the time the long-legged Scot learned their true identities, he had grown close to Butch, who often borrowed his magazines. Gardiner loathed Sundance, however, and described him as morose and sullen and "a mean, low cur." This view may have been colored by Gardiner's affection for Etta, who "was his first love and his only love," according to Irishman Frank O'Grady, whom Gardiner befriended after returning to Great Britain in 1907. O'Grady attributed Gardiner's love for Etta to the fact that "he was an educated man and she was an educated woman. Two educated people who meet in such a place in the wilderness are like two magnets drawn together. About Gardiner's age, she was. Etta was a great reader. Gardiner received books and magazines from England and shared them with her."

Gardiner told O'Grady that Butch and Sundance rode their horses hard every day around the ranch, to make them ready for anything, and always kept saddled mounts behind the cabin to ensure a quick getaway. According to Gardiner, a local sheriff received a copy of a Pinkerton Detective Agency circular with photographs of Butch, Sundance, and Etta as well as that of another Wild Bunch member, Harvey Logan. Although a $10,000 reward had been offered for the outlaws, dead or alive, the sheriff—who was also smitten with Etta—told Gardiner that he would resign rather than attempt to arrest them. According to O'Grady, Gardiner sent a note warning Butch to clear out while he had the chance, and the bandits escaped over the Andes into Chile.

By 1907, Gardiner said, they were living in open country on the coast of Chile. He told O'Grady that rumors of the bandits' deaths in South America were false, and that Butch had died in Arizona in 1937 after being "shot in the back by a skunk who feared to face him like a man."

In 1948, O'Grady wrote to the Chubut police in an attempt to ascertain the truth of Gardiner's assertion that Butch and Sundance had left a cache of gold buried near their ranch. Although the police knew nothing of the alleged buried treasure, retired policemen verified other elements of Gardiner's story. Welsh-Argentine Milton Roberts, for example, confirmed that three North Americans calling themselves Enrique Place, Ethel Place, and James Ryan came to Cholila in 1902 and established a small ranch with livestock purchased from the Leleque Company, a British-owned enterprise near Cholila. Roberts described Etta as "good-looking, a good rider, and an expert with a rifle, though not with a revolver." He wrote that Sundance was "not so much a bad character as a cold-blooded one," that he was an expert with a revolver and "a genuine cowboy, very capable with animals," and that he appeared to be the leader of the gang, because Butch seemed to take orders from him in running the ranch.

According to Julio O. de Antueno, another retired police official, Etta was an elegant woman who "never wore dresses, just pants and boots," and Butch and Sundance were always well dressed. Antueno said that they committed no crimes in Chubut. "They were comfortably established to raise livestock in a place in the mountains where they felt secure, but overnight they disappeared, when some companion warned them that their whereabouts were known."

The end of our vacation is fast approaching, but before returning to Buenos Aires to catch our plane home, we decide to drive our rented Ford to the Cochamó pass, over the route Butch and Sundance took when they drove their cattle to market. At the small town of Río Villegas, we leave the gravel highway for a narrow dirt road that climbs at an alarming angle through a series of blind curves. I grit my teeth and try not to look over the precipice.

"Don't worry," says Dan, "the fall would probably kill us."

"Thanks, dear. I feel so much better."

Presently, the land levels out somewhat, and the road follows the green Manso River. We drive for half an hour through rolling hills and small *estancias*, where livestock graze in pastures dotted with beeches and poplars. Squadrons of honking yellow-beaked *bandurrias* fly in formation overhead. Heavy rains have washed away chunks of the road and filled the potholes with muddy water. Unable to gauge their depth, we bounce and splash along and hope that the road doesn't get any worse before we reach the border.

After hitting a rock in a particularly deep hole, however, Dan is reluctant to continue.

"Come on," I chide him. "Where's your spirit of adventure?"

"I left it back there with that four-wheel-drive jeep we didn't rent."

Within moments, we hit another rock. Dan glares at me. Before driving through the next big puddle, which spans the entire road, he stops the car and gets out for reconnaissance. The hole is shallow, but as he walks back to the car, he suddenly yells, "Son of a bitch!"

What now?

"Goddamn radiator's busted."

Oops.

Fortunately, we have just passed a small house and can easily back up to get help. Only yesterday, a friend with a leaky radiator mentioned having had great success plugging up the holes with ground chili pepper, so that is what we ask for. Someone brings a big bag of red *ají molido* and a bucket of water, and several men in nearby fields drop what they are doing and gather around our car to peer under the hood. In go the *ají* and the water, and out gushes a red torrent. It's tow-truck time.

We're thousands of miles from the nearest AAA station, and no one between here and Río Villegas has a telephone. Three families in the valley, however, have radios we could use to summon help from El Bolsón or Bariloche. The men argue about what kind of temporary repair will enable us to drive to a radio. In the end, they move some hoses around to send the water directly from the antifreeze tank to the engine and back again, bypassing the radiator. A wine cork plugs a hole that would otherwise defeat the jury-rigged system.

The pass beckons, but we turn the car around and head back. When the needle on the temperature gauge hits the red zone, Dan turns off the engine; the car coasts in neutral until its momentum fades. We stop halfway up a hill and wait for the needle to fall, and then we begin again. Cows lounge in green fields behind wooden fences. Above the valley rise vertical expanses of rock broken only by larches, which sprout wherever they find purchase. Finally, we reach a house with an antenna. The owner says that his radio is on the blink but that the third house on the right, a couple of miles ahead, has one. We drive on. Waterfalls plunge down the rock faces. Firebushes glow red among the evergreens. Standing in the opaque shallows of the Manso River, a cow slakes its thirst. Butch and Sundance certainly wouldn't have had to worry about finding water for their livestock on the way to market.

We have yet to pass a single house. Gradually, the realization dawns on us that even though the needle takes a while to climb into the red zone, the engine is anything but cool in the meantime; if we keep going, we might burn out the motor. At the next wide spot on a straight stretch of road, Dan stops the car and announces that he'll jog the rest of the way to the house and radio for a tow truck, then return to the car to wait with me. If no one is home, he may have to hitchhike to El Bolsón, thirty miles south of Río Villegas.

I read for a while, but the air in the car is stifling, so I take a walk. A mare and her colt, browsing among bushes with flat pink-tipped blossoms, trot away at my approach. I follow them into a grove of willows and beeches, but they escape, leaving me with a cloud of horseflies to fend off. As I make my way back to the car, a family—mother, father, two children, and a baby—passes by on horseback, and half the swarm buzzes off in pursuit.

Three o'clock: Dan has been gone more than an hour. Probably hitched a ride to El Bolsón. He won't be back until five at the earliest, which means we'll wind up on the snakiest part of the road after dark. Maybe I should move the car ahead while there's still plenty of light. The engine must have cooled by now. I drive for ten minutes before the needle hits the red zone, then I shift into neutral and coast to a stop.

One side of the road is lined with bramble bushes, but the other side is inviting: Bright pink foxgloves and holly-leafed barberry bushes grow in the shade of tall cypresses; pale green tendrils of epiphytic moss flutter from the branches of dead beeches. Although the river isn't visible from the road, water courses nearby. I follow the sound until I see the river, narrower here, with steep banks. My presence has disturbed a small herd of sleeping cows. Lowing in protest, they stumble to their feet and slouch off. When snapping branches signal the hasty approach of a bull, I duck behind a tree. While I am considering whether to freeze, run, climb the tree, or jump into the river if *el toro* charges, a mangy white creature with grey splotches, blunt horns, and long white eyelashes crashes into view and careers by my tree without so much as a glance in my direction.

Having survived the encounter with the bull, I stiffen at the sound of human voices. Two fishermen are strolling this way on my side of the river. I melt back into the woods before they can see me. They are undoubtedly harmless, but for the first time I am aware of being a woman alone in the middle of nowhere. Did Etta ever feel this way when Butch and Sundance were away on a cattle drive? Heading for the safety of the car, I run a gantlet of brambles, thorns, and thistles. I emerge from the shade just in time to see a car full of teenage boys whiz by. They look at our car, look at me, and keep moving.

I drive as fast as I dare until the temperature gauge registers danger. The car coasts to a stop beside a dark pond. Bleached tree trunks and skeletal limbs hung with strands of moss rise from the still water. Across the road, horses graze among the beeches. Snow peaks crown the horizon. The pond has yielded a bumper crop of insects, so the windows must stay shut. I take periodic breathers but never stray far from the road. As the day wanes, the car cools off and I move inside for good. In all this time, I have seen only one house. Could others have been hidden by the trees? It must have taken Dan at least an hour to reach the house with the radio. Maybe he's still there. If I go any farther, I might pass him by and then he won't be able to find me. Better sit still. I read for a while, then lock the doors, tilt the seat back, and settle down for a nap. With any luck, Dan will be here when I wake up. If not, I may be in for a chilly night. I have just closed my eyes when a truck grinds up the road and halts before me.

Dan alights with a puzzled smile. "What are you doing here?"

Turns out the house with the radio is just around the bend, not more than a quarter of a mile away. He's been there for hours while the lady of the house, Señora Carro, tried to get through to someone in Bariloche on the radio. She could hear them, but they couldn't hear her. As soon as her teenage son returned from an errand, he and Dan set out to rescue me. Upon learning that no tow truck is on the way, I hardly feel rescued, but at least I'm no longer alone.

A gaunt woman in a loose housedress, Señora Carro invites me into the kitchen and plies me with cake and *mate*, the scalding and bitter holly tea second only to red wine as the national drink of Argentina. A chick wanders in peeping loudly and leaving a trail of white droppings on the linoleum, which Señora Carro cleans with a rag. Embarrassed, she explains that she nursed the little orphan back to health and hasn't had the heart to evict it yet.

Meanwhile, her son doctors our radiator. He tears an old shirt into strips, slathers them with epoxy, and layers them over the hole. While the glue dries, he removes the cork and shifts the hoses back to their proper places. The patch holds, but the water finds a new route of escape higher up, because (according to the mechanic who eventually fixes it) the entire *plastic* end of the radiator popped off when it hit the rock. The road between here and the highway isn't wide enough for the kind of stop-and-go game we've been playing, especially not with night coming on, so Señora Carro suggests that her son give us a lift to the inn in Río Villegas. We can call a tow truck from there and return for the car tomorrow. Then, depending on how long the repairs take, we can race back to Buenos Aires in time to catch our plane.

Within half an hour, we are explaining our plight to a policeman in Río Villegas, when the local dump truck rounds the corner. After a bit of jovial dickering, the driver agrees to haul the car to El Bolsón in the morning for $150. Now, for supper and a good night's sleep.

Gingerbread trim lends a fairy-tale quality to the aging inn, built of cypress planks, on the riverbank. Like Hansel and Gretel fresh from the forest, we open the front door and step inside. The harshly lighted room is full of handmade wooden tables and chairs—but no diners, a bad sign. Behind a counter at the back stand a pallid young man and a wrinkled woman with white hair pinned up in a bun. They stare at us without speaking as we approach them and ask for a room. The woman registers us in silence, then leads us down a musty hallway,

16

through the kitchen, up a flight of rickety stairs, along a narrow passageway, and into a small room with a dormer and a low ceiling. Two cots and a rustic nightstand take up most of the space. Unseen beneath the trees outside our window, the river surges by. "First door on the left is the bathroom," she says. And then she is gone.

Once she's out of earshot, I whisper to Dan, "They're going to put knockout drops in our dinner and cram us into a stew pot."

"Don't be silly." He sits on his cot to test the suspension and counts the blankets to gauge how cold the night will be. "This place is great."

Reluctantly, I follow him down the creaking stairs and into the dining room. In the five minutes since we last saw her, the old woman has been transformed. She seats us with a smile, animatedly recites the menu, and trots off to fetch our steaks and french fries.

When morning arrives, our first task is to find the driver of the dump truck. Rousted from his bed, he dons a plaid shirt, grey *bombachas*, and a pair of canvas *alpargatas*, the *gaucho* version of espadrilles. The handle on the passenger door of his Ford dump truck doesn't work, so we climb in through the driver's side. A rubber strip holds the hood in place, and a tin can covers the gas pipe.

At the Carros' home, the driver surveys the scene, backs his truck up to an embankment, and asks Dan to drive the car onto the truck bed. They lay thick planks alongside the car to wedge it in place, then jam spare tires between the car's bumpers and the truck's cab and gate, close the gate as far as it will go, and secure it with a lasso, a cable, and strips of rubber. With the car packed solidly in back, the truck crawls down the mountain and onto the gravel highway.

We then take what the driver describes as a shortcut for the thirty-mile trip to El Bolsón, and two and a half hours later we lumber into town. After we unload the car at the municipal dump—the only place that has a ramp—he begins whining that the fare was too low for such a long distance. After that miserable, dusty detour, we are hardly in the mood to renegotiate anything. He backs down at once. "*Adiós*," he says. "*Que les vaya bien.*"

If trailing Butch and Sundance was as tough for the Pinkertons as it has been for us, no wonder they never caught the pair.

2 · HOOKED ON HISTORY

BACK in the United States, Dan decides to write an article on the Wild Bunch in Patagonia for our favorite magazine, the *South American Explorer* (which is similar to *National Geographic*, except for being printed in black and white on cheap paper and having ten million fewer subscribers). He goes to the Library of Congress for a spot of background reading and disappears for several weeks. Once he has read every available book on Butch and Sundance and all the back issues of *True West, Old West,* and *Frontier Times,* he begins poring over old South American newspapers on microfilm.

After too many evenings and weekends alone, I am hurt by the lack of attention and certain that he has lost his mind. Finally, over supper on the tiny patio behind our Washington row house, I confront him. "What do Butch Cassidy and the Sundance Kid have that I don't have?"

"Stacks of stolen banknotes." He pats his thigh, and Boca—our green-eyed Russian blue—jumps into his lap.

"Don't try to hide behind the cat."

He winces and waits for a police helicopter to pass overhead. "I guess it's the mystery. I just want to know what happened to them."

"They robbed a bunch of banks and payroll trains and got shot."

"Maybe. But they were in South America for the better part of a decade, and nobody knows what they really did down there. Aside from a few anecdotes and robberies blamed on them with scant evidence, their South American adventures are a blank. Even the Bolivian shootout is questionable. Most outlaw historians think the movie ending was based on a fabrication cooked up by the outlaws' pals so that they could start new lives without Pinkerton detectives hounding them all over the world, but nobody has proved anything one way or the other."

"How can you hope to prove something if the historians haven't been able to prove it?"

"As far as I can tell, no one has done any original research in South America." A German shepherd barks half a block away. Boca's ears twitch, but she remains coiled in Dan's lap. "I've found all kinds of stories in the Argentine newspapers that nobody seems to have read. Maybe none of the researchers speaks Spanish."

"Okay, it's a mystery. But why waste so much time on a couple of criminals who probably got what they deserved?" The dog barks again, and Boca jumps down.

"There's no record of Butch or Sundance ever killing anybody until the Bolivian shootout, assuming it happened."

"Maybe they didn't go around committing murder in front of witnesses," I say, "but that doesn't mean they never killed anyone."

"It was a point of honor with Butch Cassidy." The helicopter is back, shining its light down through the elm next door. "He was the Robin Hood type."

"Sure, just like Jesse James." I stack the dishes and head for the door. "Steal from the rich and give to yourself."

"No really, Butch was a sweetheart."

"You mean Paul Newman was a sweetheart," I call from the kitchen. "Butch Cassidy's charm was a gift from the screenwriter."

Dan joins me inside. "Listen," he says, opening the dishwasher, "William Goldman may have invented the dialogue, but he captured the spirit of the real Butch Cassidy. If you don't believe me, take a look at the record."

The next morning, I sit down and begin reading the stacks of material Dan has amassed. By suppertime, I am addicted. Over pizza from the neighborhood carryout, we compromise: Instead of spending my evenings alone, I'll join him in the library.

Butch Cassidy was born Robert LeRoy Parker in Beaver, Utah, on April 13, 1866. His parents, Maximillian and Annie Gillies Parker, had emigrated from England with their families in the 1850s in answer to Brigham Young's plea for tradesmen to help build a new Mormon empire in the valley of the Great Salt Lake. As the first of thirteen children, towheaded Bob Parker grew up with more than his share of the chores. He inherited his mother's deep-set blue eyes, square jaw, and outgoing nature, and his father's generosity and playful sense of humor. According to cowboy folklorist Jack Thorp, Bob was a "girlish young fellow, and his companions nicknamed him Sallie."

In 1879, when Bob was thirteen, his father quit his job as a frontier mailman and bought a ranch with a two-room cabin at the foot of a hill three miles south of Circleville, Utah. At first, the Parkers used the large room with the fireplace as both kitchen and living room and slept in the small room on bed ticks stuffed with corn husks or straw. The ceilings were covered with white cloth, the windows with lace curtains, and the rough floors with rag carpets over straw padding. In time, the still-growing family added a separate kitchen and two bedrooms.

Life on the ranch in Circle Valley was difficult—the work demanding, the weather treacherous—but there were compensations. Bob, who had a gift for working with animals, became a broncobuster at an early age and trained a pet magpie to speak. And he played the harmonica on the winter nights when Max and Annie Parker gathered their children for stories and songs.

Although Annie came from a devout family, Max was a jack Mormon, one who attended church only sporadically and violated taboos, especially the ban on smoking. Bob shared his father's views on religion and volunteered for any chore that would keep him home during church services. His sister Lula wondered whether the thriftiness and caustic tongue of their extremely pious Grandmother Gillies could have sparked his opposition to restrictions. In 1880 or 1881, when a Mormon bishop awarded land homesteaded by the Parkers to a more righteous family, Max Parker nearly left the church. He relented for his wife's sake, but Bob developed a lasting grudge against what he viewed as religious hypocrites.

In the summer of 1882, while working with his mother and two of his brothers on the Marshall ranch south of Circleville, Bob met Mike Cassidy, a young drifter who worked as a ranch hand, with sidelines in cattle rustling and horse theft. Bob admired Mike's skills with animals and eagerly learned everything Mike showed him. Mike took a liking to the boy, gave him a saddle and a gun, and taught him how to shoot. Alarmed at Bob's association with a man of questionable character, Annie Parker moved her sons back to Circle Valley. When Mike later left the area, Bob wanted to ride off with him, but Mike is said to have told him, "No, the place for you is here on the farm. You're too good a kid to go where I'm going."

In 1884, at the age of eighteen, Bob Parker left home under a cloud as a result of his relationship with some cattle-rustling friends of Mike Cassidy's. Whether Bob had really committed a crime or was paid to take the rap for the actual thieves is unclear. In any event, he found work 240 miles to the east in Telluride, Colorado, hauling ore on mules down the mountain from the mine to the mill. After two years in the area, he was falsely charged with horse theft and acquitted. Max Parker attended the trial and urged his son to come back to Circle Valley, but Bob wanted more excitement than his home in Utah could offer. He began working at odd jobs and drifting north. By the spring of 1887, he was working near Miles City, Montana.

Using the name Roy Parker, he turned up in Telluride again in 1888 or 1889 and soon joined Matt Warner and Tom McCarty in a horse-racing venture that went sour when McCarty killed an Indian who had refused to accept defeat gracefully. On June 24, 1889, the three partners, perhaps with an unidentified accomplice, robbed the San Miguel Valley Bank of $20,750. They got away but were recognized. Whatever shady dealings he may have engaged in before, the Telluride holdup made an outlaw of Robert LeRoy Parker.

Once the posse went home, he left the bandits' hideout in the Mancos Mountains and rode north to Brown's Park, a high valley forty miles long and six miles wide, with fine grazing land watered by the Green River and protected from harsh weather and unwanted visitors by the rugged surrounding mountains. Its location at the intersection of Utah, Colorado, and Wyoming made the park an ideal sanctuary for outlaws, who could slip across state lines to avoid arrest. The ranchers, an independent lot with little use for land-grabbing cattle barons or the lawmen in their control, raised no objection to outlaws who behaved themselves, and good ranch hands were always welcome there.

In the summer of 1889, still calling himself Roy Parker, Bob hired on at the Bassett ranch in Brown's Park. During this sabbatical from crime, he took advantage of the well-educated Herbert Bassett's extensive library, befriended Bassett's daughters, Ann and Josie, and attended the occasional dance parties and horse races that took place in the park. It was here that Bob probably met William Ellsworth "Elzy" Lay for the first time. The tall, baby-faced midwesterner rounded up mavericks and broke horses for Matt Warner and worked as a hand on the Bassett ranch. Like Bob, Elzy was intelligent and averse to unnecessary violence, though not to larceny, and the two men became fast friends.

Later that year, Bob went to Rock Springs, Wyoming, and introduced himself as George Cassidy. He spent a few months hacking up carcasses in William Gottsche's butcher shop. People began calling him Butch, and from then on, no matter what alias he used, he would be remembered as Butch Cassidy.

Butch often retreated to Brown's Park, where he was always warmly received. Whether deservedly or not, he developed a reputation as a philanthropist. As Josie Bassett Morris later put it: "Butch took care of more poor people than FDR, and with no red tape." The list of his alleged good deeds includes paying off windows' mortgages (then stealing the money back from whoever collected it), giving hard-up ranchers money to pay their taxes, buying Christmas presents for needy homesteaders, delivering medicine to flu-stricken families, chopping wood and fetching water for bedridden settlers, counseling juvenile delinquents to go straight, saving a town marshal from a drunken mob, funding an underground railroad to Mexico for Mormons charged with bigamy, giving gold coins to little girls and a horse to a ten-year-old boy who admired it, setting the broken leg of a fawn (using an ingenious method that would cause the splint to fall off when the bone had healed), and scattering wildflower seeds in barren spots alongside the trails he rode—a regular Johnny Flowerseed. If Butch had actually done all the favors attributed to him, he wouldn't have had time to pull any holdups.

While working near Wyoming's Wind River in late 1889 or early 1890, Butch met a young fellow named Al Hainer, and they decided to homestead some land together at Horse Creek. During this period, Butch dated several young women from the Lander area. Although his intense blue eyes, blond hair, and gallantry undoubtedly made him appealing, he was not known as a womanizer. Perhaps he avoided romantic entanglements because of his work. In any event, he was a loyal friend who genuinely enjoyed the company of men and loved to play practical jokes on his buddies.

On March 13, 1890, after receiving word that his brother Dan had held up a stagecoach the previous December, Butch wrote to show his solidarity with the family's other black sheep.

> My Dear Brother.
>
> It has been so long since I have written I suppose you have done looking for a letter from me but do not dispare [sic] for you shall have one after so long a time. You must forgive me for not writing before. I have no excuse to offer only my negligence and I will try to be more punctual for the future. I was very sorry to hear that you are in hidding [sic] again, but you know that I am not one to point a finger only be carefull [sic] for I am inclined to think as Grandfather Parker did about the wild cat in Duncan woods. I do wish I could come and see you all and I intend to if nothing happens to prevent this Summer coming for I almost feel homesick when thinking how long it is since I saw my Mother it seems almost an age since I saw any of you. When you get this letter you must write me and tell me all the news and what the prospects are for a safe reunion. I hope we may have a grand revelry but I should think it doubtful according to your letter. I am now located at a good house about 18 miles [actually, it was 75 miles] from Lander and have taken to raising horses which I think suits this country just fine. [Hainer] and I have throwed our lots entirely together, so we have 38 horses between us and we would have more but it has been a cold winter with plenty of wind and snow. (And you must excuse the pencile [sic] but the ink froze.)

Business here is very dull and money hard but you know I am well. I should be in perfect health if I did not have such a good appitite [*sic*] and eat so much 3 times each day. I must draw my letter to a close. Give my love to Uncle Dan and family and tell them I should be happy to see them. Give my love to Father Mother Brothers and Sisters and receive the same yourself—

This from your Brother

Bob

P.S. Direct your letters to George Cassidy as before and burn this up as you read it.

What the letter failed to mention was the method by which Butch and his partner acquired their stock. In April 1892, they were arrested in Star Valley, Wyoming, and charged with horse theft. On July 4, 1894, after a series of delays in the legal proceedings, Al Hainer was acquitted, but Butch—under the name George Cassidy—was convicted and sentenced to two years at the Wyoming Territorial Prison in Laramie, beginning July 15, 1894. According to prison records, he cited New York City as his birthplace and did not disclose the identity or location of any relatives. After serving eighteen months of his sentence and promising to refrain from committing any more crimes in Wyoming, he received a full pardon from the governor.

Released on January 19, 1896, Butch went directly to Brown's Park and began consorting with felons and contemplating his next holdup. To the saloon keepers in nearby frontier towns, Butch and his noisy pals soon became known as "that wild bunch from Brown's Park." Six months after Butch's release, he joined Elzy Lay and a fellow named Bob Meeks in robbing the bank in Montpelier, Idaho. Having stationed fresh horses at Montpelier Pass, the outlaws easily outran the posse and got away with $16,500, which went toward their friend Matt Warner's legal fees in an upcoming trial. Soon after the holdup, Matt's wife wrote and asked Butch to come see her. Unsure of her motives and perhaps fearing a trap, Butch sent her a letter instead.

Vernal, Utah. Aug. 25, 1896

Mrs. Rosa Warner, Salt Lake:

My Dear Friend—Through the kindness of Mrs. Rummel I received your letter last night. I am sorry that I can't comply with your request, but at present it is impossible for me to go to see you, and I can't tell you just when I can get there. If you have got anything to tell me that will help you or Matt, write and tell me what it is and I will be there on time. I can't understand what it can be, for I have heard from reliable partys [*sic*] that you did not want Matt to get out, and I can't see what benefit it could be to you unless it was in his behalf. I may be misinformed, but I got it so straight that I would have to be shown why you made this talk before I could think otherwise. But that is neither here nor there, you are a lady, and I would do all I could for you or any of the sex that was in trouble. Of course, I am foolish (Which you have found out), but it is my nature and I can't change it. I may be wrong in this, but if so, I hope you will look over it and prove to me that you are all right, and I will ask forgiveness for writing you as I have. I understand you and Matt named your boy Rex Leroy after me, thank you. I hope I will be able to meet you all before long if everything is satisfactory. I [was] sorry to hear about [the cancer in] your leg. If I can do anything to help you out let me know and I will do it. Lay and I have got a good man to defend Matt and Wall, and put up plenty of money, too, for Matt and Wall to defend themselves. Write me here in care of John Bluford, and believe me to be a true friend to my kind of people.

George Cassidy

During the winter of 1896–1897, Butch stayed at Robbers' Roost, a colorful canyonland in southeastern Utah, between Hanksville and Moab. Lawmen generally avoided the arid, inhospitable region, where horses left no tracks on the hard sandstone mesas and every twisting canyon held the promise of ambush, but the outlaws knew all the water holes and seeps, the hidden trails onto the plateaus, and the parcels of relatively flat grazing land hidden within the rocky maze. Butch and his men favored an area that could be reached only by jumping their horses ten feet into Dennis Canyon, which runs into the Green River, and scrabbling up to the head of Horseshoe Canyon, where a tent measuring twelve feet by sixteen feet sheltered them from the elements. That winter, the outlaws erected a second tent for Elzy Lay and his bride, Maude Davis Lay, and a third for Sundance and his girlfriend, Etta Place.

The Sundance Kid was born Harry Longabaugh, the youngest of Josiah and Annie Place Longabaugh's five children. Although the exact date and place of his birth were not recorded, he was probably born in the spring of 1867 in a small town near Phoenixville, Pennsylvania, the home of his parents' families. Josiah Longabaugh was a common laborer who often worked as a farmhand. He moved his family frequently and never owned property.

Harry had two brothers, Elwood and Harvey, and two sisters, Samanna and Emma. By 1880, Samanna had married and begun a family of her own; although Elwood and Emma remained at home, the two youngest boys were earning their room and board elsewhere. Thirteen-year-old Harry lived as a servant with the family of Wilmer Ralston in West Vincent, Pennsylvania, about ten miles from the Longabaughs' home. The family reunited on Sundays for services at the First Baptist Church of Phoenixville, where Emma and Samanna were baptized. Harry was not baptized, which must have distressed his maternal grandfather, a church deacon. The extended family gathered for picnics and birthday parties, but Harry did not feel particularly close to his relatives, apart from Samanna, who had taken care of him when he was small and remained attentive to him after her marriage. He sometimes stayed with Samanna and her husband, Oliver Hallman, who operated a foundry and blacksmith shop, where Harry picked up ironworking skills and practiced shooting an old pistol.

Fascinated by the Civil War, Harry read about it in dime novels and even bought a one-dollar library card from the Young Men's Literary Union in Phoenixville in January 1882. Books alone, however, could not satisfy his curiosity about the world outside small-town Pennsylvania, and he went to Philadelphia that June. After finding no work there, he continued on to New York and Boston but returned home at the end of July still unemployed.

A month later, at the age of fifteen, he set off for Illinois to join cousins George and Mary Longenbaugh and their two-year-old son, Walter, on a trip by covered wagon to Colorado. (Different branches of the clan varied the spelling of the family name, as did the Pinkertons and the reporters who wrote about Sundance.) The Longenbaughs settled on a homestead in Durango, and Mary soon gave birth to another child. Harry worked with George, breeding and raising horses. By

1884, the Longenbaughs had moved to Cortez, about fifty miles from Durango and eighty miles from Telluride. Harry went with them and continued to help out on their homestead in his spare time, while toiling as a horse wrangler on the LC ranch. Also bunking in the area were several outlaws or soon-to-be outlaws, including Matt Warner, the McCarty brothers, Bill Madden, Dan Parker, and Robert LeRoy Parker. Whether Harry ran across any of these men at that time is unknown but not unlikely.

The severe winter of 1884 threw hundreds of Colorado ranch hands, including Harry, out of work. Hoping to find a job with a rodeo, he left his cousins and headed north. He soon joined a large cattle drive en route from Texas to Montana and impressed the outfit's owners so much that they offered him a job on their N–N ranch near Miles City, Montana, when the drive ended. He stayed at the ranch all summer, then was let go in the winter. Harvey "Kid Curry" Logan, the most notorious and violent man ever to ride with the Wild Bunch, lived nearby, and Harry probably met him during this period.

The N–N rehired Harry in 1886, then laid him off again late in the year. Now nineteen years old, Harry went to the Black Hills in South Dakota, near the borders of Montana and Wyoming. Unable to find a job as a ranch hand, he began working for room and board and wending his way back toward Montana. After selling all his belongings for food and shelter, he was desperate to reach friends who could help him. On February 27, 1887, he stopped at the VVV ranch on Crow Creek, near the town of Sundance in Crook County, Wyoming, and stole a light-grey horse, a saddle outfit, and a revolver. He headed northwest to Miles City and was apprehended there on April 8 by Crook County Sheriff James Ryan, who had tracked the "smooth-faced, grey-eyed boy" a distance of two hundred miles. Ryan locked Harry in the local jail for four days and then took him back by train via St. Paul, Minnesota, where the sheriff apparently had other business. At some point during this fourteen-hundred-mile detour, while Ryan was in the lavatory, Harry picked the locks on his handcuffs and shackles and jumped off the train. Ryan halted the train and offered a $250 reward for the youth's recapture but was forced to return home empty-handed, "dejected and grieved."

Once free, Harry made the inexplicable decision to return to Miles City. After two months at liberty, he was caught by Deputy Sheriff Eph

K. Davis and Stock Inspector W. Smith. On June 7, 1887, the *Daily Yellowstone Journal* described the arrest in a front-page article with dramatic headlines:

HE PLAYED 'POSSUM

HOW DEPUTY SHERIFF E.K. DAVIS

FOOLED A FLY YOUNG CRIMINAL

HE HAD IN CHARGE

THE ASTONISHING RECORD OF CRIME

PERPETRATED BY HARRY LONGABAUGH

IN THREE WEEKS

A FLY KID

AND THE WAY HE WAS CAUGHT UP BY OFFICERS

DAVIS AND SMITH

According to the *Journal,* after escaping from Ryan, Harry "made his way back to Montana over the Canadian Pacific, and just before leaving Canadian soil stole seven head of horses from an operator on the new road and sold them near Benton." The article went on to name Harry as the culprit in all the recent crimes in the area and to describe his attempt at a second escape.

> After Mr. Davis had made the arrest he took three six-shooters from the bold young criminal and shackled him and handcuffed him with some patent lock bracelets which were warranted to hold anything until unlocked by the key and which the manufacturers offered a premium if they could be opened otherwise. Eph Davis had heard a good deal of Longabaugh's prowess in effecting escape, and after taking all due precautions when night closed in upon them he lay down in one corner of a shack and Mr. Smith in another, the kid between them. Smith was tired out and soon fell to sleep and Davis played 'possum, keeping an eye on the prisoner. Soon as he thought everyone was asleep the kid, shackled and manacled as he was, managed to free himself and rising stealthily approached the window and raised it and was about to make a break for liberty when sly old Eph thought it was time for him to take a hand and

raising on his elbow with a cocked six-shooter in his hand he said in a quiet tone of voice, "Kid, you're loose, ain't you?" and then called to Smith. The kid dropped back as though he was shot and it is needless to add that the officers did not sleep at the same time during the rest of the night. Resolving not to lose his prisoner or reward this time, Sheriff Irvine has telegraphed Sheriff Ryan asking what he will give for the Kid laid down in Sundance. Talk about the James boys, this fellow has all the necessary accomplishments to outshine them all and Tom Irvine considers him one of the most daring and desperate criminals he has ever had to deal with.

On June 9, 1887, the newspaper published a letter to the editor from the "Kid" himself:

In your issue of the 7th inst. I read a very sensational and partly untrue article, which places me before the public not even second to the notorious Jesse James. Admitting that I have done wrong and expecting to be dealt with according to law and not by false reports from parties who should blush with shame to make them, I ask a little of your space to set my case before the public in a true light. In the first place I have always worked for an honest living; was employed last summer by one of the best outfits in Montana and don't think they can say aught against me, but having got discharged last winter I went to the Black Hills to seek employment—which I could not get—and was forced to work for my board a month and a half, rather than to beg or steal. I finally started back to the vicinity of Miles City, as it was spring, to get employment on the range and was arrested at the above named place and charged with having stolen a horse at Sundance, where I was being taken by Sheriff Ryan, whom I escaped from by jumping from the cars, which I judged were running at the rate of 100 miles an hour. After this my course of outlawry commenced, and I suffered terribly for the want of food in the hope of getting back south without being detected, where I would be looked upon as I always had been, and not as a criminal. Contrary to the statement in the Journal, I deny having stolen any horses in Canada and selling them near Benton, or anyplace else, up to the time

I was captured, at which time I was riding a horse which I bought and paid for, nor had I the slightest idea of stealing any horses. I am aware that some of your readers will say my statement should be taken for what it is worth, on account of the hard name which has been forced upon me, nevertheless it is true. As for my recapture by Deputy Sheriff Davis, all I can say is that he did his work well and were it not for his "playing possum" I would now be on my way south, where I had hoped to go and live a better life.

Harry Longabaugh

Ten days later, the *Journal* noted that Sheriff Ryan had arrived "to take charge of Kid Longabaugh" and would "take such precautions this time that it [would] tax the ingenuity and hardihood of a slicker chap than the Kid to get away." This time, Ryan and his prisoner traveled directly to Sundance by buckboard. On June 19, the *Journal* reported that "Longabaugh was securely shackled and handcuffed, the shackles being made of steel and riveted with steel rivets, and [that] as they got aboard Ryan informed the kid that he was going to land him or his scalp in Sundance jail. The Kid gave him fair warning that he intended to escape and told him to watch him but not to be too rough on him."

No opportunity for escape presented itself on the way to Sundance, but while awaiting the next court session, the Kid and a fellow prisoner succeeded in removing a bolt head from their cell door before a guard discovered their handiwork and moved them to sturdier quarters. After negotiations with the prosecutor, Harry pleaded guilty to horse theft and was sentenced to eighteen months at hard labor. Because he was still a minor, he was allowed to serve his time in the Sundance jail instead of the Wyoming Territorial Prison at Laramie. He continued striving to escape and nearly succeeded once, when he and another inmate assaulted the jailor who brought their dinner.

At the request of the Crook County prosecutor, Governor Thomas Moonlight granted Harry a full pardon on February 4, 1889, one day before his scheduled release. As soon as he got out of jail, Harry—now destined to be known as the Sundance Kid—took the stagecoach to Deadwood, South Dakota. Three months later, on May 17, 1889, he was with Buck Hanby and two other men in a dugout on Oil Creek, about thirty-five miles north of Sundance, when lawmen burst in looking for Hanby, who was wanted for murder in Nebraska. Hanby reached for his gun, and Deputy Sheriff James Swisher shot and killed him. The next day, Swisher swore out a complaint against Harry, who had threatened to avenge the life of his friend. The time had come for the Sundance Kid to move on.

By the end of May, he was heading south for his cousin George Longenbaugh's home near Cortez, Colorado. According to Walter Longenbaugh, his Uncle Harry had no sooner returned than he teamed up with Butch Cassidy, Matt Warner, and Tom McCarty for the 1889 robbery of the San Miguel Valley Bank in Telluride. Walter's mother, Mary, is said to have fed the outlaws when they hid out at Tom McCarty's ranch, a mile and a half southwest of the Longenbaugh homestead.

Sundance did not stay long in Colorado; he returned to Montana and hired on at the John T. Murphy Cattle Company near Lavina and later at Henry Ester's ranch south of Malta. In 1890, Sundance went north to the Canadian province of Alberta, where he broke in new horses for the McHugh brothers at the H2 ranch near Fort Macleod and for the Calgary-Edmonton Railway Company near High River. By April 1891, Sundance had become a broncobuster for the Bar U ranch, one of the biggest spreads on the Alberta frontier. Fred Ings, who rode with him there, described him as "a thoroughly likeable fellow, a general favourite with everyone, a splendid rider, and a top notch cow hand." The North-West Mounted Police, however, arrested him for cruelty to animals, a charge that was dismissed on August 7, 1891. The following November, Sundance served as best man at the wedding of Everett C. Johnson—a Wyoming pal who was now the Bar U foreman—in High River. After cowboy Herb Millar saw something glitter under Sundance's saddle and discovered it to be a hacksaw blade, a tool sometimes carried by outlaws for emergency use on handcuffs and prison bars, Sundance fell under suspicion. Whether he was fired or not is unknown, but by the next fall, he had returned to Montana.

On November 29, 1892, he joined Bill Madden and Harry Bass in the inept holdup of a Great Northern train near Malta. The deed netted the robbers about $19 in cash, two small paychecks, and a few packages of unknown value. Arrested in a local saloon two days later, Madden and Bass wound up being sentenced to fourteen and ten years, respectively, in the state penitentiary at Deer Lodge, Montana. Sundance was apprehended at the Malta train depot but later escaped and headed straight for the Hole-in-the-Wall hideout, an ancient river-bed accessible through a notch in a steep sandstone wall near Kaycee, Wyoming.

During the winter of 1892–1893, he reportedly was back in Canada, operating the Grand Central Hotel Saloon on Atlantic Avenue in Calgary. When his partner, a disreputable tough named Frank Hamilton, tried to cheat him out of his share of the profits, Sundance took the money at gunpoint and left. Where he went next is unknown, although unconfirmed reports put him in the bandlands of southern Saskatchewan, perhaps in Big Beaver, near the Montana border. By 1895, he had returned to the United States and was once again working for the N–N ranch, which had moved its headquarters from Miles City to Oswego, in northeastern Montana. He also worked part-time with a gang of rustlers who operated near Culbertson, a few miles from the North Dakota border.

Sundance spent the winter of 1896–1897 at Robbers' Roost with Etta Place. Then springtime came, the young bandits' fancies turned to crime, and their women went home. In late April, Butch and Elzy stole a payroll from the Pleasant Valley Coal Company in Castle Gate, Utah, and scooted back into Robbers' Roost with $7,000 in gold. A few weeks later, Sundance teamed up with Harvey and Lonnie Logan, Tom O'Day, "Flatnose" George Currie, and fifteen-year-old Walt Punteney to rob the Butte County Bank in Belle Fourche, South Dakota. The robbery had barely begun when the drunken O'Day fired his gun outside, alerting townsfolk that mischief was afoot. Having spooked his horse, which he had neglected to tie up, O'Day took refuge in an outhouse and was soon arrested. The other bandits, forced to leave more than $1,000 in gold and silver in a teller's tray behind the counter, got away with only $97, snatched from the hand of a customer.

After eluding a posse of nearly a hundred men, the bandits split up. Sundance, Harvey Logan, and Punteney took refuge in the Hole-in-the-Wall area for a couple of months, then rode north to Montana. Another posse picked up their trail in Red Lodge and confronted them north of Lavina in late September. Following a brief skirmish, the outlaws were captured, extradited to South Dakota, and jailed with the incompetent Tom O'Day, who was still awaiting trial. At the end of October, the bandits overpowered a deputy sheriff, escaped through the exercise yard, and rode off on horses left near the jail by a confederate.

Sundance crossed the state line into Montana and eventually headed south to join Butch and other members of the Wild Bunch at the W.S. ranch in Alma, New Mexico, near the Arizona and Mexican borders. Using the alias Jim Lowe, Butch worked as a foreman for Captain William French and hired Elzy Lay, Harvey Logan, and other pals as hands. Captain French, unaware of their true occupations, was pleased to note that rustling of W.S. livestock soon stopped—indeed, the herds seemed to increase. Although the ranch hands came and went, tending to business elsewhere from to time, the W.S. ran smoothly; Butch never had any trouble finding good men to fill in as needed.

After wintering in New Mexico, Sundance rode north and joined Harvey Logan and George Currie in Brown's Park. In July 1898, they held up a Southern Pacific train near Humboldt, Nevada, and made off with about $450 and some jewelry. Sundance then returned to the W.S. ranch, where Butch was busy making a success of Captain French's operation. Both bandits remained in Alma through the winter, but in March, Sundance met Harvey Logan and George Currie in Brown's Park to plan another holdup.

Toward the end of the month, the three men rode into Elko, Nevada, and spent a week gambling before their money ran out. They had planned to rob the bank but altered their plans upon hearing rumors that the safe at the Club Saloon fairly bulged with cash. Moments after the saloon closed, the outlaws struck. They collected a mere $550 and hied to Brown's Park, where they found Butch planning the gang's biggest robbery to date.

Shortly after two in the morning on June 2, 1899, two members of the Wild Bunch flagged down and boarded a Union Pacific train just short of a bridge between Wilcox and Medicine Bow, Wyoming. They ordered the engineer to drive across the bridge, which exploded once the train had passed over it. The passenger cars were then uncoupled and left behind; the rest of the train went on another two miles to a rendezvous with four more members of the gang. When the mail clerks and the express messenger refused to open their cars, the bandits opened the doors with dynamite. They also opened the express-car safes with a heavy charge that blew the whole car to pieces and scattered the safes' contents across the land. The outlaws—who probably included the Sundance Kid, Harvey Logan, Lonnie Logan, Flatnose George Currie, Will Carver, and Ben Kilpatrick—picked up more than $30,000 in cash, unsigned banknotes, jewelry, and loose diamonds, then rode off to the north. They were joined the next day by another man, perhaps Butch Cassidy, who is credited with having masterminded the job.

The group split up, and those led by Flatnose George hurried to Hole-in-the-Wall. A posse led by Josiah Hazen traced the remaining outlaws, apparently including Sundance, to a cabin near Horse Ranch, Wyoming. Sheriff Hazen was fatally wounded in the ensuing gunfight. The bandits escaped on foot, and rewards totaling $18,000 were offered for them. The Pinkertons sent ace detective Charles A. Siringo, who dogged the men for weeks but lost their trail after a string of false leads. Unsigned banknotes taken in the heist turned up in Colorado, Montana, and New Mexico, but the culprits were never apprehended.

Following the July 1899 holdup of a Colorado & Southern train near Folsom, New Mexico, a posse bagged the wounded Elzy Lay and slew Sam Ketchum, but Will Carver got away. Although Butch and Sundance had advised Elzy to avoid Sam and his brother—"Black Jack" Ketchum, later hung for trying to rob a train by himself—Elzy ignored the warning and wound up sentenced to life in the New Mexico Territorial Prison. Pardoned and released in 1906, after rescuing the warden's wife and daughters and ending a riot, he went straight, if you can call working as a professional gambler in Tijuana going straight.

Meanwhile, in October 1899, a Pinkerton detective had visited the W.S. ranch, and Captain French had learned that Jim Lowe was Butch Cassidy. French didn't fire Butch but declined to promote him when a better job opened up. Soon afterward, Butch resigned.

In the early spring of 1900, he called on Judge Orlando W. Powers, a prominent Utah attorney who had helped to defend Matt Warner (recently released after a forty-month stretch in the Utah State Penitentiary). Butch asked Powers to look into the possibility of amnesty for past crimes in exchange for a promise not to commit any new ones. The governor rebuffed Powers, who then approached Union Pacific officials. They agreed not to prosecute Butch for prior offenses if he would swear never to rob another U.P. train. Moreover, the officials declared, they would gladly hire Butch as an express guard.

Powers sent the tidings to Butch via the bandit's personal attorney, Douglas Preston of Rock Springs, Wyoming. Pleased, but wary of a trap, Butch asked that Preston bring the officials to meet him ten days later at Lost Soldier Pass in a rugged area forty-five miles north of Rock Springs. A storm waylaid Preston and the railroad men, and they arrived a day late. Meanwhile, Butch had become suspicious of their intentions and departed, leaving a note for his attorney: "Damn you Preston you have double crossed me. I waited all day but you did not show up. Tell the U.P. to go to hell and you can go with them."

Butch's next caper was the robbery of a Union Pacific train. Three other men joined Butch in the holdup, which took place between Tipton and Table Rock, Wyoming, in the early morning hours of August 29, 1900. After assuring the trainmen that no harm would come to them or the passengers, the outlaws went to work with their dynamite and managed to blow off the roof, sides, and ends of the baggage car and the car next to it. An hour's work earned them $55,000 and some jewelry. Two weeks later, three posses were still chasing them. U.S. Deputy Marshal Joe LeFors tracked his quarries as far as the Little Snake River near Baggs, Wyoming, before losing their trail.

Although Butch had invited him to participate in the Tipton job, Sundance had sent word that he couldn't make it. He was on his way to Nevada, where he met with Harvey Logan and Will Carver to plan the robbery of the First National Bank of Winnemucca. On September 19, the trio stole nearly $33,000 in a daring holdup that lasted no more than five minutes. Butch apparently played a role in the Winnemucca holdup: He was seen with the other bandits in the days before the robbery, although he did not enter the bank or flee with the men who pulled the job. A posse followed the bandits by train for a while and then switched to horses. After shaking their pursuers near Tuscarora, the bandits escaped into Idaho through a wild area known as the Junipers. By this time, the rewards for their capture had grown to more than $10,000 a head. Logan and Carver made for Texas, while Sundance went to California to visit his brother Elwood, a sailor on whaling ships out of San Francisco.

Later that fall, several members of the Wild Bunch gathered in Fort Worth, Texas, to celebrate their recent victories over the railroad companies. The bandits made the rounds of the taverns, gaming parlors, and brothels in the bawdy district known as Hell's Half Acre. Flushed with the joy of hard-won prosperity, Will Carver married his sweetheart, Lillie Davis, a onetime prostitute from Fanny Porter's bordello in San Antonio. The gang threw a reception for the happy couple in Maddox Flats. Five of the bandits—Butch, Sundance, Harvey Logan, Ben Kilpatrick, and Will Carver—duded up like bankers in derbies and three-piece suits and posed for photographer John Swartz. This proved to be a colossal blunder. A Wells Fargo detective soon spotted the portrait in the window of Swartz's studio and recognized Will Carver. The detective obtained copies and sent them to fellow law officers and the Pinkertons, who snipped the photo apart for WANTED circulars that found their way to posts as remote as Tahiti.

When the outlaws parted company that fall, Will Carver stayed in Texas with his bride and was killed by a sheriff the following April. In July, Harvey Logan and Ben Kilpatrick, who had headed north from Forth Worth, held up a Great Northern train near Wagner, Montana, perhaps with the help of O. C. Hanks and Kilpatrick's girlfriend, Laura Bullion. Bullion and Kilpatrick were nabbed in November 1901, after trying to pass stolen banknotes in St. Louis, and were ultimately sentenced to five and fifteen years, respectively, in a federal penitentiary. Hanks was killed while resisting arrest in San Antonio in the spring of 1902. Logan was captured and tried in Tennessee but escaped from the Knox County jail before he could be transferred to the federal penitentiary to serve his sentence of twenty years at hard labor. Following the June 1904 robbery of a train near Parachute, Colorado, the badly wounded Logan committed suicide rather than surrender (although some witnesses claimed that the body was misidentified and that Logan had actually escaped). Ben Kilpatrick was released in July 1911, only to be slain eight months later by an ice-mallet-wielding Wells Fargo messenger during a train robbery. Laura Bullion, the last known survivor of the Wild Bunch, died in Memphis in 1961.

Meanwhile, after the festivities in Fort Worth, Butch and Sundance repaired to San Antonio, where they had often romped with Fanny Porter's girls, drunk champagne, and cheered from a balcony while a member of the gang rode a bicycle in the street. Around the corner from Fanny's, in a similar establishment at 212 South Concho Street, lived a twenty-three-year-old unemployed music teacher named Ethel Bishop. A local directory of the sporting district rated Ethel's place of residence as a class-A house, one that not only offered the usual services but also allowed guests to spend the night, have their clothes pressed, and eat breakfast. Ethel had been born in West Virginia in September 1876, according to census records recently located by Sundance's relatives Paul and Donna Ernst, who believe her to have been Etta Place.

Whatever her true identity, Etta accompanied Sundance to New Orleans, where they celebrated the end of the nineteenth century on New Year's Eve. They then traveled north by train to Pennsylvania, and Sundance introduced Etta as his wife to his brother Harvey and sisters, Samanna and Emma. During this visit, Sundance told his family that he had been shot in the left leg out west and planned to see a doctor. He wanted to go straight, he said, but felt that his notoriety precluded his doing so in the United States. He had decided, therefore, to move to Argentina, where he could buy a ranch and settle down without worrying about Pinkerton detectives showing up on his doorstep.

Why Argentina? What drew Butch and Sundance as well as Teddy Roosevelt, William Jennings Bryan, Will Rogers, Anatole France, Enrico Ferri, and Georges Clemenceau there during the early 1900s? British author James Bryce visited the country during that era and wrote: "All is modern and new; all belongs to the prosperous present and betokens a still more prosperous future. Argentina is like western North America. The swift and steady increase in its agricultural production, with an increase correspondingly large in means of internal transportation, is what gives its importance to the country and shews that it will have a great part to play in the world. It is the United States of the Southern Hemisphere."

After saying goodbye to his family, Sundance and Etta went to Buffalo, New York, and checked into Dr. Pierce's Invalids Hotel, a medical clinic that offered Turkish baths and holistic remedies for "chronic diseases—particularly those of a delicate, obscure, complicated, or obstinate character." Upon leaving Buffalo, the couple visited Niagara Falls.

By the first of February, they had reunited with Butch in New York City. Using the aliases Mr. and Mrs. Harry Place and James Ryan, and posing as a Wyoming cattle buyer, his wife, and her brother, they rented the best second-floor suite in a boarding house at 234 West Twelfth Street. They then spent three weeks relaxing and touring the city. Sundance and Etta posed for a portrait at the DeYoung Photography Studio, and Butch bought a forty-dollar watch from Tiffany's. At last, on February 20, 1901, the trio boarded the British ship *Herminius* and steamed off to build a new life for themselves in the "United States of the Southern Hemisphere."

3 · GRINGOS IN PATAGONIA

ALL the taxis sailing down Second Avenue in the grey dawn are taken. Trenchcoated lawyers with fat briefcases wave in vain at the passing yellow streaks. We walk up two blocks to a corner free of sharp-elbowed rivals. After a shivery half-hour, we finally land a cab of our own and join the honking flotilla bound for lower Manhattan.

We arrive late for our appointment at the Pinkerton Detective

Agency's Church Street headquarters and find that we're not on the receptionist's schedule, which means that we have no business being here at all. Glaring at us over the black rims of her reading glasses, the receptionist scratches her head with the eraser of a number 4 pencil, then shoulders her telephone to track down George O'Neill, the man in charge of the archives. From the wall behind her desk, founder Alan Pinkerton's portrait regards us with similar disdain.

Leaving his sons Robert and William to run the agency, the senior Pinkerton retired well before the Wild Bunch's heyday. The Pinkertons had offices in all the principal cities in the United States and Canada and cooperated with North American and European police departments and with the forerunner of the Federal Bureau of Investigation. After Butch and Sundance fled the country, the Pinkertons kept tabs on them by watching the homes of friends and relatives, paying postal informants to open letters from the bandits, and even sending a detective to Argentina to verify reports that they had taken refuge there.

O'Neill appears at last and apologizes about having an urgent meeting, then leads us through quiet hallways and unlocks the door to the long, narrow room where the archives repose. Before hurrying off, he tells us which of the several oak cabinets contain files on the Wild Bunch. Guns, badges, and other relics of the agency's most celebrated feats are arrayed in glass display cases on top of the cabinets, and black-and-white photographs in burled-walnut frames tell of badmen and the detectives who chased them. Dan hauls several thick binders over to a big oak table, and we leaf through handwritten notes and memoranda typed in faded ink on paper brittle with age.

Compared with the voluminous record of Wild Bunch activities in the United States, the information about the years Butch, Sundance, and Etta spent in South America is scant, but we come away with photocopies of several interesting documents. A July 1902 report, for example, reveals not only that the trio visited Manhattan before leaving for Argentina in February 1901 but that Sundance and Etta returned to New York on the steamship *Soldier Prince,* arriving on April 3, 1902. The Pinkertons found no evidence that Butch had returned from South America. According to the report, Etta was "said to be [Sundance's] wife and to be from Texas."

After receiving this report and a copy of the 1901 portrait of Sundance and Etta taken at DeYoung's studio, William Pinkerton complained in a letter to his brother Robert that it was "a great pity we did not get the information regarding the photograph while this party was in New York. It shows how daring these men are, and while you are looking for them in the wilderness and mountains they are in the midst of society."

The most detailed report on the bandits' Argentine life appears in a memorandum written by agent Frank Dimaio nearly four decades after the events he described. Having completed an assignment in Brazil in March 1903, Dimaio traveled to Buenos Aires to follow up an informant's tip that Butch and Sundance were ranching in Argentina under the names James Ryan and Harry A. Place. Dimaio reviewed the records of the local steamship companies and met with officials who might aid his search. When shown photographs of Butch, Sundance, and Etta, U.S. vice-consul George Newbery, a dentist in Buenos Aires, said that they were "located on a sheep ranch at Cholila, province of Chubut, district of 16th de Octubre, and . . . were considered respectable citizens."

Newbery, who owned an *estancia* 130 miles north of Cholila, told Dimaio "that it would be impossible to apprehend these criminals at that time due to the fact that about May 1st the rainy season would set in and [the] country would become so flooded it would be impossible for the authorities to reach Cholila and bring about their arrest. That in order to reach Cholila it would be necessary to go to Puerto Madryn, 250 miles south of Buenos Aires, and then travel by horseback for about 15 days through the jungle. That it would be necessary to hire a peon familiar with the trail. Upon arrival in Cholila the commandant of the garrison at the 16th October would have to be seen and arrangements made for the arrest of these criminals."

The description of the route inland perplexes us, because aside from the forested slopes of the Andes, nothing in the Patagonian landscape remotely resembles a jungle. Was Newbery deliberately misleading Dimaio? Did Dimaio misunderstand what was said? Perhaps he fudged the description to avoid an arduous journey to the home of sharpshooters who would welcome him with firearms. The memorandum continues: "I called on the chief of police Beazley and explained the situation to him. He said he would render every assistance. Later I visited the various banks in Buenos Aires. At the London & River Plate I met the manager, who advised me that Harry A. Place had opened an account with the bank on March 23, 1901, depositing $12,000 in gold notes. He gave as his address Hotel Europa. . . . Place drew out his balance of $1,105.50, August 14, 1902. . . . The manager had no record of Place since, but it was believed he was still at Cholila. When shown the photographs of these people, the manager readily recognized them.''

Dimaio's handwritten notes provide further details. Butch apparently accompanied Etta and Sundance to Buenos Aires before their March 1902 departure on the *Soldier Prince*. Posing as Etta's brother, Butch spent three weeks at the Hotel Europa. On April 2, one day before Sundance and Etta disembarked in New York, Butch filed a document at the colonial land department informing the Argentine government that Harry Place and Santiago Ryan "had settled on four square leagues of government land in the province of Chubut," that they were raising livestock and improving the land, and that they wished to be granted the first right to buy it. Both men had signed the petition. Dimaio learned that the land had not yet been sold, which meant that the bandits were squatters.

After completing his business with the colonial land department, Butch caught the fortnightly steamer from Buenos Aires to Bahía Blanca and took a smaller boat to Rawson, at the mouth of the Chubut River. Near the beginning of the 450-mile journey on horseback up the Chubut Valley to Cholila, he stopped at the Welsh settlement of Trelew, where Angel M. Botaro cashed a check for $3,546 drawn on the London & River Plate account.

Meanwhile, according to other Pinkerton records, Sundance and Etta had registered as Mr. and Mrs. Harry Place in a rooming house on the lower east side of Manhattan and taken an excursion to Coney Island. They also visited Sundance's brother Harvey in Atlantic City and his sisters in Pennsylvania. Samanna's family later recalled that Sundance mentioned being treated for a gunshot wound in his leg at a Chicago hospital, but no one knows when the treatment occurred. It may have been the basis of a May 10, 1902, report by a Pinkerton operative who had obtained brief descriptions of Etta and Sundance from officials at an unnamed medical facility that had treated Sundance for an undisclosed ailment.

The DeYoung photo had not yet found its way into the Pinkertons' hands, so this may have been the first word of Etta's existence to reach their ears. The report described her as being twenty-three or twenty-four years old; standing 5'5"; weighing 110 pounds; and having medium-dark hair, blue or grey eyes, regular features, and a medium complexion with no marks or blemishes. The only new information about Sundance was that instead of being bowlegged, as numerous witnesses described him, he had small feet that turned in when he walked.

Dimaio learned that the couple had left New York again on the freighter *Honorius* on July 10, 1902, which meant that they had been in the United States for more than three months, ample time to visit not only Sundance's relatives but Etta's as well, wherever they might have been. The ship had docked in Buenos Aires on August 9. Dimaio found Mr. and Mrs. Place on the crew list, which described them as a purser and a stewardess (officially, the freighter carried no passengers). They had spent five days at the Hotel Europa before closing out their account at the London & River Plate Bank and sailing on the *Chubut* to Puerto Madryn, a Welsh settlement not far from Rawson on the Patagonian coast. Their round-trip passage to New York had cost them about three hundred dollars apiece.

According to Dimaio's notes, Newbery described Etta as "the only white woman in the province," which wasn't true, and he called Place and Ryan good fellows who were doing well and had doubled their stock. The dentist-diplomat-rancher said that he planned to return to his own Patagonian *estancia* the following November and would attempt to help Chief Beazley lure Butch and Sundance to Buenos Aires on the pretext of having them sign the title to their land. Dimaio gave the chief a list of code words with which he could discreetly notify the Pinkertons by cable if the bandits tried to leave Argentina. Before sailing from Buenos Aires in May 1903, Dimaio arranged for circulars to be printed in Spanish to alert Argentine police departments and steamship companies that Butch, Sundance, and Etta were wanted in North America and that rewards would be paid for their capture and extradition. For good measure, Dimaio included a photo and description of Harvey Logan, who had recently escaped from jail in Tennessee.

On July 1, a few weeks after Dimaio's return to the United States, Robert Pinkerton sent a letter warning the Buenos Aires police chief of the threat the bandits posed to the ranchers, bankers, trains, and lawmen of Argentina: "It is our firm belief that it is only a question of time until these men commit some desperate robbery in the Argentine Republic. They are all thorough plainsmen and horsemen, riding from 600 to 1,000 miles after committing a robbery. If there are reported to you any bank or train hold up robberies or any other similar crimes, you will find that they were undoubtedly committed by these men."

The Pinkertons then set about soliciting the help of U.S. railroad companies and the American Bankers Association to finance "the cost of running down and apprehending Harry Longbaugh, alias Harry Alonzo, and George Parker, alias Butch Cassidy." The bandits' former victims, however, preferred to leave them where they were. If extradited home from Argentina, they might well escape and again threaten U.S. banks and trains. Let the South Americans worry about them. The Pinkertons, unwilling to use their own funds for the $5,000 they estimated as the cost of mounting an expedition to Cholila, reluctantly let the matter drop.

They continued to monitor the outlaws' activities, however, and an October 1904 memorandum reported that Sundance and Etta had been sighted near Fort Worth, Texas, in late 1903 or early 1904. The Pinkertons also kept records of South American crimes and credited Butch and Sundance with robberies in Chile, Peru, and Bolivia, as well as several Argentine jobs, including various local holdups between 1901 and 1903, and bank robberies in Río Gallegos, Villa Mercedes de San Luis, and Bahía Blanca. Although Harvey Logan and Etta Place were often cited as suspects in these crimes, the Pinkertons could not document their participation in any of them. In a February 1910 letter to William Pinkerton in Chicago, for example, an official from the agency's New York office wrote that "in the robbery of the bank of Río Gallegos, Etta Place, Harry Longbaugh's wife, in male attire, is alleged to have held the horses while Longbaugh and Cassidy committed the robbery. But our information is that there were some other North American desperadoes down there with these men. We have never been advised that Harvey Logan's photograph has been identified as being in the Argentine Republic."

The other desperadoes mentioned in this letter may have been Robert Evans and William Wilson, whom Argentine police official Milton Roberts named as the perpetrators of the 1909 robbery and murder of Llwyd ap Iwan, a Welsh shopkeeper in the northern Patagonian settlement of Arroyo Pescado. In a letter to the Pinkertons, Roberts described Evans as "about 35 years of age, 5 feet 7 in. in height, inclined to be stout and thickly built, color of hair red, which we believe to be false, blue eyes, short roman nose, face red from sunburn," and Wilson as "about 25 years of age, 5 ft. 11 in. in height, slightly built, fair hair, complexion dark from sun tan, nose short and straight, walks with the right foot turned out." According to Roberts, Evans had "been in the sheep stealing line for about two years" in southern

Argentina, and Wilson "had been working [there] about two years as a wagoner and [was] a very good shearer."

Perhaps the most intriguing tidbit we find among the thousands of foxed, chipped pages in the Pinkerton archives is a September 28, 1940, letter to the agency's criminal-identification department from a man seeking information about Etta Place's background. The man had heard that Etta was either a Massachusetts schoolteacher or the daughter of a rancher, and that she "was killed by Mateo Gebhard, who broke up the Wild Bunch rendezvous in Chubut, Argentina, in March 1922, Gebhard having taken her at the battle at the ranchos 12 or 15 years before."

This is the first we've heard of a Wild Bunch rendezvous in Chubut or a battle at the "ranchos," whatever he meant by that. And who was Mateo Gebhard?

"Gebhard," says Argentine journalist Francisco "Tito" Juárez, "organized the frontier police, after Evans and Wilson killed a popular Welsh shopkeeper at Arroyo Pescado and kidnapped a rancher who lived in Chubut but was from a powerful family in Buenos Aires. The *fronterizas* arrested hundreds of brigands and rustlers and killed many others. They also tracked down Evans and Wilson and shot them in Río Pico in 1911. Of course, all that was after Cassidy's time."

A short man with dark-grey hair and a paunch, Tito has invited us to his apartment in Palermo Viejo, the Bohemian, working-class Buenos Aires neighborhood immortalized in poems by its most famous resident, Jorge Luis Borges. Cristina Juárez serves *empanadas* from a nearby deli. The family has just returned from the beach, where Tito and Cristina celebrated their twenty-fifth wedding anniversary. "A record these days, no?" Tito puts his arm around his wife, who exudes boredom with his research project, which began soon after their marriage and promises to continue until death do them part.

We have returned to Argentina in search of more information about Butch and Sundance's activities here. Although we enjoy collecting the word-of-mouth stories, learning the truth is our primary goal. The challenge is to sort out the facts from the fables; we've been told that Tito is the man to help us do just that.

"I have mountains of material on Butch Cassidy in Argentina," he says, "including a few original letters, photocopies of police reports, hotel registers, land records, and so on. I have everything on the Río Gallegos and Villa Mercedes robberies."

"What about Bahía Blanca?" Dan asks.

Tito wags his finger and makes the sucking tut-tut sound that is Argentinian for *no*. "Bahía Blanca was in the 1890s, before they came here."

"And the Comodoro Rivadavia holdup?"

"Evans and Wilson. Cassidy would not have botched it the way they did. He was in a different class, he and his *compadre*, the Sundance Kid."

"What crimes did Butch and Sundance actually commit in Argentina?"

"They robbed one bank in Río Gallegos early in 1905 and another in Villa Mercedes de San Luis toward the end of that same year. That is all."

"Was Harvey Logan with them?"

Again the wagging finger and the sucking tut-tut. "The woman, Etta Place, she went with them to Río Gallegos but never went into town. She waited at their camp with fresh horses, and they all rode back to Cholila together. As soon as they reached their *estancia*, they began preparing to go to Chile. They left Argentina through the Cochamó pass, then returned months later via Mendoza, or perhaps Curicó, to plan the Villa Mercedes job."

"Did Etta participate in that robbery, as well?"

"I know everything, *but everything*, about the assault in Villa Mercedes. It was a work of art, very well planned way in advance. They escaped quickly to Chile. I talked with the daughter of the bank manager before she died. I interviewed the man who served them at the bar before the holdup. I even know how much they left as a tip." Like many researchers we have spoken with in the United States, however, Tito prefers to keep most of the details to himself.

"We've read that Etta Place and Harvey Logan were in Villa Mercedes."

"The woman, *sí*. Logan, *no*. The other man was an Argentine who worked for them."

At one o'clock, Cristina excuses herself and turns in. I try to drag Dan away, but Tito says, "No, no, what's your hurry?"

We stay until four.

In the late 1860s, when Butch and Sundance were born, fewer than two-hundred-thousand people lived in Buenos Aires; some thirty-five years later, when the bandits went into exile, the city had a million inhabitants. The booming Argentine economy—based on cattle, sheep, grain, corn, and the processing of agricultural products—had drawn hundreds of thousands of immigrants from Italy and Spain and smaller numbers from France, Germany, Russia, Lebanon, Syria, and other parts of the Near East. Although unemployment was high in 1901, the slump soon ended, and the demand for labor was so great that many Italians found it worthwhile to sail down for the Argentine harvest each December and January, then return to Italy and work on their own farms or vineyards during the other months.

Bryce found the approach to Buenos Aires inordinately dull:

> The vessel enters a muddy, reddish brown sea, and presently the winding channel, marked for a long way by buoys, shews how shallow is the water on either side. This is the estuary, two hundred miles long and at this point about thirty miles broad, of the Rio de la Plata. . . . Approaching the Argentine shore, one sees a few masts and many funnels rising above the tall hulls of steamships, docked in lines alongside huge wharves. Beyond the open space of the wharf runs a row of offices and warehouses, but nothing else is seen, nor can one tell, except from the size of the docks and the crowd of vessels, that a great city lies behind. Nothing can be seen, because Buenos Aires stands . . . in a perfectly flat alluvial plain, with scarcely any rise in the ground for hundreds of miles.

Reading this account, I picture Etta looking accusingly at Sundance and wondering why she had left home. Her doubts would have been allayed, however, once she cleared customs and headed into the city. James R. Scobie, who has written extensively on Argentine history, described what a traveler entering Buenos Aires in the early twentieth century saw, once beyond the warehouses and grain elevators:

> The horses climbed briskly up the fifty-foot rise which marked the line where the riverbank had been before port construction reclaimed nearly 150 city blocks from the estuary. As his carriage moved around the Plaza de Mayo . . . and up the broad Avenida de Mayo, the visitor received many fleeting

impressions: of a low and columned Cabildo, the only reminder of Spain's architectural heritage remaining on the plaza; of the pillars and squatness of the Cathedral, which resembled the Madeleine of Paris; of elegance along the Avenida de Mayo, with its rows of trees and streetlights and its sidewalk cafés; of the multistory buildings . . . that lent further credence to comparisons with Paris. The narrow streets off the Avenida de Mayo . . . seemed to overflow with streetcars, carriages, huge horse-drawn carts, and automobiles. Wall posters, store signs, banners, and flags dazzled the eyes, while the cries of street vendors, peddlers, and newspaper boys, and the insistent clamor of streetcar bells, car horns, and shouting cart drivers, assaulted the ears. On all sides raged the fever of a city under full construction: sidewalks torn up for gas mains or sewer connections; piles of sand and stone half blocking thorough-fares; wrecking crews opening swaths for two newly decreed diagonal avenues or widening existing streets into avenues; paving gangs replacing cobblestones with wood blocks or as-phalt; and overhead the hum of a tangle of streetcar, telephone, and electrical wiring.

According to Scobie, "the narrowness of the streets, which had been laid out at the founding of the city in the sixteenth century, often resulted in a jostling and dangerous jumble of pedestrians, carts, streetcars, and carriages. Especially in the financial and commercial zones, the pedestrian's major concern was to avoid being elbowed into the path of a passing streetcar or horse-drawn vehicle. A few streets had served since colonial times to empty rainwater and wastes toward the estuary, and the height of their sidewalks, which were raised several feet above street level, added further hazards."

Comparing Buenos Aires with other great cities, Bryce found that it matched or exceeded their standards:

Buenos Aires deserves its name, for its air is clear as well as keen, there being no large manufacturing works to pollute it with coal smoke. The streets are well kept; everything is fresh and bright. The most striking buildings besides those of the new Legislative Chambers, with their tall and handsome dome, are the Opera-house, the interior of which equals any in Europe, and the Jockey Club, whose scale and elaborate appointments surpass even the club-houses of New York.

Buenos Aires is something between Paris and New York. It has the business rush and the luxury of the one, the gaiety and pleasure-loving aspect of the other. Everybody seems to have money, and to like spending it, and to like letting everybody else know that it is being spent. Betting on horses is the favourite amusement, and the races the greatest occasion for social display. An immense concourse gathers at the racing enclosure and fills the grand-stand. The highest officials of state and city are there, as well as the world of wealth and fashion. The ladies are decked out with all the Parisian finery and jewels that money can buy. . . . On fine afternoons, there is a wonderful turnout of carriages drawn by handsome horses, and . . . of costly motor cars, in the principal avenues of the Park; they press so thick that vehicles are often jammed together for fifteen or twenty minutes, unable to move on. Nowhere in the world does one get a stronger impression of exuberant wealth and extravagance. The Park itself, called Palermo, lies on the edge of the city towards the river, and is approached by a well-designed and well-planted avenue. . . . The Botanical Garden, though all too small, is extremely well arranged and of the highest interest to a naturalist, who finds in it an excellent collection of South American trees and shrubs.

When Dan and I first visited Buenos Aires in 1978, the Botanical Garden provided a home for hundreds of stray cats. They hid like Easter eggs under every bush, tree, and bench and dined on milk, crackers, fish, and meat delivered daily by an army of kindly neighbors. We went to the garden often until we read a newspaper article about corpses—victims of the military *junta*—turning up in Palermo Park. (More than nine thousand people died in the Dirty War, mostly in the late 1970s. Many of the victims were buried in graves marked "*n.n.*"—meaning *ningun nombre*, no name.)

The *junta* is gone, but the sidewalks are as crowded as ever when Tito Juárez takes us on a walking tour of downtown Buenos Aires to see the former locations of the Hotel Europa, the London & River Plate Bank, and other establishments patronized by Butch, Sundance, and Etta. The heat and humidity are beastly. Accustomed as they were to the arid Rocky Mountain West, I don't suppose the bandits liked the summers in Buenos Aires any more than I do. No wonder everybody leaves town in January and February. I watch for an air-conditioned ice-cream parlor while Tito and Dan swap bits of information about the Wild Bunch.

"No, no, no!" says Tito. "Cassidy did not join them here in 1902. All three of them arrived in Buenos Aires at the same time, in March 1901."

"But the researchers I've talked to insist that Butch joined them later because he was still in the United States on July 3, 1901, robbing a train near Wagner, Montana, with Harvey Logan and Ben Kilpatrick."

Tito's finger begins to wag. "I have proof that Cassidy could not possibly have been in Montana then. I have a document signed by him here in Argentina on that very day."

"Okay, the three of them came to Buenos Aires together. Then they caught a boat to Rawson and went up the Chubut Valley in a wagon."

"No. They took the train from here to Neuquén. They bought horses there and continued south to Cholila on horseback. The famous trip to Rawson happened later. That was when Sundance and Etta went back home for a visit. They rode to Rawson on horses and caught a ship from there to Buenos Aires."

"Why did they choose Cholila?"

Tito strokes his moustache. "That, I don't know."

"How did they buy their land?"

"They didn't. They were homesteaders and left before their purchase was completed."

"But they sold the land to the Cochamó company."

"No, they sold their livestock. Not the land. They didn't own it."

"What prompted them to leave Cholila?"

"Look, they lived peacefully until after Dimaio came and papered the area with WANTED posters. I talked to all their neighbors, all the people who had known them. I used to work for a radio station in Bariloche, just half a day's drive north, and all those people were still alive then. I have letters to and from the outlaws, letters about them, invoices, and other contemporary records of their comings, goings, and doings. I know where they purchased their windows."

The most famous windows in Argentina.

"I know all about Etta dancing with the governor. I know about

Cassidy's problems with the language; he didn't speak much Spanish. After giving a gun to a person who was later involved in a crime, Cassidy had to testify about the gun in court, which made him uncomfortable."

"Is that why they left?"

"No, no. They found out that the Pinkertons knew where they were."

"So when are you going to write a book?" asks Dan. "I'll buy the first five copies."

"Oh, you know, I have several other projects to finish first. The economy is such a mess now. I have to work three jobs just to make ends meet. If I live long enough, I hope to write the story of Patagonia. Not just the bandits. They were part of it, but there was much more."

We see Tito again in Patagonia, at his mother's home in San Carlos de Bariloche, an overgrown resort town that sprawls along the shore of the deep-blue Lake Nahuel Huapi beneath the eleven-thousand-foot snowcapped peaks of the Tronador ridge. Founded on the site of a German-Chilean immigrant's trading post shortly after the turn of the century, the town flourished after rail service was inaugurated in 1934. Today, Bariloche is a small city crowded with skiers in winter and boisterous teenagers in summer. When Butch, Sundance, and Etta rode through on their way to Cholila, scarcely a thousand people lived in the steep-roofed stone-and-wood buildings that still give the center of Bariloche the look of a Bavarian village. The town's first hotel opened within a year of the bandits' arrival, and a one-room schoolhouse was constructed, as well. Area residents, who included many immigrants— Chileans, Germans, Spaniards, Norwegians, Italians, Russians, Arabs, French, and North Americans—traveled on cart tracks rather than roads, and there were no bridges over the rivers.

Tito's mother-in-law, Erika Kerwitz, lives in an old two-story wooden house with a deep front yard shaded by cypresses and beeches and screened from the noisy street by tall hedges. When we arrive, Tito is out front preparing a bed of coals for today's *asado*, which will include half a goat, several slabs of beef, and a panoply of sausages. Doña Erika's cat, which has not fully recovered from last night's table scraps, dozes under the raspberry bushes. We chat amid the usual Argentine interruptions—people coming and going, kissing hello and goodbye. Tito's teenage daughter brings out wine and fruit juice. I've had enough wine in the past week to last me a good six months. Envying the cat under the raspberries, I opt for fruit juice. Dan and Tito drain a pitcher of dark red wine.

"So," says Dan, "Butch and Sundance and Etta disappeared from Argentina after the Villa Mercedes job. Then what?"

"They may have lived in Chile awhile," says Tito, "but I don't really know anything about what they did there. People in Cholila heard that they had been killed in Bolivia. And friends here stopped receiving letters and cables from them. I obtained a lot of material from the man who handled their affairs in their absence. They left their cattle with him and later sent him orders to sell it. He is the one who received word that they were killed in Bolivia."

More company arrives, their small cars slipping into the long driveway and docking like boats on the lawn. Cristina's sister goes into the kitchen and leaves her husband outside with us. He talks at a roar until Doña Erika comes out and chases him away. "Be quiet. They are discussing the *bandoleros*."

Before we leave, Tito mentions that a local photographer has a photo of the bandits in Cholila. "You should try to get a copy of it if you can."

Photo historian Ricardo Vallmitjana—a handsome man with bright white teeth, a high forehead, and a wild corona of grey-and-black hair—lives in a log house built into the side of a hill overlooking Lake Nahuel Huapi. He answers the door dressed in jeans and a yellow T-shirt that stops short of his navel, and we introduce ourselves as students of Butch Cassidy and the Sundance Kid, the North American bandits who lived in Cholila during the early 1900s.

"I am no fan of theirs," the photographer declares. "They caused trouble for their countrymen who lived in the area. For some time, all North Americans were feared in these parts because of the bandits. In the beginning, it was the fact that they wore guns all the time. Then, when they didn't do anything to their neighbors, people relaxed. Cassidy and the married couple, they were friendly, well mannered, and well dressed. They even introduced a touch of refinement to the region. Later, when it turned out that they were criminals, and especially after they kidnapped a rancher and murdered a Welsh merchant, people again distrusted all North Americans, including perfectly innocent ones."

"I understand how you feel," says Dan, "but those violent crimes—

the kidnapping and the murder—were actually committed by other bandits after Butch and Sundance left the area.''

"By that time," I add, "Butch and Sundance were probably dead.''

"*Bueno,*" says Ricardo, "come in.'' The entry is lined with bookshelves. "My library," he says with a smile as we pass through it into the dining room.

Expecting eighteen family members for dinner this evening, Ricardo's wife, Alba, bustles around in the kitchen while he sits with us on benches at the long wooden table. Colores, a pregnant calico, paces the room in search of a cozy place to deliver her kittens. Grey-and-white-striped Lucía is the daughter of Gatote, who lived his nine lives all at once—with different families in the neighborhood: Thinking him to be a stray, each family named him, fed him, and gave him a soft spot for snoozing. The ultimate in pampered pets, Gatote spent his twilight years as head mouser in a Bariloche butcher's shop.

"My only interest in the bandits has been their role in shaping Patagonia," says Ricardo. "I've often wondered why they came *here*. There was gold-mining near Esquel, and I suppose that might have been an attraction."

"*National Geographic* ran three articles about Patagonia around the turn of the century," says Dan. "Maybe Butch read one of them in a barbershop."

"I think he probably knew somebody who had visited Patagonia and said it was a great place," I volunteer.

"After a couple of severe winters in the late 1800s decimated the cattle business in the United States," Dan continues, "lots of people lost their livelihoods and had to start over elsewhere. In those days, Argentina had a promising future."

"It attracted millions of immigrants, including my great-uncle Marion Meadows," I say, "who emigrated from Louisiana in 1915 or so."

"There was a Welsh immigrant named Mansel Gibbon," says Ricardo, "who visited California and may have brought Butch and Sundance with him when he returned. His brother was a *comisario*, which was awkward because Mansel was a bandit."

"A Gibbons family lived near Robbers' Roost in Utah, where Butch and Sundance used to hide out." Dan makes a note. "Maybe there's a connection."

"I once saw a map of Esquel with the locations of all the North

American residents marked," says Ricardo. "Now, where did I see it? Maybe in that article by George Newbery."

"George Newbery, the dentist?"

"Yes."

"He's the guy who told the Pinkertons that Butch and Sundance were living in Cholila."

"We have the upper part of Newbery's stove sitting right over there." Ricardo points to an ornate piece of ironwork, with books on the shelf that once served as a bread warmer. "The Newberys were an important family, but George feuded with his neighbors, especially Jarred Jones, who owned the ranch next to his. Jones was the first person to settle here after the war against the Indians. He left Texas when he was about twenty to work as a cowboy in the Chaco. Then he signed on with the Argentine army, which killed or arrested the Indians who used to live here. The army would take the Indians' cattle, sell it in Chile, and pocket the money. Jones was one of the guys who drove the cattle over the Andes to market. After he left the army, he started a ranch and did very well. Several of his descendants still live here. As a matter of fact, Jarred Jones socialized with the bandits. The family has a photograph of the bandits taken at the cabin in Cholila."

"Actually, Tito Juárez mentioned the picture to us." Dan swallows, then plunges onward. "He said you had a copy, and we wondered whether we could get one, too."

"Juárez frustrates me," says Ricardo. "He has collected so much information, but he never does anything with it. I wish he would either write his book or donate his material to a museum where historians could use it in their research. He let me glance at some of his documents, but he whisked them away before I could read anything. He has the Villa Mercedes police file and a letter Butch Cassidy wrote urging the Argentine government to build a road to the Cochamó pass, to shorten the route for hauling cattle to Chile."

Butch's lobbying must have done the job. If he were still around, maybe he could persuade them to fill the pothole that landed us in that dump truck.

"About the photo, I don't have permission to publish it, so I can't give you a copy, but you may look at it." Ricardo starts up the steep open staircase, then leans against the steps and continues talking to us. "If Edith Jones authorizes it, I'll make a copy for you, but the family is very touchy about having known the bandits. When their true identities were revealed, nasty rumors circulated about anybody who had ever socialized with them.''

Ricardo invites us upstairs to see his archives. On the second floor, his son Diego bends over a draftsman's table and inks a trail onto an elaborate map of the region. The teenager began drawing maps as a hobby but discovered a market for them and has stayed busy ever since. While Diego shows us samples of his work, Ricardo climbs a bamboo-rung ladder to the loft, where he keeps his files in plastic bags on narrow shelves.

"The photograph was taken in 1902 or 1903." Ricardo descends from the loft, then leads the way down to the dining room and places several black-and-white pictures on the table. "The original is small and in poor condition, so the enlargements I have are not very good."

The figures lined up before the Cholila cabin in the grainy, scarred photographs are tiny, but the man on the far left is instantly recognizable as Butch Cassidy. On the far right, Etta and Sundance hold their horses' reins. In the middle stand four men and two women, probably Joneses (why else would they have the photograph?), although Ricardo insists that they aren't. A white picket fence runs in front of the cabin; neatly tied curtains hang in the renowned windows. A springer spaniel sits beside Etta, who wears a jacket and a matching skirt or culottes, perhaps a riding habit of sorts. Butch and Sundance are dressed alike in white shirts, vests, and trousers. Slung low on their hips are gun belts, and perched on their heads are Montana Peak hats—the same four-crease, straight-brimmed, felt Stetsons later worn by Canadian Mounties, Boy Scouts, Smokey the Bear, and most highway-patrol officers in the United States. Butch and Sundance were trendsetters.

I'll die if I can't have a copy of this photograph. After staring so long at the few authenticated pictures taken in the United States, after struggling to see beyond their frozen expressions into the thoughts and emotions that drove them down the curious path they chose, I can finally look at the outlaws in the place where our lives became entangled: Cholila.

I favor driving to the Jones ranch at once and asking Edith Jones straight out for the picture, but I defer to Dan, whose patience has paid off in similarly delicate undertakings. As it happens, we have been invited to an *asado* at George Newbery's old ranch at Fortín Chacabuco, just beyond the Jones ranch. Dan suggests that we recruit our host,

Roger Whewell, a banty Englishman who manages Chacabuco, to accompany us to the Jones ranch. He can vouch for our character, and if that fails to sway Edith Jones, he can simply beguile her into saying yes.

We drive north along the shore of Lake Nahuel Huapi, cross the Río Limay, and turn into Chacabuco's long gravel driveway. Newbery's house burned down long ago, but the stone foundations and the poplars he planted remain. I manage not to blurt our request the instant I've kissed Roger and Elspeth and their sons hello and greeted Roger's mother, who is visiting from England. But as we work our way through the grilled lamb, beef, and sausage, the tomato salad and bread, and the exquisite mincemeat tarts, I look for an opening to bring up the subject of the photograph. The timing never seems right.

We finish eating and wash the dishes, then wander over to the barn to watch Roger and son Stephen attempt to doctor the infected leg of a bighorn sheep. Still the opportunity eludes us. Eventually, Elspeth, Mrs. Whewell, and the boys take their leave. After telling us to stick around, Roger fetches a bottle of Scotch and settles down for some serious drinking. Ordinarily, Dan avoids hard liquor, but he hates to see a friend drink alone. I stick with water. Sensing my impatience, Dan stubbornly talks about everything but the photograph. Finally, just as he edges toward the subject, a car pulls up and several of Roger's business associates alight. They stay until the Scotch and the wine left over from the *asado* are gone. When the men drive away in a cloud of dust, Dan at last pops the question: "Look, Roger, how's about going over to see Edith Jones with us? She has a photo of our bandits, and we figure you're just the person to charm her into giving us a copy."

Roger guffaws. "I'm the last man for that job, mate. The Joneses haven't been terribly keen on me since I shot a couple of their dogs. Bloody delinquents wouldn't leave my sheep alone."

As we drive past the NO TRESPASSING sign and pull to a stop before the heavily creosoted log cabin where Edith Jones lives, I say, "Now, whatever you do, don't mention the fact that we've been consorting with Roger. If she's mad at him, she might not feel kindly toward his friends, either."

"Yeah, yeah," says Dan. "I can handle it."

I know that tone. He gets it when he's had too much to drink.

We're in luck: Edith Jones is home. The daughter of a Welsh immigrant and a Colorado River pioneer, she is the widow of Jarred Jones's son Andrés.

"*Buenas tardes.*" Pale in the twilight, she stands in the open doorway.

After we introduce ourselves, Dan says, "We were just over at Chacabuco with Roger Whewell, and we were wondering—that is, uh . . ."

I shoot Dan the dirtiest look I can muster, then turn to Señora Jones. In my broken Spanish, I explain that we are serious researchers who have seen the photograph and would love to have a copy of it, but that Ricardo will not make one for us without her okay.

"Well, I don't know," she says. "We've tried to keep it a private thing. In the family, you know. I suppose it wouldn't do any harm, but I'm expecting company and can't look for the original now. I'll find it later, when I have time, and Ricardo can mail you a copy."

Edith's daughter Carol does not share her family's reluctance to acknowledge any connection with Butch and Sundance. A lithe, intense woman with sun-bleached braids, Carol spends her summers leading week-long horseback tours across the land her grandfather homesteaded a century ago. Bandits are a perfect topic for weary tourists lounging around the evening campfire—not that she doesn't have plenty of family stories to keep her audience entertained.

"My grandfather came from Fort Worth in 1887 with John Crockett, who was the nephew of Davy Crockett. They went to Brazil, but they didn't like the Chaco. In Buenos Aires, they enlisted in the War of the Desert, but they didn't like that, either. Afterward, they bought cattle in Buenos Aires and sold it to the Leleque ranch and in Chile for five cents a head. My grandfather used his money to start the ranch here at Nahuel Huapi in 1889."

A whistle sounds in the next room and Carol stands up. "Would you like some tea?"

"Sure." So long as it's not *mate*.

From the kitchen, she continues her story. "One winter, Butch Cassidy and a friend went north to Neuquén to buy horses. On their way home, they were held up by bad weather and spent a month in my mother's house, which at that time was a store owned by my grandfather. They played cards and were very *simpático*, and the family enjoyed seeing fellow North Americans. When they returned to Cholila, they invited my grandfather to come visit them.''

Carol sets a tray of steaming mugs on a low table and passes the sugar. I take two lumps and begin stirring as she resumes the tale.

"That spring, he and my grandmother piled into a cart with two of their children and drove to the ranch in the Cholila Valley. It would probably be a week's journey on horseback, but I don't know how long it took them in their cart. They were mildly disturbed when Butch and Sundance played poker like professionals and Etta demonstrated her skill with firearms, but they didn't think too much of it at first. After a few days, however, my grandfather found a hidden corral full of cattle with different brands and realized that his hosts were not honorable people, so he gathered up his family and left. They never saw the outlaws again.''

Carol's sister wanders in and says that the bandits killed a Pinkerton agent and buried him under their house. "While Grandfather was playing cards with them, a dog came into the house with a human leg bone in his mouth.''

Carol waves her away. "The bandits were very well liked, amiable, generous, cordial, polite to the ladies, friendly with children.'' She says that some people assume that because Jarred Jones knew Butch and Sundance and socialized with them, he was an outlaw, too. "Even though the rumor was false, the older members of my family have always been sensitive about it. They don't even like to talk about the *gringo* bandits. Personally, I think it's exciting.''

Carol recommends that we see George Kennard, a British immigrant who used to have a friend who knew Butch Cassidy.

"We wrote to him," says Dan, "but he didn't answer. Where is he living now?"

We climb the stairs to George Kennard's flat for the third time today. The note we left on the door is gone, but nobody answers our knock. As we linger in the hall, arguing about what to do next, the door opens, revealing a middle-aged woman in a rumpled blouse and corduroy skirt. Clearly displeased at the interruption of her siesta, she yawns and rakes her fingers through her disheveled grey hair. We introduce ourselves and say we're looking for George.

"He's not here," she snaps in English.

"When will he be back?"

"I have no idea."

"Do you know where we could find him?"

"He's out with some tourists. If you give me your number, I'll tell him to ring you."

"We left a note earlier with our number on it."

"You're the ones looking for Butch Cassidy?"

"That's right." Now we're getting somewhere.

She shakes her head. "I've had it up to here with those outlaws." Uh-oh.

"Look, I can't promise anything, but I'll tell him to call you."

"Will he be around tomorrow?"

"No, he has another tour. You'd think he'd take New Year's off and spend some time with his wife, but I'm the last one to see him on holidays. He worked all day Christmas, too."

"That's not much fun for you." We shake our heads sympathetically. "Well, tell George we're sorry to have missed him."

"To tell you the truth, George is here now, but you can't see him. He's sleeping, and he needs his rest. He's a lot older than you think. I'm the second wife, you see." She shrugs and smiles. "He's been working so hard, and he's already had one heart attack. He won't take care of himself, so I have to protect him."

"We just wanted to say hello. We wrote to him a while ago and told him we were coming, but we didn't have this address, so he might not have received the letter."

"Oh, you can't count on anything with the Bariloche post office. Whenever the mail begins to pile up, they pitch it into the lake."

Great. That means we can kiss the Cholila photo *adiós*.

She looks over her shoulder, then turns back to us and says, "Wait here a minute, and I'll just go check on George and see if he's awake yet."

The door closes. Presently, she reappears with a conspiratorial smile. "He was asleep, but I woke him up. Come on in."

She makes tea and brings out the last of her Christmas cookies. "Give the heart-shaped one to your wife," she tells Dan.

George has twinkling blue eyes and British charm but says he doesn't know very much. "I have a few stories from Mrs. MacWilliams, who died in her nineties. For example, the Percivals, an American brother and sister living in Trevelin or Esquel, went in a buggy to Cholila to

58

visit their countrymen. The outlaws had 'fiscal land'—free as long as you farmed it. They were all seated and dining when a dog came in with a human hand. That put the wind up Cassidy. The Percivals kept mute and left the next morning.''

"Did they report the incident to the police? Is that why the bandits left?''

"The way I understand it, Jarred Jones told another Texan, a former sheriff or Pinkerton living in the area, about Butch Cassidy. The Texan then got in touch with the provincial police, who paid a visit to the ranch. Butch shot their horses out from under them, so they gave it up.''

Could a posse without horses do otherwise?

"They robbed some banks in Argentina and shot a Welshman who ran a store—sold skins and a little of everything—at Arroyo Pescado. Then they entered Chile and got jobs as paymasters for a big American mining company.''

"George,'' says the second Mrs. Kennard, "I thought you told me that one of them remained in this area.''

"There are supposedly some love letters that say Butch stayed in Bariloche, but I've never been able to verify it.''

We drive south and east on a scabrous blacktop road that parallels the Chubut River from the Andes to the Atlantic coast. This is the valley the Welsh followed inland during the last half of the nineteenth century and the route Butch, Sundance, and Etta followed to and from the ships that carried them to Buenos Aires. It is also the ''jungle'' that prevented Dimaio from apprehending the bandits.

Not far from Esquel, we detour to the scene of the crime we've heard so much about, the murder of Llwyd ap Iwan, proprietor of the Compañía Mercantil del Chubut. In a marsh beside the road, cattle browse near a sign identifying the site as Arroyo Pescado. We stop to look for information about ap Iwan, but there is no mention of him. Just beyond the marsh, a grove of poplars rises around a small brick building with Welsh dentation and a corrugated-metal roof. This must be the place. After thrashing through a field of yellow knee-high grass spiked with purple thistles, we narrowly avoid tumbling into sink-holes—root cellars, perhaps—in the dry soil. The brick building is locked tight, with boards over the door and windows. Out back sits a low mud-and-wattle house too big for chickens but too small for other farm animals. Someone must have lived here once. I poke my head through the door, but the low ceiling and dank air fill me with vague disquiet. "Let's get out of here," I say, and Dan doesn't tarry.

We barrel alongside crenulated sandstone cliffs beneath a china-blue sky. Except for the willows by the river and the poplars surrounding the widely scattered homes of sheep ranchers, the vegetation runs to grey-green scrub and an occasional yellow patch of wildflowers. In the distance, a sandstorm is brewing. We expect dry grit to blast the car when we drive into the storm, but it seems more like dirty rain than anything else. We pass through it quickly, and the sky turns blue again.

Dan pulls off the highway at Gaiman, a small town that has retained more of its Welsh character than the other Chubut Valley settlements have. At the old train station, now a museum, we find Tegai Roberts, the white-haired, blue-eyed granddaughter of Llwyd ap Iwan, which is Welsh for Lloyd Son-of-Jones. As a child, she visited the site of his murder at Arroyo Pescado. "Nothing is left now, neither the store nor the ranch. There may be a stone marker, but I was there so long ago, the marker is probably gone." Pointing to a photograph of three men with bicycles, she says, "My grandfather is the sturdy man with the hat and moustache."

To give us a sense of the language, whose paucity of our kinds of vowels has us thoroughly confused, she reads aloud from an old Welsh book. We walk through the museum, and she stops beside a harp that once belonged to Llwyd ap Iwan. Nearby sit a cast-iron pleater, a sewing machine, a typewriter, and various other tools brought by the immigrants who came between 1865 and 1911 to build a new Wales in this unlikely place. Old photographs, newspapers, letters, and ledgers spell out the hardships and joys that awaited the pioneers.

Standing amid the churns and butter molds with Tegai Roberts, whose gentle presence makes the murder of her grandfather seem all the more tragic, I'm grateful that Butch and Sundance didn't kill him. Otherwise, I would have to feel guilty on their behalf. I take no responsibility, however, for Evans and Wilson. I'd like to think that Butch and Sundance never even met them.

Oil rigs spike the countryside near Puerto Madryn and Rawson, where Sundance and Etta embarked on their way to Buenos Aires and New York. Thanks to the right whales that swim in the gulf, the seals and sea elephants that nest on the fringes of the nearby Valdés Peninsula, and the penguins that venture this far north during the winter (when the krill they feed on is less plentiful in Antarctic waters), Madryn has become a tourist haven. But Rawson, a small town with sandy streets and shuttered houses at the mouth of the Chubut River, probably hasn't changed much since the bandits' time.

We drive through Rawson to the port and park the car alongside a run-down seafood restaurant, then walk out onto the long concrete pier. Alone with the seagulls, we turn back and gaze at the painted wooden fishing boats moored in the river that leads to Cholila. The water is brown, the riverbanks low and weedy. Despite the blazing summer sun, a stiff breeze chills the air. After all this time, Bertie Perry is still right: Coming here seems like leaving the world.

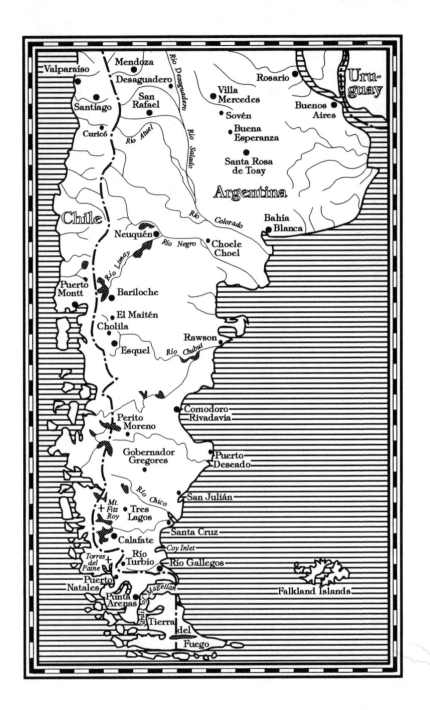

4 · BANDOLEROS ON THE RUN

WE still don't know the precise incident that sparked Butch and Sundance's return to banditry, but territorial police records offer clues about what caused them to leave Cholila. When Chubut policeman Milton Roberts received a copy of the Spanish version of the Pinkerton circular on the Wild Bunch, he sent the poster to the territorial governor, who ordered the capture of the outlaws. Policeman Julio O. de Antueno was "informed that there would be rewards for the officials who made the arrests, but before the military police squadron could take action," the bandits and Etta disappeared. According to Antueno, "Place, his companion, and Ryan stayed [whenever they were in Trelew] in the hotel 'del Globo,' owned by Angel M. Botaro, and had a close friendship with Lincoln Haward, the manager of the Banco de la Nación, where they spent hours relaxing every day, because the manager was also North American. Given this intimacy, they could have learned from him the news that their capture had been requested."

"At that time," wrote Roberts, "the *comisario* of the district was Eduardo Humphreys, a good citizen well loved by his neighbors—although perhaps weak in character—and a very good friend of Daniel Gibbon, an Esquel resident who was also close to the North Americans. It was said that Gibbon tried to terrify Humphreys with facts he knew about the band, which caused the official to renounce his position as *comisario*." According to Antueno, the governor dismissed Humphreys "for failing to carry out his orders."

Regardless of who tipped them off, the outlaws knew by late 1904 that Cholila was no longer safe: If the Pinkertons didn't come for them, sooner or later reward-hungry Argentine lawmen would. Starting over again would be costly, but Butch and Sundance had the knack of raising capital in a hurry. Using the formula they had perfected in the United States, they robbed a pair of distant but worthy targets: the Banco de Tarapacá y Argentino Limitado in Río Gallegos, near the Strait of Magellan, seven hundred miles south of Cholila, and the Banco de la Nación in Villa Mercedes, in the province of San Luis, seven hundred miles north of Cholila.

Shortly after the second crime, Buenos Aires newspapers *La Prensa* and *La Nación* and magazine *Caras y Caretas* published illustrated stories—with details provided by the Buenos Aires police and the Pinkerton Detective Agency—about Butch Cassidy, the Sundance Kid, Etta Place, and Kid Curry, who had become suspects in the Villa Mercedes holdup after witnesses said that the bandits had been speaking English beforehand. In view of the similarity of the crimes, the gang was retroactively credited with the Río Gallegos holdup, as well.

In the process of reading ten years' worth of microfilmed South American newspapers from the early 1900s, Dan has discovered several articles about the Argentine holdups. I find one of the pieces from *La Prensa* particularly interesting: To learn what the bandits had been doing before resuming their life of crime, the newspaper dispatched its Rawson correspondent to interview their former neighbors in the Chubut Territory. He reported that two men and a woman from North America had lived in Cholila from 1902 to 1904. Local residents told him that Etta "spoke a little Spanish and said she had lived in Mexico before emigrating." (The presence of numerous careless errors in the article suggests that she could just as easily have said *New* Mexico.) According to the correspondent, the governor and the police chief of the Chubut Territory stayed at the home of Santiago Ryan when passing through Cholila in February 1904. "Miss N.A. Place was also there, and it is said that she is married to one Morry Longbauch. He was then in Nahuel Huapi, and according to his wife, went to see Mr. Jones, a rancher there, in order to buy livestock." The correspondent went on to say that Etta and Sundance had traveled "in April 1904 . . . to Puerto Madryn, where they embarked on a steamship for Valparaíso [Chile], and were absent from Chubut until the end of 1904." Ships bound for San Francisco called at Valparaíso, and a Longabaugh family story has Sundance and Etta returning to the United States in 1904 and sending a postcard home from St. Louis, where they attended the Louisiana Purchase Exposition.

The correspondent said that Butch "had been arrested the latter part of March 1904 and sent before a judge on suspicion of having aided the flight of a fellow North American, Emolini Nood, who had been accused of robbing . . . the foreman of the Cholila Land Company of 6,000 *pesos*." Perhaps this is the incident Tito Juárez alluded to in his tale of Butch's having given a gun to someone who later used it in a crime. I'm delighted with my discovery until I recall that Milton Roberts told the Pinkertons that Hood was an alias of Robert Evans. If the correspondent wrote "*N*ood" when he should have written "*H*ood"— not inconceivable for a man who wrote "*Miss N*.A. Place" instead of "*Mrs. H*.A. Place"—Butch and Sundance consorted with the brutish Evans and Wilson.

The next article I read contains more bad news. According to another *La Prensa* correspondent, Hood and his cohort Grays (probably Wilson) "had headquartered at the Ryan-Place house in Cholila." In other words, Butch and Sundance not only knew Evans and Wilson but lived with them. Inasmuch as he credited Hood and Grays with the Río Gallegos holdup, which Evans and Wilson almost certainly lacked the finesse to pull off, the correspondent probably just confused the two sets of outlaws. That's what I decide to believe anyway.

Over the decades, many journalists, outlaw fanciers, and historians have recounted the Río Gallegos robbery, but almost nothing—not the number of participants, their descriptions, their aliases, their activities beforehand, the loot, the date, or even the weather—has remained constant. One early account appeared in the April 1911 issue of *The Wide World Magazine,* a British true-adventure monthly. The author had recently returned from Patagonia, where a Welshman named Thomas had told him about the Río Gallegos holdup. Two North Americans rode into town, said Thomas, secured "rooms at the best hotel, stabled their horses, and . . . deposited twenty thousand Argentine dollars" in the bank. The men spent a fortnight in Río Gallegos "entertaining and being entertained, and paying frequent visits to the bank manager, until apparently they were perfectly conversant with the habits of the employees and the plan of the building." On the eve of their departure, the pair threw a grand dinner for the town's leading citizens, including the police chief and the bank manager. The festivities bubbled into the early hours. At eleven the next morning, the bandits entered the bank, withdrew the balance in their account, then pulled revolvers and announced, "Now, we will take the rest!" After scooping $70,000 into their saddlebags, they jumped onto their horses and galloped off. "They were not heard of for some considerable time," Thomas said, "as the officials, with that praiseworthy care of their own personal safety which characterizes the Argentine, did not start out in pursuit until they had given the thieves two days in which to get clear away."

In 1937, the *New York Sunday Mirror Magazine* described the holdup under a catchy headline: THE GAUCHOS LOVED BEING ROBBED BY THE DASHING "GRINGOS"—BECAUSE THEY STOLE IN THE GRAND MANNER. According to the *Mirror,* "a party of two men and a young, good-looking woman" arrived in Río Gallegos in November 1907 and registered as Henry Thompson and Mr. and Mrs. Lewis Nelson at the Hotel Uglesich. Mr. Nelson and Mr. Thompson, who claimed to be Mrs. Nelson's brother, "presented themselves to Mr. Bishop, manager of the bank, with a letter of credit" and instantly made friends with him.

It was only a matter of hours until Mrs. Nelson met Mrs. Bishop and a round of social functions was the order. Card parties, horseback riding, dinners; it was all very gay. Only one eccentricity did the three Americans possess, and that was the harmless little pastime of riding hell-for-leather through the streets, shooting their irons into the air. The natives, grown to like the Americans immensely, only shook their heads and smiled amiably.

It was in December that it happened. The weather was very bad. It was two in the afternoon. Charming Mr. Nelson entered the bank and asked for Mr. Bishop. He was immediately shown to Mr. Bishop's office. No sooner had the door closed on him, however, than the street door opened to admit Mr. Thompson—only a different Mr. Thompson than they had known! He covered the clerks with two guns, ordered them to keep their hands well in the air, or else!

Mr. Nelson, in the meantime, was holding a razor-edged knife against Mr. Bishop's surprised throat muscles, advising that trusting gentleman to "fork over." Mr. Bishop "forked," but unfortunately the loot only amounted to 35,000 *pesos.* The bandits had picked the wrong day. Apologizing to Mr. Bishop for the inconvenience he had caused him, and asking courteously to be remembered to Mrs. Bishop, Nelson left the office and hastily departed with his confederate. They were reported seen meeting Mrs. Nelson some 22 miles out of town, and a chase was started.

The *Mirror* article found its way into the Pinkerton archives and became the chief source of information about the holdup for western historians in the United States. James D. Horan, for example, wrote three versions of the tale between 1949 and 1977. Along the way, he changed the date and hour of the holdup, shifted the bandits' lodgings from the Hotel Uglesich to the home of the bank manager, and transported Etta and the spare horses from several miles outside of town to just outside of the bank, in plain view of the manager's wife. According to Horan, Butch was armed with two revolvers, and Sundance was "waving a gun and a straight razor." As the posse approached, "Butch shot the horses of the leading pursuers," and the bandits escaped with $10,000.

In 1970, the Buenos Aires daily *Clarín* published a three-part series, "Butch Cassidy in Patagonia," by Argentine journalist Justo Piernes, who added Harvey Logan to the roster of Río Gallegos bandits. Piernes installed them in a house in the country and had them gallop to and from town twice a week, so that on the day of the holdup they could grab the money and run without alarming the populace.

These versions put the Río Gallegos holdup in 1906 or 1907, but the actual event occurred in 1905. Argentine historian Osvaldo Topcic has unearthed detailed accounts of the holdup from *El Antártico,* a six-page weekly in Río Gallegos, and from a report prepared by the police of the Santa Cruz Territory. From Topcic, we learn that at the end of 1904 or the beginning of 1905, two well-mannered North Americans calling themselves Brady and Linden checked into the Hotel Argentino. They opened an account at the Banco de Tarapacá with a deposit of 7,000 *pesos* and, according to *El Antártico,* claimed to "represent a prosperous livestock company in Río Negro and declared their intention to buy large stretches of land in the territory" of Santa Cruz. The Yankees spent freely, lavishing tips on waiters and servants, and mingled with the town's upper crust at the Club del Progreso and the Café de Farina. The visitors purchased a telescope and a compass and then, the day before the holdup, withdrew all the money from their bank account.

On Tuesday, February 14, 1905, they returned to the bank while assistant manager Arturo Bishop and cashier Alexander Mackerrow were closing out the accounts for the day. According to the twenty-four-page police report, the "two subjects armed with large revolvers, apparently Colts, presented themselves in the establishment." Mackerrow told the police that the bandits "opened the door to the office in which [he] and [Bishop] had been working in their daily occupations and . . . the taller of them aggressively jumped on the counter, with revolvers in hand, and aiming at [Bishop] ordered him to raise his hands and rest them on the railing of the same counter and, under threat of death, to stay at a distance of more or less two yards from the aggressor." The shorter bandit told Mackerrow to put his hands on the bronze grille atop the counter and to keep quiet. Mackerrow said Bishop had to put "all of the bank's money into a white canvas sack," which the shorter robber handed up to the thief on the counter. The shorter robber took "a small tin box that contained approximately 483 pounds sterling." The assistant manager disagreed about how much was stolen, but the loot was equal to at least $100,000 in today's money.

According to Bishop, after collecting the money and the cash box, the robbers made him join the cashier behind the counter. "While one of the thieves covered us, the other went outside and put the sack that contained the money on his horse. About a minute later, I heard the one who was outside say in English something like 'all set.' The other assailant at once went outside, and they immediately took off in flight on horses that they had already prepared."

Mackerrow told police the bandits "left at a full gallop . . . and went in a southeasterly direction in search of the ford that would permit them to cross the Gallegos River in the vicinity of Güer Aike," fifteen miles west of Río Gallegos. They took seven horses from an *estancia* at Güer Aike and retrieved supplies they had sent to the cook there.

Meanwhile, Mackerrow ran down the street to the Café de Paris and alerted the policeman posted in the doorway, and Bishop found a telephone and rang up the police headquarters. Within moments, calls went out for posses and for assistance from the Chilean border patrols as well as from the territorial police of Chubut and Río Negro and from neighboring towns in the Santa Cruz Territory. According to *El Antártico*, the alarm "spread rapidly in the community, and at once various residents and police agents mounted horses and took off in pursuit of the fugitives." They were soon followed by another posse led by Sergeant Eduardo Rodríguez, who continued his search for several days until his horses were exhausted. Then, benighted at a place known as Bajo de la Leona, he lost "the trail of the badmen, who relied upon elements of mobility of the first order." At la Leona, "the fugitives had left three tired horses," noted *El Antártico*, "two they rode and another one." Or was the third horse occupied?

Police patrols and trackers from the towns of Santa Cruz, San Julián, and Puerto Deseado joined two commissions of soldiers from

Río Gallegos and spent nearly three weeks searching the Santa Cruz Territory from Coy Inlet on the east to Lake Argentino on the west. They even met with Chilean police near Ultima Esperanza but found little more than a series of abandoned horses with unfamiliar brands, presumably left behind when the bandits switched to fresh horses. The fugitives stuck to remote and seldom-used routes, took shortcuts, and exercised care to avoid detection near ranches and other habitations.

Four days after the robbery, a cart driver named Francisco Cuello had found the tin box near the Killik Aike Springs. The box contained only a deposit slip and some envelopes. Cuello reported that a peon he knew had introduced him to the bandits in the Hotel Argentino three weeks earlier. At the peon's request, Cuello had hauled parcels containing sugar and horseshoes to the Sutherland *estancia* at Güer Aike. He told the police that he had later met the bandits on the road, and that they claimed to be heading for the hotel at Güer Aike and then on to Lake Argentino. The next day, he met them camping near Güer Aike, and they invited him and his crew to drink some beer. During this encounter, the men told Cuello that they had come down from Río Negro four months earlier and were now heading north to Neuquén.

Other witnesses reported having seen the bandits camped at Lake Argentino and Las Horquetas before the holdup. Daniel Gibbon swore to police that Butch and Sundance had been in Cholila when the robbery occurred. Gibbon's peon Francisco Albornoz, however, told investigators he saw the outlaws returning from the south after the holdup. While chasing a stray sheep, he had come upon Gibbon and another man, whom he had recognized as Santiago Ryan. The peon said that Ryan had kept his distance and had been disguised with a long white beard, but that his voice had been unmistakable. The peon had first met Butch, Sundance, and Etta near the Limay River in 1901, as they were traveling by wagon from Neuquén to Esquel. Albornoz led them as far as El Maitén and had seen all three at Gibbon's home many times since then.

Esquel resident Gumersindo Zenteno said he'd heard that Enrique Place and Santiago Ryan were in Cholila on the date of the holdup, but that Mrs. Place was away. He thought Evans and Wilson (alias the Grice brothers) had pulled the heist under Etta's direction. Speculation that she played a role in the crime may have been fueled by Santiago Allsop, a British patent-medicine merchant in Río Gallegos. Allsop informed police that the bandit known as Brady had mentioned having a sister in Punta Arenas, a Chilean port about a hundred miles southwest on the Strait of Magellan. Allsop described her as a loose woman nicknamed "La Americana," a tall blonde "who always went around in a veil and hat." Near the time of the holdup, he said, she sailed to Peru and then to California.

No proof of Etta's involvement has been found. We can't even be sure about the prime suspects. The outlaw known as Linden was 5′ 10½″ tall and had a narrow face, a light complexion, green eyes, blond hair, and a regular nose. This description roughly fits both Sundance and Wilson. The cashier said Brady was shorter than Linden and had green eyes, a ruddy face, and a closely cropped dark beard. Though Butch and Evans were shorter than their sidekicks, neither had a dark beard (unless it was part of another disguise). Evans had a bushy light-brown moustache and blue eyes; Butch had a sandy moustache and "eyes like gimlets." Witnesses estimated the Río Gallegos bandits' ages at twenty-five to thirty, but Butch and Sundance were in their late thirties, Evans was about thirty-five, and Wilson was just nineteen. Moreover, Wilson had only recently left the United States and didn't come to Chubut until a couple years after the holdup. In any event, the modus operandi points to Butch and Sundance. If anybody had the charm to con a whole town and the stamina to ride that far through rugged country, they did.

Guided by the old newspaper articles and the police report, we plan to retrace the bandits' journey to Río Gallegos. We set off from Cholila and drive south in a rented Renault on a gravel road that cuts across forested slopes and along the rims of dazzling green lakes and rivers. At Esquel, we pick up Route 40, which winds through the Andean foothills. Route 3, the asphalt highway on the coast, carries most of the traffic today, but the western road offers access to fresh water and shelter from the notorious Patagonian wind, factors that undoubtedly influenced the bandits as they planned their crime. Although the journey would have taken them through one of the most sparsely inhabited regions on the continent, the trail had been well established by nomadic Indians who traveled back and forth between the Strait of Magellan and the Negro River, hunting *guanacos* in the south, gathering pine nuts and wild apples near Lake Nahuel Huapi, and trading with other tribes on the island of Choele Choel in the Negro, downstream from Neuquén. The Indians used the coastal route only during the winter, the rainy season, when the western route might be blocked by snow.

Some stretches of Route 40 are paved, but mostly the road's surface varies with the terrain: shingle where the land is rocky, sand where the land is sandy, dirt where the land is loamy, mud where the land is marshy, and so on. The occupants of every car we meet seem to wave at us. Friendly place, Patagonia. Several cars with screens over their windshields pass by before we grasp that the wavers actually are just putting their hands against the glass to keep it from shattering if flying gravel hits it. They're not at all happy to see us or the dust we're kicking up. Even with the windows closed, it seeps in through the tiniest openings, and the car is filthy before we have logged fifty kilometers.

After wrestling with the steering wheel for five hours, Dan begins to flag. I volunteer to spell him, but he says, "It's like driving a bucking bronco. You couldn't handle it."

Naturally, I insist that I can. We trade places. I shove the gearshift into first and peel out in a spray of gravel. Within minutes, my shoulders knot and my arms tremble from trying to keep the wheel steady. On the horizon, a brown plume marks the approach of a truck. Terrific, more dust. The truck startles a troop of horses into flight across the plain, and the sight lifts the tension from my shoulders. Nonetheless, when Dan is ready for another shift at the wheel, I don't protest.

The distance between the small towns stretches out, and we meet fewer vehicles. Eventually, the only signs of life are the sheep nibbling the scrubby vegetation on the increasingly arid hills. At dusk, hares spring from the earth and dash into our path.

"Slow down," I nag. "Watch out for the bunnies."

"Considering the weight differential, you'd think they'd watch out for us." Dan turns on the headlights, but they seem to attract even more hares. He turns off the lights and drives without them until the twilight gutters out.

According to our map, we're not far from a paved road leading to the town of Perito Moreno. A sign looms encouragingly. BADENES, it says. "Where the hell is Badenes?" asks Dan. "Are we lost?"

"I don't know. It's not on the map."

We plunge abruptly downhill, then uphill, and the car is momentarily airborne before we jolt back onto the rocky road. Mile after mile, the *badenes* continue, a roller coaster of hills and gullies that must be traversed slowly or not at all.

At last, we hit pavement and triple our speed. "We're home free now," I say. "And it's every bunny for himself."

The minutes tick by, and the car skims over the asphalt. How peaceful the night seems without the clatter of stones in the wheel wells. Suddenly, a lamb sprints across our path, then doubles back and freezes in the headlights' glare. In an instant, we are upon it with a terrible thud and bumping; then there is nothing before us but the empty road sliding underneath the car.

Dan blanches and feels guilty enough to slow down but not enough to stop.

"Maybe we just stunned him," I say. "The wheels didn't hit him. What do you think? Could he had survived?"

"Perhaps."

"What if he's maimed? We should go back and put him out of his misery."

"With what?"

"Maybe we could run over him again." I shudder at the notion.

"No thanks."

"But we can't just leave him there suffering."

"His suffering stopped when he hit this big hunk of metal."

"I thought you said he could have survived."

"I thought you wanted me to say so."

We drive the rest of the way to Perito Moreno in silence.

The town seems shut tight, but we eventually spot an open bar. Dan goes inside and asks directions to the best hotel in town. The bartender says, "*Señor*, you have come to the right place. I have a room out back you can sleep in for two dollars American."

"Let me put it this way," Dan parries, "what's the second-best hotel in town?"

Minutes later, we pull up to a restaurant that has several guest rooms in back. Instead of the carnage we expected to find on the front of the car, the grill and bumper are spotless, wiped clean by their woolly encounter. The rest of the car is coated with dust, as are we. To our surprise, we have a private bath with hot water and a firm bed with clean sheets.

We set out again early in the morning. So few people live in the region that the map shows virtually every building located between the small towns. A place called Las Horquetas, which has a hotel symbol beside it, catches my eye. Wasn't that one of the spots where Butch and Sundance camped? "What does *horquetas* mean?"

"I don't know," says Dan. "Why don't you look it up?"

"The dictionary is in the trunk. *Horquetas, horquetas.* Sounds like orchids to me."

"Could be."

"Let's spend the night there and give the wildlife a break."

Aside from those that say BADENES, few signs appear along the road. The islands of civilization are so scarce that we top off the gas tank whenever we see a filling station. At the village of Baja Caracoles, we buy gasoline from the police and *empanadas* from a general store.

Sheep and cattle graze on the low shrubs and sparse ground cover. The only fences are the ones between the *estancias*. Where the road meets these fences, rubber strips have been laid across the asphalt to keep the livestock from straying from one ranch to the next. The occasional solitary *gaucho* rides the fence lines or hunkers by a campfire with a gourdful of *mate* and a loaf of crusty bread. When Butch and Sundance rode through here, the evidence of human habitation must have been slight indeed. A census taken nine years after they left found a mere eighty-one thousand people living in the whole of Argentine Patagonia and Tierra del Fuego—an area roughly twice the size of California, which has some twenty-four million inhabitants.

At seven o'clock, we finally reach Las Horquetas, which turns out to be a squalid truck stop. *Horquetas*, it seems, means crossroads. I'd rather sleep in the car than in this dump. We drive on through ferruginous hills. As we climb a long slope under a blue sky, Dan spots a bicyclist on the horizon. We soon catch up with him and stop for a chat. He's a Swedish student biking from Bariloche to Tierra del Fuego and collecting adventures along the way.

His most recent one, he tells us, occurred at Las Horquetas, where he stopped for provisions. While in the store, he heard a gunshot ring out. When he cautiously stepped outside a few minutes later, he found the body of a dog lying in a pool of blood by the stoop. The owner of the truck stop was tending to chores nearby, and the Swede asked what had happened.

"Had to shoot him. Killed one of my chickens."

"But why did you do it beside your own front door?"

"Had to teach him a lesson, didn't I?"

We manage to avoid suicidal sheep and hares and reach Gobernador Gregores before nightfall. After Las Horquetas, we expect the worst, but we find a modern hotel with every amenity from laundry service to a billiard room. From here, the Indian trail followed the Chico River to the coast, but Butch and Sundance took the back road, to Lake Argentino, so we return to Route 40 and drive southwest toward some of the wildest terrain on the continent. At this latitude, the Andes still bear the scars of the ice ages, when glaciers four thousand feet thick mantled the mountains. Under the weight of all that ice, the western range sank into the Pacific Ocean until only the highest peaks remained, in the form of rain-drenched, heavily forested islands and archipelagoes. On the east, the glaciers carved a snaggled wall of granite spires, gouged out what are now the basins of a series of great lakes, and carried the resulting rocky debris far out onto the Argentine plains. Countless glaciers, like wrinkled blue arms, still reach down from a vast ice field.

Against this massy backdrop, flocks of sheep share their scrubby grey-green pastures with *guanacos*, the wild cousins of the *llamas* and the other camelids of the central Andes. Ninety years ago, *guanacos* roamed the Patagonian plains in such abundance that it was "scarcely possible to pass out of sight of them." Today, the few small bands we spot along Route 40 skitter over the nearest ridges before we can get a good look at them, let alone take a photograph. Finally, we come upon twenty-two *guanacos* that seem reluctant to abandon the succulent grass in a flat lea west of the road. In three hours of driving, we have encountered no cars or trucks and only two men on horseback. Maybe these *guanacos* have never seen a vehicle before. They might not know enough to be afraid of us. Dan pulls the car off the road and kills the engine. We step out into the silence and slowly walk toward the animals. They retreat somewhat but do not flee. While Dan waits atop a boulder, I try to move in with my camera for a close-up. If I walk very slowly and approach them from an angle, rather than head-on, they hold their ground. A few go back to grazing, but most of them watch me intently.

Curiosity got their ancestors into trouble and helped thin their ranks to about six-hundred thousand from more than thirty million. Charles Darwin, who visited the region in the 1830s while sailing around the world on the HMS *Beagle*, wrote that the ship's crew shot scores of *guanacos* lured into shooting range by men who lay on the ground and wiggled their legs in the air to pique the animals' interest. Luckily for this band, we don't pack anything stronger than a telephoto lens.

Standing there listening to the *guanacos* chitter, the sunlight warm on my face, the wind soft in my hair, I try to imagine how Butch and Sundance felt as they rode through here to resume their careers as outlaws. Did they lament their impending exile from this exotic landscape? Or did they see Patagonia as a big, useless prairie separating them from their goal? If Etta was with them, did she make them wait while she tried to edge close enough to pet a *guanaco*? And how did she feel about leaving Cholila? As often as she and Sundance sailed back to the States, she must have been homesick. Living with a wanted man and never knowing when he might be arrested—or killed—couldn't have been easy.

According to Butch's old bandit pal Matt Warner, "a man who has had an outlaw past is never safe, no matter how straight he goes afterwards. That's the price he pays. Something out of his past life may raise up against him and wreck his life any time." Not long before his death, Warner told Charles Kelly "what it means to be hunted. You can never sleep. You've always got to listen with one ear and keep one eye open. After a while you almost go crazy. No sleep! No sleep! Even when you know you're perfectly safe you can't sleep. Every pissant under your pillow sounds like a posse of sheriffs coming to get you!"

Back on Route 40, we encounter innumerable rheas, flightless birds that resemble ostriches (and are called ostriches here). The rheas seem drawn to the relatively smooth surface of the road and cut across country only when the road won't take them where they want to go. Each time we come upon a flock, the rheas run along the gravel ahead of us. The mother chases her tots off the road one at a time, and only when they are safe does she hop out of harm's way.

We gas up and grab lunch at Tres Lagos, then detour west for a better look at the pale-green Lake San Martín and the slab-faced Mount Fitz Roy, named for the captain of the *Beagle*, which sailed north through the archipelagoes on the far side of the ice cap. We pass an upended butte, its tilted strata even older than the ice, then cross a one-lane swinging bridge and wend through fields of grass and wild-flowers. Near the base of the mountain, a swollen stream has washed out a bridge, cutting off access to the lodge where we have hoped to spend the night. We return to Route 40 and pass Bajo de la Leona—where Sergeant Rodríguez gave up the chase for the Río Gallegos bandits—then drive on toward Calafate, the jumping-off town for visits to the nearby glaciers.

"The brakes are squishy," says Dan as he negotiates the sandy shores of the turquoise Lake Argentino, where the bandits camped on their way south, according to the police chief, and where they told the cart driver they planned to stay on their return to the north. Unless they crossed the glaciers, they couldn't have picked a more uninhabited escape route. Not long before the holdup, two scientists from Princeton University had spent a leisurely five months traveling from Río Gallegos to Lake Argentino without bumping into a single other human being.

By the time we reach Calafate, the sky has turned pink.

Once our brake fluid has been replenished in the morning, we set off—on a circuitous route dictated by geography and the highway department—from Calafate to Río Turbio, a coal-mining town in the southwest corner of Argentine Patagonia. We drive east, then south, then west, and find ourselves heading straight for the granite needles of Chile's Torres del Paine, near the southern end of the ice cap. Cresting a hill, we see the massif's jagged profile reflected upside down in a broad pond where flamingos troll for algae. Clouds hang darkly over the horizon, but the rain doesn't cross the border today.

We swing south again and drive through a valley dusted with daisies like light morning snow. Firebushes and evergreen beeches crown the grassy yellow hills. Horses munch on clover in small pastures, and fragrant wood smoke swirls from the chimneys of corrugated-metal dwellings. At length, the vegetation thins out, and we are in sheep country again. The sky glowers, but still the rain doesn't fall. In the gathering dusk, we round a curve and see the town of Río Turbio rising from what looks like a slag heap, beyond a welter of railroad tracks. We spend the night in a motel room with the stink of a hundred previous guests, all of them chain-smokers.

A short distance across the Andes from Río Turbio is the thirty-mile fjord Ultima Esperanza (Last Hope), named in 1830 by British seamen seeking an outlet to the Pacific that would bypass the treacherous western half of the Strait of Magellan. After the Río Gallegos holdup, Argentine soldiers met with Chilean police and scoured this area to no avail. We follow the posse's route through a low pass and descend to the town of Puerto Natales, which sits on a hill overlooking the blue bay at the mouth of Ultima Esperanza.

Sheets of painted metal, corrugated or flat, form the outer skins of most of the buildings. Stunted beeches grow crooked under the force of a wind so strong that we can lean into it at a forty-five-degree angle without falling. This place must be wild during storms. At dusk, we walk along the shore. Black-necked swans glide through the water, and steamer ducks paddle nearby. Overhead, Antarctic geese fly south for the summer. Across the bay sit snowcapped islands. As the light wanes, mist descends, until only the birds are visible.

In the morning, we undertake an excursion in a dubious wooden vessel whose one lifeboat is equipped with a single broken oar. When gale-force winds halt us halfway up the fjord, we dock at an isolated *estancia* and literally crawl off the boat and across a rickety pier to dry land. The ranch owner and his sons move their sheep from one field to another with the help of two border collies while we wait in vain for the wind to die down. In the end, we clamber back aboard and return to port. Even if the bandits reached Puerto Natales undetected, they would never have relied on escaping by boat in these waters.

We make our way back to Argentina and head for Río Gallegos. Beyond Río Turbio, our route takes us through rolling hills that smooth out until we seem to be on a long slope running straight down toward the ocean. Although the fertile land in northwestern Patagonia supports large herds of cattle and sheep, much more rangeland per animal is needed here in the sparsely vegetated south. As a result, the *estancias* are huge. Signs at the entrances give the distances—often fifty miles or more—to the ranch houses and indicate whether first aid, telephones, radios, or airstrips can be found on the premises. Alongside these signs sit gaily painted mailboxes, some as elaborate as dollhouses and others large enough to shelter a couple of people from the wind while they wait for rides.

The *estancias* were established during the late 1800s, under the fiscal-land program, by a small number of individuals who prospered with the help of the free or low-cost transportation provided by the Argentine navy for products shipped from Río Gallegos. Despite its isolation, the town became a hotbed of commercial activity. In the year before the holdup, some twenty thousand bales of everything from lambs' wool and sealskin to horsehair and "ostrich" feathers left the port, which the government made duty-free to encourage the development of the region. But as the landowners grew wealthy, their poorly paid peons struggled to survive.

Coasting toward Río Gallegos, I finally come to terms with what the outlaws did here. Until now, I have wondered how anyone as nice as Butch supposedly was could have toyed with people the way the Río Gallegos bandits did. Robbing someone impersonally is bad enough, but making friends with your intended victims beforehand is cruel. If Butch viewed the big shots in Río Gallegos as Argentine versions of the U.S. cattle barons and bankers, however, he might have enjoyed making monkeys of them. And yet, at some level, Butch and Sundance must have envied the class they professed to despise. Why else would they have dressed up like bankers for that Fort Worth photograph or posed as wealthy ranchers in New York and Buenos Aires? Were they putting on airs the way they put on aliases, as camouflage? Or were they acting out their fantasies of how life might have been if they had stayed on the straight and narrow?

I'm still musing when we reach Río Gallegos, now a busy city of forty-two thousand people. The Banco de Tarapacá has become Lloyds, and the few square blocks of 1905 have multiplied enough to permit traffic jams. We check into a hotel and have supper at a crowded restaurant in the center of town. When we leave at midnight, the restaurant is still full of families with young children.

We poke around Río Gallegos for a day without learning anything new about the robbery, then head north on Route 3, bound for Villa Mercedes, the scene of the bandits' second Argentine holdup. Between us and the lush alfalfa fields of the San Luis province, however, stretch hundreds of miles of two-lane blacktop in a barren landscape whose tallest structures are occasional windmills and gigantic trucks with double trailers. Thousands of penguins live along the coast a few miles to the east, but the only wildlife we have seen are a few rheas until Dan shouts, "Flamingo alert!" To the west is a pond stippled pink with a veritable flamingo convention. We pull off the road and dash down the hillside for a closer look. The birds rise from the water and fly into a head wind so strong that no matter how furiously they beat their wings, they cannot escape. Antoine de Saint-Exupéry, who did a stint as a mail pilot in Patagonia, flew into the same kind of wind and found himself standing still: "I saw the landscape freeze abruptly where it was and remain jiggling on the same spot. I was making no headway. My wings had ceased to nibble into the outline of the earth. I could see the earth buckle, pivot—but it stayed put. The plane was skidding as if on a toothless cogwheel."

After eluding the Río Gallegos posses, the bandits returned to Cholila and began wrapping up their affairs. In a note dated April 19, 1905, Butch asked merchant Richard Clarke to give Daniel Gibbon some clothing Butch had ordered but not yet received. On May 1, Butch wrote his neighbor John Perry, who owed him money, and asked him to give it to Gibbon instead. "We are starting today," Butch told Perry. A short time later, ranch hand Wenceslao Solís accompanied Butch, Sundance, and Etta to Lake Nahuel Huapi, where the *gringos* caught a boat bound for Chile. Solís returned to Cholila with their saddles, which were given to designated friends. Having left two hundred sheep and thirty mares with Gibbon, the bandits sold the rest of their holdings to a Chilean land company for an amount that would be worth about $200,000 today. According to Gibbon, the trio left behind a box of letters from North America. The box, alas, has vanished.

Authorities investigating outlawry in the territory obtained a letter Sundance had sent to Gibbon from Valparaíso, Chile, on June 28, 1905. The original is missing, but we have converted a Spanish translation of the letter back into English, reproducing Sundance's sentiments, though not necessarily his exact wording.

Dear Friend:

We are writing to you to let you know that our business went well, and we received our money. We arrived here today, and the day after tomorrow my wife and I leave for San Francisco. I'm very sorry, Dan, that we could not bring the brand R with us, but I hope that you will be able to fetch enough to pay you for the inconveniences.

We want you to take care of Davy and his wife and see that they don't suffer in any way. And be kind to the old [spaniel] and [give him] pieces of meat once in a while and get rid of the black [dog]. I don't want to see Cholila ever again, but I will think of you and of all our friends often, and we want to assure you of our good wishes.

Attached you will find the song "Sam Bass," which I promised to write down for you. As I have no more news, I will end by begging that you remember us to all our friends, without forgetting Juan and [Wenceslao], giving them our regards and good wishes, keeping a large portion for yourself and family.

Remaining as always your true friend,

H A. Place

Witnesses reported that Sundance had returned to Cholila in 1906 to sell the livestock he and Butch had left there. According to Gibbon, Sundance said Etta was in San Francisco and Butch was in Chile, en route to Bolivia. Several accounts put all three on the coast of northern Chile in 1905, between their Argentine holdups. Although next to nothing is known about what they did there, the bandits apparently spent time in Antofagasta, a seaport and rail center that bustled with foreigners, most of them employed in the region's lucrative nitrate industry or the import-export business.

According to a January 1906 Pinkerton memorandum, a Pennsylvania postal worker who was reading the Longabaugh family's mail reported that Sundance had recently run into an unnamed difficulty with the Chilean government, but that he had settled the matter for 1,500 *pesos* or dollars with the help of Frank Aller, the U.S. vice-consul in Antofagasta. Sundance, who was using the alias Frank Boyd, had then returned to Argentina. In view of how long it took letters to reach the United States by ship, his Chilean misadventure must have occurred before December 19, 1905, when he joined Butch, Etta, and another friend in robbing the Banco de la Nación in Villa Mercedes.

Dan's weekends in the library have yielded several stories from Argentine newspapers, including *La Prensa* and the caustic English-language *Buenos Aires Herald*, both of which covered the holdup and the pursuit of the bandits in detail. The *Herald* reported that "four well-mounted horsemen rode up to the [bank] and, knife in hand, entered, taking the employees by surprise. The safes were open and two of the brigands emptied them whilst the other two covered the employees. The manager . . . offered resistance [and] was wounded. Before any policemen arrived, the four robbers had re-mounted and disappeared in a cloud of dust."

After remarking on the failure of the police to capture the bandits who had held up the bank in Río Gallegos ten months earlier, the *Herald* added:

> Whilst a fussilade was kept up between the robbers and the bank defenders for four long minutes, only two people were wounded, not by bullets but by blows struck with the butt-ends of revolvers. This exhibit of bad marksmanship may amuse our Texas visitors [from a touring rodeo show], but we fear it will encourage some bold bad men to practice straight-shooting and go forth on similar expeditions. Four minutes work, however hot, cannot be said to be thrown away when the robbers successfully scoop the Bank with apparent impunity at the end of the melee. It remains to be seen whether the Provincial police, hard on the tracks of the robbers, will succeed in bringing them to justice, or restore the plunder to the coffers of the Bank.

La Prensa reported that the amount stolen was 12,000 *pesos*—

equal to about $137,500 today—and that "one of the assailants was seriously wounded by an employee who was defending himself from the assault." Just before the robbery, according to *La Prensa*, the bandits "were drinking whisky in a bar two blocks from the bank." After riding to the bank and dismounting in front of it, three of the bandits went inside; the fourth remained with the horses.

At the time, the only people on the premises were the employees and an Italian named Carlos Ricca. Two bandits entered the treasurer's office, and one entered the manager's office. Mr. García, the treasurer, could not understand how they could have jumped with such speed and agility over the counter and grating that separates the public area from the offices. As he was stamping a check, Mr. García spotted the bandits, but they were already on top of him and fired three shots, none of which, fortunately, found its target. Mr. Ricca, who had money in his hand, suffered a strong blow to the jaw and dropped the money. Other customers arriving at the cashier's window were enraged by what they saw. The bandit who entered the manager's office struck him on the head, causing a minor wound. Ventura Domínguez, who was in his office across the street from the bank, heard the gunfire and ran to the bank. Upon entering the bookkeeper's office, he was detained by one of the bandits, who stuck a revolver in his chest. Happily, he was able to sneak out and run to his office, where he grabbed a revolver. When he returned, the bandits were just leaving the bank and gathering their horses. Mr. Domínguez got off five shots, which were answered by the cowboys, who quickly mounted their horses and made their escape.

When the posse came near them, the bandits dismounted and began firing. According to *La Prensa*, "their early fire was abundant, but upon seeing that their pursuers were few and not well-armed, they let up. While two of the bandits continued shooting, the others saddled the horses, and then they all mounted and resumed their flight." *Caras y Caretas*, a Buenos Aires weekly magazine, reported that the bandits shot and killed a horse being ridden by a local official named Belisario Oliveros. (This incident probably was the germ of truth in James D. Horan's report that "Butch shot the horses of the leading pursuers" after the Río Gallegos holdup, as well as George Kennard's story that provincial police visiting the Cholila ranch were deterred when "Butch shot their horses out from under them.")

Two days after the Villa Mercedes holdup, *La Prensa* reported that nothing had been heard from the posses, who were traveling in rural areas where communication was difficult, but that success was anticipated. A second story disclosed that one of the bandits had been so badly wounded that his companions had tied him to his saddle. The next day, under the headline FRUITLESS PURSUIT, *La Prensa* lamented that the results of the chase were unknown. All that could be said was that one bandit had been shot in the arm and that five posses had been dispatched by four towns. Crisscrossing the provinces of San Luis and Mendoza, the posses were thought to be "closing in" on their quarries. The *Buenos Aires Herald*, which campaigned for stronger and more professional police protection in the provinces and territories, voiced skepticism about the likelihood of the culprits' capture.

> The police ... went in pursuit of the bandits, who were reported to be hemmed in, surrounded, and, with one of their number wounded, just about to be taken. But the arrest has not yet been effected, and the noise of the pursuit seems to be dying away in the distance. The amusing part of this otherwise unpleasant business is the guesses made as to the nationality of the outlaws. Whilst described as "Gauchos" by the [wire service], some local Sherlock Holmes declares that are English or Americans, because they were observed, just before the exploit, indulging in various glasses of whisky. Only people of these nationalities could possibly carry so much camp "whisky" under their belts, and at the same time move, with incomparable celerity, the contents of a Bank safe. Really we do not know whether to take this as a compliment or not.

On December 23, the *Herald* revved its sarcasm up to full pitch.

> Those bad, bold, whisky-drinking, hard-riding, round-the-corner-shooting, Anglo-American, gaucho, Bank robbers have not been captured yet. The whole Republic has been astonished by the depravity of those four buccaneers, and all the horses and men of the Province of San Luis have, it would appear, been turned out upon their trail. The authorities of the adjoining provinces have volunteered to co-operate: and yet ... the rob-

bers are still at large, and their valuable booty unrecovered. After this one must not be surprised to hear that Bank robbing has become a Provincial "industry" second in importance to cattle-stealing. It is to be hoped that this new enterprise will not, later on, ask for Government protection to favour its development.

The chase continued in earnest, and Argentine posses from different jurisdictions reported encountering the gang as it galloped south and west, apparently intent on escaping over the Andes and into Chile. According to local residents, the bandits had been in the area three months earlier studying the roads and "target shooting three or four hours a day." Ostensibly looking for land to buy, they had actually been caching supplies along the way and arranging for peons to meet them at strategic locations and provide reinforcements during their flight. After the robbery, whenever the gang changed horses, one member would separate from the group and scan the horizon with powerful binoculars while the others cared for their wounded companion, cleaned their weapons, and saddled up the new mounts.

A witness quoted in *La Prensa* said that "one of the bandits was beardless, had small feet and delicate features." The reporter then added, without explanation, that "it is supposed that the woman was in charge of cooking the meals," and that "said woman is a fine rider, to the extent that she is widely admired by the Argentines for her skill and natural ability."

Torrential rains swelled the rivers and flooded the pampas, complicating the pursuit, and the posses returned home empty-handed, some of them having ridden a hundred miles or more. Major Cipriano Sosa, whose posse finally lost the trail between the Salado River and Mendoza, complained that the bandits had set fire to the brush as they rode through it, which would have caused terrible damage if the weather had been dry. He also reported that they had rustled or picketed fresh horses en route, and that when a horse became tired, they shot it, presumably so that it could not later be used to chase them.

By the end of January 1906, the bandits were allegedly bivouacked between two arms of the Desaguadero River, south of Mendoza. A second report had the gang camped where the Salado River joins the Atuel, west of Santa Rosa de Toay. Lawmen were dispatched to both sites, but the floods had left the entire region so swampy that pursuit was impossible. Three weeks later, *La Prensa* reported that a witness had seen the bandits, including a woman, cross the Salado on a raft, after which they stole four horses from an *estancia* and bought 60 *pesos'* worth of supplies from a store. The trail ended on the Argentine side of the border, but the outlaws were thought to have crossed into Chile.

When shown photographs from the Pinkertons, the owner of the bar where the bandits had been drinking before the holdup recognized Butch, Sundance, and Etta but not Harvey Logan. The foreman of a nearby ranch also recognized the Cholila trio, who he said had spent three days at his place and departed mere hours before the assault on the Banco de la Nación.

"The *bandoleros* stayed awhile at the Estancia de Luna without the owners' knowing that they were criminals," says Eduardo Cornejo, the publisher of *La Voz del Sud*, a venerable Villa Mercedes newspaper. "It was common to seek lodging at ranches in those days."

Señor Cornejo, a keen student of the holdup, lives in a nineteenth-century house on a green plaza in the oldest part of Villa Mercedes. A portly man with wavy grey hair and dark-framed eyeglasses, he leaves the cool comfort of his book-filled home office, with its twelve-foot ceilings and working shutters, to show us the scene of the crime.

"Because it had rail service to both Buenos Aires and Rosario, Villa Mercedes was an important transportation center for cattlemen," he says as we drive along the shady, cobbled streets. "Livestock fairs were held every month, and ranchers came great distances to attend them. During the fairs, a lot of money passed through the bank, and that was undoubtedly what attracted the bandits to Villa Mercedes. There were two cowboys and a woman. They came here by train under the pretext of buying a hacienda and spent several days in town. They attended one of the fairs and bought some horses before the holdup."

We pull up to the corner of Belgrano and Riobamba, and Señor Cornejo points to a modern white building with a furniture store on the ground floor. "That is where the Banco de La Nación stood in those days. They tore it down ten years ago; all that is left is part of the fence. There was a garden in front of the bank, and the entrance was on the side, where the gate is now. The manager's home was in the same building and shared the entrance with the bank. The porter was shot, but he survived. The woman held the horses. Some people have said that when the *bandoleros* escaped, they tossed *pesos* on the ground to distract the police, but I don't know how reliable that story is."

"You know," says Dan, "we started out looking for the truth, but collecting the folktales is just as much fun. They're almost always more entertaining than the banal reality."

Following the bandits' route, we drive west on Riobamba Street. At Señor Cornejo's instruction, Dan turns north through an area that in 1905 consisted of country estates with big houses. "The police chased them down Betbeder Street to the Quinto River, which they crossed on a wooden bridge that no longer exists. From there, they rode on to what is now Nueva Escocia, detoured around Lavaisse, and rode south, with the police on their heels. At Sovén, they had a shootout, but no one was injured. The bandits escaped, and the police returned to Villa Mercedes after losing the trail on the way to Buena Esperanza. The bandits crossed at Desaguadero, went west to Mendoza, then south to San Rafael, where there is a well-traveled pass."

After saying goodbye to our guide, we cross the new concrete bridge over the Quinto River and head out into the countryside in search of the bandits' escape route. We easily find the few modest brick homes and *pulperías*—combination bars and general stores—that make up Nueva Escocia and Lavaisse. The trees alongside the dirt road become smaller and then disappear altogether; green fields reach to a horizon broken only by wire fences and ruminating cows. The road deteriorates, and the weather turns muggy. Eventually, we come to an *horqueta*. According to the rusty sign, we can continue on this narrow trail to Sovén or turn left to reach the paved road that parallels it a mile or two away. Dan favors the highway. "The way this gearshift keeps popping into neutral makes me leary of getting too far away from civilization. I'd hate for you to have to push us all the way to Sovén."

"But the bandits didn't take the highway," I plead. "If anything happens, we can always cut across country and flag somebody down on the paved road."

"All right, but if the car breaks down, it's your ass."

Within ten minutes, we reach a steep twenty-foot stretch of road that trucks have churned into a braid of ruts. Dan stops the car and gets out to examine the obstacle. The road is too narrow for turning around, so we will have to drive backward for several miles if we chicken out. "I don't think the Society for the Prevention of Cruelty to Autos would approve," says Dan, "but we can probably make it." He shifts into reverse and backs up a ways, then drops into first gear and stomps the accelerator. We bounce and grind up the hill. "Well," says Dan, at the top, "there's no turning back now. Let's hope it doesn't get any worse."

It gets worse. No more hills await us, but we are soon bogged in an endless series of mud holes, some of them forty feet long. I take off my shoes, roll up my jeans, and resign myself to pushing the car out of the mess I've got us into, while Dan graciously refrains from saying he told me so. According to our map, a short spur up ahead connects this miserable track with the real road. We must reach the spur, however, if we are to escape from the escape route. At least we don't have a posse on our heels.

Eventually, we negotiate an enormous lagoon at the intersection of the trail and the spur, only to find our path blocked by a large truck. Dan somehow manages to maneuver the car around the truck, and we rattle out onto the highway and straight to the nearest gas station, where the attendant announces that the transmission has lost all its fluid. "I can put in some more fluid," he says, "but I can't fix the leak."

We should start picketing fresh rental cars along our escape routes.

"I don't suppose there's a mechanic nearby," says Dan.

"Not at this hour. If you can make it to Santa Rosa, you shouldn't have any trouble finding somebody to take care of you there."

If we can make it.

"Well," says Dan, "I reckon we just nailed down first place on Avis's LEAST-WANTED list."

5 · NOWHERE TO HIDE

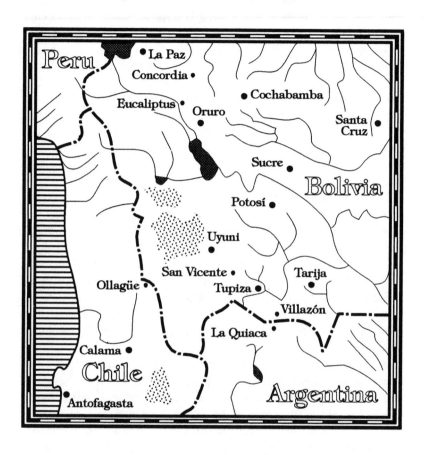

AFTER the Villa Mercedes holdup, the bandits apparently returned to Antofagasta and may have lived there for a while. In 1914, the Pinkertons wrote to Antofagasta's police chief to verify a report that Butch Cassidy was imprisoned there. According to the Pinkerton's informant, who had visited the prison in 1913, the warden told him "that Cassidy with two other North Americans and a woman had been in Chile, Ecuador, and Bolivia, that these men were desperadoes, that one night the three Americans, after drinking a lot of native liquor, started fighting among themselves." The informant was unsure whether Butch killed his companions or they left town, but only he remained. "Cassidy went to work for the Nitrate Mining Company as a packmaster and conveyed the mineral to Antofagasta and guarded the money going back. Cassidy worked at this for some time and made himself very well acquainted and very well liked. He did considerable business at the bank in Antofagasta and in this way got acquainted with the officials of the bank. One day Cassidy appeared at the bank with an American woman. Under some pretext or other, she got the cashier or one of the bank officials into a separate room and Cassidy then robbed the bank. In attempting to escape, Cassidy killed the mayor of the town or the man who occupied the position of mayor." According to the informant, Butch's horse stumbled and fell, breaking Butch's leg and leaving him unable to avoid capture.

This report seems dubious to us, but we try to run it down anyway, as did the Pinkertons. They asked the Antofagasta police chief for whatever information he had about this crime and for photographs of anyone implicated in it, but if the chief answered the letter, we cannot find his response among the thousands of documents in the Pinkerton archives. Nor do the Chilean newspapers in the Library of Congress go back far enough to help us ascertain whether the report was true, what happened to Etta Place (who disappeared during this period), or what Butch and Sundance did in the months before they turned up in Bolivia, where they spent the last two years of their lives.

Because the route from Antofagasta to Bolivia crosses one of the driest, coldest deserts on earth and climbs from the seacoast to an altitude of more than thirteen thousand feet in the space of a couple hundred miles, most people in the early 1900s made the journey by train. An account by an anonymous Chilean journalist from that era gives us an idea of what Butch and Sundance saw as they made their way up onto the *altiplano*—a vast, high plateau in the central Andes—and north to the Bolivian city of Oruro.

> Antofagasta gradually recedes below. The lines of its streets are distinguished and then rapidly, as the train moves away, become confused in a thousand lights separated by a black

band [the beach] from the dim radiance of the bay. Beyond, magnificent and barely illuminated by the last light of the afternoon [is] the Pacific Ocean. . . . We climb in an impenetrable darkness. In vain all faces approach the windows, which are covered with a whitish veil [of fog]; outside the only things visible, in the illumination from the train's lights, are the crags of the ravine. There is nothing for it but to recline in the seats and endure, without sleep, a long conversation, increasingly monotonous as topics are exhausted, and fatigue sets in. From time to time, the locomotive's whistle heralds a populated center. . . . The windows are opened, and an icy air bathes our warm brows; the poor wood-and-tin buildings of the first way stations on the plains are dimly lit with oil lamps; some night-walkers . . . wrapped in shawls and scarves approach the train and look with curious eyes at the travelers.

Farther ahead stretches an immense plain lit by a splendid moon, which stands out beautifully over a clear sky spangled with stars. . . . If not for the penetrating cold, the traveler would stay in the open on the deck of the car. . . . At midnight the first nitrate *oficinas* appear, looking like ghostly castles, illuminated with thousands of electric lamps. We see, perfectly delineated, the superb constructions of these works, in which the activity is never interrupted. . . .

We continue the trip, turning toward the San Pedro volcano. . . . This region is very interesting because of . . . the varied colors of the mountains. On top of the volcano, white smoke continuously appears, rising slowly and turning into flakes that remain suspended over the crater for some time. . . . Well before coming to the Bolivian border, the traveler . . . will encounter in the stations small groups of natives, almost all women, dressed with an infinity of short skirts of loud colors, their heads covered with small white string hats, and their bodices wrapped in shawls. These people travel constantly, and in the stations we see their luggage—wide boxes of leather with carved designs and bags that get their color, so we are told, from *llama* hair.

Just across the border, we find ourselves in an extensive plain whose horizon is much broader than in any other part, owing to the low air density. Seen first are some mountains, then others behind, and many more in a chain that seems infinite. . . . There is a curious optical phenomenon in which the traveler perfectly distinguishes lakes in which the nearby mountains are clearly reflected. These lakes do not exist.

As the train rolls through this arid plain, where not the slightest sign of traffic is noted, we see every so often some curious monuments made . . . with the corpses of animals, which have been placed on foot and propped up with rocks and sticks in such a manner that—semi-mummified—they remain poised to run across the plain.

If Butch and Sundance believed in omens, they might have looked twice at these fellow fugitives.

The countryside is extensive and lonely. . . . Long stretches of it are covered by *yareta* and *tola,* the only plants in almost the whole way to Oruro. The *yareta* is a species of resinous moss that grows [in] . . . outcrops up to six feet wide; the *tola* . . . is scrub that rises a few centimeters in small unobtrusive branches. Both plants are harvested by the natives and used as quick-burning fuel. Upon arriving at Julaca . . . we see great heaps of *yareta* ready for consumption.

From Julaca, we continue toward Río Grande, crossing fields more intense in the growth of these plants; we cross over a low bridge and continue toward Uyuni, the first Bolivian city of importance. Now it is night, and the cold obliges us to leave the quixotries for another occasion. We bundle up well and jump onto the platform to receive the agreeable surprise of seeing several Chilean acquaintances who have come to await the night train to procure fresh fish. . . .

After a brief detention in Poopó . . . we pass new native hamlets and come into Machacamarca, where . . . a traveling companion asks us to join him in discovering what is happening among the numerous Indian women who, seated in a long row across from the train, dispense bread, milk, cheese, *chicha,* and many other things. The man . . . displays enthusiasm for a girl dressed in who knows how many skirts, wrapped in a clean shawl, and speaking Quechua with another girl of her age. Both are *chicha* vendors. Our companion, believing that [his Spanish] will not be understood, begins to praise the almond eyes of the Indian girl and the sweetness of her voice. A youth approaches to buy *chicha*. She speaks in perfect Spanish and looks, smiling, at our companion. At the same time, a bare hand and arm of an unimaginable grime come out from under her shawl to deliver the goods; at least eighteen years must have passed in which not even the slightest drop of water has fallen on them, as a result of which a horrible black scale has formed. We take one look at this masterpiece of filth and return to the car.

The train begins to describe some curves, crossing through picturesque fields to . . . the base of beautiful, softly shaded mountains, which complete an admirable panorama. Half an hour later, we are in the outskirts of Oruro [where the outlaws spent time], and the homes of the Indians are closer together. To the west of the tracks, Oruro forms a strange grey ensemble, over which several towers stand out. The train has slowed its march, and the first part of the city that comes into our view is the cemetery, a square reserve whose walls are all niches, distinguished in the center by a type of chapel or mausoleum. On the other side of the line is an ample area devoted to sporting games, provided with a grandstand painted green.

Inasmuch as the penalty for losing at their favorite sport was death, how fitting that Butch and Sundance entered the city by this route.

We have arrived in Oruro after thirty-eight hours of travel . . . to find ourselves for the first time in a city located at 12,126 feet above sea level, an altitude at which a man from the coast cannot engage in vigorous exercise without suffering enormous fatigue and sometimes bloody noses. The . . . plaza is spacious, perfectly paved and adorned with small trees protected by high iron fences. At the center is a great fountain with beautiful bronze figures representing lions and other animals, and in the corners are smaller fountains with sculpture groups of true merit. All have waterworks and electric lamps, with which a splendid effect is achieved at night. On the west, forming a magnificent base for the plaza, is the Government Palace. . . .

The narrowness of the streets, nearly all of them flanked by stone buildings with colonial escutcheons and adornments, attracts the traveler's attention. . . . Swarming incessantly through the streets are enormous numbers of Indians of different types and with varied clothing. Most notable are the vendors who come from the environs of La Paz wearing dark suits and short hair covered with a cap over which they place a cloth hat. . . . The municipal market [is] an area composed of several patios, crowded with an infinity of Indians of every countenance. The sites next to the walls are divided into distinct posts separated with canvas and thin partitions built by the merchants, who are almost all women, except for a few Arabs . . . who are discordant notes, with their modern suits, amid the variety of loud colors of the native finery. We examine the goods of the Indian women and purchase some curious miniature dolls made with a Chinese thoroughness. Nearly everyone sells clothing and herbs. In the center of the unpaved patios numerous Indian women sit on the ground before small mounds of potatoes. In some corners, we see tables covered with glasses and bottles with yellow and red liquids. They are *chichas,* highly esteemed by the common man, despite the fact that their preparation [in which corn is chewed and spit into jars to ferment] is anything but clean. . . . We are also struck by the scarcity of resources for nourishment, as articles of the most indispensable necessity are seen in only a few of the posts, the majority of the vendors being devoted to the sale of trinkets and herbs. . . .

Leaving this neighborhood and passing through the streets, we see several modern buildings that make a strange contrast with the florid [colonial] facades. Among others, we note . . . the Hotel Americano [Sundance's last known address] and the Argandoña Bank in Bolívar Street. . . . The police are scarce, [and] we see only a few soldiers, all of them poorly dressed and not very military in appearance.

If Butch and Sundance judged the soldiers' competence by their looks, the mistake could have proved fatal. Some thirty years earlier, Jose Domingo Cortes had observed that "without doubt the soldiers of many countries are more disciplined and warlike than the Bolivian soldier, but none is more humble, patient, and long-suffering. . . . As for suffering, the Bolivian soldier can take first place in the world. He crosses the most fiery desert and the coldest plain on forced marches, and withstands hunger and thirst beyond belief. [Forty miles] on steep and dangerous trails are a day's journey that the Indian conquers on foot without rest or fatigue."

Most of the stories about Butch and Sundance in Bolivia have come from Percy Seibert, an American engineer who met the bandits working at the Concordia tin mine, fifty-five miles north of Oruro and seventy miles southeast of La Paz, as the crow flies, or about a hundred miles from either city by cart roads and mule trails. In a series of conversations that took place over the course of more than thirty years, Seibert told western writers Arthur Chapman, Charles Kelly, and James D. Horan about the pair of American cowboys known at Concordia as Santiago Maxwell and Enrique Brown. Some of Seibert's tales have been verified; others are demonstrably false; the remainder fall somewhere in between.

In 1906, Butch rode into the Concordia camp, sixteen thousand feet up in the Santa Vela Cruz range of the central Bolivian Andes, and said he was looking for a job. Manager Clement Rolla Glass needed someone to buy livestock for hauling material and feeding the workers. Butch, who introduced himself as Maxwell, said he knew mules as well as he knew horses, and Glass hired him for $150 a month, plus room and board. The next morning, Glass sent his new stockman to La Paz with $200 and three muleteers. Within a week, Maxwell returned with a herd of fine mules and $50 change. He clearly knew mules and could drive a bargain, to boot. Glass found him capable, trustworthy, and pleasant and thought about making him a foreman. Soon, Maxwell was carrying Concordia's payroll remittances and scrupulously accounting for every cent entrusted to him, even though the amounts often temptingly exceeded $100,000.

Meanwhile, Sundance had been working as a muleteer for a Bolivian Railroad construction contractor. Roy Letson, who had hired him in northern Argentina to help drive a herd of mules to La Paz, later wrote that Sundance had been "well dressed, without funds, had a crust of bread in his pocket for his next meal. He did have a very fine Tiffany gold watch." Letson found Sundance shy but able:

> Longabaugh kept very much to himself most of the time. I told him my destination was Bolivia and he said that he would be glad to go along. We were several weeks on that trip. Travelling without any guide we would frequently come to a point where trails branched out in several directions. Longabaugh would suggest a trail and in each case he was correct. Shortly before reaching our destination, and while sitting around a camp fire, he told me that he knew every foot of the country and that he had been over the same trail many times. He was employed by our company to break the mules to harness and saddle and done a very good job. Naturally he grew restless and it was not long before he was on the go again.

According to Seibert, Letson bought some mules for Concordia and brought Sundance along to the camp, introduced him as Enrique Brown, and asked Glass whether he could use another hand. The Concordia manager found Brown somewhat sullen but hired him anyway. Glass sensed that Maxwell and Brown already knew each other and, from the way they handled animals, that they had been cowboys in North America.

At some point, Glass learned their real identities. According to one report, he simply put two and two together after hearing descriptions of the culprits in a series of holdups in the region. We doubt this account, however, because Bolivian newspapers described very few significant holdups while Butch and Sundance were at Concordia, and the articles never mentioned their names. More plausible is the report that an engineer who had seen a Pinkerton circular in Buenos Aires told Glass that Maxwell and Brown were Butch Cassidy and the Sundance Kid. In any event, Glass decided not to act on the information, so long as they continued to behave themselves. After all, the mining camps were full of *gringos* with unsavory pasts, and workers as capable as this pair were hard to find.

Then one night, a longtime employee with a heavy grain-alcohol habit overheard Maxwell and Brown talking about a holdup and thought they were planning to rob Concordia. The agitated man woke up Clement Glass. After quieting the fellow down, Glass walked to the bunkhouse with a loaded Winchester and confronted the bandits.

"I don't care who you are," he said, "but I heard you were planning to rob the mine."

As Sundance watched silently from his bunk, Butch calmly affirmed their identities but said the eavesdropper had been mistaken. "We don't rob the people we work for."

After declaring that he was no policeman, Glass agreed to keep them on as Maxwell and Brown. That settled, the manager took his leave. On his way out, he noticed the tip of the gun Sundance had been aiming at him from beneath a blanket the whole time.

In late 1906, Percy Seibert—who was Glass's assistant—returned to Bolivia from a long trip to the United States. He found the Concordia crew celebrating Christmas in La Paz. When Glass introduced him to all the men who had been hired in his absence, Seibert felt that the two named Maxwell and Brown tried to avoid him. Back at the mine, he asked Glass about them and learned their secret. Initially shocked, Seibert came to like Butch immensely. Although he had difficulty striking up a friendship with the taciturn Sundance, Seibert "never had the slightest trouble getting along with" either of them.

Not that their real occupation didn't sometimes discomfit their employers. Once, for example, Butch came into the office while Glass and Seibert were counting out a payroll. According to Seibert, Butch took one look at the hundreds of thousands of dollars' worth of gold on the table and "jokingly remarked that it was the easiest money he had ever seen, but we continued our work and he finally asked us if we would give him the gold in exchange for paper currency. We told him we would gladly accommodate him, but we would have to fulfill our obligation to certain of our men and pay them in actual gold. Cassidy then volunteered to see these men and get their consent to the exchange. This he did within an hour or two, and when he came back we made the exchange, much as we disliked being parties to such a transaction."

After Glass left Concordia, Seibert became the manager. By then, his wife was also living in the camp, and Butch and Sundance had become regular guests for Sunday dinner at the Seiberts' home. At the table, Butch always sat in the seat overlooking the valley and the trail up to the house. In the sitting room, he "would invariably take a seat on a small sofa which was placed between two windows. This seat gave him a survey of three doors and one window. He always seemed to be cool and calculating, and protected his back very well."

The bandits gradually let down their guard, and even Sundance relaxed enough to talk about his past, though not enough to tell the truth about it: He said he had come from a good family in New Jersey and had a sister married to a congressman. Sundance also told Seibert of having run away from home to become a cowboy "after reading some thrilling novels on the West" and of having taken part in a couple of holdups "just for excitement" before joining Butch's gang.

The bandits had intended to go legitimate in South America, Butch said, but left Cholila after a former deputy sheriff from the United States immigrated to a nearby ranch and recognized them. Butch believed that this man had informed the authorities of their whereabouts, probably in hopes of collecting the reward for their capture. The bandits felt they had no choice but to come out of retirement. "There's no use trying to hide out and go straight," Butch told Seibert. "There's always an informer around to bring the law on you. After you've started, you have to keep going, that's all. The safest way is to keep moving all the time and spring a holdup in some new place. In that way you keep the other fellows guessing."

Musing about his outlaw career, Butch said that he had never been so closely trailed as after the holdup in Villa Mercedes, where—contrary to the opinions expressed by the *Buenos Aires Herald*—the pursuit had been organized quickly and well. He also told Seibert of having tried, apparently without success, to induce Harvey Logan to come to South America. Butch said that Logan was the coolest and most able man he'd ever known. Evidently, Butch didn't mind riding with a psychopath, provided he was a cool and able psychopath.

Nonetheless, Butch struck Seibert as "an exceptionally pleasant and even cultured and charming man. He used good language and was never vulgar." Only once did Seibert see Butch "under the influence of whisky . . . and then he seemed to be very much ashamed of himself because he could not walk straight." In a 1964 letter to an acquaintance, Seibert wrote that Butch "took well with the ladies and as soon as he arrived in a village he made friends with the little urchins and usually had some candy to give them. When he visited me he enjoyed hearing the gramophone records, as I had a large selection of choice music."

At Seibert's request, the bandits demonstrated their marksmanship by shooting beer bottles in the air, and Butch explained their preference for .45-caliber Colt revolvers: "The long barrel can be used as a club." If anyone offered resistance during a robbery, they would hit him across the nose with a Colt, and he would invariably raise his hands to protect his face. The result: no noise and minimal bloodshed.

Butch told the Seiberts about Etta Place, whom he called a great house-keeper with "the heart of a whore," and said that Sundance had taken her to Denver for an appendectomy. After installing her in the hospital, he proceeded to get roaring drunk. The next morning, hung-over and irritated by the lack of room service in his boardinghouse, he fired a few rounds into the ceiling. When the landlord threatened to call the police, Sundance hightailed it out of town and returned to South America. Butch said they didn't know what became of Etta after that.

Butch and Sundance periodically left Concordia, but they always came back, usually bearing Indian jewelry or other trinkets for Mrs. Seibert. Sometimes, their return would be followed by reports that a payroll had been stolen or a train had been robbed. Although Seibert had no proof of their involvement, he credited them with virtually every holdup that occurred during their tenure at Concordia, as well as a Peruvian job that took place before they ever set foot on the continent. Seibert did not, however, convey his suspicions to the authorities. "It was sort of a game we played," he told Horan. "While we would never betray them, they also knew they were fair game. If the police or the army came in to take them, we would cooperate with the law; if we heard they planned to rob a bank, train, or store, we would somehow get word to the intended victim. It was accepted that we were on one side, they were on the other."

In October 1907, Butch and Sundance went with another American to Santa Cruz, in the sugar, rice, and coffee region of eastern Bolivia. Seibert said that, while looking for a place to stay, they visited the sheriff's office, where they saw posters offering large rewards for the notorious Butch Cassidy and Harry Longabaugh. According to their companion, although the descriptions of the wanted men were good, Butch had a heavy beard at the time, and Sundance had grown much stouter. Butch brazenly joked that he would be on the lookout for the thieves, but the sheriff evinced not the slightest suspicion about his visitors' identities.

A letter Butch wrote from Santa Cruz on November 12, 1907, wound up in a thick scrapbook with other mementos of Seibert's years in South

America. Whether the man referred to as Ingersoll in the letter was Sundance or the other American is unknown.

To the Boys at Concordia:

We arrived here about 3 weeks ago after a very pleasant journey, and found just the place I have been looking for for 20 years, and Ingersoll likes it better than I do, he says he won't try to live anywhere else. This is a Town of 18,000, and 14,000 are females and some of them are birds. This is the only place for old fellows like myself. One never gets too old if he has blue eyes and a red face and looks capable of making a blue eyed Baby Boy.

Oh god if I could call back 20 years and have red hair with this complection [*sic*] of mine I would be happy. I have got into the 400 set as deep as I can go. The lady feeds me on fine wines, and she is the prettiest little thing I ever seen, but I am afraid Papa is going to tear my playhouse down, for he is getting nasty, but there is plenty more. This place isn't what we expected at all. There isn't any cattle here. All the beef that is killed here comes from Mojo, a distance of 80 leagues, and are worth from 80 to 100 Bs. But cattle do very well here. The grass is good, but water is scarce, there isn't any water in this town when there is a dry spell for a week. The people here in town have to buy water at 1.80 per barrel. They can get good water at 40 feet but are too lazy to sink wells.

Land is cheap here and everything grows good that is planted, but there is damned little planted. Everything is very high. It costs us Bs100 per head to feed our mules, 250 each for ourselves. We rented a house, hired a good cook and are living like gentlemen.

Land is worth 10 cts. per hectare 10 leagues from here and there is some good Estancias for sale, one 12 leagues from here of 4 leagues with plenty of water and good grass and some sugar cane for Bs5,000, and others just as cheap, and if I don't fall down I will be living here before long.

It is pretty warm and some fever but the fever is caused by the food they eat. At least I am willing to chance it.

They are doing some work now building a [railroad] from Port Suarez here and they claim it will be pushed right through, so now is the time to get started for land will go up before long.

It is 350 miles from here to Cochabamba and a hell of a road, just up one mountain and down another all the way, not a level spot on it big enough to whip a dog on, and most of the way thick brush on both sides. But there is people all along and lots of little towns. In fact it is thickly settled. There is plenty of game on the road but it is safe for it is impossible to get it for brush. I killed 1 turkey, 1 Sandhill Crain [sic] and 1 Buzzard. We could hear the turkeys every day and seen some several times but I only got one shot. It won't do for Reece [a fellow employee] to come over that road for he would kill himself getting through the brush after birds. We would of left here long ago, but we had a little trouble with the old mule. Ingersoll hobbled her and tied her to a tree and wore a nice green pole out on her, but I didn't think he had done a good job so I worked a little while with rocks. Between us we broke her jaw and we have been feeding her on mush ever since, but she can eat a little now and we will leave in a few days for a little trip south to see that country. I am looking for the place Hutch wants, 8 leagues long, ½ league wide with a big river running through it from end to end.

We expect to be back at Concordia in about 1 month. Good luck to all you fellows.

J. P. Maxwell

Butch seems to have forgotten that he was a *gentleman* bandit. Would a gentleman joke about whipping a dog and breaking a mule's jaw? Would a gentleman brag about his affair with one of the many apparently interchangeable fish in his sea? Robbing banks is one thing, but there are limits! I suppose he might have been telling the boys in Concordia's "locker room" what he thought they wanted to hear. I'll give him the benefit of the doubt just this once.

In 1908, two holdups occurred near Eucaliptus, a way station on the *altiplano* about fifty miles southwest of Concordia via a mule trail and cart roads. In May, according to an Oruro daily, "some Yankee contract employees, who had worked on the railroad line and had disagreements with the firm, confronted the paymaster in the manager's tent with guns drawn and forced him to turn over all the money," an amount equivalent to $90,000 today. In August, "the paymaster of the South American Construction Company was robbed [on] the new rail line from Viacha by two masked men, said to be the same who stole a sum of money from the same line's paymaster" earlier in the year.

While asserting that Butch and Sundance were innocent of the second job, Seibert blamed them for the first one, which he inaccurately described as a train robbery. According to Seibert, after forcing the engineer to detach the express car and haul it away from the rest of the train, Butch and Sundance compelled the cashier to open the safe and hand over its contents. Seibert said that the bandits asked about several packages and envelopes with names on them and were told that they contained watches, money, jewelry, and other personal effects of the construction workers. Naturally—Butch being Robin Hood and all that—those packages went back into the safe.

To hear Seibert tell it, passing up the workers' money and jewelry at Eucaliptus wasn't Butch's only good deed in Bolivia: He also foiled a plot to kidnap a mine owner in 1907 and rode some forty-eight hours on a mule to warn a Concordia official of a plan to assassinate him. And, Seibert wrote, Butch was selective about his victims:

> He went to a mining camp owned by a pair of wealthy Scotch-men, to get the lay-of-the-land and to learn where their payroll remittance would arrive so as to pick it up. They gave him a job as a night watchman, and told him they really needed no one, but wanted to give him a chance to make a little money so he could continue prospecting for mines, as on applying for work he told them he was a prospector and had run out of money and supplies. They told him the meal hours, told him the sideboard had a supply of whiskey, appolinas water, gin and beer and whenever he felt like a drink to help himself. He told me after that he had not the heart to hold up people who treated him so kindly.

Butch's loyalty to his employers at Concordia outweighed even his fellowship with other bandits. Seibert said that when his "camp was visited by two embryo American bandits on horseback, horses being very rare in the high altitudes of Bolivia, Cassidy promptly approached

100

them and told them to get out of camp. He informed them that he did not want them or any other would-be bandits to cause people to get the impression that our camp was a rendezvous for outlaws. These unwelcome visitors informed Cassidy that they realized they had not done right . . . but, as they had to have food, there was no alternative for them. I afterwards learned that Cassidy gave them one hundred dollars, with a warning never to appear in camp again.''

Seibert said that Butch and Sundance left Concordia after their own status as outlaws became widely known. This came about when Sundance got drunk in Uyuni, 165 miles south of Oruro, and bragged to another American about the Argentine robberies he and Butch had pulled off. Butch paid their tabs at Concordia's commissary and the two men rode away for good. Seibert later heard that they had gone to southern Bolivia and found work with James "Santiago" Hutcheon, a Scot whose company hauled passengers and freight in mule-drawn wagons and coaches.

Hutcheon knew them as Maxwell and Brown, but they introduced themselves as the Lowe brothers to other people in the region. According to Horan, a Norwegian missionary named Wenberg, who had met Butch in northern Bolivia, bumped into him in the lobby of a Tupiza hotel and called him Mr. Maxwell. When Wenberg asked how he was, Butch "gave him a cold stare. 'I am fine,' he replied, 'but my name is Lowe.' And then walked away.'' Soon afterward, the news reached Seibert that Butch and Sundance had been killed in a shootout following the holdup of a payroll remittance belonging to the Aramayo mining company.

Other than a few rumors that wafted northward, virtually nothing about the shootout was known in the United States until a couple of decades later, when Seibert described the event to Arthur Chapman, a New York journalist. In the April 1930 issue of *The Elks Magazine,* Chapman related Seibert's tale. After stealing the Aramayo remittance in early 1909, Chapman wrote, Butch and Sundance "proceeded to Tupiza, where they took employment with a transportation outfit" for the next few weeks. "Learning that they had been identified as the perpetrators of the Aramayo holdup, they hurriedly departed for Uyuni,'' some 120 miles northwest of Tupiza. Halfway to their destination, the "two heavily armed Americanos, on jaded mules, rode into the patio of the police station at the Indian village of San Vicente, Bolivia, and demanded something to eat. It was not an unusual demand, for the police station was also an inn, and there was no place else in the village where wayfarers could find food and shelter.''

Chapman described what happened next:

> After making it known that they intended to pass the night at the station, the strangers stripped their saddles, blankets and rifles from their mules. They piled their equipment in a room at one side of the little courtyard which was soon to become a shambles. Then they sat at a table in a room across the patio and called for a speedy serving of food and liquor. . . .
>
> The constable in charge of the station at San Vicente happened to catch sight of one of the strangers' mules, then rolling in the dust of the courtyard to relieve his saddle-galled back. He recognized the animal as having belonged to a friend of his—a muleteer who was helping transport the Aramayo mines' remittance when the holdup took place. . . . There was a company of Bolivian cavalry just outside of town. The constable would send an Indian messenger to the captain. Then the Americanos would have to explain how they came into possession of that mule.
>
> On receipt of the message, the Bolivian captain brought up his command and quietly surrounded the station. Then the captain himself walked into the room where Cassidy and Longabaugh were eating and drinking.
>
> ''Surrender, señors,'' came the demand from the brave captain.
>
> The outlaws leaped to their feet. Longabaugh was drunk, but Cassidy, always a canny drinker, was in complete command of his senses.
>
> The captain had drawn his revolver when he entered the room. Before he could fire, Cassidy had shot from the hip. The captain fell dead and Cassidy and Longabaugh stationed themselves where they could command a view of the patio.
>
> A sergeant and a picked body of cavalrymen rushed through the gate, calling upon the outlaws to surrender. Revolvers blazed from door and window, and men began to stagger and fall in the courtyard. The first to die was the sergeant who had sought to rescue his captain.

Cassidy and Longabaugh were firing rapidly, and with deadly effect. Those of the detachment who remained on their feet were firing in return. Bullets sank into the thick adobe walls or whistled through the window and door. Other soldiers began firing, from behind the shelter of the courtyard wall.

"Keep me covered, Butch," called Longabaugh. "I'll get our rifles."

Shooting as he went, Longabaugh lurched into the courtyard. If he could only reach the rifles and ammunition which they had so thoughtlessly laid aside, the fight would be something which the outlaws would welcome.

Blood was settling in little pools about the courtyard. The sergeant and most of his file of soldiers were stretched out, dead. A few wounded were trying to crawl to safety. The mules had broken their halters and galloped out of the yard, among them the animal which had been the indirect cause of the battle.

Soldiers were firing through the open gate and from all other vantage points outside the wall. Longabaugh got halfway across the courtyard and fell, desperately wounded, but not before he had effectively emptied his six-shooter.

When Cassidy saw his partner fall, he rushed into the courtyard. Bullets rained about him as he ran to Longabaugh's side. Some of the shots found their mark, but Cassidy, though wounded, managed to pick up Longabaugh and stagger back to the house with his heavy burden.

Cassidy saw that Longabaugh was mortally wounded. Furthermore it was going to be impossible to carry on the battle much longer unless the rifles and ammunition could be reached. Cassidy made several attempts to cross the courtyard. At each attempt he was wounded and driven back.

The battle now settled into a siege. Night came on, and men fired at the red flashes from weapons. There were spaces of increasing length between Cassidy's shots. He had only a few cartridges left. Longabaugh's cartridge belt was empty. So was the dead Bolivian captain's.

The soldiers, about 9 or 10 o'clock in the evening, heard two shots fired in the bullet-riddled station. Then no more shots came. Perhaps it was a ruse to lure them into the patio within range of those deadly revolvers. The soldiers kept on firing all through the night and during the next morning.

About noon an officer and a detachment of soldiers rushed through the patio and into the station. They found Longabaugh and Cassidy dead. Cassidy had fired a bullet into Longabaugh's head, and had used his last cartridge to kill himself.

6 · LIFE AFTER DEATH

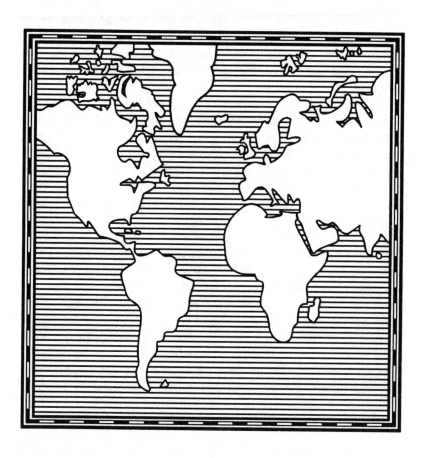

B UTCH died for the first time on Friday the thirteenth of May 1898, when a posse trailed a rustler named Joe Walker to Robbers' Roost and shot him in his bedroll, which he happened to be sharing that night (a common sleeping arrangement in the Old West, two bodies being warmer than one). His sandy-haired, lantern-jawed bedmate caught one of the bullets meant for Walker. Inspecting the bodies, the lawmen were delighted to see that, in addition to reeling in Walker, they had hooked an even bigger fish: the famous Butch Cassidy. On their way back to town, the men calculated their shares of the reward. News of the gun battle preceded them, and a crowd had gathered to see the outlaws' corpses by the time they arrived on Saturday. The burial took place on Sunday, but Butch was exhumed on Monday and, to the posse's dismay, identified as a law-abiding cowboy named Johnny Herring. The real Butch, joking that he wanted to attend his own funeral, was said to have sneaked into town while the bodies were on display.

Before the troops closed in on him in San Vicente, Butch had died several more times, according to reports we have found in various newspapers, magazines, and archives: He was shot by another posse near Vernal, Utah, in the late 1890s; slain "in a tropical saloon brawl" in the early 1900s; and "filled full of holes on the bridge at Green River, Wyoming," in the winter of 1905–1906. By the fall of 1908, he was also said to have paid "his reckoning in the Paris slums," where "a gendarme found him face downward, the hilt of a long crooked knife fast between his shoulders." Both Butch and Sundance had supposedly died when "surrounded by soldiers near the Argentine-Chilean border in 1904," attacked in a ranch house on the eastern side of Andes in 1906, or ambushed by bounty hunters while driving cattle to market in Brazil. Meanwhile, Sundance and an unnamed associate were reportedly slain in Venezuela.

After Chapman's article about the Bolivian shootout appeared in *The Elks Magazine* in 1930, other writers began embellishing the story. The location, date, circumstances, and participants changed with each retelling. The battle took place in a saloon or a corral; at a railroad station, a bank, or a ranch; in Bolivia, Chile, Argentina, Peru, Uruguay, or Mexico. The slayers were "Chilean soldiers who suspected them of cattle rustling," "native officers and a couple of United States rangers," and Argentine *fronterizas,* among others. Generally, Butch was said to have used his last bullets to put Sundance out of his misery and commit suicide, but once in a while the bandits "shot each other to keep from falling into the hands of the law." In the most fanciful version, Butch fired his gun from a swiveling holster, Sundance was shot in the groin, and Etta Place was killed by a stray bullet.

Charles Kelly's friend Otis "Dock" Marston once observed that the outlaws' occupational need for secrecy "opened the field around the

Wild Bunch to much more hokum than the general run of history.'' Perhaps the hokum is part of the attraction outlaw history holds for many of its practitioners; there is no denying that historical yarns are entertaining. G. Ezra Dane went so far as to issue a warning to readers of his 1941 book, *Ghost Town*: "Do not expect historical accuracy—this is not a history. There is some history in it; there are even whole pages of what we know to be plain, honest truth. A great deal more of it may be true; we shouldn't be surprised if it was. Some of it we know to be absolutely false, and that is the best part of all."

In attempting to discover where fact and folklore diverge, we find most accounts of Butch and Sundance's deaths—or survival—too vague to pin down or too ludicrous to take seriously. We pay close attention, however, to a story told by Victor Hampton, a mining engineer who worked in San Vicente from 1922 to 1925. Having heard about the shootout from Malcom Roberts, the manager of the company whose payroll had been stolen, Hampton later passed the details along to writer James D. Horan.

> After robbing the payroll they followed the trail which leads from Atocha, a small village on the Bolivian-Argentine Railroad, to San Vicente. Roberts said the soldiers arrived as darkness was closing in. The . . . payroll's guard [who had followed the bandits from the holdup site] went inside and found the mule. He came out and told the officer in charge of the detachment that the two Americans cooking inside the hut were surely the robbers.
>
> Cassidy and the Kid were in the adobe hut, their rifles outside.
>
> They were using a small beehive-type baking oven and could be seen eating by the glow of a candle. The officer led his men into the gate and shouted an order to surrender. That's when the shooting started. Roberts said they found the pair dead the next morning.
>
> They were buried by the soldiers in the Indian graveyard. I made a trip up there and found the two graves. A German prospector is buried on one side of Cassidy. He was thawing out a package of dynamite on a stove in his house over the hill from San Vicente. As he entered the door the dynamite went off.

A Swede prospector is buried on the side of the Kid. One Sunday as he got off his mule, his gun accidentally fired, killing him. When the Indians found him, the condors had eaten all the flesh from his face and neck.

I went over Cassidy's trail from San Vicente to Atocha. Even in the 1920s it was rough. The silver mines of San Vicente have long been abandoned and the settlement has completely reverted to the Indians.

From the beginning, the report that Butch and Sundance were dead met with skepticism. In the 1930s, after Percy Seibert's tale was first published, dozens of witnesses stepped forward to say that they had seen the bandits alive during the years that had elapsed since the shootout. Butch was said to have become a businessman, a draftsman, a door-to-door salesman, a lumber dealer, a banker, a rancher, a trapper, a miner, a chiller in a foundry, a civil engineer, a railroad engineer, and a Hollywood movie extra.

Unverifiable reports have him showing his cousins' kids how to tie knots, whittle sticks, and perform rope tricks in 1909; asking a postal detective in Salt Lake City to buy a wagon, harness, and camping outfit for him with money he peeled from "a big roll of bills" in 1910; saving Jesse James's grandson "from five kidnappers in the St. Louis railroad station," after receiving a coded telegram about the plot while getting a medical checkup in a nearby hospital; then returning to Utah to work in a saloon in Price in 1915 and to sell shoes in Delta in 1918. Later, he supposedly went to Wyoming and spent two days in Baggs, drank whisky in a Lander bar, looked up an old flame, and had his Model-T Ford repaired in Rock Springs, while hauling around a two-wheel trailer full of camping gear. He also attended a Wild West show in San Francisco; prospected with Wyatt Earp in Alaska; popped up in Nogales, Arizona; visited Albuquerque, New Mexico; and drifted to Europe.

If but half of the reports were true, Butch certainly got around: In the 1920s, he traveled to Mexico, ate blueberry pie with his family in Utah, showed up at a church picnic in Montana, and lived "like a desert rat" in Nevada. In the 1930s, he lived in Idaho, spent a lot of time in Wyoming, visited the La Claire Ranch several times, had a drink in the bar of Lander's Nobel Hotel, went fishing in Meadow Creek, visited the Fort Washakie Indian Reservation, walked down a street in Seattle, minded his own business in Vernal, and lived in California. He was said to have disrobed, from time to time, to show off the scars from the Bolivian battle. In 1936, when he would have been seventy, Butch supposedly resided in Seattle. Other reports had him "feeble and living alone in a house in Portland, Oregon," in the spring of 1937; spending a winter in Fredonia, Arizona, during the late 1930s; and being sighted in Rawlins, Wyoming, in 1946. To sustain him in his old age, he was said to have received a pension from an unnamed source so that he wouldn't have to choose "between starving and robbery."

In addition to the accounts of his dying in various shootouts, being decapitated with Sundance in Argentina, having "his neck stretched" in Wyoming, getting shot after walking "into a quarrel between two native gangs," and being killed "in New Mexico in a house of prostitution where he was causing trouble," several reports have Butch dying of natural causes, including pneumonia, a heart attack, cancer, and old age. He supposedly died on a ranch near Vernal in 1927 or 1928, in Oregon in 1930, on an island off the west coast of Mexico in 1932, near the Manso River in the Chilean Andes in 1935, in Denver and Lander in the late 1930s, once in Tombstone and twice in Spokane in 1937, and three times in Nevada—at Goldfield, Johnnie, and Las Vegas—in the late 1930s or early 1940s.

Although he was seen much less often than Butch, Sundance was said to have made his way north through Central America on trains and horseback, run guns for Pancho Villa in Mexico, won and lost a gold mine playing poker in Alaska, "migrated to Europe with $50,000—his share of the loot of a dozen train robberies," fought for the Arabs against the Turks in World War I, and become "a gray-haired, dignified . . . country squire" on a plantation near Tennessee. After visiting England, France, and India, Sundance supposedly was arrested under the name George Hanlon for rolling a drunk in San Francisco in 1919. He spent a year in prison, then adopted the name Hiram BeBee and wandered through California, Nevada, and Utah. Along the way, he was charged with malicious mischief and using vulgar and abusive language. He sold mineral water, led a pseudoreligious cult, and was run out of town more than once. During the 1940s, still using the BeBee alias, he lived in Rockville, Fountain Green, and Spring City, Utah. At the age of seventy-seven, eighty-one, or ninety-four, he shot an off-duty town marshal or a sheriff from a parked pickup truck or a second-story window in Mount Pleasant, Utah, and was dragged off to jail, where he eventually died. Meanwhile, he had reportedly married Etta Place, died in 1957, and been buried in Casper, Wyoming. When last seen, in the 1960s, he "was mean as hell . . . and nearly blind and . . . had shot several men fooling around his place" near Valier, Montana.

Naturally, none of these things would have been possible if Butch and Sundance had died in South America years before. To explain how the bandits survived, aficionados have propounded more theories than a roomful of science-fiction writers could dream up in a decade of working around the clock. The simplest is that Butch and Sundance started the death tales so that they could come home without worrying about the law. According to one old-timer, the outlaws bribed the head of the Bolivian army to declare that they had been killed in a fictitious gun battle. A variation is that a friend deliberately misidentified the victims of a real shootout to give Butch and Sundance a fresh start.

The flaw in these theories, however, is that very few people in the United States knew anything about the shootout until 1930. The Pinkertons heard many death tales, but as late as 1921 the agency maintained that Butch and Sundance were alive and well in South America—which might surprise the old-timer who recently asserted that the Pinkertons "fabricated [Butch's] death because they wanted to close the books. It was an embarrassing situation." The old-timer was half right: It *was* embarrassing. As the *Steamboat Pilot,* a Colorado mountain-town newspaper, put it in 1910, "The best men of the Pinkerton detective service have been detailed to capture the leaders [of the Wild Bunch] from time to time, but have failed. They have had all three men [Butch, Sundance, and Harvey Logan] killed or in prison, according to the reports, several times over, but each day they bobbled up in some other place."

The most common theory is that one or both of the outlaws lived through the shootout. One writer claimed, for instance, that Butch and Sundance were eating lunch at San Vicente when *gringo* bandits Harry Nation and Dick Clifford rode into town. Soldiers shot all four outlaws, but only Clifford and Nation died. Another way to survive was to be elsewhere when the shooting began. William French asserted that the man who died with Butch was not Sundance, but Tom Capehart, an alias used by Harvey Logan. Other accounts also cited Logan as Butch's ill-fated partner at San Vicente. In one, Butch and Logan spent several months with a Briton named A. G. Francis, who was overseeing the transportation of a gold dredge in the San Juan del Oro River in southern

110

Bolivia. After the holdup, the bandits returned to Francis's camp to spend the night, then forced him to accompany them as a guide halfway to San Vicente, where they met their doom hours after setting him free.

More often, in the tales we read, the survivor was Butch. He usually switched clothes with a dead soldier and sneaked away under cover of darkness. In one version, he spent several days hiding in a tree before he could effect his escape. Indians nursed his wounds, if necessary. According to author Charlie Rile, Sundance died in the gang's South American hideout, but Butch snatched some money and jumped out the back window of their adobe house. From a nearby gully, he watched the troops surround the hideout and slaughter its occupants, including a newly hired drifter wearing clothes borrowed from Butch. After checking the personal effects found on the corpses, the soldiers identified the dead men as Butch and Sundance and buried them quickly, "since bodies don't keep long in that climate." (Actually, in the high, cold Andes, bodies keep rather longer than necessary.) The Pinkertons looked into the matter and closed the case, leaving Butch free to rejoin his family and eventually die "in his own bed, with his boots off, at the age of eighty-seven."

My favorite explanation comes from Art Davidson, a Wyoming miner who claimed that Butch—using another alias—told a visiting North American journalist that one of his countrymen, "a fellow named Butch Cassidy," had been "killed in a nearby mountain village while robbing a bank." According to a long-winded manuscript that surfaced after Davidson's death, the reporter wrote up the story without verifying the information, and in no time the word spread throughout the United States that the leader of the Wild Bunch had croaked in South America.

Davidson was full of tidbits about his outlaw pal. Before embarking on his career in banditry, for example, Butch did some mining near Moab, Utah, and sold more than a ton of high-grade uranium ore to Madame Curie, who shipped it back to France and discovered radium in it. A short while later, he hired on as an undercover agent and tracked down rustlers for the Wyoming Cattleman's Association. When the Pinkertons came after him, he changed his alias and joined the navy, then jumped ship in a South American port. It was during his brief stay in the city that he planted the false tale about his own death. According to Davidson, Butch returned to Utah and settled in Salt Lake City under the name of Bob Mullins. He was married for a couple of years, but the relationship didn't work out, so he went to Goldfield, Nevada, and made "one of the greatest gold strikes on the continent." Next, he amassed a fortune from the silver mines near St. George, Utah. This enabled him not only to repay all the money he had ever stolen, but also to tithe belatedly to his beloved Mormon Church for his ill-gotten gains. He spent his last years running a small store in Leeds, Nevada, where he died in 1956 after a short illness. His friends buried him in the desert.

Long before the rest of North America learned about the Bolivian shootout, the outlaws' friends had heard rumors about it. At first, they dismissed it as a lawman's pipe dream or a ruse; after all, Butch had written about maybe coming home one day. But when the bandits' letters ceased and mail sent to them in Bolivia was returned unclaimed, their friends had to face the possibility that the story was true. Finally, Matt Warner, Elzy Lay, Bert Charter, Charley Gibbons, and Dr. J. W. K. Bracken reportedly took up a collection and sent an emissary to South America to find out what had really happened. Identified variously as Burton, Walker, or Sawtell, the man traveled to Bolivia and interviewed soldiers who had participated in the shootout. He allegedly returned to Utah with a photograph of the outlaws' corpses and declared that Butch and Sundance were, in fact, dead.

Upon seeing the picture, however, Bracken reportedly thought that the one identified as Butch was actually an outlaw named Tom Dilly. By contrast, Gibbons said that the evidence supported Percy Seibert's description of the shootout and that Butch had indeed died in San Vicente. Although Lay's account of the shootout differed somewhat, he agreed that his friends had died in it. Historian Charles Kelly tried to obtain a copy of the photograph but failed, and no one has ever produced any solid evidence that the expedition actually took place. In any event, although he believed Bracken to be mistaken, Kelly acknowledged the "bare possibility that Longabaugh's companion in that last stand was some other American outlaw and that Cassidy was satisfied to let the world believe he had been killed."

In a December 1937 note, Matt Warner advised Kelly to "forget all the reports on Butch Cassidy, they are fake. There is no such man living as Butch Cassidy. His real name was Robert Parker, born and raised in Circleville Utah and . . . killed in South America, he and a man by the name of Longbow were killed in a soldier post there in a gun fight. This is straight."

In his autobiography, *The Last of the Bandit Riders,* Matt wrote that Butch Cassidy and Harry Longabaugh "ranched and robbed in Bolivia and Argentina and was finally killed in a fight with soldiers that had been chasing 'em. They stole an army mule and a reward was offered for their capture. Soldiers got on their trail and one night found the mule near their hide-out in some deserted army barracks. Butch and Harry held the whole company off for hours and killed a lot of 'em. But their ammunition give out, and they was killed. Some say Longabaugh was killed first and that Butch kept his last shot for himself. That don't sound like Butch to me. The Butch I knew would keep all of his shots for the men that was trying to get him."

An old-timer swore that he had seen Butch at Matt's saloon in Price between 1915 and 1919, and that Matt had specifically pointed him out, saying, "That's Butch Cassidy. He's staying with me for a while, but keep it under your hat."

And yet, Matt wrote in 1938 that there were "a lot of false legends about what become of Butch. Some believe today that he is still alive. Some men claim they have seen Butch recently. Once in a while some hombre claims he is Butch. It's all poppycock."

Brown's Park native Ann Bassett told Kelly that "Matt Warner was full of baloney, always windy. Nobody believed his stories."

But which story should we disbelieve—that Butch came back or that he didn't?

Matt's daughter, Joyce Warner, claimed that after her father's death Butch visited her family and that she had last heard from him in 1941. Because she wasn't born until Butch had already left the country, she could have been mistaken about the identity of her visitor, who said that he and Sundance had split up in South America, and that he had gone straight, while Sundance had found another partner and called him "Butch" as a joke. "Because of Sundance's 'little joke,' " the visitor told Joyce, "I was wanted on two continents." After his death was erroneously reported in the United States, he came back and settled in the East under the alias Frank Ervin. Joyce heard he had died in 1944 in Nevada.

Butch's relatives don't offer much help. Dr. B.V. McDermott, a friend of the Parker family, "swore they believed Butch was dead—and that he and the 'Sun Dance Kid' had been killed together in South America." Yet Lula Parker Betenson, one of Butch's sisters, insisted that he visited the family in Circleville in 1925. "My brother . . . came

113

back to the United States in 1912," she said. "He never married. He worked as a trapper and as a cowboy. He spent some time in Alaska." According to Lula, Butch told the family that there *was* a shootout but that he wasn't present. " 'I heard they got Percy Seibert from the Concordia Tin Mines to identify a couple of bodies as Butch Cassidy and the Sundance Kid all right. I wondered why Mr. Seibert did that. Then it dawned on me that he would know this was the only way we could go straight. . . . He knew I'd be hounded as long as I lived. Well, I'm sure he saw this as a way for me to bury my past along with somebody else's body so I could start over.' "

Lula, who was a baby when Butch left home, never provided any evidence to substantiate her stories, which were contradicted by other relatives. According to Wyoming rancher Jim Regan, "before Cassidy's father died [in 1938] he said that if Butch had gotten back from South America he would have been to see him and look up his own people." A niece characterized Lula's views as "controversial within the family" and said that several of Butch's other siblings had attempted, without success, to determine what had happened to him. Max and Ellnor Parker, son and daughter-in-law of Butch's brother Dan, informed outlaw historian Jim Dullenty that "Lula was not telling the truth about Butch. Ellnor said she wrote to Lula asking why she was saying so many things that weren't true. Ellnor said Lula wrote right back telling her to keep quiet and not say a thing and let Lula do the talking for the family." Nevertheless, Max and Ellnor believed that Butch *did* come back from South America. "They 'knew' he had died in Spokane," they told Dullenty. Max told another researcher that his father had confided to Ellnor that Butch was living in Spokane under the alias William Phillips.

Mart Christensen, who ran the WPA's Wyoming Writers' Project in the 1930s, heard scores of reports that Butch had recently visited the state and was using the name Bill Phillips. After assigning several writers to look into the claims of Butch's return, Christensen wrote to Charles Kelly about what they had found. When Kelly dismissed the accounts as fictional, Christensen fired back an angry letter, saying that Butch had spent time with an old friend named Hank Boedeker and others during a visit in 1934. "He talked to Harry Baldwin, Wyoming merchant, who sold him a bill of grub, and to Ed Farlow, a former mayor of Lander, who knew him during his early days. Now, if I were interested enough in the life of Butch Cassidy to write a book I would forthwith visit Hank Boedeker, Ed Farlow, and Harry Baldwin in Lander." After assuring Kelly that interviews with these men would "explode all the 'bunk' put out by the several writers who finish the life of Cassidy in South America with such dramatics," Christensen vouched for the reliability of his sources, whom he called "reputable, well-known and responsible citizens and not the type who would expoit any sort of story for publicity or for gossiping purposes. They knew Butch Cassidy well and they are not mistaken."

Because so many people believed that Phillips was Butch Cassidy, Kelly began to think that Butch might indeed have returned from South America, but Phillips died before Kelly had a chance to interview him. Kelly sent off for a copy of the death certificate, which indicated that William Thadeus Phillips was born in Michigan on June 22, 1865, to Celia Mudge and L. J. Phillips. This convinced Kelly that Phillips was not Butch, but the historian wrote to the man's widow to make doubly sure.

Gertrude Phillips replied that both she and her late husband had known Butch Cassidy, but that William T. Phillips was not the famous outlaw from Utah. Instead, she wrote, Phillips had been "born and raised in an eastern state until he reached the age of 14 years, at which time (owing to dime novel influence) he ran away and headed for the Black Hills." She wrote that Phillips had met Butch Cassidy "at the time of the Johnson County War, and I've heard him express himself as being entirely in sympathy with the 'little fellows' instead of the stock association. He thought he knew Cassidy very, very well, and considered he was much more sinned against than sinning. As to just how long he was associated with him I am unable to say, for my memory is none too good." Phillips, she wrote, had done "mural decorating in New York City for two or three years [and] at one time had a machine shop in Des Moines, Iowa, for about seven or eight years. After he and I were married, we lived in Arizona for a year [then] came to Spokane, and have been here ever since, until his death last year."

Friends recalled Phillips's saying that he had applied gold leaf to the domes of several capitols in the Midwest and had lived in Globe, Arizona, before moving to Spokane, where he operated a machine shop. The shop prospered during World War I and the 1920s, but Phillips went broke during the Depression and died of cancer at the county poor farm in 1937. Between 1925 and 1936, he visited Wild

Bunch haunts in Wyoming several times in search of loot cached by the gang. He wrote a biography of Butch—*The Bandit Invincible*—but could not find a publisher. Although the manuscript was written in the third person, Phillips told friends in Spokane and old-timers in Wyoming that he was Butch Cassidy.

Phillips, who resembled Butch and knew a lot about his early life, wrote that Butch had survived the Bolivian gun battle that took the lives of Sundance and two other outlaws. According to Phillips, "a detachment of Bolivian cavalry" surprised Butch and three companions in the act of robbing a mule train near La Paz. After his pals died in the ensuing fight, Butch crawled away through the darkness. Once he had reached his horse, he escaped down the eastern side of the Andes, made a long, perilous journey through the Amazon jungle, sailed to Paris for plastic surgery, and returned to the United States to marry his sweetheart.

In the 1970s, western writer Larry Pointer marshaled considerable evidence that Phillips was indeed Butch Cassidy. Despite a diligent search, Pointer could find no documentation of Phillips's existence earlier than May 14, 1908, when he married Gertrude Livesay in Michigan. A sculptor compared photographs of Phillips and Butch and told Pointer that the two men had the same basic bone structure, although the ears appeared to have been altered, perhaps as a result of a face-lift. After analyzing the handwriting in two letters—one from Butch to Maude Davis and the other from Phillips to Mary Boyd, an old girlfriend of Butch's with whom Phillips (calling himself George Cassidy) carried on an affair during visits to Wyoming in the 1930s—a graphoanalyst concluded that the same person had written both letters. Pointer tracked down a ring with the inscription "Geo C to Mary B" and found Butch's brand carved on the handle of a revolver once owned by Phillips. Phillips's adopted son asserted that "the fact that his father was Butch Cassidy was accepted in their home. He had never been told otherwise, by either William or Gertrude Phillips. It was, however, a well-guarded family secret." As for his mother's statement to Charles Kelly, she had deliberately misled him: "She just didn't want the notoriety."

In an effort to document the circumstances of the San Vicente shootout, Pointer wrote to the U.S. embassy in Bolivia. A cultural attaché replied: "We have attempted to find out from several sources any information that might be available here about these now famous outlaws, and we have drawn blanks everywhere." In the mid-1960s, according to British author Bruce Chatwin, Bolivian president and outlaw-history buff René Barrientos had reportedly ordered a search of Bolivian military records and visited San Vicente—with similar results. After ascertaining that the Pinkerton archives also lacked "a single verification of the legendary shootout," Pointer concluded that it had never happened, and he laid out the results of his extensive research in his book *In Search of Butch Cassidy*.

Although the older Wild Bunch researchers—including Chapman, Kelly, and Horan—considered the survival stories to be fiction, most modern outlaw historians apply that label to the shootout. According to Ed Kirby, "the reports that Butch Cassidy came back to the United States are now so numerous and so definite that few researchers maintain any longer that Butch died in South America. If Butch did not die, then why think that Sundance did? Both were to have perished in the same gun battle. . . . But there is no evidence of any gun battle with local police or soldiers, no evidence the two men died, no evidence of any graves. . . . As the evidence mounts that Butch and Sundance returned, there will have to be very solid evidence they met their deaths in South America before researchers will return to the older view."

Evidently, we have our work cut out for us.

Having read all the Wild Bunch books and articles he can find, Dan begins writing to everyone who might know something about what Butch and Sundance did in South America. A letter to Bruce Chatwin elicits the information that he learned about the Barrientos expedition to San Vicente from Kerry Ross Boren, an outlaw historian in Utah. Although Chatwin's health is fading, his response to our inquiry is prompt and gracious: "I felt that [Boren's] imagination tended to get the better of him, but mustn't malign him because he was very kind. It was he who showed me, in photostat, a text by a U.S. mining-engineer . . . who accompanied Barrientos on the trip."

Jim Dullenty sends us a copy of the document, a 1972 notarized statement by a sixty-year-old Californian named William Frank Hutchens. According to his statement, Hutchens was a guest at a Buenos Aires dinner party hosted by a Polish doctor named Samuel Tornapolski in 1964. At the party, the doctor allegedly declared that "Cassidy did not die in Bolivia as reported but had instead lived to [a] ripe old age in the States [and] that he had positive proof that such was the case. I had heard such rumors before the war in Arizona." The next year, according to Hutchens, Bolivian president René Barrientos gave a speech to a military audience and "mentioned that they had once fought a ferocious battle with a gang of bandits from North America."

Hutchens averred that he had written to Barrientos and challenged him to prove the claim, and that the Bolivian president had responded by organizing a trip to San Vicente in mid-1966. With him were Dr. Tornapolski and Hutchens. They questioned elderly residents, all of whom said that "there had never been any gun battles in the village or anywhere else that they could recall involving *norteamericanos.*" Hutchens went on to say that only two Europeans had been buried in the local cemetery before 1910. The team dug them up and found a mummified Swede and the skeleton of another man of unknown nationality.

From their observations of the remains, wrote Hutchens, "President Barrientos was convinced that no gun battle had ever taken place in San Vicente, however he continued to have old Army reports and records searched for any indication that anything had ever taken place." Barrientos died in a helicopter crash in 1969, two years after directing the Bolivian army to hunt down and kill the Cuban-backed Argentine guerrilla Ernesto "Che" Guevara.

In a 1982 letter to *True West,* Hutchens claimed to be the only surviving member of the expedition and suggested that the magazine publish an article about it. The editor wrote to Hutchens and expressed interest in having him write the article and supply photographs to illustrate it, but Hutchens did not respond.

Unable to locate Hutchens or any newspaper accounts of the expedition, Dan interviews Bolivian historians, Barrientos's colleagues in the Bolivian air force, one of his personal helicopter pilots, and retired diplomatic and military personnel who had been stationed at the U.S. embassy in La Paz in the 1960s. An American who knew Barrientos socially and professionally verified that the Bolivian president *was* a western-history buff and that he "could have dashed to San Vicente, puttered around the cemetery, and returned to La Paz without much notice, because he was always flying around the country," but Dan finds no one who can confirm the expedition or provide more information about it.

Meanwhile, I compare what *The Bandit Invincible* says about the outlaws' years in exile with what we know to be true. The manuscript contains only five brief paragraphs about Argentina, misplaces the Cholila ranch by several hundred miles, and says nothing about Chile, but Phillips included many details about Bolivia that would not have been known to the average North American. I stare at the pictures of Butch and Phillips. Although there is a strong resemblance, the photographs were made decades apart, and I can't tell whether they're the same person. Having worked at the post office in my youth, I pride myself on being able to decipher any kind of handwriting, but poring over photocopies of letters written by Butch and Phillips leaves me confused. Despite the fact that some of the letters (including the f and W) are markedly different, both men often used an ϵ in place of an e, the writing slants at the same angle, and several words look as if they had been traced. If I had to guess, I'd say the same man wrote everything, but I wouldn't bet the row house.

As I am mulling this over, the telephone rings. The caller says, "This is Bill Goldman."

Goldman, Goldman. Do I know anyone named Goldman? Suddenly, it hits me. "William Goldman, the screenwriter?"

"Don't act so surprised. You wrote to me."

I did? Oh no, not again. Dan signed both of our names to a letter and forgot to show it to me. Wonder what it said.

"You wanted to find out if anyone who knew about the South American end of it got in touch with me after the film came out. There was a lot of interest, but I didn't find out anything I didn't already know. What have you found?"

"We've been trying to figure out whether William T. Phillips—the man who claimed to be Butch Cassidy in the 1930s—was real or a fraud. Most of the outlaw historians we've talked to think either that somebody else was killed in San Vicente and misidentified or that the shoot-out was just a lie Butch dreamed up so that he could come back to the United States."

"Given Butch's distaste for violence, he might have had the motivation to fake his own death. That would fit with his character. He didn't need to prove his manhood with a gun. But the notion that he survived is probably just wishful thinking."

At this point, someone comes into Goldman's office with a problem needing his attention. "May I call you back in fifteen minutes?" he asks.

As soon as he hangs up, I phone Dan at work. "Grab a cab and come home immediately!"

When Goldman calls again, we ask how he became interested in Butch and Sundance. He says he read about them in the late 1950s and spent several years researching them in a haphazard way. "I was drawn to the story because, instead of toughing it out like John Wayne, Butch would rather run than fight. He was such a *nice guy*—unusual for an outlaw—and yet he was successful. I still find him fascinating. You haven't by any chance learned what became of Etta Place?"

"Not really," says Dan. "She's hard to find, because nobody knows who she was."

"I don't think she was a prostitute," says Goldman. "In photographs from that era, even the young prostitutes look old, because their lives were so hard. Etta was too pretty for that. I really believe she was a schoolteacher."

"We've heard several theories about what happened to her," I say, "but none of them holds up. She's a mystery woman, all right."

"Well, if you ever solve the mystery, let me know."

Tracing Etta is particularly difficult because we don't know her real name or where she came from. She has been described as everything from a Boston finishing-school grad to a Wisconsin "gal who got mixed up in a bad crowd." More than one writer has speculated that Etta was Eunice Gray, who ran a bordello and then a hotel in Fort Worth before dying in a fire in 1962, but historian Richard F. Selcer spent ten years researching the city's red-light district and found no sign that Etta had ever been in Forth Worth. According to rancher John F. Gooldy, however, Sundance wrote a friend in Slater, Colorado, to say he'd married a woman from Texas.

Researcher Doris Burton believes that Etta Place was Ann Bassett, who left Brown's Park for a couple of years in the early 1900s. Ann returned to Brown's Park in 1903 and died in 1956. Although she wrote a memoir revealing many spicy details about her life, she never claimed to be Etta. In any event, Ann didn't leave Utah until the day after Etta signed the guest register at a New York boardinghouse in February 1901.

Ignoring the obvious—that Etta acquired her surname by becoming Sundance's wife (common-law or otherwise) while he was using his mother's maiden name in his alias—a few outlaw enthusiasts have postulated that Etta and Sundance were cousins. One version names her as the illegitimate daughter of Emily Jane Place of Oswego, New York, and George Capel, son of an English earl. A variation has a

Scots-Irishman named George Capel moving to Arizona and fathering Etta in an affair with a Mexican woman. (Apparently, the fact that Capel is an anagram of Place is one basis for these theories.)

Wherever Etta came from, she was last seen crossing Argentina's Salado River on a raft after the Villa Mercedes holdup. From then on, the path of speculation forks regularly. Some say that she went back to Denver to have not an appendectomy but a baby, or an abortion, perhaps as a result of her alleged affair with her Cholila neighbor John Gardiner, and that she was still living in Denver as late as 1924. Others say she returned to the United States and had several children, including a daughter who carried on the family trade and headed a minor gang of bank robbers in the Midwest in the 1920s and early 1930s. In addition to moving to Tacoma with Sundance and cadging money from elderly relatives who didn't have any to spare, Etta supposedly spent six years fighting in the Mexican Revolution, with or without Sundance, depending on whether he survived Bolivia or not.

Some accounts leave her in South America. After marrying an "Irish adventurer who [had] led Argentine troops to one of [the Wild Bunch's] strongholds and killed Longabaugh, her husband," for example, she was slain in a Buenos Aires hotel by *fronteriza* Mateo Gebhard. In another version, after Butch and Sundance died in a shootout with Argentine soldiers, Etta met Elzy Lay in Buenos Aires; they married, moved to La Paz, and lived happily ever after. While residing in Argentina in the late 1940s, Welsh novelist Richard Llewellyn (*How Green Was My Valley*) heard that Etta had wed a Paraguayan government official. No one has found any evidence to support this story or a related tale that married her to an American fight-promoter in Paraguay. Boxing-impressario Tex Rickard temporarily retired to the Chaco region in 1910, but his wife, Edith Mae, accompanied him there and returned to the States with him five years later. An outlaw named George Musgrave, recruited as a cowboy for Rickard's ranch, remained in Paraguay and was married for a time to Janette Magor, who later ran an Arizona sanitarium with Elzy Lay's second wife and briefly drew attention as a possible Etta Place, but proved to be too young for the job.

Another candidate was the mother or aunt of a man who once swore on a Bible in a California rescue mission that the Sundance Kid was his father. A garrulous fellow with a slight build and an uncanny resemblance to members of Sundance's family, he had spent a lot of time riding freight trains and bouncing in and out of drunk tanks before wandering into the Rocky Mountain states in 1969 or 1970 and volunteering colorful lectures at county libraries. Calling himself Harry Longabaugh II, Harry Thayne Longabaugh, or Robert Harvey Longabaugh, he described his mother as a young schoolteacher named Anna Marie Thayne or Mary Tryone who was briefly married to Sundance but left him because he had taken up with her half sister Hazel, alias Etta Place. Sundance Jr. said that he had been born in early 1901 and raised by relatives or friends after his mother's accidental death when he was three years old, and that Etta had abandoned a husband and two children to go to South America with Sundance. According to Sundance Jr., Etta returned alone and drifted to Marion, Oregon, where she died in 1935.

Butch and Sundance, he said, also came back to North America. He met his father in 1940 and 1947 and served as a pallbearer for Butch Cassidy, known to him as William T. Phillips. (A neat trick, inasmuch as Phillips was cremated and his ashes were unceremoniously buried at the county poor farm.) Sundance Jr. claimed to own maps showing buried Wild Bunch loot, but he said that he had dug up only one cache before U.S. Treasury agents began following him. He spoke of going back for the rest—supposedly $300,000—if he had "any assurance any of the money could go to reduce the national debt or for bonuses for Vietnam veterans." The alleged son of Sundance died in 1972 in a hotel fire in Montana, and all his papers perished with him. Except for his death certificate, which was based on his own statements, nothing has been found to support any of his yarns.

While agreeing that Etta died in Oregon, Art Davidson said that she was the younger sister of one Marion Bennion. According to Davidson, Marion was married to Butch Cassidy, and the couple had a daughter who became a silent-screen star. Furthermore, Davidson asserted, Etta and Marion were the sisters of Hiram Bennion, also known as Hiram BeBee, George Hanlon, and the Sundance Kid.

Condemned to life imprisonment for the 1945 murder of an off-duty town marshal in Utah, BeBee died of natural causes at the age of eighty-eight in 1952. According to Ed Kirby, BeBee told fellow inmates that he was the Sundance Kid. At first, Kirby doubted the claim because Sundance's height was described as between 5'9" and 6' and his weight as 160 to 190 pounds, whereas Utah State Prison records showed

Hiram BeBee as being 5′3″ and weighing 103 pounds in 1947. Kirby discovered, however, that BeBee had been listed as being 5′5″ and weighing 135 pounds two years earlier, at the time of his arrest, and former neighbors estimated BeBee to be as tall as 5′9″. After learning that the effects of old age and diseases like spinal osteoporosis can considerably decrease an individual's height, Kirby declared that Hiram BeBee was indeed the Sundance Kid, returned from South America.

We are skeptical, not only about BeBee's shrinkage, but also about whether the years could have transformed Sundance into this haggard tramp. After noticing that BeBee, alias George Hanlon, served time in San Quentin in 1919, we send off to California for his mug shot and vital statistics. Back comes a glossy photo of a forty-five-year-old man who looked nothing like Sundance but a lot like Jimmy Durante and who stood 5′2¾″ and weighed 128 pounds. Instead of shrinking, BeBee came through old age with a net gain of a quarter inch.

Although debunking this fake Sundance has been easy, William T. Phillips presents a greater challenge because so many people who met him in the 1930s were positive he was Butch. We find a few dissenters, including Butch's sister Lula, who said that Butch died in 1937 in Spokane, as did Phillips, but that he was *not* Phillips. We find three accounts identifying Phillips and Butch as two separate people. The Rife brothers in Mt. Carmel, Utah, told Charles Kelly that their mother knew Phillips and that he sometimes posed as Cassidy for kicks. Wyoming rancher Jim Regan said that Phillips had run a poker game at Lost Cabin during shearing time and that he was taller and heavier than Butch. In 1934, said Regan, "Phillips came to my place at Burris with Bill Boyd. He wanted to see me. I recognized him as he drove in the yard and called him by name. He was looking for a cabin in the mountains . . . but they couldn't find it. . . . Phillips made the remark, 'If we find the cabin we'll all be well-fixed.' He wanted to find this cabin which presumably was the landmark for a cache of the outlaws." Wyoming writer Blanche Schroer contends that Butch's alleged girl-friend Mary Boyd Rhodes, who went with Phillips and her brother Bill on this treasure hunt, confided to a close friend that she and Phillips "had planned the phony identity."

If Phillips was not Butch, who was he? According to records at the Elks and Masonic lodges in Spokane, he was born to Celia Mudge and Laddie J. Phillips in Sandusky, Michigan, which conforms with his death certificate and marriage license. Although no Laddie J. Phillips is listed in Michigan census records, a Celia Mudge was born in Sanilac County in 1852. Because she would have been only twelve and a half at the time of William T. Phillips's birth and her descendants knew nothing about him, author Larry Pointer dismissed the notion that she could have been his mother. But outlaw historian Jim Dullenty, who has scoured Michigan in an attempt to verify or disprove Phillips's statements about his background, says that his in-laws thought he had been raised by Indians in Canada. Dullenty views this as the tale of a man who was trying to conceal his past, though not necessarily a bandit past. "If he had been of illegitimate birth, he could have been the type who fabricated much about his background all his life and letting it spin into having been an outlaw was a natural progression of things."

I don't know what to think. Dan says Phillips was a fraud. Having grown quite fond of Butch, however, I would like to believe that he *didn't* die in Bolivia. Thanks to Pointer's work, we know for certain that, despite Gertrude Phillips's disclaimer, her husband privately claimed to be Butch. And then there's the handwriting. Dullenty, however, says two graphoanalysts not mentioned in Pointer's book also analyzed the handwriting; one said the letters were written by different people, and the other was unable to reach a conclusion. Dan consults a retired Federal Bureau of Investigation questioned-documents examiner, who disparages graphoanalysts as correspondence-school psychologists divining character traits from the way people loop their loops, close their *o*'s, dot their *i*'s, and cross their *t*'s. Moreover, says the expert, any two individuals who went to school during the same era and learned to write from the same penmanship book could have had handwriting similar enough to fool a graphoanalyst.

Two of Butch's letters came from Percy Seibert's scrapbook. Wondering what else is in the scrapbook, Dan sets out to track it down. He traces Seibert's daughter, Stella Seibert Graham, to California and sends her a letter asking whether she has any of her father's memorabilia about Butch and Sundance. When told about the tales that the bandits had come back from South America, Percy Seibert said, "Rubbish!" But in her reply to us, Stella Graham says her father believed that Butch was *not* killed in Bolivia. As if that wasn't startling enough, she adds this bombshell: "My husband will be writing you soon. He knew Bill Phillips very well."

If Percy Seibert's son-in-law knew Phillips, maybe Seibert did, too. In fact, Phillips could have found out a lot about Butch and Sundance's activities in Bolivia from either man. Then again, if Seibert told his daughter that Butch didn't die at San Vicente, maybe he *was* in cahoots with the bandits, and the tale he told Arthur Chapman and the other writers was a hoax. Either scenario would be a major discovery in the arcane world of outlaw history. Waiting for Mr. Graham to write us is out of the question. Pad and pencil at hand, Dan picks up the phone.

Hovering over his shoulder, I read his notes as he scribbles them. Wayne Graham says that Percy Seibert never met Phillips, never even heard of him. Nor did the Seiberts ever say anything to Graham about Butch and Sundance. Moreover, Graham had left Spokane and moved to Chile before he met Stella Seibert in the 1930s. Earlier, Phillips had sponsored Graham's membership in the Elks and the Masons, and the men sometimes got together of an evening, but they never discussed Butch Cassidy. Phillips was talkative about generalities but closemouthed about his personal life. He never mentioned his past. Graham found him "a very generous person and smart and an exceptionally good friend to those he liked."

"Phillips never told you he was Cassidy?"

"No. I heard it from other people, but that was much later."

"Do you think he could have been Cassidy?"

"I don't know. He could take care of himself. He was all man, but I never saw him with a gun or anything like that."

Okay, Phillips didn't have any secret ties to Percy Seibert. What about Stella Seibert Graham's comment that Butch didn't die in Bolivia?

"I'm not sure her memory is reliable. If it conflicts with what her father said in the history books, I'd stick with her father's version."

For a week, I vacillate. Every time I conclude that Phillips was a con man, I look at his photograph and letter again and then I'm not so sure. Finally, I hear a whoop from the living room and rush downstairs to find Dan holding a torn manila envelope and a magazine published by the Historical Society of Michigan.

"Remind you of anyone?" He hands me the magazine and points to a photograph of an elderly woman in a shirtwaist dress. Her eyes, her eyebrows, her smile, even her hairline—they're all identical to Phillips's.

"William T. Phillips in drag?"

"Celia Mudge."

So she *was* his mother! That means he couldn't have been Robert

LeRoy Parker, who looked as much like Annie Gillies Parker as Phillips looked like Celia Mudge. William T. Phillips was an impostor. What a relief to finally *know*. But relief gives way to sadness. "Then Butch and Sundance didn't come back."

"Looks that way."

"Sigh."

"I know."

Later, two separate computer-assisted comparisons of photographs of Butch and Phillips verify our conclusion. Dr. Thomas Kyle, a researcher at Los Alamos National Laboratory, conducts the first comparison in his spare time. He uses a computer to adjust the magnification of the photographs until the distance between Butch's eyes and mouth is the same as that between Phillips's eyes and mouth. Grids are then placed over the faces to aid the comparison of their various components. After observing that the two men's noses were quite similar, which might have accounted for Phillips's ability to pass for Cassidy, Kyle notes significant differences in their ears and hairlines. He also concludes that Butch had small features in a big head, whereas Phillips had more normally proportioned features in a smaller head.

The second comparison is conducted by Dr. Lewis Sadler at the University of Illinois at Chicago. Sadler has developed a computer program that counts the similarities between digitized photographs of different individuals and a target individual, then ranks the photos in order of the number of similarities to the target photograph. Two photographs of the same person do not match in every aspect, but when Sadler runs the program with photographs of Butch and Phillips, the computer determines that of two hundred people selected at random, fifty looked more like Butch than Phillips did. For there to be any possibility that two photographs are of the same person, the gap would have to be no greater than fifteen or twenty.

Eventually, Jim Dullenty's efforts to identify Phillips yield a letter from a Sandusky, Michigan, man named Bob Phillips, who says his great-grandfather William J. Phillips reared (and may even have sired) the impostor. Bob Phillips says his great-grandparents lived across the street from Celia Mudge's family. Upon noticing that thirteen-year-old Celia was unable to provide proper care for her illegitimate son, Mr. and Mrs. Phillips—who had fifteen kids of their own—volunteered to take the baby in and give him a name (as well as the nickname "Butch"). The boy lived with his adoptive family until he was fourteen, then went north to work in logging camps. After throwing an axe at a man during a fight, "Butch" Phillips lit out for the West, and his family never saw him again.

Thinking that news of Butch and Sundance might have turned up in the correspondence of U.S. diplomats in South America, Dan drags me off to the National Archives. We wind up spending a summer of Saturdays and evenings in the company of historians, genealogists, graduate students, private investigators, Civil War buffs, conspiracy theorists, and the other researchers who inhabit the cavernous reading room. Seated at a large table, a stack of material piled on the wooden cart beside us, we leaf through books of letters sent or received by U.S. embassies and consulates. Most of the letters are typed originals or carbons, but some are copies of handwritten documents made by placing the original in a letterpress along with a damp cloth and a sheet of onionskin paper; the ink bled onto the blank sheet and made a sepia-toned facsimile, which was then bound with hundreds of similar pages in a letter book.

We run through all of the State Department's Argentine and Chilean diplomatic post books for the relevant period and find several circulars seeking information about embezzlers, bail jumpers, runaway husbands, and other missing persons, but not a single document directly related to Butch and Sundance. This seems odd in view of the attention U.S. newspapers of that era gave to the Wild Bunch's escapades in South America.

We then turn our attention to the Bolivian post files.

"Bingo!" Dan has found a letter from Alexander Benson at the American legation in la Paz to Frank Aller—who, as vice-consul in Antofagasta, had helped Sundance out of his 1905 scrape with the Chilean government. Writing in September 1910, Benson relayed the text of a letter he had recently sent, at Aller's request, to the Bolivian minister for foreign affairs: "I have the honour to request that I be furnished with a copy of the death certificate of the American citizen, [H.A.] Brown, who was killed by the Bolivian police at San Vicente, near Tupiza, over a year ago. Legal proof of his death is wanted by a Judge of the Court of Chile, in order to settle his estate. Brown and Maxwell were the men who held up several of the Bolivian Railway Company's pay trains and also the stage coaches of several mines, and I understand were killed in a fight with soldiers who were detached to capture them as outlaws." Benson also copied the reply from the Bolivian minister, who had ordered the prefect of the Potosí province to obtain the death certificate. As soon as the minister sent the certificate, Benson wrote, he would forward it to Aller.

The photocopiers hum and whoosh, the wooden book-carts creak, and the shadows deepen outside the big windows overlooking Pennsylvania Avenue as we search for the letter transmitting the death certificate. The next thing we find, several volumes later, is a letter from Aller thanking Benson for his "interest in the matter of H.A. Brown or Frank Boyd, the name used by him while in Chile. I have a letter from him in which he stated that he would use the former name in Bolivia, in order to get 'honorable employment,' and so will be in a position to prove that they are identical persons. I take the liberty of enclosing a copy of my letter of July 31, addressed to the American Minister, and about which I spoke to you while in La Paz."

In other words, Aller had written to Benson's predecessor, but the letter had apparently been lost, and Aller had renewed his request upon meeting Benson later in La Paz. Aller's original letter, dated July 31, 1909, provides more details:

> An American citizen named Frank Boyd is wanted in Antofagasta and letters addressed to him in Bolivia have failed to receive reply. I have been informed by Mr. Wm. Gray of Oruro, Mr. Thomas Mason of Uyuni and many others that Boyd and a companion named Maxwell . . . were killed at San Vicente near Tupiza by natives and police and buried as "desconocidos" [unknowns].
>
> I have endeavored by correspondence to obtain confirmation and a certificate of death, but this has been impossible as it seems that the authorities are endeavoring to hush up the matter.
>
> It is very important to locate Boyd alive, or failing this, to produce legal proof of his death. Everybody in Bolivia, except the authorities, seem convinced that the larger of the two men was Boyd and that possibly he had assumed the name of Brown.
>
> I regret exceedingly to trouble you in this matter, but I see no other course of having light thrown on the matter. I would therefore esteem it a great favor if you would use your kind offices with the proper authorities to have this matter investigated and the identity of these two men established, and a death certificate duly legalized by a Chilean official accredited to Bolivia, sent to me.

This is it! These letters tie Butch and Sundance—under recognized aliases—to the shootout. Now all we need to know is exactly what happened to them and when. We eagerly read the letter sent to Aller a month later by Benson, but it merely acknowledges the receipt of Aller's letters and says that the Bolivian Foreign Office has not yet obtained the death certificate.

After pawing through another thousand pages, Dan taps my shoulder.

"What?" I whisper.

He points to a letter, dated January 21, 1911, from Benson to Aller:

> Dear Sir:
>
> In compliance with the promise made to you in the Legation's letter of September 3rd, last, I am pleased to enclose herewith a complete record of the case of Maxwell and Brown, drawn up by the authorities of the district where they were killed, and which I hope will be of some use to you.
>
> This document had not previously been sent to you because we had been unable to obtain it from the Bolivian Foreign Office until now.
>
> Yours very truly,
Alexander Benson
>
> Enclosure: Testimony to the diligencies of investigation and identification of the Americans killed by the Uyuni Police during their assault of a remittance.

Before I have finished reading the letter, Dan lifts the page to see the report. It isn't there.

Frantically, we search for the report. Our hopes rise momentarily when we find a December 1910 letter in which the Bolivian minister informs Benson in La Paz of an enclosed ten-page report and death certificate for American citizens "whose names are unknown," but the report and the certificate are nowhere to be seen. Apparently, neither the Bolivian minister nor Benson bothered to copy them before sending them on. By the time Aller received them, he was no longer the vice-consul in Antofagasta, so we are not surprised that nothing is in the State Department's Chilean post files. He probably filed the documents with a judge in Antofagasta. We'll have to go to South America and search the archives there.

7 · THE ROAD TO SAN VICENTE

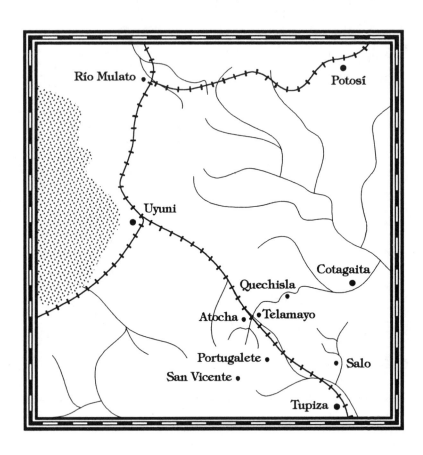

ON November 15, 1908, after a long train journey from Buenos Aires, Hiram Bingham III and a friend checked into a hotel at La Quiaca, an Argentine border town sixty miles south of Tupiza. Bingham—who would later uncover the Incan ruins at Machu Picchu in Peru—wrote of a chance encounter that evening with "two rough-looking Anglo-Saxons who told us hair-raising stories of the dangers of the Bolivian roads where highway robbers, driven out of the United States by the force of law and order and hounded to death all over the world by Pinkerton detectives, had found a pleasant resting-place in which to pursue their chosen occupation without let or hindrance." Bingham later learned that one of the men he had met was himself an outlaw.

> He put his case quite emphatically to us that it was necessary for them to make a living, that they were not allowed to do so peaceably in the States, that they desired only to be let alone and had no intention of troubling travelers except those that sought to get information against them. They relied entirely for their support on being able to overcome armed escorts accompanying loads of cash going to the mines to liquidate the monthly payroll. This they claimed was legitimate plunder taken in fair fight. The only individuals who had to suffer at their hands were those who took up the case against them. Having laid this down for our edification, he proceeded to tell us what a reckless lot they were and how famous had been their crimes, at the same time assuring us that they were all very decent fellows and quite pleasant companions.

Bingham left at dawn the next day in an eight-mule coach owned by James Hutcheon, who had supposedly hired Butch and Sundance after they left Concordia. At six in the evening, the coach clattered into Tupiza, where Bingham heard more news of *gringo* outlaws:

> Two weeks before our arrival a couple of bandits, one of whom had been hunted out of Arizona by Pinkerton detectives, had held up a cart containing twenty thousand dollars, on its way to pay off the laborers in a large mine. The owners, wealthy Bolivians, immediately offered a large reward for the capture of the bandits, dead or alive, notwithstanding that the robbers and their friends, of whom there seemed to be a score or more, let it be carefully understood that they would take a definite revenge for any lives that might be lost in pursuit of the highwaymen. This did not deter the mine owners, however, and a party of fifty Bolivian soldiers went on the trail of the robbers, who were found lunching in an Indian hut. They had

carelessly left their mules and rifles several yards away from the door of the hut and were unable to escape. After a fight, in which three or four of the soldiers were killed and as many wounded, the thatch roof of the hut was set on fire and the bandits forced out into the open where they finally fell, each with half a dozen bullets in his body. Their mules were captured and sold to [Hutcheon] who let me have one of them for my journey. He turned out to be a wonderfully fine saddle mule. When his former owner had had the benefit of his fleet legs and his splendid lungs, there was no question of his being caught by the Bolivian soldiery.

Dan finds this account while browsing through our South American travel and adventure books. Perhaps because Bingham neglected to name any of the bandits he met or heard about, his story has escaped the attention of outlaw historians for eight decades. While fixing the time of the shootout as early November 1908, however, the report raises as many questions as it answers. If one of the slain bandits was "hunted out of Arizona by Pinkerton detectives," for example, was his partner *not* wanted by the Pinkertons? Did Bingham or the person who told him the story say *Arizona* instead of *the West* the way people always seem to think I'm from *Tennessee* no matter how many times I tell them I'm from *Kentucky*? And who were those guys at the border? Were they friends of Butch and Sundance? Was one of them Butch or Sundance?

Hoping to find the outlaws' names in Bingham's research notes or journal, we track down his papers, which he donated to Yale University. Unfortunately, neither his family nor the Yale library has anything related to his 1908 trip to Latin America. We'll never know the identities of the men he met at La Quiaca.

We have better luck locating Percy Seibert's scrapbook, which is actually an old U.S. Department of Agriculture yearbook in which he pasted letters, calling cards, business cards, dance cards, invitations, tickets, and the like, along with some eighty newspaper articles. Seibert was the son of a Maryland sheriff, and the collection reflects a longtime interest in crime, politics, and the Civil War. The scrapbook used to contain letters written by Butch Cassidy. One was his letter from Santa Cruz to the Boys at Concordia. The other was a brief note to Clement

Glass about Concordia business. Another note, signed "D. J. Myers," has sometimes been attributed to Butch, but the handwriting isn't remotely similar to his.

Seibert's nieces stored the small, thick volume in their attic for forty years before donating it to the American Association of University Women for a used-book sale in the early 1970s. A member of the AAUW wrote to outlaw historian Jim Dullenty to inquire about the value of the letter and the note that Seibert had attributed to Butch. Dullenty verified their authenticity and put the AAUW in touch with Craig Fouts, a California dealer in Old West memorabilia, who bought the scrapbook. Fouts tells us that he photocopied Butch's correspondence and some of the articles, then sold the scrapbook to collector Brent Ashworth in Utah. We call Ashworth, who says he removed and sold several letters—including Butch's—before trading the scrapbook to Nyal Anderson, an antique dealer in Salt Lake City. Anderson wants $10,000 for the denuded book. The price is not only way out of our reach but also preposterous.

Meanwhile, however, Fouts has kindly sent us photocopies of Butch's letters and two articles. This time, I have no doubts about the handwriting: It matches Butch's in every way. The letters are genuine. Although the articles are in Spanish, they so clearly relate to the Aramayo holdup and the San Vicente shootout that we can't believe another historian hasn't beaten us to them. Fouts had rough translations made, but he says he never got around to writing anything. Both articles appear to be from *La Prensa* of Oruro. According to the first one, Carlos Peró was carrying a large cash shipment from Uyuni to Tupiza and was held up "at a bend in the road at a place called Salo." Once the bandits had left him, Peró "hastily returned to Uyuni to report what had happened." A posse of policemen found the outlaws resting in San Vicente. "Upon seeing the patrol approaching, the thieves went for their guns, resolved to battle heroically . . . for the stolen money. And without further notice, the bandits unleashed a veritable hail of bullets at their pursuers, who answered with a blaze of fire as if hunting wild animals. The fight was intense; a tremendous din and the furious shouting of the bandits and the police were all that could be heard. In the end, after a battle of more than an hour, the bandits fell lifeless, their bodies riddled with bullets. One policeman died, and two others were wounded. The stolen shipment was found beside the bodies of the bandits, whose faces were frozen in rage, and whose lips formed a last grimace of hate." According to the reporter, "the names and nationalities of these two birds so fiercely bound together are not yet known."

The second article from Seibert's scrapbook says that Carlos Peró, accompanied by his son and a servant, was en route from Tupiza to Quechisla with a cash shipment when two masked men confronted him at the foot of the Salo hill. The bandits tied up Peró's party and departed with the money and the company's best mule. Once free, the victims walked to the smelter at Cotani. Peró sent a message to the Aramayo company via the administrator at the Salo ranch and the Tupiza officials sent a telegram requesting help from the Abaroa regiment stationed in Uyuni. Several patrols went out, and two *gringos* were captured in Salo. "They were armed to the teeth: Each one had a fine rifle, two revolvers and a dagger. They also had a pack mule, leather cords for binding hands, chemicals sufficient to drug someone, and a total of five hundred *bolivianos* in cash." Meanwhile, another patrol went to San Vicente, where two other *gringos*—the actual robbers—"put up such a ferocious and tenacious resistance that it lasted more than an hour and resulted in the deaths of one soldier and both bandits." This article places the holdup on November sixth and the shootout on the tenth.

Now that we know approximately when these events took place, we return to the microfilm room of the Library of Congress for another look at the Argentine newspapers. A series of four brief articles in *La Prensa* of Buenos Aires adds little to the Bolivian stories except that the two *gringos* captured in Salo claimed to be a North American named Ray Walters and an Englishman named Frank Murray, that they had a woman's saddle (but no woman) with them, and that they were freed after the real bandits (described as Americans or Chileans) were killed in San Vicente "in a scuffle with the forces who were pursuing them."

Although we have found proof that a shootout took place in San Vicente in November 1908 and that acquaintances in South America believed that Butch and Sundance were the bandits slain there, the water has been muddied considerably by Walters, Murray, and the men Hiram Bingham met at the border. Moreover, while taking the point of view of the military heroes rather than the bandit antiheroes and exaggerating somewhat less than the North American versions, the South American newspaper accounts differ from one another nearly as much as those in the United States do. Unless we find the report sent to Aller, we may never know exactly what took place in San Vicente.

134

And unless we dig them up, we may never know for certain who the bandits were. The first step is to find their graves.

We climb down off the plane into the freezing night and wobble across the tarmac into the world's highest commercial airport, at an altitude of more than thirteen thousand feet on the *altiplano* above La Paz. By the time we have stumbled through customs and loaded our backpacks into a taxi, my head throbs. When we visited Bolivia in the late 1970s, we journeyed by land, which gave us a chance to acclimate gradually to having less oxygen in the air we breathed. By contrast, this visit promises to give new meaning to the term *jet lag*.

After a night's rest and two cups of *coca* tea with a breakfast of *salteñas* (the ultimate in *empanadas*), we head out in search of the elusive truth about the fate of Butch and Sundance. A day of huffing and puffing up and down steep streets, weaving through throngs of businessmen in suits and pigtailed *cholas* in iridescent skirts and bowler hats, and poring over old newspapers at the San Andres University, the Bolivian Library of Congress, and the La Paz Municipal Library leaves us with full-blown *soroche* (altitude sickness) and a few more articles about the shootout. According to these accounts, the bandits were Americans, Yankees, a Chilean and a Dane, or two unidentifiable masked men. The holdup took place three leagues from Salo, "on the road from Tupiza to Quechisla," or "at an appropriate spot" between Uyuni and Quechisla. Once free, Carlos Peró reported the robbery to the Tupiza police, or he went to Quechisla to organize a posse and then returned to the scene of the crime and tracked down the bandits. They were killed "on the field of combat" or in "a spirited battle" by agents of the Uyuni police, by armed men, or by one of three patrols sent out from Uyuni. When the shooting stopped, the bandits were found "with their guns in their hands, prepared to defend themselves to the last moment," or "one shot in the forehead and the other in the chest, the latter with seven bullet wounds in different parts of his body."

In the most detailed account, which appeared in *La Mañana* of Sucre, Sheriff Timoteo Rios, Captain Justo P. Concha, and two soldiers marched from Uyuni to San Vicente, a "strategic point for those who seek the most deserted frontier." At eight o'clock on the evening of the sixth, the patrol received word that two well-armed foreigners had just arrived. The posse confronted the bandits, who shot and killed one of the soldiers. The captain told the *gringos* to give up, but they answered with more shots. The battle continued for more than half an hour, until the bandits died. Along with their weapons and the stolen payroll, the *gringos* had in their possession a map of Bolivia with penciled notations of the places they had visited in the departments of La Paz, Santa Cruz, Cochabamba, and Potosí. Their route was well marked to San Vicente and from there, via Santa Catalina, to La Quiaca. The newspaper congratulated Captain Concha and Sheriff Rios "for their brilliant conduct in such a risky undertaking" and said that they had brought honor to "the Uyuni police and the country in general."

After reading all the old newspapers we can find, we turn to the government agencies whose archives might contain relevant documents. Unfortunately, any files that the Ministry of Justice might have had were lost in a fire in the 1960s, and the death certificates at the Ministry of the Interior date back only to the 1940s. At the main gate of the Estado Mayor—the Bolivian equivalent of the Pentagon—we ask whether we can visit the army's archives. The machine-gun-toting youthful guards take our cameras and passports and direct us to the administrative building, which is down a long drive near the front of the compound. The building has two front doors; we climb the steps to the wrong one, then start over again to reach the correct one. No one knows what to make of our curious quest, and we are sent up several additional flights of stairs. Thoroughly winded, we are introduced to a gracious colonel, who serves us *coca* tea in an elegantly appointed salon. He leaves briefly, then returns to say that the commander in chief of the armed forces wants to see us.

He does?

"Swallow your gum!" I whisper to Dan as the colonel leads us down the hall, past a cadre of generals and arms merchants, and into a long office with sofas and chairs at one end and a big desk at the other.

The commander in chief, smacking his own wad of gum, greets us warmly and says he loved the film *Butch Cassidy and the Sundance Kid.* "I saw it in the United States, when I was there for some training. It was banned here, you know, because it was thought to present an unflattering and distorted picture of Bolivia."

"The movie certainly exaggerated the number of Bolivian soldiers it took to kill two puny *gringos,*" says Dan. "I don't suppose that went over very well here."

"Especially not," says the commander in chief, "when the soldiers were wearing German uniforms and speaking Mexican Spanish. Even worse was the part where Butch suggested going to Bolivia and Sundance asked, 'What's Bolivia?' In English, Butch's answer was 'Bolivia's a country, stupid!' But in the Spanish translation, they dropped the comma, so the sentence turned into 'Bolivia's a stupid country!' ''

With that, he shakes our hands again and turns us back over to the colonel, who takes us to the officer in charge of the archives, who turns us over to his assistant, who takes us to the building where the files are kept on shelves that reach to the ceiling. A clerk makes a cursory search for anything having to do with the Abaroa regiment during the relevant years, but he announces that what we need is neither here nor anyplace else he can think of, and that is that. After retracing our path across a broad lot where soldiers march in formation, we climb several sets of stairs to report back to the various officers who have helped us. By the time we have walked up the long drive and retrieved our gear from the guards at the main gate, we are breathless again and more than a little dazed.

Later, at the archives of the Ministry of Foreign Relations, we finally score. In a drafty room with a high ceiling tinged green by fluorescent lighting, row upon row of metal shelves hold thousands of books containing hundreds of thousands of letters, including several related to Frank Aller's inquiry about Sundance, alias Frank Boyd or H.A. Brown. The American legation in La Paz relayed Aller's request for a death certificate to Bolivia's foreign relations minister, who delegated the task to the prefect of the department of Potosí. The prefect turned to the subprefects of the provinces of Sud Chichas and Porco, which had jurisdiction over the matter.

On September 30, 1910, the Sud Chichas subprefect in Tupiza sent the prefect ''a certificate of the clerk of the magistrate's court, which intervened slightly in this business.'' According to the certificate, the Tupiza magistrate's ''investigation into the deaths of two North Americans in San Vicente did not discover their names; no document was found that would shed any light in that respect. The individuals had been killed in a fight with the force that came from Uyuni and, having taken all of the papers, cards, money, etc., the Uyuni authorities are the ones who could provide some information about the particulars.''

The first sign of trouble appears in an October 7 letter from the Porco subprefect in Uyuni. He reported ''that none of those who participated in the San Vicente mission are here, some because they have completed their military service, and Captain Concha because he has moved to Santa Cruz, and the policemen because they have retired.''

On October 18, the minister wrote to the prefect in Potosí: "As I still have not received the certificate necessary to discharge my duty, that is the death certificate for the [American citizen] Brown, issued by the priest of the place he was buried, I suggest that you might want to give precise orders that said document be sent up to this ministry as quickly as possible.''

Three weeks later, the subprefect in Uyuni reported that "the priest as well as the *corregidor* of San Vicente, a canton under the jursidiction of the Sud Chichas province," had not been forthcoming with respect to the death certificate or information about the deaths of the two Yankees: "The *corregidor* says that he has not a single document in his power, the Tupiza judges having taken them, without leaving any papers in the canton. The curate has not answered my repeated notices which is why I have not completed your repeated orders. . . . It would be useful if the Sud Chichas subprefect suggested to the priest that he comply with his duties.''

After receiving this report, the prefect wrote to the subprefect in Tupiza: "Such conduct being intolerable, please send a notice to the San Vicente priest demanding the death certificate. . . . At the same time, with the district attorney's assistance, you should obtain the certificates and copies of documents that shed some light on this business, taking the appropriate steps that must exist in the court of that city. These documents have been requested repeatedly by the foreign relations minister, and it is urgent that you preoccupy yourself with obtaining them.''

The Sud Chichas subprefect wrote back: "I have made inquiries in that regard and have been assured that the death certificate does not exist and that the identification has still not been proved and that the names of the victims are not known. Nonetheless, I will look into the matter and find a way to obtain a certificate.''

The district attorney in Tupiza wrote that he had "asked the magistrate's court to provide a transcript of a report prepared against the individuals who robbed a cash shipment belonging to the Aramayo, Francke and Company, and who were later killed in San Vicente in a fray with the force . . . from Uyuni commanded by Captain Justo P. Concha; having been buried in that place. It should be noted that the

138

cash shipment, effects, weapons, and papers that were found with the assailants were taken . . . to Uyuni, where a report was also prepared, and which should still be there, and from which better information could be obtained. In the files of this district, there are no documents or [other material] related to this matter.''

As usual, each new document answers a few questions and poses many others we hadn't thought of. This series of letters shows what drove Frank Aller to write that the local authorities seemed to be "endeavoring to hush up the matter," but the correspondence also raises the issue of where the outlaws were buried. Although many of the comments imply that they wound up in the San Vicente cemetery, others suggest that the corpses were taken to Uyuni.

On December 20, 1910, the prefect in Potosí finally sent the foreign relations minister the death certificate and the ten-page report we first read about in the National Archives back home. We are disheartened, but not surprised, to find that the report is missing from the files in La Paz. We have amassed quite a few cover letters, but the report seems to have passed from one official to the next without ever being copied. In this latest addition to our collection, the prefect wrote, "I hope that these documents will be able to satisfy the wishes of the chancellery, for it has not been possible to obtain other information about [the matter], and it only remains to seek equal testimony from the criminal file that must exist in the courts of Uyuni, for which I have sent an immediate request by mail to the subprefect of the Porco province.'' The letters from the Porco subprefect in Uyuni, however, have already shown his inability to find anything that would clear up the case. If the Bolivian government couldn't locate the Uyuni records barely two years after the shootout, how can we possibly find them three-quarters of a century later?

Before leaving La Paz, we have cocktails with Roberto and Isabel Arce in the small library of their penthouse above the Isabel la Catolica plaza. Don Roberto, who was vice president of Bolivia for one day in 1952 and ambassador to the United States in the late 1970s, is now writing a history of the Bolivian mining industry—a subject in which we have taken a sudden interest because of its relevance to our two favorite outlaws.

Doña Isabel pours sherry for us and Scotch for them, and we munch on crackers with blue cheese and trade travel stories. After a *coup d'état* cut short Don Roberto's vice presidency, he spent a period of exile in Burma, Malaysia, and the United States, where he headed up the United Nations mining organization.

"Why Burma?" asks Dan.

"In my youth, my grandfather gave me the choice of a new car or cash. I took the cash and set off around the world. I ran out of money in Burma and then found work at a mining company there."

Doña Isabel passes a platter of cheese *empanadas* and a bowl of smoked almonds while her husband cheerfully answers our questions about the mining companies Butch and Sundance worked for or held up. "The Concordia Mine was abandoned long ago, and the Aramayo company was expropriated and nationalized in 1952. Today, its mines are operated by COMIBOL, the Corporación Minera de Bolivia, the government mining agency. Back at the turn of the century, Aramayo was one of the three companies dominating the mining industry here. Patiño and Hochschild were relative newcomers, but Aramayo had been around since 1850, when the silver market was still strong. In the early 1900s, Aramayo had the biggest outfit in southern Bolivia. Patiño and Hochschild operated farther north, taking part in the boom sparked by the demand for tin for cans and industry and such."

In his research into the history of Bolivian mining, Don Roberto is currently addressing the question of why the city of Potosí was the focus of so much attention during the seventeenth century, when Mexico had equal quantities of silver. The answer apparently has something to do with politics in Spain.

Potosí prospered in the shadow of Cerro Rico, a mountain full of tin, silver, bismuth, and tungsten, discovered in 1545 by an Indian named Diego Huallpa. By 1611, nine years before the Pilgrims landed at Plymouth Rock, Potosí had 160,000 inhabitants, making it one of the biggest cities in the world at the time. Although it fell into a decline when the silver played out, Potosí bounced back with the tin boom in the early twentieth century. Today, the population is about 110,000.

Hoping that the archives in Potosí will contain as many nuggets as Cerro Rico, we board a *ferrobus*—a cross between a train and a bus, with neither the comforts of the former nor the speed of the latter—and climb through tumbledown, litter-strewn neighborhoods that cling to the walls of the Choqueyapu River Canyon, which cleaves La Paz. Children, many-skirted *cholas,* and leathery old men scatter when the driver leans on the horn. After passing through sun-dappled eucalyptus groves and finally reaching the flat, brown *altiplano*, we are startled to see a troop of *vicuñas* lounging in a bed of spiky *ichu* grass. They usually stay much farther away from civilization. More typical is the menagerie of sheep, burros, and bedraggled *llamas* urged on by a *campesino* who has forsaken the traditional woven *chullo* for a red baseball cap bearing the Coca-Cola logo. Nearby, farmers scour and comb their fields with primitive implements, and a boy chops *tola* for firewood with a pickax as big as he is. Trucks whir across the plain, and flamingos stroll like boulevardiers along the saline shore of a shallow river. The *ferrobus* picks up speed and flies by adobe huts with TV antennas and abandoned villages bombed out by wind and rain.

We halt on the outskirts of Oruro, where disgruntled residents have blocked the tracks with rocks to protest an injustice perpetrated by—depending on whom we ask—the railroad company, a landlord, or the city government. We wait for the railroad people to sort things out, but they don't even bother to speak to the demonstrators. The waiter serves lunch—chicken or pork chops with french fries and salad—and the engineer turns on his cassette player, removes his jacket, sits in his seat, and swats flies with a towel. His assistant jumps off the *ferrobus* and walks toward the train station, but no railroad officials show up, and a passenger who goes to check on the situation finds the assistant drinking in a bar. The police, with lights flashing, come and go. A massive diesel slides up to the rocks, then backs off. Inside the *ferrobus*, "*La Bamba*" plays on. Finally, after three hours, the army comes to our rescue. A truckful of soldiers outfitted with tear-gas cannisters and shotguns roars onto the scene, and the officer in charge chats with the demonstrators, while the German shepherd and Doberman pinscher by his side strain at their leashes. The rocks are moved.

Just beyond Oruro, the tracks run on a raised strip of land through Uru Uru Lake, where gulls flit and ducks glide among islands of golden reeds, and flamingos and herons wade in the shallows. We pass a village plumed with mimosas and poplars, and then the land flattens out completely. The first patches of *yareta* appear, followed by *tola* bushes and acres of mud. Beside a hut sit a tractor and a 1968 Chevy. The *ferrobus* rolls on past an abandoned mine, an old smelter, a white-washed church, hamlets with thatched adobe huts, and scores of *llama* herds.

At Río Mulato, where the spur to Potosí turns east, we pause for a few minutes. Two *cholas* climb aboard and walk tentatively down the aisle saying, "Don't you want some cheese?"

Only one passenger evinces any interest in the pungent white disks being proffered. "What kind of cheese are they?" she asks.

"Sheeps' milk, *señora*."

"Are they fresh?"

"*Sí, señora*, from lambs."

Wait till the baby-vegetables crowd hears about this: lactating lambs!

Apparently impressed, the *señora* takes a disk. But the *chola* doesn't give her enough change, and, they begin arguing over her arithmetic. As the horn blasts and the wheels roll, the *señora* takes the disk out of her plastic bag and hands it back to the *chola*, who returns the money and jumps off the moving train. As we pull away, her associate is berating her for botching their only sale of the day.

The delay in Oruro has cost us considerable daylight, and night falls long before we reach Potosí. At the station, all the luggage is ripped out of the bowels of the *ferrobus* by a gang of teenagers—brazen thieves, we think, until we notice that they're heading straight for the baggage-retrieval area. This burst of energy and organization bewilders even the Bolivian passengers, who begin demanding their bags right there on the platform, claim tickets or no.

We check into a hotel in a renovated colonial mansion, and Dan unpacks and falls into bed. Meanwhile, I soak my foot in hydrogen peroxide in an attempt to cure an infection that recently developed in one of my toes after some minor surgery. The next morning, a red line still runs from my toenail up onto my foot. Thinking sun and fresh air might help, I take off my shoes and sit for half an hour in the hotel's bright courtyard. Nothing happens to the red line, but—thanks to the power of the sun at high altitudes—I wind up with a deep tan that starts at my toes and stops at my ankles.

Dan fetches me from the patio, and we stroll down a narrow, cobbled street to a plaza flanked by government buildings and a sandstone cathedral and filled with pine trees and flowers. Taxis prowl the square, and cops in white helmets and olive drab direct the vehicles even when the traffic light is working. Across from the northwest corner of the plaza are the heavy wooden doors of the main entrance to the Casa de Moneda. Since its construction in the eighteenth century, the building has housed a mint, a prison, a fortress, the army's headquarters, and now a museum and historical archives. We pass through an arched tunnel and a wrought-iron gate into a colonnaded courtyard with a fountain in the center. From the far wall, a huge mask bearing a distinct resemblance to Chico Marx grins down on us. Although its significance is uncertain, the mask has become a symbol—along with Cerro Rico—of Potosí's faded glory.

In a dimly lit room off the courtyard, we find copies of many of the same telegrams and letters we saw in La Paz. An 1859 map of Bolivia shows Uyuni on a trail jutting northeast from a road between Potosí and Calama and puts San Vicente near what is now the Chilean frontier. The Casa de Moneda also contains broken sets of early 1900s newspapers, which yield a few articles about the Eucaliptus robbery but only one report of the San Vicente shootout. According to the article, the bandits' bodies were taken to Uyuni for identification.

We buy tickets to Uyuni on a Bluebird bus—the kind used in the United States for hauling schoolchildren—with thinly padded bench seats and no legroom. Dan stays outside to ensure that our backpacks go into the luggage compartment, and I stake out our seats. When a Swiss tourist carelessly leaves her purse on a nearby seat and steps outside to chat with a Dutch couple, I silently appoint myself as guardian of the purse and keep my eyes fixed on it. A commotion momentarily distracts me, however, and when I turn around again, the purse is gone. No one has entered the bus in the meantime, so the thief must be a fellow passenger. I study the *cholas* with their belongings tied up in huge cloth bundles, the elderly couples in threadbare suits and finely knit sweaters, the young *altiplano* James Deans wearing leather jackets and smoking cheap cigarettes. Which of them looks like a thief? But wait—the window is open. Anyone could have reached in and snatched the purse. While I am mulling over the possibilities, the tourist discovers her loss. The bus driver carries out a quick, unsuccessful search for the thief, and then we are off.

The bus has been oversold, and several people must stand—bad enough for the short Bolivians but torturous for a tall Norwegian who has to stoop for the entire eight-hour trip. Whenever we hit a rut or a rock, his head bumps the roof. On a narrow dirt road, we cut through sandy hills and high meadows where *llamas* forage. The bus pitches and turns and crosses one corrugated streambed after another. We pass through a region of volcanic outcrops and wind-sculpted rocks, then break for lunch in a small town where eateries have been set up in roadside tents. All the trucks parked nearby have Rambo on their mud flaps. (The last time we came through here, Che Guevara was the truckers' hero.) In the field across from the unpaved square, sheep bleat at unseen annoyances.

We reboard the bus and continue our journey west. The terrain flattens out, beige and dusty, and we cross numerous dry riverbeds, then climb into mountains again. The bus snakes through the gritty mining town of Pulacayo at dusk, then descends toward the *altiplano*, where dazzling arc lights make the town of Uyuni look like a giant shopping mall on the moon.

As soon as our backpacks come off the bus, we hasten to the Hotel Avenida, whose owner, Jesús Rosas Zúniga, is an old friend of ours. A short, barrel-chested adventurer with noble bearing and a full head of white hair, he has climbed El Misti (altitude, 19,102 feet) and rafted the Madre de Dios River, and he once took us to see the James flamingos at the Laguna Colorada, an isolated lake tinted red by algae and ringed by volcanoes in the Atacama Desert. A few months back, when we wrote and asked him whether he knew anything about our *bandoleros,* Don Jesús drove all over southern Bolivia in search of information. Visiting San Vicente, Tupiza, Salo, and the Aramayo headquarters at Quechisla, he was unable to find anyone who knew anything about the holdup or the shootout. Nonetheless, he has sent us this tantalizing piece of news: "I recently learned that the grandchildren of these men came to Bolivia conducting an investigation and offering two thousand dollars for the same facts you are seeking, but that they did not locate any information."

We are alarmed to find our friend limping around with a cane.

"What did you do?" says Dan. "Twist your ankle in a marathon?"

"I was driving up to Oruro in that same old truck we took to the *laguna,*" Don Jesús says in his gruff voice, "and I ran off the road. Rolled the truck and broke my hip. I'm going to the United States soon to get the hip replaced, but in the meantime I've had to interrupt the work on the hotel. I'm doubling the number of rooms and adding some private baths."

The Avenida was already the cleanest hotel with the firmest, widest beds on the *altiplano*. The new addition will make it the most comfortable small-town hotel in the Andes. Uyuni has changed a lot in the decade since we first visited it. Back then, it was a sleepy burg with little more than third-rate movies for entertainment. Today, youngsters in Uyuni ride skateboards and motorbikes, listen to Walkmen and walkie-talkies, play video games in adobe huts with dirt floors, and wear running shoes, stonewashed jeans, and *Tortugas-Ninjas* T-shirts. We spot one lad wearing an earring. Growing numbers of tourists, drawn by the town's proximity to a vast salt flat and the lunar Atacama Desert, support four or five tour companies. And Uyuni now offers a choice of stores that make photocopies for researchers like us—all we have to do is find something worth copying.

Our first stop is the provincial administrative office, where the staff is preoccupied with an upcoming visit by the minister of mines, whose name they can't remember. In any case, their records go back no further than 1911. Next, we visit the subprefect. He is just leaving to see the visiting minister, whose name escapes him. The subprefect's secretary helps us sort through their records, but the oldest ones date from the 1940s. Although the Abaroa regiment is no longer stationed in Uyuni, the army maintains a fort here; an officer promises to search for records about the shootout and let us know what he finds. We put little faith in such promises, which are always well intentioned and almost never fulfilled.

Hoping to learn something from the descendants of Timoteo Rios, the Uyuni policeman said to have participated in the shootout, we begin asking around and discover that Uyuni has many residents named Rios, but none of them are related to Don Timoteo. He died forty years ago and left no widow or children. Another impasse. We climb the stairs to the judicial offices above the post office. Panes are broken in most of the windows, the hallway is dark, and many floorboards are missing in the large anteroom we must cross to reach the magistrate's office. The magistrate is away for the afternoon, but his secretary helps us search the archives, which amount to two cabinets full of papers bound with twine. The oldest documents date from the 1940s. The district judge across the way has records that go back further, but only to 1916.

Our only hope now is the cemetery—an odd place for hope, but this is an odd business. The weather is hot, a surprise at twelve thousand feet, as we walk north past the soccer fields and the municipal dump. In front of the walled cemetery is a dreary plaza: A weathered angel stands atop a grey pedestal fenced in by a chain and barbed wire, and flagstone walks forming crosses are laid out in squares landscaped with cacti, rocks, and stone benches. In large letters above a huge cross on the wall facing town is the following message: QUIET! ENTER HERE LADEN WITH PAIN, YOU WHO TREAD PROUDLY, LET THE DIN OF THE LIVING NEVER DISTURB THE PEACE OF THE DEAD. Small hand-painted signs nearby read WARNING: ENTERING WITH BICYCLES, THE CONSUMPTION OF ALCOHOLIC BEVERAGES, AND INEBRIATED PERSONS ARE PROHIBITED and WARNING: ENTRANCE IS PROHIBITED TO MINORS AND YOUNG COUPLES WITH NEGATIVE INTENTIONS.

The cemetery is huge, and most of the graves are relatively new. Along the back wall, in an area where the monuments date from the early part of the century, we find a great many empty niches. Nearby is an igloo-sized oven, which leads us to speculate that the bandits' remains might have been burned. And what happened to the bodies that were in those niches?

The local curate insists that corpses are never cremated. "That would be a sin."

"But what about that huge oven in the cemetery?" asks Dan.

"It is used for burning dead flowers."

"Do you have any records that might tell us where the outlaws are buried?"

"What interest would the parish have had in the burial of two *bandoleros*? They were not Catholics, were they? In any event, we have only birth records, not death records, from that long ago."

"Is there an older church whose records might go back further?"

"This is the oldest church. It was founded in 1906."

"Uyuni was here long before then," says Dan. "It was on an 1859 map we saw in Potosí."

"No, that's wrong," barks the priest. "Either you are mistaken or the map was wrong. There was nothing here then. It was an empty plain until the 1890s, when the railroad came."

Over lunch, however, Don Jesús tells us that before the railroad was built, Uyuni was a way station for travelers. "There were just a few houses and corrals. *Uyuni* means corral in the Aymara language. When the Pulacayo mine opened, the owner did not want the miners living nearby, because they stole silver ore, so he moved them all to Uyuni, which took off after that. Then the railroad came, and the town grew even more. Today, there are about twenty thousand inhabitants."

146

If the priest was wrong about Uyuni, the rest of his claims are suspect. In the afternoon, we track down the cemetery guard, a toothless man gumming his lunch. He says that when relatives don't pay for the upkeep on crypts, the corpses are removed and burned in the big white oven. He knows nothing about any outlaws buried in the cemetery but speculates that, as unknown indigents, they would simply have been tossed out on the plains anywhere.

Great. Butch and Sundance wound up as buzzard bait, and we don't have a prayer of finding what's left of them.

While wandering around town on our various fruitless missions, we keep noticing a fellow guest from the hotel: a chubby man with black hair, a drooping moustache, and aviator sunglasses. He has such a fetching smile and teddy-bear look that we begin saying hello to him when our paths cross. On the morning of our departure, while I soak my still-infected toe, Dan walks over to the train station to buy our tickets for the trip to Tupiza. He finds himself in line ahead of the teddy-bear man, who turns out to be a civil engineer named Francisco Vega Avila. Ticket windows in Bolivia rarely open until a long line has formed, which gives Dan and Francisco time to strike up a conversation. When Dan mentions that we're looking for Butch and Sundance, Francisco says that he has seen their grave—not in Uyuni, but in San Vicente.

"The first time I saw it," he says, "I had a spiritual sensation. Later, I dreamed of *bandoleros*. That grave is enchanted." He recalls having heard that the bandits were lost and broke and making for Potosí when they were killed in San Vicente. According to Francisco, the government mining agency, COMIBOL, has all of the Aramayo company's records in Quechisla, which used to be the Aramayo headquarters. As a COMIBOL employee, he can help us get access to the records. There is no public transportation to either San Vicente or Quechisla, but he feels certain that he could arrange a ride from his office near Atocha, which is roughly halfway between Uyuni and Tupiza. And we could sleep at his place.

Dan eagerly accepts the invitation, buys tickets for Atocha, and runs back to tell me the good news. I am less than thrilled about staying in the home of a bachelor. Who knows what shape the bathroom will be in—or whether he has one? But I suppose I can survive a couple of days without a shower if it will help us discover what happened to

Butch and Sundance. The news of the encounter at the train station is greeted enthusiastically by Don Jesús, who calls it *suerte de chancho* (pig's luck), which apparently is better than it sounds.

The *ferrobus* purrs south past a broad plain of sunbaked red mud, which gives way to shingle and then windblown sand, freckled with *tola* bushes. The tracks parallel a line of low, mineral-streaked hills; cumulous clouds billow in the blue sky above them. In sheltered meadows, *llamas* with red tassels tied to their ears nibble *tola* and sheep graze on stunted tufts of *paja*. Francisco points out a sharp triangle of a mountain and says, "Chorolque, the highest peak in this area."

Presently, we find ourselves in a region of badlands. Following a dry riverbed, the *ferrobus* twists in and out through narrow ravines. At the tiny Chocaya station, the conductor snags mail from a wire loop. On the edge of Atocha, a sunlit cemetery covers a steep hillside within spitting distance of the tracks. Wreaths of plastic flowers, left over from All Saints Day, lend the place an eerily cheerful air.

Within moments, we arrive at Atocha's shabby train station. A tiny, elderly porter hefts all our packs and bags onto his back, secures them with a rope, and trots like a mobile mountain of luggage across the one-lane bridge to Telamayo, where COMIBOL maintains its regional offices and a tin-concentrator. We pass a huge slag heap and several large buildings, then turn into a residential neighborhood, where the COMIBOL workers live. Francisco has a modern two-story flat with a comfortable guest room and a shower with plenty of hot water.

Our host introduces us to his supervisor, Juan Cabrera, who shares our interest in Butch and Sundance and agrees to take us to San Vicente and Quechisla the next day, Sunday, if we will buy the gas and pay for a driver. Meanwhile, Juan suggests that we see Wálter Gutiérrez, a fifty-eight-year-old bookkeeper who is the local authority on the Aramayo holdup and the San Vicente shootout. On the way to his house, Juan describes Señor Gutiérrez's scheme to tap volcanic steam for heating homes and says COMIBOL is developing a pilot project that shows promise. We reach the house just as Señor Gutiérrez pulls up in his battered 1958 Willys jeep.

A wiry man wearing a sports jacket over a shirt and sweater, he alights and shakes hands all around. He has worked here more than thirty-five years, since before the mines were nationalized. His father, he tells us, worked for Félix Avelino Aramayo and said that there was a safe full of documents at the *patrón*'s house, Chajrahuasi, located this side of the entrance to Tupiza.

When asked where the 1908 holdup took place, Señor Gutiérrez says, "North of Tupiza on a trail that branches off from the road between Salo and Cotagaita near Almona. At Salo, there is a *hacienda* that belonged to the Aramayos. Don Félix was on a mule; there was another mule with a blanket and a Winchester, another mule with a servant, and a fourth mule with the cash shipment. That mule carried two *petacas* [small rawhide trunks]. The *bandoleros,* one of whom was armed, were hidden behind the rocks. It is said that they greeted Don Félix very courteously: 'Pardon us, but we know that you have a lot of money, and we have a great need.' The one who spoke had a foreign accent. 'Don't turn back for a while.' Both men were masked. After they took the money and left, Don Félix returned to Tupiza, and the police sent telegrams to Cotagaita and Uyuni, and soldiers went out from Uyuni."

"Did the bandits take a mule?" asks Dan.

Señor Gutiérrez lifts his flat cap and scratches his head. "I don't remember anything about Don Félix's mule."

"How did the shootout come about?"

"The *bandoleros* arrived in San Vicente at seven, very tired. They spoke English, according to the landlord of the place where they ate. One wanted to continue; the other wanted to sleep. They stayed. In the night, the soldiers came from Uyuni. The landlord notified the soldiers, and at dawn they attacked. I don't know whether both *bandoleros* died or just one."

"What about the soldiers?"

"There were fifteen or twenty soldiers. None of them died. The *bandoleros* offered no resistance. The soldiers just shot them, that's all. They must have been buried in San Vicente, but I don't know the cemetery there. If you go to Tupiza, you should visit my uncle, Fausto Gutiérrez, who worked for Aramayo for a long time. His memory is failing, though, so you might want to talk to his son—who is named Wálter Gutiérrez, just like me. He works in the Tupiza office of COMIBOL and might know something about the papers at Chajrahuasi."

"I thought the archives were in Quechisla," says Francisco.

"Some of the records are there, too. You must have two keys to

149

open the building, and both keyholders must be there at the same time. The files are very disorganized and contain nothing but papers related to the business. I doubt that you will find anything of value there."

Francisco is more optimistic. "You have two chances: the archive in Tupiza and the one in Quechisla."

Early in the morning, we set off in a Toyota jeep with Francisco, Juan, and a driver called Pancho. In this part of the Andes, the smoothest surfaces are usually the riverbeds, or *lechos,* which serve as roads in the dry season. In the rainy season, when the rivers contain more than a token amount of water, many routes become impassable. During the winter months, June to August, snow and ice can also make travel difficult. Today, the weather couldn't be finer. We follow the Atocha River *lecho* south through a sandy region where the vegetation runs to yellow *ichu* grass and huge clumps of *cortadera,* which is used for thatching roofs. Near Escoriani, we turn west into dry hills. *Alpacas* munch on *tola* beside the winding dirt road. Although vastly better than the cart track followed by mining engineer Victor Hampton in the 1920s, the road has only one lane much of the way, even on the numerous blind curves. Pancho enjoys driving as close to the crumbling edge as possible, which—without guardrails in the way—is pretty damn close.

The hulking Chorolque is visible for much of the ride. Francisco points out another local landmark, a low, dark ridge known as the Sleeping Monk. After passing several old mines that still yield lead or silver or both, we come upon a brown valley where hundreds of adobe huts stand roofless beneath the bright sky. "Portugalete," says Francisco. "The Spaniards abandoned it in the seventeenth century. According to legend, the town's *patrón* had two sons, and when one of them killed the other, the river dried up. The residents left and never came back. Lead, zinc, and silver are still mined here, but people say the place is haunted."

Pancho wheels the jeep west along the narrow Honda River. Cacti and purple lupines festoon the fractured orange walls of the ravine. A lovely xeroscape. Or is it? Runoff from nearby mines has turned the river into foaming sludge in some places. Is this a recent development, or did mining poison the land back in Butch and Sundance's day, too? As we make our way down a series of hairpin curves into the Angosta Mica River Valley, Francisco points out a ridge to the west. "There was a wagon trail up there running from Tupiza to Uyuni," he says. "The police came south on it."

"How long would it have taken to get from Salo to San Vicente?"

"The shortest route would require two days of walking. With mules, I don't know. The *bandoleros* could probably have ridden about thirty kilometers a day across country or fifty kilometers a day with a trail."

We pass boggy meadows where *llamas* browse on *tola* with yellow blossoms. The jeep stops to let a train of burros shuffle past, then we crest a hill and see snowcapped mountains lining the southern and western horizons. Below us, stretching across the bottom of a barren bowl are the corrugated roofs of San Vicente. On the far end of the town is the entrance to the mine, from whose depths COMIBOL extracts zinc, copper, lead, and silver. About half a mile east of the town, a few huts and a whitewashed church fringe an empty square. The adobe-walled cemetery sits alone on a brown slope. What a godforsaken place to spend eternity!

We drive through the dusty streets looking for elderly residents. A weather-beaten, canvas-skinned sixty-five-year-old knows nothing of *bandoleros* and says that San Vicente looks very different today from the way it looked in 1908. "The old part has been more or less destroyed. Most of the houses here now were built in 1980 or so, when the mine became much more active. Some of the older residents, they didn't like the new development, so they rebuilt the old town on the other side of the soccer field. The Risso family, one of those over in the *pueblo civico,* has been here a long time and might be able to help you."

Fifty-year-old Froilán Risso—a small man in a ragtag combo of shirts and sweaters with a suit jacket, baggy pants, and a brown *chullo*—says his father witnessed the shootout. "He was ten years old and lived next door to the place where it happened. He saw everything. After it was over, he looked for bullets."

"Can you show us where the battle occurred?"

"The house has been rebuilt, but the patio is still there, if you want to see that." Señor Risso has an animated face with supple skin the color of mahogany, a wispy moustache and eyebrows, a pointed chin, and very few teeth. *Coca* spume coats his mouth like vegetable lipstick.

Juan motions him into the back of the jeep for the five-minute ride to what is left of old San Vicente: a few adobe huts surrounded by the

151

tin-roofed plywood shacks that COMIBOL built for its workers. "The shootout took place in the home of a man named Casasola," says Señor Risso, "at about seven in the evening." He signals Pancho to stop on the main street.

"They were at a house?" asks Dan. "I thought they were at an inn."

We climb out of the jeep and troop after Señor Risso through a sheet-metal gate with a wooden frame into a patio littered with crates, cans, laundry paraphernalia, and other junk.

"No, it was a house, just like it is now, with rooms that opened into this patio, which was bigger then. Anyhow, the *bandoleros* were in a room against the back wall. The original room has been torn down, but the front of it was right where this concrete wall is. The door was where I am standing. There was an adobe bench built into the wall inside the room, and the *bandoleros* were beside an oven, which used to be in the corner."

Dan and I climb onto crates and peer over the wall into a vacant lot full of trash.

"The *bandoleros* were in their room when a squadron of twenty soldiers came looking for them. A soldier named Victor Torres came through the gate first, like this." Señor Risso goes out through the gate, then comes back in. "They shot and killed him at once. The other soldiers immediately began shooting from the gate and surrounded the house."

"The bandits were already here when the soldiers arrived?"

"No, the soldiers came first, and the *gringos* came later."

"How did the soldiers know who the bandits were? Did someone recognize the mule?"

"They recognized the *gringos* by their color. The mules had nothing to do with it. The foreigners had four mules, but they were in a corral outside when the shooting began."

"How long did the shooting last?"

"I don't know. The next morning, the soldiers went in and found the *bandoleros* dead, one on the bench and the other by the oven. The corpses were laid out in the patio and later buried in the cemetery."

We pile into the jeep and head uphill to the cemetery. On the way, Señor Risso tells us that his parents lived here before the town was founded, and that the San Vicente mine goes back to the time of the Spaniards. "The mine has two hundred and thirty employees now, but they have been on strike for the past eight days."

Pancho brings the jeep to a halt in front of the cemetery. The gate is shut, and a padlock and chain hang from the bars at the center.

"Does the cemetery close for the *siesta*?" asks Dan.

"It certainly looks that way," says Juan.

The gate swings open.

"A good omen," says Francisco, jumping out of the jeep. "The *bandoleros*, they want to be found."

"Probably just the wind," I say.

"What wind?" says Pancho. He's right. The air is perfectly still. And the temperature must be at least 60 degrees Fahrenheit—downright balmy at more than fourteen thousand feet above sea level.

Walking briskly, Señor Risso leads us through a maze of crosses and tombstones and then under an adobe arch to the oldest section of the cemetery. He stops beside a small, fissured, concrete monument wedged between two large and relatively new slabs. "Here it is," he says. "It used to have a cross on top and a plaque engraved with words in a foreign language." He insists that the grave contains both bandits, which contradicts Victor Hampton's statement that Butch and Sundance were buried side by side between a Swede and a German.

"My father showed me the grave when I was about fourteen. He said he wanted me to know where it was, because someday *gringos* would come looking for the *bandoleros*."

"What are these?" asks Dan, pointing to a pair of U bolts that protrude from the concrete at ground level.

"The people from the town attached padlocks to them and put a chain around the grave to lock the outlaws' evil spirits inside."

"Well," says Dan, "mission accomplished. Now all we need to do is get somebody to dig them up and figure out if they're Butch and Sundance."

I'm excited at the prospect of solving the mystery once and for all, but being here in the cemetery has made me ambivalent about exhuming the bandits. Having always been fairly unsentimental about death, I suddenly find myself feeling like an intruder in an unfamiliar realm. Perhaps the padlocks were meant not only to keep the spirits in, but also to keep us out.

8 · THE ARAMAYO PAPERS

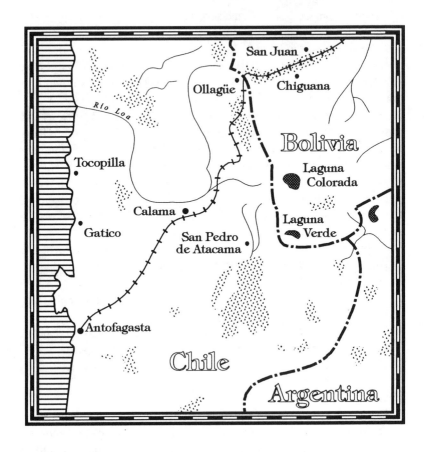

W E stop to buy bottled water in Atocha, then drive north and east
around Chorolque and into the Quechisla valley. The gravel *lecho*
widens out and the hills on either side grow steeper and rockier with
every passing mile. At last, we round a bend and see the tidy, whitewashed town of Quechisla huddled at the base of a mountain on a small
peninsula that juts into the confluence of two dried-up rivers. "If you

followed that *lecho*," says Francisco, pointing beyond a small cemetery, "you would eventually reach Salo."

Pancho stops the jeep in a deserted square, and we walk through empty cobbled lanes past vacant tile-roofed buildings set among unkempt rose gardens and shaded by poplars, pines, eucalyptus, and palm trees. Sheltered from the wind by the surrounding mineral-laden peaks, Quechisla is a verdant paradise compared with San Vicente. "This was the manager's house," says Juan, pointing to a two-story house with a wide porch and a bamboo trellis. A huge ficus tree dominates the garden in front. "The payroll that Butch and Sundance robbed would probably have been headed here."

Two burros meander up the lane, but their owners are nowhere in sight, and all the buildings at this end of town are shuttered. We walk past the old radio room and print shop and the residences that once housed the company's lawyers and middle managers. Finally, in a garden protected by a fence of thorny *churqui* branches, we encounter a couple of women whose husbands are employed by COMIBOL to watch over the place until the agency decides what to do with it. When we find the watchmen in a bar on the main plaza, they inform us that the Aramayo records once stored in Quechisla have long since been carted away to Tupiza. Juan Cabrera says he will write us a letter of introduction to the COMIBOL manager there, asking him to assist us in our research.

The *ferrobus* won't pass through again for several days, so Francisco suggests we take *el tren mexicano* for the fifty-mile ride to Tupiza. "The train has no reserved seats. It's a free-for-all, a jungle, but it will get you there just the same."

Sounds charming, especially at six in the morning.

"Don't worry," he says. "The *mexicano* never comes on time. You don't need to be at the station until quarter after seven at the earliest."

Sure enough, the train chugs up to the platform at half past seven. We say our goodbyes and climb aboard. The coach is jammed, but two military policemen insist that we take their seats. I gratefully settle in by the window to watch the scenery roll by. Twenty *llamas*, trotting bundles of brown and white fur, raise a low cloud of dust on the plain beside the Atocha River *lecho*. Dust seeps through the windows, and we are soon coated with it. At Escoriani, the road to Portugalete branches off to the west, but we continue south, shifting back and forth across the riverbed and flying past hills whiskered with *ichu* grass. The train clips across a bridge and into a canyon, where cacti poke up like barber poles from the steep slopes. We stare into each ravine and wonder whether Butch and Sundance passed through it on their way from Salo to San Vicente. The train ducks through a series of tunnels and runs along a ledge high above a narrow riverbed; foxtails beside the *lecho* and scree from the slate walls paint the landscape in orange, ecru, and grey. We pause in small towns, where rows of thatched adobe huts with tin doors and stiff paper over the windows parallel the tracks. As the elevation drops, willows and mimosas sway along the riverbank, and *churqui*-fenced fields of corn nestle among apple and peach orchards. Adobe buildings spread out at Oro Ingenio and cluster in a ravine at Hornos. Near Oploca, the *lecho* opens into a lush valley of small fields green with corn. Then we are back into badlands, where wind and water have carved red clay and rock into thousands of giant horns. Beneath a dark-red ridge shaped like a pair of stegosaurs, *tête-à-tête*, lies Tupiza.

There are no taxis at the train station, but men and boys with handcarts clamor for the privilege of hauling our baggage four blocks to the hotel. Along the way, we dodge several bicyclists and carts carrying everything from wine bottles to sides of beef.

After we check into a room off a patio filled with bougainvillea and pansies, I decide to take a quick shower before tackling the COMIBOL research. The shower and the toilet share the same small space, and the water sloshes into the plastic mesh receptacle for used toilet paper (which the plumbing can't handle) before slowly gurgling down the clogged drain in the middle of the grimy floor. I hobble around with my infected toe in the air.

By the time we reach the COMIBOL office, which occupies a one-story building with a pink stucco façade, it has closed for the *siesta*. Looking for the judicial archives, we are directed to the old customs house, an arcaded building that faces the shady main plaza and contains most of the government offices. We climb the stairs to the second floor and note that Tupiza, at an elevation of only 9,813 feet, is easier on the lungs than anyplace else we've been in Bolivia. In the subprefecture, we ask where the judicial archives are kept. The clerk asks what we are looking for and then tells us to take a seat. Moments later, he ushers us into the office of the subprefect, a lean, middle-aged man with a

Napoleonic fringe of reddish bangs and a white linen suit. We shake hands and sit in boxy chairs around a modern steel-and-glass coffee table.

A Bolivian of French descent, Gastón Michel Alfaro serves as the subprefect for the equivalent of twenty-five dollars a month. He also teaches grade school and, in his spare time, writes poetry. "Many of the judicial records were destroyed in a student revolt a few years ago," he tells us. "For a while, they were stored at the jail, and some of them were used as toilet paper. The others are totally disorganized, but I will ask the judge to let you review them."

This does not sound promising.

"Our newspaper may also have something about the *bandoleros,* although it did not exist in 1908." Don Gastón picks up his telephone and begins calling elderly *Tupizeños* and asking them whether they know anything about the holdup or shootout. They don't. "I will talk to my mother tonight," he says. "She was born in Salo but lives in Tupiza now." Meanwhile, he calls a pal who owns a local television station. "I have a couple of foreigners up here—Germans, I think—whom you should interview. They are looking for information about some *bandoleros* who held up an Aramayo remittance eighty years ago. You could put them on the news and ask for anyone who knows anything to come forward." He turns to Dan and says, "Can you meet the reporter at your hotel at two o'clock?"

"Sure."

Before eating lunch, we stop by the COMIBOL office and find it still closed.

The two-man television crew shows up on bicycles. While the cameraman aims a handheld video camera, the reporter asks several questions about our project, then moves on to the obligatory "What do you think of Tupiza?" and "Is this your first visit?" The whole thing is done within five minutes. They bike off down the street, and we miss the broadcast, which elicits no information.

Meanwhile, we return to the subprefect's office to find out whether he has arranged permission for us to see the judicial archives. He is busy, so we walk down the hall and ask the district-court clerk, who says we must obtain a court order, which necessitates hiring a lawyer to draft a *solicitud* asking the judge to issue the order. As we leave the clerk's office, we run into Gastón Michel, who volunteers to introduce

157

us to a lawyer. While crossing the plaza, he spots an elderly man on a bench and says, "Let me see if he knows anything. You wait here, because he is very cranky." The dapper subprefect strides over to the *anciano,* chats with him briefly, then rejoins us beside the life-size statue of José Avelino Aramayo, founder of the Aramayo dynasty. "Well, the old man knows nothing. We'll go to my friend. He won't charge more than two dollars. Besides, he has nothing else to do."

We find the lawyer alone in a long, dark room with a door opening onto the street. Don Gastón introduces us as good people who need a hand, then takes his leave. After shuffling three pieces of onionskin with two carbons and rolling them into his portable typewriter, the lawyer runs through a list of questions: What are your names? Passport numbers? The nature of your research? What are you looking for? Finally, he stops typing and asks, with a note of incredulity, "*Why* are you doing this?"

"It combines our love of South America with our interest in popular history," says Dan, "and the role of word-of-mouth stories in shaping legends."

"Also," I add, "we're suckers for a good mystery."

Apparently satisfied, the lawyer resumes pecking on the typewriter. He absolutely refuses payment and sends us back to the court.

The clerk takes the *solicitud* and says, "For the judge's order, you must buy a *cartula* [a blank piece of official paper, which costs a penny]. The order should be ready sometime tomorrow afternoon."

"But that means half the day will be gone before we can begin our search!" Dan has had enough of bureaucracy.

"Well," says the clerk, "come back in the morning, and I'll do what I can."

We stop by the COMIBOL office, which has closed for the day.

In the morning, when the paperwork is complete and the judge's three-dollar fee has been paid, we are finally allowed to enter the judicial archives, where case records dating from the seventeenth century to the present are piled in no particular order in stacks up to five feet high. The documents vary from loose pages covered with dust to pages sewn together in two- or three-inch case files. While Dan sifts through this hodgepodge, I go to the room housing the prison records, which are in similar chaos. At five o'clock, after hours of searching without encountering anything relevant, we throw in the towel.

The COMIBOL office is closed again, but as we are standing on the sidewalk discussing what to do next, a balding man in a plaid shirt and khaki trousers pedals up to the curb on a bicycle. "May I help you?" he says.

"Do you know when the COMIBOL office is open?"

"Or where Fausto Gutiérrez lives."

"He's my father. I am Wálter Gutiérrez. But what do you want with him?"

After Dan introduces us and explains our project, I say, "Your cousin and some other COMIBOL people in Telamayo told us that the Aramayo company's records were here in Tupiza and that you or your father could help us find them."

"There are no records here. They were destroyed in 1952, when the mines were nationalized, but my father worked for the Aramayo company for a long time. I suppose he might be able to tell you something about the robbery."

"Where can we find him?"

"As a matter of fact, I am on my way over there right now, but he is nearly ninety and has lost much of his hearing. He may not feel well enough to receive company. I could ask him and then meet you in the plaza at about six o'clock if you wish."

"We'll be there," says Dan.

In the meantime, we walk down the street to see Francisco Salazar, a retired journalist and amateur historian. We find the eighty-three-year-old *Tupizeño* sitting in the small odds-and-ends shop that occupies the front room of his house and opens onto the street. Although the weather is quite warm, he wears a brown cardigan sweater over a long-sleeved shirt buttoned to the neck. He has a thatch of white hair and thick eyeglasses, which are tinted green and tied onto his head with a network of strings. Behind the counter stands his daughter, Dora, who is slight, delicate—waif-like, even—with big dark eyes. She wears a finely knitted pink vest over a skirt and blouse, and her black hair is pulled away from her pale face.

"I know all about the Aramayo *asalto*," says Señor Salazar. "I wrote a pamphlet about it. The gang had six members, North Americans and Chileans. The holdup occurred at Salo, and the posse consisted of ten *Tupizeños*—volunteers, not military men—led by Carlos Peró. They caught and killed one of the bandits in the old town of Tatasi.''

"No, Papa," says Dora, who is cradling a black cat in her arms. "It was San Vicente, and *two* bandits were killed. Two members of the posse also died."

"They were brothers," says her father, "from Tupiza."

"You know," says Dora, "some other *gringos* came here ten or fifteen years ago looking for information about these *bandoleros*. I can't recall the name of the man, but he told us he was Butch Cassidy's grandson. He and his wife were traveling in a *casa rodante*."

A rolling house?

"A trailer," says Dan.

"They came and interviewed me and went to the court, but they could not find anything," says Señor Salazar. "Later, he took my picture. He was in the *casa rodante*, and he leaned out the window with his camera and took my picture." Señor Salazar gives us a copy of his pamphlet about the holdup and says, "I know the *bandoleros* were famous in North America, but why did they come here?"

"It's a long story," says Dan, but he tells it anyway.

At quarter to six, we plop down on a bench in the plaza. Half-hour later, we are still waiting for Wálter Gutiérrez. Bicyclists circle the plaza like dragonflies, but Don Wálter is not among them. "This is a waste of time," says Dan. "Let's go."

"No. Everybody in Quechisla and Telamayo said the records were here, and I'm not leaving until I see them."

"But he already said there aren't any records."

"Maybe he just didn't want to be bothered."

At six-thirty, Dan stands up. "He's not coming."

"Why are you in such a hurry? There's nothing else to do. We might as well sit here awhile. Maybe he'll turn up."

Just then, Don Wálter whips around the corner on his bicycle and stops in front of our bench. "I'm glad you are still here. I feared that I would miss you."

"Not a chance," says Dan. "How is your father?"

"He went to bed. He isn't up to seeing you, but I asked him about the holdup, and he said he had heard of it but doesn't know any of the details. I wish I could be more helpful."

"Do you know where 'Santiago' Hutcheon lived?" asks Dan. "He was a Scot who owned a transportation company here and apparently knew the bandits.''

"I'm not familiar with the name, but the corral for the muleteers used to be behind the train station, between the river and the mountains.''

"Are there any historical organizations around here that might have something about life in Tupiza in 1908?"

"There is no interest in history or conservation here. Almost all of the old buildings have been torn down and the old records destroyed. There were several hotels and banks on the plaza, but they are gone now. Of course, the old Aramayo *hacienda* Chajrahuasi is still here. I could take you there if you wish.''

Don Wálter arrives at our hotel in the morning as we are finishing our *café con leche* and soda bread. We walk a few blocks to the edge of town and cross the Tupiza River *lecho* on a modern bridge. Sunlight spills down over the ridge of dark-red conglomerate that walls the eastern side of the green pasture where Hutcheon kept his mules. No mules are in sight, but uniformed soldiers exercise a herd of horses in a field this side of the Aramayo *hacienda*. "The army has taken over Chajrahuasi," says Don Wálter, "so we probably won't be able to enter the house, but we can look around the grounds.''

We turn into a long drive flanked by eucalyptus trees and stroll toward the once-grand Italianate villa. A litter of piglets romps in the courtyard of the rustic adobe stable to our right while a sow drinks water from a metal tub nearby. The iron gate at the head of the drive is locked, but a soldier eventually responds to Don Wálter's shouts and lets us in.

Mildew creeps up the beige walls of the house, which sits on a hill. A fortress-like retaining wall supports the flagstone porch that runs across the front of the building, wraps around the side, and culminates in a graceful stairway. Built in 1876 by Félix Avelino Aramayo, who ran the company after his father's demise, Chajrahuasi was a country estate a stone's throw from town. Don Wálter leads us around back, where a swathe of gravel separates the villa from the walled compound that once housed the offices of Aramayo, Francke y Compañía.

"Could there be any records here?" I ask.

"No. This place was ransacked when the mines were nationalized.''

We pass through an arched doorway beside a huge willow and find the offices in ruins. At the end of the corridor, Don Wálter points to a tumbledown room now open to the sky and says, "This is where the manager would have picked up the remittance. The money would have come from La Paz, via Oruro and Potosí, to Tupiza and then to Quechisla."

On the way out, Don Wálter says, "I've been asking around and found out a few things for you. After the *bandoleros* stole the remittance, the Aramayo company turned the miners loose, because it was their payroll that had been stolen. When the two foreigners were cornered near San Vicente, they tossed out the money in hopes of causing confusion. During all the commotion, they managed to escape through the roof."

This sounds like a relative of the folktale we heard about the Villa Mercedes holdup.

"The miners collected all the money," he continues, "and later returned it to the company. The remittance was not guarded, because every family in the region had somebody who worked for the company, so the Aramayos felt completely safe. Only strangers could rob them without being recognized."

We take a shortcut, crossing a tree-trunk bridge over the trickle of water in the river, and walk to the COMIBOL office, once the home of the Aramayo family. Don Wálter unlocks the street door, and we enter a tiny anteroom created by glass and wood partitions. A swinging door leads into the outer office, which holds a couple of empty desks and an old wooden chair. We pass through to his office, furnished with a more substantial desk, a bookcase, a couple of cabinets, and a wooden settee. A door at the rear gives onto a sunny courtyard with French doors leading to the old bedrooms and a passageway leading to the rest of the house.

Back in the front office, Dan has already begun saying goodbye, when I ask, one last time, "Are you absolutely certain that there are no Aramayo records here? The COMIBOL people in both Telamayo and Quechisla specifically said that the documents we need are here."

"I can't imagine what they were talking about," says Don Wálter, "unless they meant the old letter books in the shed out back."

"*¡Exactamente!*" Dan and I say in unison.

Don Wálter leads us back through his office, across the courtyard, and all the way down the passage to an adobe shed the size of a one-car garage. He unlocks the door, and we find ourselves in a dimly lit room with a high ceiling. Against the back wall, beyond the oil drums and old office furniture, hundreds of dusty letter books and ledgers are stacked in random order on broken shelves.

The Aramayo company used the same letter-book system we saw at the National Archives in Washington. In fact, the original letterpress is here on the floor—in our way and too heavy to move. Working by flashlight, we begin pulling out all the books we can get at without bringing the whole mess crashing down on us. The job raises thick clouds of dust, and we encounter a prodigious quantity of rat turds and dead bugs. I begin sneezing at once, and all my Kleenex is soon black and tattered. Don Wálter directs me to an immaculate bathroom with an elegant claw-footed tub and an old-fashioned washbasin, where I scrub my face and hands. With my pockets full of fresh toilet tissue, I return to the shed just as Dan finds a volume labeled "*Noviembre* '8" and shouts, "This is it! This is it!"

But it isn't. The '8 stands for 1898, not 1908.

Shaking his head, Don Wálter comes and goes. He undoubtedly thinks we're crazy.

About thirty books remain in the section we can get at. If what we need isn't among them, we'll have to bring a ladder in here and dismantle the shelves—or give up. But we didn't come this far and get this filthy just to leave without any answers. If the letter book is here, we'll find it. With only five books left in the accessible area, I wipe the dust and dead flies off a battered volume with no jacket. This *is* it: The book contains handwritten copies of all the letters and telegrams sent from the Aramayo company's administrative headquarters in Tupiza in November and December 1908.

We carry the disintegrating book out into the sunlight and gingerly turn the onionskin pages. Don Wálter helps us to decipher the archaic Spanish and florid script of a November 4, 1908, telegram to the Aramayo company's agent in Uyuni: "This morning Mr. Peró was robbed between Salo and Guadalupe by two tall individuals, one slender and the other heavyset, a *gringo* and a Chilean; armed with rifles, they made Mr. Peró hand over the fifteen-thousand-*boliviano* remittance in cash, along with a dark-brown mule, which they took with them. Ask the authorities to capture them. . . . The heavyset man's name is said to be Madariaga."

If one of the bandits was Chilean, then maybe Butch or Sundance or both really *did* survive! Eagerly, we turn the pages and watch the story unfold. A follow-up message advised the Uyuni agent that "an armed force is departing here to pursue the remittance robbers. Make sure that the Uyuni subprefect dispatches armed men to the roads that lead to the train station.'' A letter of confirmation the next day contained more details:

> In a gully between Salo and Guadalupe two Yankees robbed our administrator Carlos Peró of the cash shipment . . . he was delivering to Quechisla for us. This happened yesterday at 9:30 A.M., when our administrator was forced, at rifle point, to open his bags and hand over the company's cash shipment as well as a company-owned dark-brown mule he had with him. Both [bandits] were tall, one thin and the other heavyset. In addition to the rifles, they had revolvers and well-stocked ammunition belts. One also carried binoculars.
>
> Last night a six-man patrol from the Abaroa Regiment departed, and today at 10:00 A.M. five from the same regiment left here following the road to Salo. It is said that some of these soldiers are going through the ravines between Salo and Guadalupe. We hope that you have also asked the Uyuni subprefecture to spread out the patrols along the roads to the main train stations between Uyuni and Antofagasta.

What happened to Madariaga? This letter calls both of the bandits Yankees. That means Butch and Sundance are still in the running—at least until we read the letter sent to the general administrator at Quechisla that same day:

> Mr. Peró was yesterday robbed by two bandits, but he and his son and servant were not harmed. As for the fifteen-thousand-*boliviano* cash shipment that [was stolen], we have taken every measure possible to see the bandits captured. From what information we have, one must be English and the other Chilean, perhaps the same two who asked Mr. Peró for work here in Tupiza. Two patrols have been dispatched . . . by the Abaroa Regiment. One should be near Cotani and the other in Salo, where we have information that two armed individuals who fit the descriptions in his letter were seen.
>
> Mr. Roberts is now operating in Salo and a favorable result is hoped for. The subprefect and, above all, Colonel Baldivieso

have been very helpful in providing support, so necessary in this country without organized police forces. . . . We have just learned that the robbers have not gone toward Oploca.

The Chilean is back. I wish they would make up their minds. And what about the men who asked Peró for work? Could they have been Butch and Sundance casing the joint? Or could they have actually been an Englishman and a Chilean who became the prime suspects simply because they were foreigners? Or were they the real culprits?

On November 6, the Tupiza office wired Roberts in Cotagaita: "A patrol in Salo detained suspects who seem not to be those whom Mr. Peró encountered near Cotani, but they are of the same profession. They are in jail and the judges demand that Mr. Peró come identify them. These bandits are equipped with everything to kill and disable whomever. It has been a good catch . . . even if they are not the same men who attacked Mr. Peró. It would be useful to organize an Indian posse against these evildoers."

This pair must have been Walters and Murray, the suspects mentioned in the Bolivian and Argentine newspaper stories we read back home. They were also the focus of a letter to the general administrator at Quechisla:

> The patrol that went to Salo to arrest the two men (who through certain indications Mr. Roberts believed could be the two who assaulted Mr. Peró) arrived in Salo after Mr. Roberts had left. The patrol arrested the two after some resistance. They are . . . so well armed, munitioned, and equipped to kill and maim that there can be no doubt they belong to a large outlaw gang. . . .
>
> The laborer Llave, who came on his own, saw the two suspects and, according to him, they slept in Cotani Tuesday and were in Cotani Wednesday at 9:00 A.M. From this we infer that they cannot be the two who attacked Mr. Peró and stole the shipment. Regardless, the authorities say that Mr. Peró and his servant must come and identify these two, who resemble the robbers of the remittance. Mr. Peró met both the former and the latter; in view of the hour and the day that they were in Cotani, see whether his coming is necessary.
>
> In the meantime, all necessary measures are being taken.

Another patrol and military detachments have left Uyuni to cover the roads that lead to the railroad stations. We suppose that you must have dispatched the Indian herders from Cotani, Atocha, etc., to search for and capture the robbers.

You should send an employee . . . with the next shipment, which we need to make, along with a good cargo mule and two or three saddled mules for the remittance guards, because we don't have any more company mules here. All Don Manuel's private beasts and Don Avelino's wagon mules are out on patrols.

On November 7, the Aramayo manager wrote a note asking the *corregidor* in the canton of Estarca to "wholeheartedly take up the investigation and call out every available force in pursuit of" the bandits. "It is believed that they may have taken the road to Argentina or the coast." The company hoped to recover, in addition to the cash, the "dark-brown mule, with our Q brand. If you could dispatch a patrol of five or six armed men, have [the bandits] rounded up, and then bring them here under your careful custody, we will pay a handsome reward to their captors." A similar note asked the *corregidor* in Esmoraca to maintain "forceful vigilance and keen scrutiny over the transients from the north who pass through your jurisdiction," as the bandits might be among them. The official was advised to "spare no expense or effort in the investigation and, if possible, dispatch posses of five or six armed men on the roads you think most traveled down to Argentina." The company, naturally, would "cover all expenses."

Finally, on November 8, a telegram to the Uyuni agent broke the news of the shootout: "Yesterday, the seventh, in San Vicente, the payroll bandits were killed by Concha's patrol after putting up resistance. One soldier was killed. If the commander and the soldiers return [to Uyuni] from [San Vicente], reward them well. Find out whether the dead soldier had a family, so that we may help them."

Yes, we know all this. But what *happened* in San Vicente? Maybe we'll find out in the letter sent that day to Carlos Peró, who had reached Quechisla.

Last night we received your letter of the sixth, delivered by Lt. Alcoreza, whose return gave us deep displeasure at the thought that a patrol like that would return without having accomplished its mission as we had expected by continuing to investigate . . . the route that we had thought the bandits who assaulted you must have taken. As we were thinking about this and trying to make the best of lost opportunities, the messenger from Cotani arrived with the note transmitted from San Vicente by Captain Concha, who came from Uyuni, announcing the capture of the bandits in San Vicente on the seventh of this month, yesterday, which means that it was a groundless assumption that the bandits could not have passed by Salo at 12 noon on the fourth. South and west as far as La Quiaca and Esmoraca, precautions had been taken, but along the same road to the south it was more difficult to do so without being seen, which is why the expedition marched toward Tambillo between Cotani and Guadalupe in order to pick up the route from there, cutting off the roads to Uyuni.

In the end, as luck would have it, the Uyuni patrol came to San Vicente, whence we hope it will come hither to report to the authorities in whose jurisdiction the robbery and the capture of the criminals, May They Rest In Peace, took place. . . .

We managed to obtain information, relayed privately to our Manuel E. [Aramayo], that the bandits who had offered their services to you and asked what day you would return [to Quechisla] had expressed willingness to go to the mine in Concordia (Corocoro) once they had finished a job or business they had pending here.

With what happened in San Vicente, calm has returned, and there is no longer any reason to be worried about those bad moments that you have had, nor about the agitation that we have had until this morning at 10:30.

Calm will not return to this patio until we find out just what *did* happen in San Vicente! But the letter adds only that a messenger had brought ''an official letter for the subprefect and district attorney, confirming the gunfight in which the bandits died,'' and that Captain Concha's whereabouts were unknown. ''He should have come here, because San Vicente is under the jurisdiction of Sud Chichas.''

After petitioning the minister of war to provide police patrols to accompany future remittances and sending word of the shootout to officials in all the communities that had been on the lookout for the bandits, the Aramayo administrators in Tupiza set about trying to recover their money and mule from the authorities in Uyuni, where Captain Concha evidently went. A letter from Tupiza manager Manuel E. Aramayo to the company's Uyuni agent said that the "only objective we are pursuing is the recovery of that which has been stolen from us. Judges there cannot address matters of other jurisdictions. . . . The district attorney orders the case to be judged here. We do not want to happen with our cash shipment what happened with the bismuth. And you must see that the remittance, mule, etc. are returned here without delay. We do not understand the judge's tenacity in adjudicating the captors and retaining our recovered property there."

In a letter to a member of the Aramayo family who was living in Antofagasta, the Tupiza manager wrote that "every report from Uyuni you have received about this disagreeable incident is correct. We have passed some truly bothersome days and even now we are almost back to where we began, because to recover the cash shipment, we must fight the judges, a task more difficult than the operation against the bandits." We find nothing to indicate whether the company ever recovered its property.

According to a November 15 letter, Carlos Peró, his son Mariano, and his servant were to meet the magistrate and district attorney in San Vicente "to clarify matters, identify the bandits, and carry out the judicial process so that [they] might regain the payroll that was recovered but incorrectly sent to Uyuni." The book contains nothing about the outcome of this proceeding. The last letter of interest is dated November 24:

> Enclosed is a certificate from the chief magistrate of Talina and a letter from Liborio Aramayo at Churquipampa establishing that the bearer, Juan de Dios Torres, is the father of the soldier Victor Torres, who died at San Vicente and who was the legitimate son of [Juan de Dios Torres] and Francisca Avilez.
>
> In case you have not yet paid the settlement or reward (lump sum) granted the parents of the soldier Torres, please deliver it to them with the necessary conditions and send us a receipt in duplicate.
>
> From all the investigations to date, we know that the captain of the patrol did not comport himself in the capture of the

bandits with the stature that we had thought, and he is not deserving of the reward that we had been thinking of giving him.

Not only did they fail to tell us what happened in San Vicente, but they left us this bombshell about Captain Concha! What could he have done to disgrace himself? Did he solicit a bribe from the bandits? Did he run when the shooting started? If only we had the Aller report.

The punctilious Don Wálter is reluctant to let us copy the documents, despite the letter from his boss instructing him to give us every assistance. His telephone is not working, so the three of us troop down to the old customs house and wait in line to place a call by radiophone to Telamayo. Eventually, we reach the radio room in Telamayo, and someone there relays Don Wálter's question to Juan Cabrera and runs back to the radio room with his favorable reply.

Once Don Wálter is satisfied, we set off to photocopy the fifty pages related to the holdup and shootout. The Telamayo office wants a set of copies, and we decide to make two sets for ourselves and carry them in different bags for insurance. Unfortunately, the only photocopier in town has a broken paper tray, so 150 sheets of paper must be fed into the machine one at a time. And because the documents are on onionskin, each page must be backed with an opaque sheet to prevent other documents in the book from showing through. The operator of the machine frequently takes time out to sell phonograph records, cassette tapes, and film. Prints from every roll of film he processes are displayed under glass on the counters, and the small store swarms with giggling teenagers who have stopped by to look for themselves in the latest batch of snapshots. After an hour, the end of the copying job is nowhere in sight. I'm so hot, I feel faint. "I'll meet you in the plaza," I tell Dan.

I find a shady spot among the pines and palm trees on the bench opposite the door of the shop. Shoeshine boys scurry around looking for customers, and ice-cream vendors in white smocks pedal by on bicycles outfitted with coolers. There aren't many cars in Tupiza, but everyone in town must own a bike. Kids race theirs through the streets, and old men wheel theirs along at a leisurely pace. Teenagers stream in and out of the photo store, but another hour passes before Don Wálter and Dan emerge.

Having eaten nothing since breakfast, Dan and I head for the nearest café. We gulp cold beer and devour ham-and-cheese sandwiches, then begin transcribing the old-fashioned script into something we can read more easily. Meanwhile, day turns into night, the café turns into a bar, and brawls break out around us. Absorbed in our task, we notice none of this until a drunk crashes into our table.

Dawn finds us sitting in Froilán Martínez's red Toyota pickup, waiting for the gas station to open. Assorted plastic and metal containers are lined up at the pump, and their owners pace back and forth to shake off the morning chill. Once the tank is full, Martínez starts the engine, and we set out for Salo, where he grew up. He worked as a miner in Potosí for a time, but the conditions were so dangerous and unhealthy that he quit, moved to Tupiza, opened a small restaurant, and moonlights as a driver for hire.

Beyond Tupiza, we pass a police checkpoint, then thread our way through low sandstone hills. Like Gaudíesque gateposts, two dark red spires frame the entrance to a broad valley planted with beans and corn. The road skirts the valley and then drops us onto the Salo River *lecho*. We drive north on the gravel riverbed, soft green hills on one side and clay buttes bristled with cacti and thorn bushes on the other. Periodically, Martínez stops to buy *chicha* from vendors in tents made from leafy branches propped up in the middle of the *lecho*.

"Do you want some?" he asks.

I shake my head. I'm thirsty, but not *that* thirsty.

"No thanks," says Dan.

"This valley is so peaceful," I say. "Why did you leave it?"

"There is no electricity, and the only activity is subsistence farming. The young people, they all move to Tupiza or Argentina. Years ago, Argentines came with wagons and recruited entire families to go south to work cane or cotton. They were treated badly, like slaves."

Beside a stretch of sandstone palisades, Martínez stops the truck and jumps out to study the underside of the vehicle. "Just as I suspected," he announces, "the spring is broken." He has brought no tools or spare parts but, with Dan's help, manages to jack up the truck with a piece of wood supported by an ever-higher pile of rocks. While the two men wrestle with the task of fixing the spring, I watch a herd of goats drinking from a rill on the edge of the *lecho*.

At Salo, mimosas and willows surround the ruins of the Aramayo *hacienda*, where Carlos Peró spent the night. A drainage ditch separates the *hacienda* from the rest of Salo, which comprises little more than a few adobe huts and a soccer field. A *campesino* tells us that it takes twelve hours to walk to Cotani, on the slopes of Chorolque near Guadalupe. The man doesn't know anything about the Aramayo holdup, let alone where it took place.

We return to the truck and drive west into the amber hills. From a roadside butte abloom with cactus flowers, Martínez points out the trail followed by Peró's party in 1908 and still in use today. Telegraph poles along the path remind us that the records made no mention of the lines' having been cut. This troubles us because, in view of their reputation for careful planning, we feel certain that Butch and Sundance would have cut them.

"Can we drive closer to the trail?" asks Dan.

"No, the road cuts away to the north just around that curve up ahead."

In other words, if we want to see where the holdup happened, we'll have to walk to Guadalupe. Still sneezing from our day in the shed, I'm not in any shape for a twelve-hour hike at ten thousand feet—especially when we would walk right past the spot without recognizing it.

9 · CHILEAN HOPSCOTCH

B ETWEEN Tupiza and Antofagasta lies the Atacama Desert. Attempting to cross it in Martínez's truck would be foolhardy, if not
downright suicidal, so we opt to return to Uyuni, where we can hire a
sturdier vehicle or, if necessary, take a train. I fall asleep shortly after
boarding the *ferrobus* and don't wake up until it squeals into the Uyuni
station. While I wait with our bags and chat with Don Jesús in his hotel,

Dan looks for transportation to Chile. Rail service to the coast may have been first-class in Butch and Sundance's day, but the train no longer has heat, let alone the luxury of dining cars and sleeping compartments. A seat assignment doesn't guarantee a seat, and smugglers sometimes throw luggage off the cars to make more room for contraband. Furthermore, the change of trains at the border can leave passengers scrambling for seats or waiting for hours in the freezing cold. I still haven't recovered from breathing the dust in the COMIBOL shed and would just as soon avoid all this.

At Don Jesús's suggestion, we hire tour-company owners Ciprián and Antonia Nina to drive us to a mining camp at Laguna Verde, a spectacular green lake in the southwestern corner of Bolivia by the Chilean border. From there, we should be able to hitch a ride on a mining truck to Calama, where we can easily find transport to Antofagasta. This is not the quickest route, and we will run the risk of being stranded at the lake for a couple of days, but the austere scenery should more than compensate for any delay.

Dressed in blue all the way up to his baseball cap, Ciprián collects us at midday in a 1981 Datsun double-cab pickup stocked with barrels of gasoline, a winch, camping gear, eight liters of bottled water, two dozen *salteñas* for snacking, and enough provisions for several meals. We stop by the Ninas' house to pick up Antonia, who has jet black hair with bangs and a ponytail tied back with a white scarf. Her hair, her blue jeans, and her gold fingernail polish seem incongruous in this town where most women her age wear braids, skirts, and bowler hats. Although Antonia grew up nearby, she and Ciprián lived in Buenos Aires for years and only recently returned to Bolivia, fleeing the overheated pace and perils of urban life.

The first leg of our journey takes us some fifty miles across a wedge of the Salar de Uyuni, the crystalized remains of a vast inland sea. The blinding white expanse is broken only by rocky islands, where chinchilla-like *vizcachas* dart among cacti and *ichu* grass. "People always assume the rock is volcanic, because it is porous, like pumice," says Ciprián, "but actually it is fossilized algae."

Antonia points to a marker in the middle of nowhere and says, "The grave of a man who tried to walk across the *salar*. He thought he could make it, but he died of thirst halfway."

Although drivers prefer this smooth surface to the sand and mud of the other routes, the *salar* exacts heavy penalties from anyone who underestimates its dangers. Chief among these is the possibility of breaking through the crust of minerals—mostly salt, borax, and gypsum, with a dash of lithium—and sinking into the plasticine mud that lies below it. The crust varies in thickness from six inches to about two feet, and a recent rainfall has left some areas distinctly unstable. Whenever we hit a weak patch, Ciprián immediately changes direction, as if piloting a dodgem car. Sometimes he stops the truck and tests the crust on foot before proceeding.

As we approach a small town on the southern edge of the *salar*, the top layer of salt turns to slush and then to water. Two hundred yards from the shore, a rusting bus with bags piled on the roof is marooned in half a foot of brine. The passengers—women in fringed shawls and bright skirts and men in everything from homespun clothes to jogging suits—struggle to push the bus out of the mire. Unable to slow down, lest we wind up in the same predicament, we splash past the bus and head for shore. From the safety of dry land, I gaze back at the forlorn tableau reflected in the salty pond, and our rattling truck suddenly seems like a limousine.

The dirt road runs past low hills covered with *ichu*; the stone walls of abandoned corrals are laid out like rosaries on the slopes. In a small field watched over by a ragged scarecrow, a *campesina* in a celery-colored sweater, pink skirt, and battered brown fedora tends a field of orange and green *quinoa*, a type of millet. "*Quinoa* is good for you," says Ciprián. "The people around here live to be a hundred and twenty, and they are very intelligent."

"You can make salad with the young leaves," says Antonia.

Eleven *vicuñas* browse in a fan of *tola* bushes on a yellow plain as whirlwinds dance across the sand. Blue hills mirrored in the wet *salar* shimmer on the horizon.

At a small fort, Antonia passes out Jehovah's Witness pamphlets to the soldiers who come to check our papers before allowing us to proceed. "Now don't throw them away," she admonishes the youths. "Give them to the library."

We spend the night in an adobe compound in the village of San Juan. The whitewashed walls of our room, which opens off a large patio, are decorated with pictures of Christ and the Virgin Mary as well as a pink-and-green crepe-paper clown made by the owners' nine-year-old daughter, Elvira. Standing in the patio, Ciprián points to a cluster of fifty strange rock formations on a nearby mesa and suggests that Elvira give us a tour.

"Oh yes!" says Antonia, who is setting up a camp stove. "You must see the *chullpas!* Dinner will take nearly an hour to prepare, so there is no need for you to hang around here."

Unsure of what *chullpas* are but inferring that they are related to the arrowheads Elvira and her sister have shown us, we set off across the brown field. The sun's rays slant low across the mountains and gild the herds of sheep and *llamas* converging on San Juan after a day of chomping *tola* and *ichu* under the watchful eyes of shepherd children. Wrapped in a blue-and-white blanket that hides everything but her eyes and her thin, bare legs, Elvira is hard to draw out. By the time we have covered the half-mile separating the town and our goal, all we have elicited is that the *chullpas* are connected to "the grandfathers."

Coughing, gasping for air, and wishing I had stayed behind in San Juan, I follow Dan and Elvira up onto the mesa. More like beehives than rocks, the formations look almost as if they had been made by hand with coral and mud. Farther into the petrified apiary, some of the hives have cracked open, revealing hollow interiors. They *must* be man-made.

"Good Lord!"

Dan has spotted a hive that is hollow but not empty: It contains a sun-bleached human skull atop a pile of bones. We pause to gape at them and then move on through a necropolis littered with the remains of Elvira's ancestors: not her grandfathers—they're buried in the town cemetery—but grandfathers of grandfathers of grandfathers, dating who knows how far back. To my surprise, I don't feel squeamish at the sight of all these bones. They are so white that they look unreal, almost plastic. But the sensation I experienced in the San Vicente cemetery— the feeling of being an intruder—floods over me again.

After a meal of spicy *llama* stew and a chilly trip to the municipal outhouse under an orange sky, Dan and I curl up in a narrow bed borrowed from Elvira, who is bunking with one of her seven siblings. The mattress is lumpy, and the pillow is as hard as a sandbag. Dan falls asleep at once, but I lie awake coughing until long after the electricity has died for the night.

Before dawn, we hurriedly wash a breakfast of cookies down with orange juice and coffee, then load the truck. The sun rises as we head southwest through the beige Salar de Chiguana. Beyond the salt sits the town of Chiguana, which is little more than a military outpost and checkpoint. The soldiers eye us suspiciously, check our papers, and wave us through.

Shortly after turning south into the Atacama Desert, we spy smoke wisping from the Ollagüe volcano. The leathery skin of the nearby hills appears to be peeling off, as if the earth were sunburned. We pass saline ponds and peaks marbled green with copper, pink with manganese, orange with iron, and yellow with sulfur. Two *vicuñas* lope across a gravel plain, where the only plants are ground-hugging clumps of *yareta*. And then there is no vegetation at all, nothing but sand—pale, luminous sand—and the soft-hued mountains.

We break for lunch at the pimento-colored Laguna Colorada. Dan and I carry our food up onto a hillside with a commanding view of the lake. The short climb, at an altitude of nearly sixteen thousand feet, is almost more than my lungs can handle, and I reach our picnic spot exhausted. Sitting on a boulder among golden tufts of *ichu* grass, nibbling on a piece of goat cheese, and watching the James and Andean flamingos feed on the algae that tints the water, I wish I felt well enough to enjoy the trip. I can't remember the last time I had such a bad cold. Feverish and weak, I inch down the hill, rinse my hands in a hot spring beside the shore, and return to the truck for a nap.

I awaken as we drive across a tawny plain strewn with boulders. Ciprián stops the truck, and we follow Antonia to a rumpled patch of ground where the soil seems to have melted. Noisome vapors rise from dozens of salt-encrusted cauldrons of bubbling cement soup. "Don't get too close," admonishes Antonia. "People have been known to fall in or be splattered." As if on cue, a quart of grey mud belches from the nearest hole.

We drive on through increasingly barren terrain: Only the occasional mineral-stained pond and the pastel mountains provide any color, and the temperature often drops below minus 20 degrees Fahrenheit at night. In the Pampa Chiviri, wind-carved boulders rise from the sand to form a Martian sculpture garden. In the late afternoon, the 19,410-foot volcano Licancábur grows larger and larger in the frame of the windshield. At last, Ciprián stops the truck on a bluff opposite the volcano. In the gypsum-rimmed bowl beneath us lies the Laguna Verde. A stiff breeze ripples the deep-green water as we follow the sandy road around the eastern shore and up to the small mining camp on the shoulder of the volcano.

We have planned to spend the night here, but Señor Félix Colque, the owner of a local sulfur mine, is just about to leave for his home in Chile. He says he would be happy to give us a lift to Calama, which has good hotels and buses to Antofagasta. If we don't go with him now, we might have to wait several days for a ride. All I want to do is lie down, but I'll feel wretched no matter where I am, so we might as well push on to a place with comfortable beds.

"Do you still have the *vicuña*?" Antonia asks the camp's caretaker.

"*Sí, sí.* It's down below."

"May we give it some of this stale bread?" she asks, then turns to Señor Colque. "You can wait five minutes while we visit the *vicuña*, no?"

"Of course."

Antonia leads us past a couple of outbuildings and down a scree-covered slope to a ledge overlooking the adobe pen in which the *vicuña* is imprisoned. The animal looks up with baleful eyes. While Antonia tears the bread into chunks and tosses them into the pen, I study the gate that stands between the *vicuña* and liberty. There is no lock, just a piece of wire twisted around a post. Compared to a Patagonian gate latch, this would be a cinch to open.

"Dan," I whisper. "Let's stay here tonight and turn it loose."

"We can't do that."

"Why not? *Vicuñas* were meant to roam the plains, not waste away in cages where they can barely move. Isn't it a protected species?"

"Probably, but we're not game wardens. Besides, how long would it last all by itself in the desert with no *tola* to eat?"

"I bet it would rather die in the wild than spend its life locked up."

As we debate the animal's future, Señor Colque honks his horn. Leaving the *vicuña* to fend for itself, we pile into a big grey pickup.

"I must stop here for a moment," says Señor Colque. He turns onto a side road and drives up to a flat mountaintop surrounded by volcanic peaks. Chunks of sulfur stream from the tilted bed of a dump truck and fill the air with yellow dust. The resulting heap seems strangely inviting, like a pile of leaves waiting for kids to jump into it.

Once Señor Colque returns to the truck, we coast downhill about thirty miles to the sixteenth-century village of San Pedro, garden spot of the Atacama. This oasis with sixteen hundred residents has been so overrun by gringo tourists that multilingual signs saying HOT WATER or PLEASE RETURN BOTTLES HERE decorate the hotels and stores lining the few narrow streets. We pass through customs unscathed and, as the sun drops below the horizon, race along a gravel road overlooking the volcanic sand dunes and gnarled rocks of the Valley of the Moon.

I sleep most of the sixty miles to Calama, a city of a hundred thousand near the province's only significant river. When Señor Colque asks where we want to go, Dan says, "Take us to the best hotel in town." The hotel is full, and Dan asks me if I'm up to a bus ride.

"I don't care where we go, so long as I don't have to arrange it."

Señor Colque drives us to the bus station, where we learn that the last bus has already left. In the end, we hire a taxi for the 130-mile journey. After all the bouncing we've done in the past couple of weeks, the paved road is hypnotic. I put my head in Dan's lap and fall asleep.

The route from Calama to Antofagasta takes us through a bleak region where dense fogs and lightning are common, but rain falls only once or twice in the space of fifty years. The sun is fierce, the wind impetuous, the soil highly radioactive. Most of the necessities of life—water, fuel, and provisions—must be imported. And yet, between 1880 and 1920, more than half of the Chilean government's revenue came from export duties paid by the largely foreign-owned companies mining the area's vast deposits of sodium nitrate, a rich natural fertilizer and (along with sulfur and charcoal) a basic ingredient of gunpowder.

The development of synthetic methods of fixing nitrogen decimated Chile's nitrate industry during World War I, but in Butch and Sundance's day, the boom was still on. Workers blasted *caliche*—a mixture of raw nitrates, sulfates, halides, and sand—from beds about seven to ten feet thick near the surface of the ground. Dressed in twilled baize pants, loose shirts (or none at all), wide belts to help prevent hernias, Andalusian hats with holes for ventilation, kerchiefs, gaiters, and bulky shoes made of pigskin with thick, rigid soles, the laborers removed the broken mass of material and discarded the useless pieces. After packing the remaining blocks of *caliche* into sacks and hoisting them onto their shoulders, the workers ran several yards with loads weighing as much as three hundred pounds and boosted them onto carts or tramcars to be hauled to *oficinas* for processing. Once there, the *caliche* was pulverized by huge crushers, dissolved in boiling water, decanted in tanks, and crystalized in flat basins. The liquid that remained yielded iodine, another profitable commodity.

The *oficinas* were more than mere refineries: They were industrial towns with houses, shops, stores, schools, hospitals, police barracks, theaters, workshops, and even magazines of their own. Unfortunately, as company towns are wont to do, the *oficinas* controlled the workers' lives to a degree that bred bitterness. In the early 1900s, the nitrate workers clamored for wages commensurate with their physical exertions and for better living conditions, including clean, comfortable dwellings and potable water. Perhaps the greatest sources of discontent were the overpriced company stores, the *pulperías,* at which employees were required to do all their shopping. Anything purchased elsewhere was considered contraband, and workers were subject to dismissal if caught buying it. A 1904 government commission put a stop to this system.

In view of Butch and Sundance's populist leanings, the nitrate companies would have made natural targets for Wild Bunch holdups, but we have found no evidence that the pair ever robbed a nitrate payroll or a bank full of nitrate-company money. Of course, the scarcity of water would have made a getaway over this terrain particularly difficult to arrange: The bandits could hardly have picketed a series of fresh horses on the desert for any length of time.

In the early part of the century, a shortage of labor in the mining, agricultural, and manufacturing industries impelled the Chilean government to encourage immigration and even to furnish free transportation and guarantee jobs for experienced tradesmen and professionals. During 1907, this policy attracted more than eight thousand immigrants to Chile, but the number declined rapidly when the requirements were tightened to bar "the arrival of undesirable, useless, and dangerous elements." About a thousand North Americans resided in Chile when Butch and Sundance were here. Those who lived in Antofagasta tended not to mingle with the local population except in the course of their work as engineers, *oficina* managers, or agents for international firms. Unlike the Germans, Italians, French, Greeks, and Yugoslavs, who remained and became Chileans, most of the North Americans and Britons who came to northern Chile stayed for a while and then went home.

Perhaps the Anglos had difficulty adjusting to a landscape without trees or grass. In those days, water was too precious to waste on plants. Before 1905, when a local company began piping potable water from the mountains to Antofagasta, the city's twenty thousand residents drank water brought by ship or collected in barrels from condensation machines installed at various points in the city to harvest moisture from the fog.

In 1904, when Butch and Sundance probably first came to Antofagasta, the city had recently converted from gas to electric lighting. Modern streetcars ran alongside horse-drawn coaches and wagons on unpaved streets so dusty that the wooden sidewalks had to be swept twice a day. Clubs and hotels offered "warm and cold baths," and restaurants served everything from caviar and truffles to German potato salad and chateaubriand. Irish whiskey, Havana cigars, Argentine milk, Oregon pine, Portland cement, Scottish explosives, and whatever else a homesick immigrant might yearn for could be found in the shops and galvanized-iron warehouses stocked by the hundreds of sailing ships and steamers that came to pick up the nitrate, borax, silver, copper, and other minerals mined or smelted nearby. Launches ferried merchandise from the ships to the wharf, and the bundles and boxes destined for local merchants or the *oficinas* often wound up stacked in the street, causing traffic jams.

Although the nitrate industry has dwindled, Antofagasta has grown into a city of two hundred thousand, and the turn-of-the-century buildings are interspersed with modern shopping galleries. The sidewalks, now made of concrete and no longer swept twice daily, are spattered with pigeon droppings, but the city has two universities, a grand stadium, and several parks.

"We're here, kiddo," says Dan, shaking me gently. While he pays the taxi driver, I follow our bags up a few steps and into a hotel that looks like a giant brick with windows. The desk clerk has left his post momentarily, but the bellhop, a beefy man in a navy jumpsuit, says, "What kind of room do you want, *señora?*"

"A double."

"What kind of double?" He points to a board listing at least a dozen types of rooms and suites and their prices, which vary according to location, beds (twin or *matrimonial*), and whether a minibar has been installed.

"I can't think about it right now," I say. "You'll have to talk to my—"

As I ponder the nuances of *marido* (husband) versus *esposo* (spouse),

the bellhop finishes my sentence with the phrase *jefe, él que manda* (chief, he who commands).

"Whatever."

Dan and the desk clerk join us and take charge of the matter. "Would you like a room with an ocean view?" asks the clerk.

The alternative being a room with a busy-street view, Dan says yes.

The clerk hands a key to the hovering bellhop as several women in evening gowns and men in dinner jackets cross the lobby to the terrace, where scores of waiters attend dozens of tables arrayed around a large swimming pool.

"Is somebody having a wedding?" Dan asks.

"No, no," the clerk assures him. "Just a little celebration to inaugurate the pool for the Christmas season."

Even when I'm not sick, Christmas always seems surreal in the Southern Hemisphere, where the seasons are upside down.

"Is there a band? We need a quiet room."

I feel so rotten, I don't give a damn where we sleep. I just want to lie down—anywhere. The floor of the lobby would do.

"Oh no. There is no band."

But there is a disc jockey with a phonograph and a stack of North American disco records. The hotel's air conditioning apparently hasn't been inaugurated for the season, so we must open the window or swelter. The music throbs incessantly.

After a night of hacking and wheezing, I drag myself down to breakfast in the coffee shop, where small speakers on the walls play soft rock and Las Vegas tunes but nary a note of Latin American music. Although no more than two of the sixteen tables are occupied at any one time, the coffee shop is staffed by a team of obsequious waiters, who bring us Nescafé and a platter of pastries instead of the *café con leche*, orange juice, and *media lunas* we have ordered. When Dan points out the discrepancy, the headwaiter berates the underlings, and the food goes back to the kitchen. Ten minutes later, a new tray appears with one cup of *espresso*, three *media lunas*, and one glass of freshly squeezed juice "enhanced" by Tang.

Dan takes the *espresso*; I take the juice and choke it down between coughing fits.

"Are you okay?" asks Dan.

"I'm afraid you're on your own today. I'll be lucky to make it back upstairs."

While I cough nonstop and soak the sheets with sweat, Dan goes to the vital-statistics office to find out whether a death certificate was issued for anyone with an alias used in South America by Butch or Sundance. The clerk searches the records and finds only one entry that might be related to the bandits: The 1908 death of "*n. n.* Madariaga." Not only was Madariaga the name of the mysterious Chilean cited in some of the Aramayo papers, but *n. n.—ningun nombre* (no name)—was the designation under which the Aramayo bandits were buried, according to the cover letter that was sent to Frank Aller with the missing ten-page report on the San Vicente shootout.

Dan next stops at the local headquarters of the *carabineros,* the federal police force, and checks the registration cards of foreigners living in Antofagasta. The cards go back no further than the 1940s. He then visits the Antofagasta jail, which was built in the early 1900s. We wrote to the warden last year in an effort to verify the Pinkerton tipster's claim that Butch served time here, but we received no answer. In an office where an artificial Christmas tree stands beside a window with a view of palm trees and sunshine, Dan learns that the warden is no longer here. A guard remembers our letter, however, and says, "Many of the records were eaten by rats, and others were lost in the course of being moved." Five staff members join the search but find nothing earlier than 1960.

At the office of the provincial *conservador* and *archivero,* Dan looks for information about any wills, estates, or property the bandits might have left. Because the diplomatic correspondence mentioned that a judge needed Sundance's death certificate in order to settle his estate, we have had hopes of finding the Aller report here. A staff member says, however, that all files dating back thirty years or more must be sent to the Archivo Nacional in Santiago. Dan heads for the nearest travel agent and books passage on the next morning's plane to Santiago.

Having been up all night coughing, I can barely make it into the shower. The cough syrup Dan picked up for me has had no effect whatsoever. Every breath feels like broken glass scraping across the lining of my lungs. If I could push a button and instantly cease to exist, I would do so. The taxi ride to the airport seems interminable, the wait in the departure lounge intolerable. The plane ride is torture, and the descent leaves me with a double earache.

While Dan uses a pay phone in the airport to line up a hotel room,

I guard our bags nearby. Several taxi drivers begin pestering me to hire them for the ride into Santiago. I point to Dan and croak, "You'll have to ask my *jefe, él que manda.*" Without a moment's hesitation, they scurry off in his direction and leave me in peace.

Once we have settled into our hotel, which occupies several floors of an office building in the heart of Santiago, Dan heads for the Archivo Nacional. My left ear soon pops open and I can almost hear again. The right ear, however, continues to hurt and is still fogged when Dan comes back to the hotel during the *siesta.* "How are you feeling?" he asks.

"Not so hot. I think I need a doctor."

"I'll call Mike." Dan picks up the phone and dials his brother-in-law's office in Virginia. After describing my symptoms, Dan listens for a moment and then turns to me. "He wants to know whether the phlegm is green or yellow."

"Pink," I gasp.

"She says it's pink." Dan watches me and listens to Mike, then announces, "It's pneumonia."

Mike prescribes antibiotics, and I ask Dan to find out how to unplug my ear.

"Take a decongestant, wait an hour, hold your nose, close your mouth, and blow."

I carry out Mike's instructions and my ear opens at once. The antibiotics—available over the counter in Latin America—quickly cure what's left of the infection in my toe and, after a couple of weeks, beat the pneumonia, which I apparently picked up from the COMIBOL dust.

In the meantime, Dan continues researching alone. At the Archivo Nacional, the curator advises him to look for Sundance's property first and his will afterward. "If there was a problem with the death," she says, "they probably would have gone to court in Antofagasta to have him declared dead, and the records would be in the Archivo Judicial. You should also try the Registros Conservatorios, because property transfers are sometimes recorded there but *not* here."

When he finishes skimming the ancient leather-bound volumes containing Antofagasta's real-property and notarial registers for the relevant years, he checks the property transfers recorded in the Registros Conservatorios but finds nothing. In his letters to the American legation in La Paz, Frank Aller never specified what Sundance's estate comprised: It could have been anything from a house to a bank account. Upon learning that estates not containing real property would have been addressed only in the court records, Dan visits the Archivo Judicial, where he is told that Antofagasta's judicial records from 1821 to date are still in Antofagasta.

Eventually, we return to Antofagasta. In a modern office building on the main plaza, the *conservador* and *archivero* tells us, "For information about property, you must go to the Archivo Nacional in Santiago." After we explain the circumstances, he says that we might be able to find a record of the bandits' deaths by looking at the index to civil cases in the offices of the court known as the *primer juzgado de letras*, which is above the nearby post office. "The two types of cases you should look for in the index are *posesión efectiva de herencia* [actual possession of inheritance] or *muerte presunta* [presumed death]. If you find such a case in the name of any of the parties you are seeking, you can use the case number to locate the file."

At the *juzgado*, a friendly clerk in the cramped records office finds the criminal- and civil-case indexes under the counter.

"You may read them in the hall if you want. You might be more comfortable there."

Dan takes the civil index and hands me the criminal index, and we repair to a long wooden bench in the wide hall. A born speed-reader, Dan zips through his volume and begins helping me read mine. Peering over my shoulder, he says, "You look at the dates and the types of cases, and I'll read the names."

The index isn't alphabetized or arranged in chronological order; on any given page, the dates jump around through several decades between the late 1890s and the 1970s. Although turn-of-the-century cases pop up throughout the book, the cases at the end tend to be older, so we read the volume backward. Many cases are identified only by number, with no clues as to what they were about or who was involved. If Butch and Sundance had any dealings with the criminal court of Antofagasta, you'd never know it by looking here. As the *siesta* break approaches, we race through the remaining pages and call it quits.

"Maybe the indexes in Santiago will be more useful," says Dan as we walk to the nearby office of Horacio Chávez. A middle-aged lawyer in a bulging sharkskin suit, Señor Chávez overheard us discussing our project with the *conservador* and *archivero* and invited us to visit him later to discuss approaches to legal research in Chile. Heaven knows, we could use some tips.

Señor Chávez shakes Dan's hand and greets me with a big wet kiss on the mouth, and we sit on overstuffed chairs upholstered in lawyer's leather. "The information you seek might be in Iquique," he says, lisping like a Spaniard. As he speaks, his eyebrows jump up and down. "The Archivo Nacional in Santiago has titles to residential property before 1945. You could also check the register of mortgages." He raises his legs and claps his feet together. "Of course, if the property was in the form of bank deposits, that would not be in any register."

On our way out, I get another kiss and a smothering embrace.

The overnight bus from Antofagasta to Santiago has every convenience, including the services of a steward and a television set playing old movies dubbed in Spanish. We reach Santiago during the morning rush hour, check into our high-rise hotel, and hie to the Archivo Judicial. Our search begins in a basement room jammed with people who are waiting for record books at a long counter. The clerks joke with one another and toss red-jacketed volumes around like slabs of meat while the patrons jockey for position and yell out their requests. I feel like a country girl on her first visit to a New York deli. When a clerk finally notices us, we describe what we're looking for. He says that we're in the wrong office, then tells us where we should go, but we have difficulty following his heavy Santiago accent, with its truncated words and breakneck delivery. When he repeats his instructions for the third time, we still don't catch the name of the office, but we grasp that it is on the first floor.

We walk upstairs and begin looking at the signs on the offices lining a cavernous atrium. A security guard crosses the marble floor to ask whether we need help. We launch into our spiel, and the guard says that the office we should visit is on the second floor. Up we go. Eventually, we find ourselves at the supreme court librarian's office in what seems to be the attic. The librarian advises us to contact Bernardino Bravo Lira, a Chinese-Chilean professor of history and law. Before lunch, we stop by the professor's office, but he is out.

In the afternoon, armed with lists of the various registers we've been told to check, we take a taxi to the Archivo Nacional. Although Dan spent hours looking through files here on our previous visit, the clerk in the reception area tells us that we cannot enter the archives. We find this hard to believe, but the supervisor confirms it. Our only recourse is to pay a fee equivalent to three dollars and file a *solicitud* specifying the documents we need, then wait for the staff to find them. "The search will take at least twenty days," says supervisor Ricardo Valenzuela. "If we find anything, we will write and tell you the costs of photocopying the documents."

Back at the hotel, a message from Professor Bravo Lira awaits us. When we finally reach him, he suggests that we revisit the Archivo Judicial and ask to see the indexes of the civil cases located there. "Good luck," he says.

But luck is scarce in Chile. We return to the archives, only to be told that although the files we want are here in this office, the indexes are in Antofagasta.

"Couldn't we just look at all the files for the relevant years?" asks Dan.

"No," says the clerk. "In order to look at any file, you must have the case number. And to obtain the case number, you must look in the index."

"And to look in the index," I say, "we must go to Antofagasta."

"Exactly."

"Well," says Dan as we leave the basement, "that's the end of that."

"Why?"

"We read the indexes in Antofagasta and didn't find anything."

"But we were in a hurry and might have missed something. The indexes were so disorganized. We really should have spent more time and gone over them from cover to cover."

"It never dawned on me that they wouldn't have an index in the place that had the files."

"Well, we don't have time to go back to Antofagasta, so let's hope the staff at the Archivo Nacional is better than we are at figuring out what to look for and knowing where to find it."

We return to the States with our fingers crossed, but each day that passes without a letter from the Archivo Nacional dims our hopes that the *solicitud* will yield what we are looking for. Finally, after two months of waiting, we call Ricardo Valenzuela and ask whether they have found anything for us. "We're not finished yet," he says. "A lot of people are on holiday, but I will advise you by mail as soon as the research is complete." He doesn't write, and our follow-up letter asking him to let us know the results of the search elicits no response. Six months later, we still haven't heard from him, so we telephone his office and learn that he is on vacation. After his return, we place another call. "Señor Valenzuela is ill today," his colleague informs us, "but he said to tell you that he found nothing. *Nada.*"

By this time, however, we have no faith that he actually bothered to look. We enlist the aid of a high-ranking official—the friend of a friend of a friend—in the Chilean Ministry of Justice. She writes a letter asking the director of the Archivo Nacional to ascertain whether the archives contain the registers where the information would appear if it existed and whether we could hire a professional researcher to check the relevant volumes. The director never responds.

In the end, we decide to make one last trip in search of the report sent to Frank Aller. We'll stay in Antofagasta for a week, retrace all of our previous steps, and follow the new leads we've developed since our last visit. If we find a case number, we'll return to Santiago.

After arriving in Antofagasta, our first task is to recheck the indexes for the court cases. We make our way up to the second floor of the post-office building, down the wide hall, and into the crowded records office of the *juzgado*. The friendly clerk who helped us last time has been replaced by someone who doesn't know the ropes yet. A well-dressed woman with dark hair pulled back into a bun approaches the counter. She speaks softly to the clerk, who says, "I wouldn't know about that," and turns to help a man with a stack of paperwork. The woman meekly steps to the rear of the room. After everyone else has been served, the clerk asks what we want.

"She was before us," says Dan, gesturing to the woman, who is fighting back tears.

"She will have to wait," says the clerk.

Dan asks to see the indexes for the old court cases.

"*No hay,*" says the clerk. There aren't any.

"Sure there are. They're about so big," says Dan, shaping a rectangle in the air, "and they list all the cases tried in this court since the late 1800s."

187

"No, we have nothing like that here."

"Yes you do. One of them has a green cover. I think the other is black."

"Never heard of them. Next?" The clerk turns to three men who have just walked in.

Once the office has cleared out again—except for the sad-eyed woman—Dan says, "The indexes must be here somewhere. We saw them last year."

"You must have seen them somewhere else."

I've been letting Dan handle this transaction, because his Spanish is better than mine and he has more patience with bureaucrats than I do, but something inside me finally snaps. "Look," I say, "the indexes are here. We held the damn things in our hands. If you can't locate them, then please find someone who knows his way around the office."

Dan zaps me a look that says, "Now, you've done it. We'll never see them."

"I'm sorry," I tell him. "I guess I'm just not the shy, retiring type."

"My sweetheart," he says, "the shrieking violet."

My outburst has attracted the attention of another clerk, who gets up from his desk and comes over to find out what the trouble is. "*Sí, sí,*" he says, "I remember seeing something like that once." He begins rooting around under the counter and comes up with a twenty-page list of civil cases from the 1950s through the 1970s.

"No," says Dan. "There are two books full of lists. About this thick. One was green."

The door to the inner office opens, and the *jefe*—an elfin man with large eyeglasses—emerges. The clerk beckons to him and says, "These folks are looking for some kind of index of old cases, and I don't know where it is."

"You have to go to Santiago for that," says the *jefe*.

"We have seen them here in this office before," says Dan. "They go back to the turn of the century."

"Well, the *juzgado* wasn't located here then. At that time, this was part of the post office."

Huh? What does that have to do with anything?

"We saw them here, in this very office, last year." I fantasize about leaping over the counter and strangling the officious twerp, but I don't want to embarrass Dan. Besides, I'd rather not spend my vacation in a Chilean jail.

188

The man shrugs and makes a cursory search below the counter. Within moments, he produces a green book labeled "*Causas Criminales Remitidos al Archivero* 1891–1976."

"That's it," we say. "That's one of them."

After opening the book in the middle, to a page full of cases from the 1930s, he says, "See? There's nothing here from the early 1900s."

When the new clerk asks him a question, the *jefe* abandons us. I seize the book and open it to the back, where the cases date from the late 1800s. I take the volume into the hall and check it slowly, page by page. Meanwhile, Dan continues trying to persuade the clerk to look for the more important civil-case volume, which contains the *posesión efectiva* and *muerte presunta* listings. In the end, he is told to write a *solicitud* to the *jefe*.

We accept defeat. Our failure to come up with a case number makes another visit to Santiago pointless. The Aller report will just have to stay wherever it is, and we must resign ourselves to never seeing it. As we leave the office, the sad-eyed woman walks down the hall with a uniformed officer and a boy in handcuffs.

If Sundance had an estate in Chile, he might have had a family—perhaps Etta—living here, as well. After all, *somebody* in Antofagasta had to enlist Frank Aller's aid to track down Sundance, and who more likely than Etta? On the admittedly slim chance that she remained here for the rest of her life, we visit the city's huge, walled cemetery to look for her name on the tombstones. Blackbirds roost on the *botonée* cross atop the domed entryway. Inside, mausoleums range up the hillside, but the oldest niches are set into the wall near the front. They underscore the international character of Antofagasta during Butch and Sundance's time; mingled with the Chileans are dear departed souls from Australia, Austria, China, Denmark, England, France, Germany, Italy, the Middle East, Portugal, Scotland, Spain, the United States, and Yugoslavia. The names chiseled into the marble read like a roster of United Nations delegates: Juan Abat, Emilia Abuhadba, Aldo Bassino Colongo, George Boswell, Emilito Bravo McGill, Selwyn Bucknall, Miguel Carayanopulos, Adelaida Cartacho, William Caruthers, Ysmael Chabez, Luis Cortes Pizarro, Hilda Darlingston, Harold Dixon, Johann Heinrich Wily Flinn, Jorji Garafulich, José Han, Carlos Fitz Henry, Arthur Nevil Horner, Juan Kegevic, James Kennedy Kerr, Isac Levi, Pedro Losihc, Janot Louis, Sixto Ly, Manuel Mazuela, Thomas Mejnertz, John Morong, Salomon Nodelmann, Erich Ohle, Letitia Margaret O'Neill, Patrick Oxborough, Constantino Piperaki, Raymond Ritson, Otto Rummel, Elias Siede, Edward Stanley, Nonziata Sticco de Sillitti, Julio Vong, Richard Watson, and Herrmann Wessels.

They died in accidents, epidemics, or childbirth, from disease or despair, or even peacefully in their sleep. A few had lived into their fifties or sixties or beyond, but most died young, many in infancy. By now, all the inconsolable spouses, parents, children, and colleagues who erected these memorials have also passed on. We find no trace of Etta, but our stroll through the quiet, orderly maze leaves me with a visceral appreciation of the inevitability of death and the brevity and sweetness of life.

In the evening, we meet José Antonio Gonzales, who teaches law at the Universidad Católica del Norte. Over beer at a sandwich shop, the youthful professor promises to look through the university's collection for information on Butch, Sundance, and Etta. "Our best chance is to find their immigration files. All foreigners had to register and have their photographs taken for the files."

"I looked at some immigration registration cards the first time we came to Antofagasta," says Dan, "but they didn't go back far enough. I guess the old ones are in Santiago."

"Actually, they were donated some time ago to the university, which is exempt from the requirement for sending old files to Santiago. They're right here in Antofagasta. I'll go through them and let you know what I find."

He finds files for 114 North Americans who registered in Antofagasta during the early 1900s. Thirty-four of the files contain pictures, none of which resembles Butch, Sundance, or Etta. Unless they were using aliases we don't know about, the bandits weren't registered. In other words, on top of everything else, they were illegal aliens.

We may have failed to locate our outlaws in the immigration or court records, but perhaps we can find judicial notices or other information about them in old newspapers that are not available back home. If the bandits committed any crimes, attended any social functions, or had wills probated here, we should be able to read all about it in the pages of *El Mercurio,* which has been published since 1906. Because of bomb threats, the newspaper employs tight security measures. We state our

190

business to a guard at the door, then repeat it to a clerk in a bulletproof reception cage, and wind up in the outer office of the managing editor. His secretary says that he is in a meeting but that we may leave a written request and come back later. Dan takes out a sheet of stationery and begins drafting yet another *solicitud*. Before he has finished, the meeting ends, and the secretary goes in to see her boss. She returns to say that because our time in Antofagasta is limited, he has decided to allow us to look at whatever we want, beginning immediately. Dumbfounded by this display of openness and left holding a half-written *solicitud*, Dan asks her to repeat what she has just said.

Moments later, we follow a clerk through a security door, around a corner, and down a flight of stairs to the cellar. He turns a key in a large padlock, slides back an enormous bolt, and the heavy metal door creaks open, revealing a dimly lit low-ceilinged room crammed with bound copies of newspapers dating back to 1906. Books are piled on shelves, on a small table, and on the floor. There is only one chair and not enough room for another. While Dan remains in this dungeon, I take a volume out into the stairwell, which is equipped with a small desk and a hard chair. Aside from the occasional arachnid visitor and the dust swept down the stairwell by a janitor who doesn't know I am here, my little office is quite cozy. The guards not only refrain from kicking us out for the *siesta*, but also say that we can toil as much as we please between seven in the morning and ten at night—good news for a pair of workaholics in the land of *siesta*, *mañana*, and *no hay*. If the door is locked, all we need do is ring the bell.

Although our bandits probably first came to Antofagasta in 1904, the oldest issues of *El Mercurio* date back only to December 1906. By that time, Butch and Sundance were in Bolivia, according to Percy Seibert, who met them at a Christmas party in La Paz that year. Of course, if Etta was here, Sundance might have visited her on occasion. In any event, we read every issue from the newspaper's inception to the end of 1911, the year in which Frank Aller finally received the John Doe death certificate with which to settle Sundance's estate. The fine print on the fragile pages is difficult to read under the low-watt bulbs in the ceiling, so we begin bringing flashlights with us every day. From time to time, a brief power failure occurs. We hear groans from upstairs every time the presses stop running and the lights go out, but our flashlights allow us to keep working.

Strife in the Balkans dominated the international news, but *El Merc-*

191

urio found room for stories about the rioting that took place in Rio de Janeiro when women there began wearing harem pants. Other hot topics included the scourge of alcoholism, the arrival of gypsies in Valparaíso and Antofagasta, the capture of pirates who had been robbing launches in Chilean ports, and outbreaks of bubonic plague, black vomit, and cholera in Europe and yellow fever in Chile. In the personals columns, amateur boxers named Kid Mitchell, Clown Perry, and Kelly the Rake sparred over who was the brawniest. Police departments advertised for information about runaway wives, and angry merchants sought the whereabouts of customers who had purchased Singer sewing machines on credit and then disappeared before making all the payments. Letters to the editor complained of random gunfire in the night, the shooting of cats, and the "badly maintained archives at the *juzgado de letras*." Amen to that.

Aside from reports about government actions and the nitrate industry, the local news was devoted chiefly to crime. Arrests for drunkenness, assault, robbery, disorderly conduct, and discharging firearms were common. Not only was Antofagasta a port with a revolving contingent of sailors at liberty, but it attracted gangs of single men from the *oficinas* every weekend. Brawls occurred regularly, and the combination of guns and alcohol was deadly. Corpses turned up periodically; from a distance of more than eighty years, we watch the cases being investigated and the culprits being caught, tried, and executed. "The most horrible crime ever perpetrated in Antofagasta," *El Mercurio* said of a man's strangling his mother for her money. Personally, I would have saved that designation for the case of the chinchilla hunter who shot a man and left his body to putrefy in a tank from which drinking water was piped to Antofagasta.

I find myself becoming emotionally involved in the tragedies of people who are long gone: the young wife whose husband died on their honeymoon; the bankrupted businessmen; the families of the workers who died when a scaffold collapsed beneath them. Saddest of all were the suicides. Sometimes, any residents not actively engaged in killing each other seemed bent on killing themselves. Guns, poison, and dynamite were the weapons of choice, but more than one person jumped into the path of a streetcar, and a young girl hung herself from one of the town's few trees. Dogs got to her first; by the time her distraught family arrived, little more than bones dangled from the rope.

Of Butch and Sundance, we find very little. We encounter people named Lowe, Parker, Brown, and Boyd on passenger lists, but they invariably were bank managers, insurance agents, octogenarians, or fathers of six. After a while, I am so desperate to find something linking the bandits to Antofagasta that I fixate on the advertisements for *Boyd Lejitimo,* a fruit-juice concoction promoted for its "smooth, delicious, and aromatic flavor" and its lack of alcohol or artificial substances. When I show Dan the ad and explain my theory that the estate of the Sundance Kid—alias Frank Boyd—consisted of the company that produced *Boyd Lejitimo,* he hoots at the idea.

"Okay, smart-ass," I say. "You find something better."

Two hours later, he comes out to my stairwell office and spreads one of the 1910 volumes out on my desk. He says nothing but points to a small ad that says in Spanish, "Notice: Enrique Braun would like to know the whereabouts of his son Carlos Guillermo Braun."

"Braun? That's German. Sundance called himself Enrique *Brown.*"

"So what? It's better than a fruit drink."

Another ad, printed three days later, includes information eliminating Enrique Braun as a possible Sundance. This is just as well: The ad came out *after* the gun battle in San Vicente.

And what did *El Mercurio* have to say about the shootout? Surprisingly, although Antofagasta had belonged to Bolivia until the 1879–1883 War of the Pacific and the city remained a major conduit for trade with Bolivia, little Andean news found its way to the coast. We see only two references to Bolivian crimes that were eventually attributed to Butch and Sundance. The first was a June 1908 report that "the paymaster of the Viacha-Oruro railroad line was robbed of twenty thousand *pesos bolivianos* at the Eucaliptus station by three Yankees who had been employed as contract workers. The assailants escaped to parts unknown."

The second report was a single sentence buried in an article about four Chileans who had killed an innkeeper and raped his wife near Uyuni at "a miserable outpost of four huts and two corrals where travelers could find disgusting lodgings (but lodgings nonetheless) and fodder in the cold and forsaken expanse of the *altiplano.*" After describing the role played by the authorities of San Vicente in capturing the murderers, the article mentioned that "not long ago, two Yankee bandits robbed the Quechisla general manager and carried off a fifteen-thousand-*boliviano* payroll, but they were cornered in San Vicente and committed suicide a short time later." *El Mercurio* then quoted a

Bolivian newspaper's statement that " 'the Yankees are the only ones capable of giving the Chileans competition in the art of coveting what is not theirs.' "

While leafing through a late-1910 volume, I spot an article entitled "The English Equestrian Circus," which announced the arrival of performers "directed by the intelligent artist Mr. Harry LaPlace." The article provided no additional information about LaPlace except that he would appear in that evening's program in an act called "Horse on the Loose." As good as Sundance was with horses, he might well have been able to ride in a circus. And Harry LaPlace is *so* close to Sundance's Argentine alias, Harry Place, that we can't ignore it. The Pinkertons certainly would have looked into it.

"Hey, Dan," I call, "get ready to research old-time traveling circuses from England."

"Did you find something?" He is by my side in an instant. Once he has skimmed the article, we page through a week's worth of issues until we spot a follow-up story, "The Clown LaPlace," which describes the mystery man as "a charming and intelligent artist who has received applause in the principal cities of the world." According to this article, LaPlace is the stage name of Harry Filey:

> He was born in London in 1854 and ran away from home at the age of ten after an unhappy life, in which his parents caned him daily to force him to perform graceful acrobatic exercises.
>
> While earning a living as a slack-wire dancer, Harry . . . suffered a fall and broke his leg. His father took him from the hospital and put him into a reform school in punishment for his flight. At the age of fifteen, Harry worked in a circus from Bombay. He left for Europe, the ship wrecking in high seas and the young acrobat being saved by the opportune help of another boat. . . . Roving the seas and nations of all the world without putting down roots anywhere, Harry suffered reverses and curious adventures too long to tell. He traveled often as a collier or sailor, until he encountered the circus that hired him.
>
> Viewed as a whole, LaPlace's life can be seen as an interesting tale, very sad and dolorous. Nevertheless, whoever deals with this artist finds him a jovial man, affable and sincere in his affections. It would be understandable if, having been

mistreated by fate during most of his life, he were stubborn, hard, and selfish, even an enemy of humanity; but LaPlace isn't like that, because he has healed his troubles with the balm that only those devoted to the public comprehend: applause. That clown who makes us cry with laughter in the English Circus has been acclaimed in the five parts of the world, as to all he has brought happy notes with his unfailing grace.

Harry LaPlace seems to have had a lot in common with Harry "Place" Longabaugh. Both fended for themselves from an early age and suffered hardships that might have defeated individuals who had weaker spirits, but the two men chose different paths to fame and fortune. What does it say about our values when the fellow who took the honorable route is dead and forgotten, while the scoundrel lives on in legend?

Now that our last outlaw candidate is out of the running, we have to accept the fact that unless Butch and Sundance did an excellent job of staying clear of reporters, they weren't here after December 1906. Several supporting characters, however, left footprints in Antofagasta during those years. Santiago Hutcheon, the Scot who knew the bandits in Tupiza, registered at the Hotel Maury, which stood on the site now occupied by our hotel. William Gray, one of the men who told Frank Aller that Butch and Sundance had been killed at San Vicente, came in on the train from Oruro, where he served as the treasurer of the chamber of commerce and as the British vice-consul. Malcom Roberts, the Aramayo company official who coordinated the 1908 search for the bandits near Salo and later told engineer Victor Hampton about the San Vicente shootout, passed through Antofagasta twice while vacationing with his wife. And various members of the Aramayo family lived in or visited the city.

In the earliest volumes, U.S. vice-consul Frank Aller often made news—socializing with the Aramayos, partying at the Club Union, lunching on the beach, watching a polo match, and attending a funeral—and his wife was mentioned for her part in a concert given by the women of the local English colony. After the Allers' 1907 or 1908 move eighty miles north to Gatico, where his employer had a copper smelter, they appeared in *El Mercurio* only occasionally, in the lists of passengers on ships and trains.

* * *

In a rented car the size of a doghouse, we run up the coast to Gatico to see whether Mr. Aller left anything that might help us. Our map—nearly as long and skinny as Chile itself—doesn't show Gatico, but we ask around and learn that it is north of a town called Cobija. "If you pass the cemetery," says a taxi driver, "you've gone too far."

"How can we tell which cemetery it is?"

"Don't worry. You'll know it when you see it."

Gulls and crows wheel in the bay as we drive north past beaches that look more like landfills. Signs warning No Apta Para Bañarse (unfit for swimming) rise from the debris. A few fishing boats bob offshore, beyond an uninviting belt of brown foam. "Remind me," says Dan, "not to order seafood tonight."

Not far from Antofagasta, we cross the Tropic of Capricorn and officially enter the tropics. But where are the turquoise waters and pristine beaches? Shouldn't there at least be a coconut palm or two? Devil's Island is Shangri-La compared with this lifeless desert. At least we're not on foot—unlike the poor souls lamented in the eighty-year-old pages of *El Mercurio*.

> At the end of their journey, [the travelers] are totally covered with white dust, their eyes swollen and red from the dirt and lack of sleep. They walk slowly, debilitated, fatigued, with their heads down, looking at the ground. . . . It is the spirit of adventure . . . that usually inspires and drives such long trips. Sometimes, they listen intently in the shadows of the tavern to the stories about other nitrate mines. . . . They become excited, thinking of earning a better salary, of finding a splendid post, and they set off over the land, crossing league after league on a harsh and arid soil where not a single scrap of shade can be found in which to rest from the fatigue of the journey. During one season, the temperature in the desert falls to about [20 degrees Fahrenheit] at night and, I am told, rises to [140 degrees Fahrenheit] in the daytime.
>
> They leave with hopes and joys aplenty but with no money and little food. They take the long white path, full of faith as they follow it down. They never fear getting lost nor think for one moment that they could run out of water; they have confidence in their stamina and in the triumph that awaits them.

196

But many have fallen victim to their intrepidness, lost and without water on these sandy plains and harsh ridges of the desert. The water often fails to last long enough to meet the necessities of the trip; desperation sets in, a sad desperation that ends in madness; they think of the coast, the sea, without thinking that one can die of thirst in the immense salty waters of the ocean! But they do not arrive at the coast; they fall on the road and are never seen again. On remote paths, it is not uncommon to find the white skeletons of the unfortunates conquered by the desert. . . .

Last June, three workers left [an *oficina* near Antofagasta] and headed for Toco. They carried their bedrolls on their backs with two bottles of water apiece. Not knowing the terrain, they became lost and, overcome by fatigue, decided to abandon their gear in the middle of the plain. By the second day, they had run out of water and decided to head for the coast. They were walking in this direction when they began to experience the horrible martyrdom of thirst. After a while, having nothing with which to satiate the enemy, their skin became wrinkled, dry as parchment, dessicated, and colorless. One of the three, the strongest, abandoned his companions and changed direction. Soon his vision began to play tricks on him; he began to hallucinate; an inexplicable confusion seized him; and in the delirium of his desperation he cut the veins in his wrist with a penknife and, eager for death, sucked his own blood, believing it would quench the thirst that was killing him.

Almost dead, the poor man arrived at the Barriles train station . . . where he was tenderly cared for . . . and his life was saved. Search parties were sent out . . . but the other men were not found. They remain lost forever, and soon their skeletons will be whitened by the sun on the sand and rough marble of those plains.

The road cuts through tarnished ridges that run down into the sea. Tents and trailers cluster in sheltered coves with tiny beaches. Beyond Cobija, an abandoned Victorian mansion with a hipped roof rises from the rocks in the crook of a crescent bay. A water tower stands nearby. "Could this be Gatico?"

"I don't know," says Dan. "There should be a smelter."

"What about that place on the right?" A small building sits in a dusty yard of sorts fenced by sheets of corrugated metal.

"Too small. Probably a fisherman's house."

No sign identifies the spot, so we follow the road around the bay, only to stop before a landmark that no one could possibly miss: scores of crosses and tombstones, each one surrounded by a wooden fence the size of a baby's crib, planted on the beach scarcely a hundred yards from the ocean. The sun-silvered water, the bleached wood, the very sterility of the sandy soil—everything shrieks of loneliness and death.

While wandering through the cemetery, we see the ruins of several stone buildings across the bay, built into the cliff below the abandoned mansion and invisible from the road above. "Maybe that's where the smelter was."

"Yes, this is Gatico," says Felicindo Muñoz, who lives in the house across the road from the mansion, which used to serve as the administrative office of the American Smelting and Refining Company and the home of the manager and his family. "But I don't recall anyone named Frank Aller."

"He was the manager long before your time."

"I have been the caretaker here for twenty years now." A small cat with mottled black-and-brown fur saunters over to the retaining wall beside us. "The smelter shut down in 1934, and the copper mine closed in the 1940s."

"Was there a town?" asks Dan, reaching out to pet the cat. A white mutt romps across the yard, noses the cat out of the way, and tries to coax Dan to pet him instead.

"There used to be a church, a theater, and two schools." Several more dogs join us. "Take a look at the big house if you want to. It is open."

Tails wagging furiously, the dogs follow us across the road and down the sloping gravel driveway. The mansion looms above like a lighthouse. The battered stone foundations seem to grow out of the chiseled rock, which is as rusty as the corrugated roof. We walk past the side porch, with its decorative triangular braced supports, and around the ungainly square lookout-tower to the front, where a bulky concrete staircase leads up to the house.

Most of the floorboards are missing from the wide front porch, so we tiptoe across the joists to the large foyer. The glass has long since disappeared from the windows, but a few shards cling to the lead framework in the transoms. A rectangular hole gapes in the ceiling where the stairs to the second floor used to be. The walls are covered with graffiti, mostly of the basic Kilroy-Was-Here and Juan-Loves-María variety, with a sprinkling of philosophy and poetry: "Distance is to love as wind is to fire: It makes the great one burn brighter and the small one go out," and "Ghosts of the past, pardon those who make a spectacle of their ignorance in these ruins of yours."

"They say the place is haunted," says Muñoz, appearing suddenly in the doorway.

Standing by the bay window in the onetime dining room, gazing across the remains of the smelter to the fog-shrouded cemetery on the beach, I wish that the ghost of Frank Aller would materialize and sit down with us for a nice long chat.

10 · OLD-TIMERS AND ANCIANOS

T H E Pinkertons quit chasing Butch and Sundance in 1903, when the agency's banking and railroad clients declined to foot the $5,000 cost of mounting an expedition to Cholila. Seven decades later, however, the Pinkertons forked over $5,000 to Wild Bunch enthusiasts who had banded together as the National Association for Outlaw and Lawman History (which is commonly, if illogically, called NOLA).

Founding members included descendants of Matt Warner and Elzy Lay as well as researchers Jim Dullenty, Kerry Ross Boren, and others who had picked up where historians Charles Kelly and James D. Horan had left off. Among the guests of honor at NOLA's first rendezvous, as its annual convention is called, was Butch's sister Lula Parker Betenson.

Dan joined NOLA back when he first became interested in Butch and Sundance, but my introduction to the world of outlaw historians comes in San Jose, California, at the fifteenth NOLA rendezvous. The meeting room at the Red Lion Inn is filled with young women in ruffled blouses, denim skirts, and boots; older women in stretch pants and seersucker blouses; and men of all ages wearing shirts with snaps instead of buttons, blue jeans with buttons instead of zippers, and tooled-leather belts with heavy buckles. Long sideburns, drooping moustaches, cowboy hats, string ties, and turquoise jewelry abound.

Dan and I sit on folding chairs behind a woman with curly white hair and a squash-blossom necklace and a one-legged man wearing a tan-and-ivory boot, a western shirt with an embroidered bear, and a raffia hat with a horsehair band. The speakers toss around names like Rattle-snake Dick, Highwayman Jim Webster, and Cherokee Bob Talbott, and talk about legendary gun battles, including the sad tale of an innocent-bystanding shepherd dog shot in a saloon. Although his master was a teetotaler, Toodles apparently was not, and he got caught in the line of fire when a fight erupted. As we break for lunch, people are arguing over the heresy that *High Noon*–style showdowns were invented by Hollywood—to build suspense and slow down the action by cutting from one man to the other, with close-ups of their hands, their guns, and their eyes—and that most gunmen in the Old West simply waited for their enemies to get liquored up and then plugged them in the back under cover of darkness.

Dealers at tables along the walls hawk Old West memorabilia, including sheriffs' badges; playing cards drilled with bullet holes and autographed by John Wesley Hardin; scale models of the Montana territorial gallows, complete with tiny coffins; historical photographs, tintypes, and newspapers; western paintings; arrowheads and nineteenth-century barbed-wire mounted on planks; rifles and derringers; leather stirrups, saddlebags, cartridge belts, and holsters; posters advertising Smith & Wesson revolvers and Hamilton's Old English Black Oil, "The greatest Healing Liniment of the Age, treats everything from Piles to Frost-Bite to Foot Rot in Cattle and Sheep"; and vintage western clothing—a red-

and-black silk shirt, black vests, derbies, and even a black sombrero with dangling green pompoms. A skinny gent wearing a GUNFIGHTERS OF THE OLD WEST T-shirt, black jeans, wire-rim glasses, tan boots, and a matching hat with a snakeskin band purchases a belt-and-holster set. A dark-haired woman in a ruffled red denim skirt, a flowered blouse, white leather boots, and a black hat with a red feather studies a table full of new and used books with such titles as *Triggernometry; Wild, Woolly and Wicked; Last of the Bad-Men; HellDorado; 45-Caliber Law;* and *Bible in Pocket, Gun in Hand.*

That evening, eleven of us convene in a Howard Johnson's bar to discuss our particular interest, the Wild Bunch. In the dim yellow light of ersatz Tiffany lamps, we compare notes on Butch, Sundance, and Etta. "Etta supposedly had two daughters in South America," says Ed Kirby, a retired high-school principal who has been on the NOLA board for years and served as president several times. "One was the bandit Betty Weaver, who died in the early 1980s. I met her widower. He never knew that his wife had been a bank robber."

"Talk about a failure to communicate!" says Dan.

"My wife just don't have the interest in it that I have," says Colorado old-timer Ray Merrick. "She's in the room watching television."

"Not knowing where Etta came from," says Dan, "makes it hard to evaluate the claims about what happened to her. We have much more to go on with Butch and Sundance."

"Aside from the case of Hiram BeBee and the claims of Sundance's so-called son, there weren't many sightings of Sundance after he went to South America," says Jim Dullenty, a Montana bookseller and NOLA's publications director. "And most, if not all, sightings of Butch Cassidy were really of William T. Phillips. Except for the sightings by Josie Bassett, Tom Vernon, and Lula."

"At least Josie knew Butch before," says Ed. He has a booming voice, a square jaw, and a handlebar moustache. The outdoors is burnished on his skin.

"Whereas Lula was a baby when Butch left home," says Dan. "Even if a man claiming to be Butch *did* visit her, how could she have known who he was?"

Ed's daughter Kaki says, "You don't argue with a ninety-one-year-old woman. She believed what she wanted to believe."

"On our last visit with Lula," says Barclay Pringle, a Connecticut insurance agent who could pass for a cow-town gambler, "she baked Ed and me a cherry pie. I remember leaving and seeing her waving on her porch in the distance."

Nevada housewife Lenore Conway says, "I heard that they dug up a grave behind Lula's house and established it was Butch." Lenore's father was Vic Button, who as a boy had unwittingly helped Butch case a bank job and received a splendid white horse in return.

"Lula used to hint that Butch was buried in a pile of rocks at the old Parker ranch in Circleville," says Jim, "but as all the neighbors—and Lula—well knew, the occupant of that grave was a horse."

"According to Barbara Ekker," says Ed, "Lula went to Johnnie, Nevada, and asked questions about Butch being buried there, while at the same time she was telling reporters that he died in the state of Washington."

"What evidence is there that Butch died in Johnnie?"

"Josie Bassett is the origin of that story. In the 1930s, she said Butch was living in Johnnie. Later, she said he died there. When I first went to Johnnie, in the early 1980s, it was practically abandoned. The only person there was an old guy named Fred S. Cook, who claimed to be a former reporter at the *New York Daily Mirror* and declared himself mayor of Johnnie and his dog chief of police. He told me about a grave some people think is Butch's. It sits beside the highway near Johnnie, by a little picket fence. There's a wooden cross with the name Bill Kloth on it. Cook said Kloth was a miner who was setting a dynamite charge when it blew up. According to local legend, they let his body sit there for a week, and then some guy from the coroner's office came down there and said, 'Yup, he's dead.' Since then, someone has opened up a combination saloon and restaurant in Johnnie, and a lot of people talk about Butch being there, but they don't really know anything. I'll stick with Josie Bassett. The Bassetts always struck me as pretty reliable, and they did know Butch before he went to South America."

"How did you folks become interested in the Wild Bunch?" I ask.

"My father first told me about Butch Cassidy in 1934," Ed replies, "but I didn't get going on my research until 1968. I started with the Wildcat Boozing and Gorging Society while I was doing geology work in the late 1960s near Hanksville. Everywhere we went, people talked about Butch Cassidy, and I got hooked."

"I became interested when I saw Butch," says Ray Merrick. "He was in a Model T touring car without a top." Merrick has a fluffy fringe of white hair, intense blue eyes, and thin lips and talks out of the side of his mouth. "In 1923 or 1924, when I was six years old and the autumn colors were just starting, an old Model T loaded down with camping gear came steaming up the road fifty miles east of Grand Junction to where I was watching my father and another man fix a culvert to work off their poll tax. Butch and his passenger took shovels and dug in several places. They scooped up a pile of gold coins and put them on a horse blanket to carry to the Model T. Then Butch— who was clean-shaven and looked like my Uncle Ivan—came over and said to me, 'Here, kid, here's a ten-dollar gold piece for you.' He gave a twenty-dollar piece to each of the men and said, 'Remember, you never saw a thing.'

"A couple of weeks later, my father brought some old cardboard WANTED posters home from the post office to patch the cracks in the henhouse with. He was standing on a barrel and I was handing the posters up to him when we saw a picture of Butch Cassidy. My father said, 'Why, that's the man in the Model T!' Even though Butch had a moustache in the picture, my father was sure he was the same man."

"Did he call the police?"

"Or save the poster as a souvenir?"

"No, he just nailed it up in the henhouse and went on about his business."

On the last night of the rendezvous, we sit with the Merricks and Jim Dullenty at the banquet. Grace Merrick mentions having smelled a skunk in the hotel lobby, and Ray says, "What gets rid of the smell is tomato juice. Of course, you may have to take a bath in tomato juice, but it works."

Jim is worried that the James-brothers faction is packing NOLA's board of directors, changing the focus, and plotting to move the head-quarters and the library. "I'm losing interest in NOLA," he says. "This may be my last year."

Diamond Lil, a chesty blonde dolled up in a low-cut, Gay Nineties red dress, rhinestone jewelry, and a black feather boa, sings bawdy songs and flirts with the men while strolling through the room. She pauses by our table long enough to kiss the blushing Jim on the top of his bald head.

* * *

Hollywood calls—that is, North Hollywood calls. NBC's popular program "Unsolved Mysteries" plans to run a segment on whether Butch and Sundance returned from South America, and the producer has lined up interviews with several outlaw historians: Larry Pointer will make the case that William T. Phillips was Butch; Ed Kirby will say that Hiram BeBee was Sundance; and Jim Dullenty (who has left NOLA and founded a rival group called WOLA, the Western Outlaw-Lawman History Association) will provide an overview of the Wild Bunch in the United States. The producer asks Dan and me to lay out the evidence that Butch and Sundance died in South America.

Having heard that television makes you look even heavier than you already are, I head for the beauty salon and submit to an herbal body wrap guaranteed to take inches off your body, if only temporarily. As I stand naked and middle-aged before an unforgiving full-length mirror, two anorexic "estheticians" pull strips of cloth from a basin of steaming brown liquid and wrap them tightly around my legs, my torso, and finally my arms. The more mummy-like I become, the less mobility I have. By the time I am completely swaddled, the herbal brew has cooled down and left me as stiff and cold as a Popsicle. The estheticians bundle me into a rubber bodysuit and hoist me onto a table. Encased in rubber, I quickly heat up and begin to sweat off the pounds and inches. After a haircut, a manicure, and a session with a makeup artist, who tells me how to fool the camera and minimize flaws (including ones I've never noticed before), I'm ready for my television debut.

I feel positively svelte during the flight to the West Coast, but the emaciated, bronzed Californians in the L.A. airport make me feel like an albino heifer. The show has provided us with a rental car and a room in a motel conveniently located near several freeways. We have lunch in the motel's dining room, which has all the charm of a New Jersey truck stop. The only clue to our actual location—the seedy edge of the glamour capital of the USA—is the man wearing a rabbit-fur bomber-jacket and doing drug deals via a cellular phone at the next table.

After lunch, I cram myself into control-top pantyhose, put on a slenderizing dark skirt and top, and coat my face with makeup. If any of my friends see this show, they won't recognize me. We drive to the home of an "Unsolved Mysteries" staff member in Van Nuys, where most of the interviews are being taped. The crew sets us up on a sofa in the den, and the director asks Dan several substantive questions about Butch and Sundance and the impostors, then turns to me and asks how I like traveling in South America. As I am stumbling through my answer, I catch sight of Dan's reflection in the glass door of a bookcase across the room. What I am saying obviously sounds as idiotic to him as it does to me, so I stop in mid-sentence and ask to start over. The rerun is better, but I'm not surprised to wind up on the cutting-room floor. Next time, I'll try the come-as-you-are approach. Also cut is Ed Kirby, whose interview is scrapped after the producer sees the mug shot of George Hanlon, alias Hiram BeBee, and decide to focus on William T. Phillips as Butch Cassidy and forget about Sundance.

After the "Unsolved Mysteries" segment airs, viewers call in to report that Sundance is buried in the northwest corner of the Latter-Day Saints Cemetery in Salt Lake City, and that Boy Scouts "reset" his grave site; that Butch's family knows exactly where he is buried (in Utah); that Sundance was executed in the 1940s in the Utah State Penitentiary under the name of Orson Beebe; that Butch is buried in Arizona, where he died of natural causes; that an elderly man in St. Mary's, Idaho, has told several people that his father or grandfather was the Sundance Kid and was buried under another name in the local cemetery; that Butch was an artist who lived on a ridge above Minersville, Utah, and was killed in about 1913; that a man who died in 1978 (when Butch would have been 112) was "identical to Cassidy in the Fort Worth portrait" and called himself Ula, which rhymes with the name of Butch's youngest sister (Lula); that Butch was sighted in the lobby of the New House Hotel in Salt Lake in 1936; that Butch was last seen in 1979 at a store in Talkna, Alaska; that a viewer's grandmother married Sundance, who was using the alias Charles Ford, a few months after the death of her first husband, Jesse James; and that Phillips and Cassidy were one and the same, because both of them parted their hair on the right.

When the show is rerun, another tipster reveals that Butch came back from South America, only to be run down and killed by a "big limousine" near Castle Dale, Utah, and that Sundance came back and got a job operating a streetcar in Denver. When a passenger began beating a woman one day, Sundance killed the man, abandoned the streetcar, and fled to Green River, Utah. He eventually became a well-to-do real-estate agent in Southern California.

The "Unsolved Mysteries" staff then faxes us a newspaper article about a new Butch Cassidy sighting. It seems that a locked trunk, bought at a garage sale in the early 1970s in the Midwest and opened some twenty years later in Wyoming, contained the skeleton of a man who had been shot through the left eye at least forty years earlier. In an attempt to identify the victim, an artist used the skull as a guide to reconstruct the man's face. A reporter, struck by the supposed resemblance between the reconstructed face and Butch's mug shot, postulated that the bandit's relatives had dug him up and put him in the trunk to keep him near. In support of this theory, the reporter cited the fact that the trunk also contained a cottonwood leaf and the outer part of a tulip bulb—significant, apparently, because cottonwood trees and tulips grew near Butch's boyhood home. Moreover, the skeleton had lost all his teeth long before dying at the age of fifty to sixty-five, and because Butch's prison records contain no entry under the heading TEETH, he might have "had none" when he was thirty-two.

Later, genealogist Nuala Cassidy White proclaims that President Bill Clinton is related, via his mother (whose maiden name was Cassidy), to the leader of the Wild Bunch. White says all Cassidys in the United States descend from Lucas Cassidy, who left Ireland for North Carolina in 1750. Never mind that Butch Cassidy was born Robert LeRoy Parker. Maybe she had him mixed up with Hopalong.

Since we first began thinking of exhuming the outlaws, we have been clipping articles about forensic experts, including Dr. Clyde Snow, a forensic anthropologist who has identified the remains of thousands of murder victims, unknown soldiers, and casualties of airplane crashes. He has participated in high-profile cases—identifying Nazi war-criminal Josef Mengele in Brazil, uncovering new information about Custer's last stand at the Little Bighorn, and reviewing the scientific evidence related to the assassination of President John F. Kennedy—but is best known for identifying the remains of victims of political death squads and Third World dictators. Clyde's pioneering and sometimes dangerous human-rights work has taken him around the globe, from the Atacama to Zāhkō.

While exhuming and identifying Argentine *desaparecidos*, victims of the Dirty War, Clyde and an associate named Eric Stover happened upon reports of a Patagonian grave in which Butch and Sundance were purportedly buried. Now, hoping to discover what really happened to the famous outlaws, Clyde and Eric have decided to take a busman's holiday and excavate the grave. Before they have firmed up their plans, however, Eric sees an article about Butch and Sundance in the *Buenos*

Aires Herald. The piece contains portions of an article Dan and I wrote for *The South American Explorer* and mentions our belief that the bandits died in Bolivia. Eric telephones the editor of the *Herald,* who puts him in touch with the editor of the *Explorer,* who tells Eric that we live across town from him.

Clyde lives in Oklahoma, but the next time he visits Eric, they come to our house for a Sunday-afternoon slide show and steak fry. A tall man with an upturned nose and battered green canvas hat, Clyde looks like an outsized leprechaun. Eric, who has honey-blond hair, a moustache, a square jaw, and wire-rimmed glasses, works as a consultant for Human Rights Watch and Physicians for Human Rights. Also present is Eric's wife, Pamela Blotner, a soft-spoken sculptor with shoulder-length brown hair and steely blue eyes. She and Eric are newlyweds, which explains why she sits patiently on our sofa for hours despite the fact that Rio—our ruddy Abyssinian cat—has triggered an allergy that leaves her itching, sneezing, and watery-eyed. Clyde, a three-pack-a-day smoker of unfiltered Camels, is equally miserable because our house is a cigarette-free zone; he must make do with periodic nicotine fixes on the patio.

Eric describes their work helping the mothers and grandmothers of the Plaza de Mayo in Buenos Aires find out what had become of their children and grandchildren.

"Those women were so brave," says Pamela.

"Did anybody ever attack you," I ask, "for dredging up the past and making people confront what had been done in their names?"

"Sure," says Clyde. "In fact, at one point the cemetery guard started telling callers, 'Sorry, we only take death threats between the hours of ten o'clock and two o'clock. You'll have to call back later.' "

"You know," says Dan, "we were in Argentina for a couple of months during the height of the Dirty War."

"The authoritarianism was palpable," I say. "Everywhere we went, teenaged soldiers with guns were telling us what to do. There were signs everywhere saying MILITARY ZONE: SENTRIES OPEN FIRE WITHOUT WARNING! The country has changed a lot since then. Thank goodness."

"Let's talk about something more cheerful," says Dan. "Didn't we read somewhere that you've had previous experience with dead outlaws?"

"That would be the McCurdy case," says Clyde. He takes a swig of beer before plunging into the story. "It started when they were

208

shooting a television program on location in this old fun house in Long Beach, California, and there was a dummy hanging in the way. They went to move it and grabbed it by the arm, but the arm came off, and there was a bone in it. They took the dummy down to the medical examiner's office and found out that it was a mummified human. The people who owned the fun house thought it had been a dummy—or claimed they did. It was all very suspicious: He'd been shot, he had a hangman's noose around his neck, he was painted Day-Glo red, and the 'tox' report showed he was loaded with arsenic.''

"Talk about overkill,'' says Dan.

"The authorities checked with previous owners of the fun house and finally came up with this old guy who lived in a retirement home in Arizona and had owned the show in the 1930s. He told them he had acquired the mummy from some down-and-out carny who had been making his living by exhibiting the mummy as a famous Oklahoma outlaw. The carny put the mummy up as security for a loan he never got around to repaying, and the fun house guy found himself stuck with the stiff. He had to do something with it, so he put the noose around the neck and painted him so he would glow in the dark, and then hung him in the tunnel.''

"How did you get involved in the case?'' I ask.

"When all this came down, the medical examiner out there, Tom Noguchi, called me and asked if could I do some research and find out if there was anybody from Oklahoma that would fit this bizarre set of circumstances. We started checking into it and found out there was a guy named Elmer McCurdy, who robbed a train in Oklahoma around 1910 and was killed in a shoot-out in a barn a couple of days later. Then, because nobody claimed the body, they took him down to the local funeral home. Elmer was such a celebrity by then that the guy who ran the funeral home embalmed him in arsenic, which makes a body just about as stiff as a board. Then he dressed Elmer up in the same clothes he was killed in and stood him in the back corner of the storeroom. Elmer stayed there for a number of years, and people could go in and visit him. He was a big attraction. One day, the carny—who was kind of a con man—came through town and paid his nickel to see Elmer, then came back out and started carrying on and claiming to be Elmer's brother. He said he wanted the body to bury it up in Kansas. The funeral home guy believed the story and gave him the body, and for the next twenty or thirty years the so-called brother made his living exhibiting Elmer. We got him all identified, brought him back to Oklahoma, then we buried him and put concrete on top to make sure he wouldn't go anywhere.''

From Elmer McCurdy, the conversation moves on to Butch and Sundance, and by the end of the evening, we have convinced our guests that the Patagonian grave contains Bob Evans and Willie Wilson, who killed Welsh shopkeeper Llwyd ap Iwan at Arroyo Pescado.

"We are virtually certain," says Dan, "that Butch and Sundance are in the San Vicente cemetery. Whether they're in the grave that Froilán Risso has identified is anybody's guess, but he has a lot of fairly specific information that rings true. We've seen pictures—taken in 1984, a few years before our visit—in which he is showing a *gringo* mining engineer the same sites he showed us. So if Risso is wrong, at least he is consistent.''

"There's only one way to find out if he knows what he's talking about," says Clyde. "Let's dig 'em up.''

Dan and I agree to accompany Eric and Pamela on a preliminary visit to Bolivia to obtain whatever government permission will be needed and to arrange for the exhumation team's transportation and lodging. Before leaving the United States, we call on the Bolivian ambassador, Jorge Crespo Velasco, who we hope will pave the way for us with the officials in La Paz. Señor Crespo and his legal adviser, Fernando González, receive us in the modern wing attached to the ambassador's Italianate residence on Embassy Row. After Eric describes the project and we show our slides, the ambassador asks what he can do to help us.

"We need to know whether there are any special requirements or procedures we'll have to follow in shipping the remains to the United States," says Eric.

"I'm not sure I understand you," says the ambassador. "Can't you just dig them up and determine their identities on the spot or in a local hospital?''

"No," says Eric. "It's a very complicated process, and Dr. Snow will want to do the testing in his own laboratory, where he has his equipment and access to other experts he might need to consult.''

"We have two questions to answer," I say. "The first is whether the grave contains the Aramayo bandits. If we find bullets and evidence of gunshot wounds, we can be fairly certain that we have found the

210

bandits. The second question is whether the bandits were Butch and Sundance. To answer that, the remains will have to be compared with what we know about the physical characteristics of Butch and Sundance. And that part must be done in the laboratory.''

"I see," says the ambassador. "Well, if you get authorization from the Ministry of Justice in La Paz, that should be sufficient for taking the bones out of the country. I can provide the necessary letters of introduction to the minister and other officials who might be of service."

His legal adviser says, "I think it would be a good idea for you to take along a Bolivian scientist, to make the exhumation a joint project rather than a matter of outsiders coming in."

"An excellent suggestion," says the ambassador.

"I know the perfect man for the job," says Señor González. "His name is Roy Querejazu Lewis. He is a highly respected Bolivian archaeologist and an old friend of my family's. He can go with you and help you deal with the local officials, as well as provide scientific support."

Just what we need, a chaperon to keep watch on us for the government. But what can we say? "We'd be delighted to have him."

We arrive in La Paz and find that Señor Querejazu has been delayed in Cochabamba, where his father has recently undergone surgery. While we wait, Dan and Eric meet with Vice-Minister of Justice Roger Pando, who agrees to draw up the necessary papers for the exhumation and removal of the remains. We also visit our pal Francisco Vega Avila, who is now living in La Paz. Since we last saw him, he has married and become a father. He still works for COMIBOL and is able to steer us to the right people for arranging lodging at Telamayo and a jeep and driver to take us to San Vicente.

Francisco also mentions that Fernando Peró—a grandson of Carlos Peró and son of Mariano Peró, both of whom were present at the Aramayo holdup—has an office in La Paz. We find Señor Peró in a small room on the third floor of a drab building with a broken elevator. A short man of about sixty, he says that his father told him the story some thirty years ago. "My father was thirteen or fourteen at the time of the holdup. There was a party of six people—a couple of *gringos* and some others whom they couldn't see. My father told me that the *bandoleros* split up and got away. At that time, there was a very good telegraph system, and they were pursued by the police for three or four days. The battle in San Vicente was two or three nights long. Instead of two hundred soldiers, there were maybe thirty or forty. The *bandoleros* were buried in San Vicente. My grandfather went to San Vicente to check on whether the men who were killed were the same ones who robbed him." Señor Peró promises to go through his father's files and mail us a copy of anything useful.

Over drinks at our hotel, we meet Roy Querejazu Lewis, who is nothing like the government spook we have been dreading. A good-humored, wiry man with short dark hair and a close-cropped beard, he is only forty-six. Moreover, having lived in London for eight years, he speaks excellent English, which is a relief to Pamela, who doesn't speak Spanish. Roy bubbles with helpful ideas. He suggests, for example, that we clear our work with the local authorities in Tupiza and San Vicente—purely as a courtesy, because Vice-Minister Pando's order is all we really need. "But courtesy," he adds, "is everything."

The next morning, we catch the *ferrobus* heading south. The sun slices the clouds as we labor up out of the La Paz bowl onto the *altiplano*. A blue-jacketed steward with a black bow tie serves breakfast. Two drunks sitting in front of us ask for the first of many liters of Pilsner Nacional that will enliven their journey to Tupiza. We opt for *coca* tea and mortadella sandwiches and open the morning newspaper, which informs us that President Jaime Paz Zamora has fired eight of his ministers. We anxiously skim the list to see whether Roger Pando's boss is among them; a new minister would bring in his own people, and they might not want a bunch of *gringos* to come in and start digging up graves. Luckily, Pando's boss is safe—until the next purge, anyway.

Roy specializes in prehistoric rock art and has written or edited several books, including *Bolivia 30,000 Years Ago,* which makes him an ideal guide for time traveling. "The *altiplano* used to be under two hundred feet of water," he says. "This part was under Lake Ballivián. The Salar de Uyuni is what's left of Lake Minchin. Ten thousand years ago, preagricultural gatherers called the Viscachani lived on the bluffs."

As we pull out of the Oruro station, I load my camera with extra-fast film and make my way back to the second-class coach, which is less crowded and has a door facing the marshy Lake Uru Uru. To avoid the telephone lines that intrude on the timeless landscape, I open the door,

Top: The Fort Worth Five, photographed by John Swartz in 1900. *Left to right:* Harry A. Longabaugh (the Sundance Kid); Will Carver; Ben Kilpatrick; Harvey Logan (Kid Curry); and Robert LeRoy Parker (Butch Cassidy) (*Rocky Mountain House*). *Bottom left:* Sundance at age four, with his father, Josiah Longabaugh, in Pennsylvania (*courtesy Paul and Donna Ernst*). *Bottom right:* Elzy Lay, Butch's best friend in the early days (*Rocky Mountain House*).

Facing page: Sundance and Etta, alias Mr. and Mrs. Harry A. Place, photographed at the DeYoung Studio in New York, 1901 (*Rocky Mountain House*). *Top left:* The Bar U Ranch in Canada. Sundance bunked in the cabin on the right during the early 1890s (*Glenbow Archives* (*NA 466-3*), *Calgary, Canada*). *Top right:* Calgary's Grand Central Hotel Saloon, operated by Sundance and a partner in 1892 and 1893 (*Glenbow Archives* (*NA 4035-141*), *Calgary, Canada*). *Bottom:* Butch's boyhood home at Circleville, Utah (*Rocky Mountain House*).

Top left and right: William T. Phillips, the Spokane machine-shop owner who claimed to be Butch Cassidy (*Rocky Mountain House*). *Bottom left:* George Hanlon, also known as Hiram BeBee, said by some to have been the Sundance Kid (*California State Archives*). *Bottom right:* Butch Cassidy, mugshot taken in 1894 at the Wyoming Territorial Prison in Laramie, where he served eighteen months for horse theft (*Rocky Mountain House*).

Top left: John and Bertie Perry, the bandits' nearest neighbors in Cholila (*courtesy Inés Mirta Cea*). *Top right:* George Newbery, the U.S. vice-consul in Buenos Aires, who told the Pinkertons where the bandits were living (*Archivo Histórico Regional, Ricardo Vallmitjana*). *Bottom left:* Annie Gillies Parker, Butch Cassidy's mother (*Rocky Mountain House*). *Bottom right:* Celia Mudge, William T. Phillips's alleged mother (*Rocky Mountain House*).

Top: The bandits' ranch at Cholila in 1903. *Left to right:* Butch (alias James Ryan); six visitors; Sundance (alias Harry A. Place); and Etta (alias Mrs. Place) (*author's collection*). *Middle:* The Cholila ranch today (*Anne Meadows*). *Bottom left:* Daniel Gibbon, the Welsh immigrant who was the outlaws' best friend in Argentina (*courtesy Violeta Gibbon de Aranea*). *Bottom right:* Jarred Jones, the Patagonian rancher who sold cattle to Butch and Sundance and put them up during a storm (*Archivo Histórico Regional, Ricardo Vallmitjana*).

Top: The Banco de Tarapacá in Río Gallegos, Argentina. Butch and Sundance held up the bank on February 14, 1905 (*author's collection*). *Bottom:* The Hotel Argentino, where the bandits stayed while planning the holdup (*courtesy Osvaldo Topcic*).

Clockwise from top left: The Banco de la Nación in Villa Mercedes de San Luis, Argentina. Butch, Sundance, Etta, and a companion held up the bank on December 19, 1905. A compass dropped by the outlaws and recovered by a posse. One of several posses who chased the Villa Mercedes bandits for weeks. Butch later said that no other posses had ever trailed him so closely. Ventura Domínguez, who fired upon the outlaws as they left the bank. Major Cipriano Sosa, who led a posse. Belisario Oliveros, a posse member whose horse was shot out from under him. Carlos Ricca, a customer who was pistol-whipped during the holdup. (*All photos Caras y Caretas*)

Left: Frank Aller, the U.S. vice-consul who helped Sundance out of a jam in 1905 and later launched an investigation to verify rumors that Butch and Sundance had been killed in Bolivia. *Middle:* Antofagasta, Chile, circa 1900. *Bottom:* The Antofagasta train station, from which Butch and Sundance departed en route to Bolivia in 1906. (*All photos author's collection*)

Top left: The Grand Hotel Guisbert, where Butch, Sundance, and other *gringos* stayed while in La Paz, Bolivia. *Top right:* Santa Cruz, Bolivia, circa 1907. Butch wrote his letter to the Boys at Concordia from here. *Bottom:* The main plaza in Oruro, Bolivia, circa 1907. Sundance's last known address was the Hotel Americano in Oruro. (*All photos author's collection*)

Right: Percy Seibert, who knew Butch and Sundance at Concordia. Seibert was the source of the 1930 report that Butch and Sundance had been killed in Bolivia (*The James D. Horan Western and Americana Collection*). *Below:* The Concordia Tin Mine. Butch and Sundance bunked in the first white building on the left (*Percy Seibert & The James D. Horan Western and Americana Collection*). *Bottom:* The compound in San Vicente, Bolivia, where Butch and Sundance were said to have died (*Victor Hampton & The James D. Horan Western and Americana Collection*).

Clockwise from top left: Santiago Hutcheon (with pipe) and Fanny Hutcheon (in hooded coat), with friends on the *altiplano* (*courtesy Ian L. Hutcheon*). The main plaza in Tupiza, Bolivia, circa 1908. The old customs house is on the right (*author's collection*). Carlos Peró, the man in charge of the Aramayo payroll held up by Butch and Sundance on November 4, 1908 (*courtesy Florencia Peró Urquidi*). Quechisla, center of the Aramayo mining operation and Carlos Peró's destination at the time of the holdup (*courtesy Carmen Diaz de Poklepovic*).

Top: San Vicente today (*Anne Meadows*). *Bottom left:* Roger McCord, the man in the *casa rodante* (*Anne Meadows*). *Bottom right:* The bandits' putative grave in 1972, when it still had its cross and other adornments (*courtesy Roger McCord*).

Top: Froilán Risso, indicating the grave where he said the bandits were buried. *Bottom left:* Burney McClurkan, with one foot in the grave. *Bottom right:* Clyde Snow, examining an intrusive skull. (*All photos Anne Meadows*)

Top left: Eduardo "Lalo" Mostajo, the Tupiza city employee who accompanied the exhumation team to San Vicente (*Anne Meadows*). *Top right:* COMIBOL engineer Francisco Vega Avila (*Anne Meadows*). *Bottom:* The scientific and historical team, gathered around the remains of SV1 in the Oklahoma Medical Examiner's Office. *Left to right:* Paul Goaz; Burney McClurkan; Eric Stover; Roy Querejazu; the author; Clyde Snow; Skip Palenik; Dan Buck; Chris Boles; and Henry Asin (*Harold Eiseman for WGBH*).

Top: Verdugo, Bolivia, where Butch and Sundance headquartered for several weeks while planning the Aramayo holdup (*author's collection*). *Bottom:* Cucho, Bolivia, the last stop before San Vicente (*Anne Meadows*).

sit down on the steps, and aim my camera at the flamingos, ducks, and egrets among the reeds. I manage to shoot most of the roll before the *ferrobus* clacks off the levee and onto solid ground. As the lake recedes into the distance, I grab the handrails and begin to stand up. When my left foot leaves the step for a moment, however, the heel of my shoe flops loose, and a gust of wind snatches the shoe off my foot. I watch helplessly as the purple suede flutters like a leaf and then drops from sight. My favorite pair of shoes! These pictures better be worth it. My only consolation is the dubious honor of amusing my fellow passengers by hopping back to the first-class coach with my bare foot in the air.

My hiking shoes are locked away in the baggage compartment, so I resign myself to remaining barefooted for the next several hours. Then I remember having stuffed a pair of mail-order shower shoes into the pocket of my carry-on bag at the last minute. Made of white plastic netting attached to thin rubber soles, they look extremely goofy, but this qualifies as an emergency.

Near Uyuni, Roy points out a long stone building with trapezoidal windows and end walls and says that it is an Incan church he discovered some time ago. "It used to have a grass roof." He is collaborating with his father, renowned historian Robert Querejazu Calvo, on two books—one detailing the history of the church in the colonial era and the other containing photographs of Bolivian churches.

Our next bit of excitement comes when the *ferrobus* stops in the middle of nowhere, and the conductor climbs down and begins chasing a stray lamb through a field of *tola* bushes. Periodically, the man lunges for the lamb. Even when he manages to grab the fleece, the lamb slips out of his hands and dashes away. When, like an Andean Buster Keaton, the conductor falls flat on his face in the dust, the passengers cheer. In the end, however, he is victorious, and the lamb winds up riding second-class with its ankles tied.

"It was separated from the flock," says the conductor after one of the drunks in front of us needles him. "It would have died out here all by itself."

As if it wasn't on its way to market at this very moment.

We make a few more unscheduled stops to clear the tracks of stray *llamas* and windblown sand. At dusk, the *ferrobus* finally pulls into the Atocha station. Exhausted, we alight, collect our bags, and scurry across the bridge to Telamayo. Sand and dirt sift through the net in my shower shoes and, stopping frequently to empty them, I fall behind. The sun sinks quickly, darkness descends, and the temperature plummets. I catch up with the rest of the team at the entrance to the COMIBOL complex. Unfortunately, the gate is locked, and the guard doesn't know what to make of us. "Hey, Roy," says Eric, "how do you say 'We don't need no stinkin' badges' in Spanish?"

He gives the guard our letter of introduction from the head office in La Paz, but the guard sends for someone with more authority to take the responsibility for letting in a gang of *gringos*. We stand there shivering, Eric and Pamela in unlined parkas, Roy in olive drab, Dan in a thin cotton shell, and I in a down jacket, with the wind whistling through my shower shoes.

We are eventually admitted and shown to the home of COMIBOL's regional director, Joaquín Vargas. All we want is to get cleaned up and go to bed, but Señor Vargas tells his wife to set five extra plates. Half a dozen men join us, and we all sit around the table in our coats. During the soup course, Eric explains our project, and Dan describes the grave Froilán Risso showed us in San Vicente. Señor Vargas says, "Didn't Alberto Jara take the plaque from that grave as a souvenir two or three years ago?"

"No, there was no plaque," says an engineer in a brown leather jacket, "but the names of the *bandoleros* were known by legend. It is said that one was a Chilean and the other a North American."

"In the United States," says Dan, "we heard a story that President Barrientos led a 1966 expedition to exhume some graves in San Vicente. Have you ever heard anything about that?"

"Nobody has ever been exhumed in San Vicente," declares the company's doctor, a pale-faced man with slick jet-black hair and a charcoal-grey overcoat. "It is not done in Bolivia."

"About ten years ago," says a man in a woolen jacket, "family members of the two *bandoleros* came here in a *casa rodante*. They were looking for information about the shootout."

"I read an article," says the engineer in brown leather, "about a woman and two assistants who were here recently looking for information about an inheritance left by Butch Cassidy."

I open my mouth to ask a question, but only three words come out before I see the unmistakable shock on the faces of the COMIBOL officials. What have I said? Nothing that could have given offense. They must be startled by the fact that I am speaking. Come to think of it, Pamela and I are the only women at the table. Señora Vargas has overseen the serving of the meal, but she isn't eating with us. As everyone stares expectantly at me, I forget every word of Spanish I ever knew. I lean over to Dan and whisper, "Will you finish my sentence for me?"

"What were you trying to say?" Dan whispers back.

"I have no frigging idea. Do me a favor and just change the subject."

When at last dinner is over, Pamela and Eric are shown to a small green house, and we wind up with Roy in the two-bedroom home of some employees who are away. One of them returns unexpectedly in the middle of the night and, like Baby Bear, finds someone sleeping in his bed. Luckily, his roommate's bed is still empty and, after Roy introduces himself and explains his presence, all is calm and we snuggle back down under the thick wool blankets that are needed year-round in these parts.

The next morning, the COMIBOL jeep arrives to cart us to San Vicente, and the driver is none other than Pancho, who took us to San Vicente and Quechisla on our last visit to Bolivia. He still drives as close to the edge as possible, but this time I don't have to worry about it; Roy does the fretting for all of us. "Watch this curve," he tells Pancho. "Slow down. Stay away from the edge."

"What exactly does an exhumation entail?" I ask Eric. "What can we expect to find when the grave is opened? Should we bring barf bags?"

"When a grave is fresh, it can be fairly disgusting. A ripe body gives off a smell like what you get if you set fire to fingernail clippings. But after all these years, the only thing left of the bandits will probably be bones. Of course, at this altitude, they might be mummified."

"What would happen then?"

"We'd put the bones in a big pot of water and boil the tissue off."

Upon reaching the barren bowl that holds San Vicente, we head straight for the cemetery. The small patch of earth in front of the tombstone on the grave we plan to excavate is littered with rusty cans and other trash. Eric picks up a flattened can and uses it to sweep away the other debris. "This *must* be the bandits' grave: The locals are using it as a garbage dump."

"Not at all," says Roy. "Those were offerings to appease the out-

215

laws' spirits." Having knocked around the Bolivian outback for years, Roy has come prepared: He checks his altimeter and announces that the altitude is 4,380 meters, or 14,370 feet, then pulls out a loupe and begins examining a couple of rusted metal rods or nails that protrude from the top of the tombstone. "They were sawed off, not broken. Someone must have removed the cross deliberately."

"Does anybody know if they used concrete here in 1908?" asks Eric. "The tombstone is obviously old, but without a plaque to give the date of death, we can't be certain *how* old."

Pamela removes her gloves to sketch the tomb in pencil on a notepad. Her thin fingers are soon white with cold, and she blows on them to warm them up.

Most of the tombs have relatively recent dates, so Eric is worried that the cemetery might have been somewhere else when Butch and Sundance were killed. To reassure him, we point out the niches of Froilán Risso's grandparents, who died before 1908.

When we have finished poking around the cemetery, we drive to the local COMIBOL office and check in with Hector Arandia, the superintendent. Roy asks him how long the town has been here, and Señor Arandia says, "*Bueno,* the Spaniards mined silver between 1820 and 1830 at the Guernica Mine. And the area has three other mines: the San Vicente, the Confianza, and the San Francisco."

"What was here in 1908?"

"There were only about ten houses back then, and few people worked here. A Chilean company came in the 1920s, and the activity picked up for a while."

After arranging for us to stay in a vacant COMIBOL house, Señor Arandia accompanies us to the *rancho,* as every Bolivian mining-camp commissary seems to be called. No other customers are in the main dining room, where cold air rushes through several broken or missing windowpanes. The *dueña* invites us to eat in the family's dining room, which is warmed by a space heater and proximity to the kitchen. We gather around the table and tuck into steamy bowls of soup. Roy ladles hot sauce, known as *llajua,* into his bowl. A poster of Pablo Ruiz, a teenage Argentine heartthrob, catches Pamela's eye. She turns to me and says, "That's a nice change from all those naked busty blondes that seem to adorn most of the posters around here."

"Isn't it, though?"

On a desk nearby, a child's half-finished homework lies beside a desiccated rabbit wearing a dress and bonnet and carrying a bouquet of roses and a tiny basket. "My daughter's class project," says the *dueña* while serving chicken and rice.

"Do you have any more *llajua*?" asks Roy. He loves the stuff so much that I wouldn't be surprised to see him put it on his dessert.

Since our last visit, San Vicente has acquired a satellite dish, and one of the channels the town receives is CNN. "It has a very North American viewpoint," says Señor Arandia, "but we find it interesting anyway. We saw the whole Gulf War on television."

"In Cochabamba," says Roy, "people bought beer and watched the war as if it were a soccer tournament."

After lunch, we track down Froilán Risso and he gives us his standard tour of the shootout site and the cemetery. Eric questions him closely in an effort to determine how reliable his information is. "After the shootout, did anyone come to identify the bodies?"

"No, no. Nobody. The shootout lasted from eight o'clock until nine or ten at night, and they were buried the next day. My father told me everything. His name was Calixto Risso. He was ten years old when it happened."

"How did your father know where they were buried?" asks Eric.

"He was a sacristan, and the sacristan always took care of the cemetery. He lived here all his life." He leads us to his grandparents' niches in the small building at the back of the cemetery. "They were originally entombed at the church, but they were moved to the cemetery when the church was torn down."

So much for our proof of the cemetery's age. Aside from the inscriptions on these niches, the oldest date we've found is from the 1920s. According to Roy, however, bodies are often buried on top of old graves in cemeteries like this. And the surface of the ground inside the adobe walls appears to be about four feet higher than the ground outside, which lends support to his statement.

"Why did your father make a point of telling you about these *bandoleros* and the exact location of their grave?" asks Eric.

"So that I could tell anyone who came looking for them later."

"Did anybody ever come here in a *casa rodante* and ask about the grave or the shootout?" asks Dan.

"Not that I know of," says Risso.

"What happened to the cross and the plaque?" asks Eric.

"The cross fell off, and the plaque was taken to Tupiza twenty or thirty years ago by a committee." This conflicts with what we heard in Telamayo about Alberto Jara's taking the plaque as a souvenir two or three years ago, but that story is contradicted by the mining engineer's photos showing that the plaque was already gone in 1984.

Eric is concerned that we have only one person's word about where the bandits were buried, so Dan asks the *dueña* at the *rancho* whether anyone else might have information about the shootout or the grave. She says we should talk to a man named Toribio Ziso over in the *pueblo civico,* the rebuilt version of the old San Vicente, beyond the soccer field. "His family has lived here for generations."

We set off in search of Señor Ziso. When at last we locate him, he turns out to be Toribio Risso, the younger brother of our guide, Froilán Risso. The confusion arose because the *R*'s that are rolled elsewhere are pronounced like *Z*'s by some of the inhabitants of this area.

"Well, Eric. You wanted another source," says Dan. "Two Rissos are better than one."

Eric says, "Just keep thinking, Dan. That's what you're good at."

We haul the brothers up to the cemetery, and Toribio Risso says that the bandits are buried in a grave—with a plaque inscribed in Greek—below the one his brother has identified.

"He doesn't know what he's talking about," says Froilán Risso. "I know everything."

Let's hope so.

At dusk, we settle into our thin-walled COMIBOL house. The two bedrooms are furnished with cots and nightstands, and the living room has two additional cots as well as a Formica table and five or six chairs. The kitchen has been turned into a storage area, in which we find two space heaters. We plug them in at once, but what little heat they produce is immediately gobbled up by the icy air that blows under the door and through the many chinks and cracked windows; when the municipal electricity shuts off for the night at about ten o'clock, the space heaters lose any value they might have had. We are grateful to have a working toilet (with a cardboard box for the used toilet paper), but the lack of hot water renders the bathtub useless in this climate.

"Oh well," says Eric. "We don't need no stinkin' showers."

"Speak for yourself," says Pamela. "I can't wait to feel clean again."

Roy breaks out a bottle of *singani* (the local equivalent of grappa)

218

and a big bag of peanuts, and we sit around the table shelling peanuts and griping about how cold it is. We wrap ourselves in our sleeping bags, but they would have to be ten inches thick to ward off this chill. How can anyone live here day after day, year after year? The mines are the big draw, but with a starting wage equivalent to about three or four dollars a day, you'd have to be awfully hard up to take a job here. So far as I can tell, the best thing about San Vicente is the fact that the open sewer running along the main street freezes over at night, which cuts down on the smell.

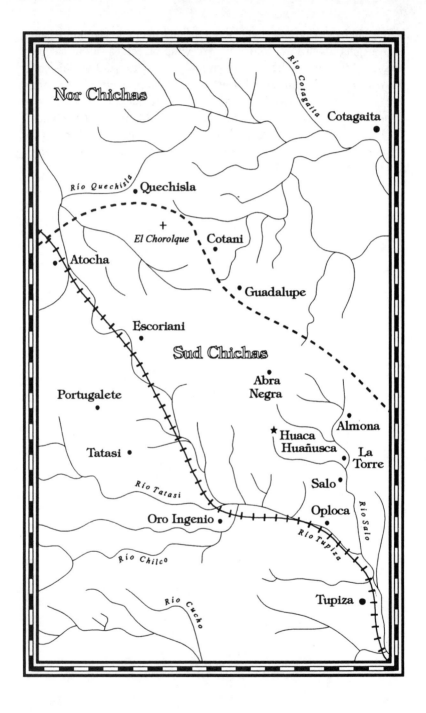

11 · THE DEAD COW

WHEN morning comes, Dan and I shiver into our clothing and join Eric, Pamela, and Roy for breakfast at the *rancho*. Afterward, Pancho brings the jeep around, and we set off for Tupiza to complete the arrangements for the exhumation. In the scrubby yellow hills halfway there, we meet a thirty-*llama* pack train and stop to chat with the drovers, who tell us that they haul salt from Uyuni south and goods from Tarija north in the space of about six weeks. Sleeping in the open on the *altiplano* must be miserable, but walking alongside these graceful beasts, with their colorful ear-tassels and tinkling necklaces, would be infinitely more pleasant than spending six weeks working in a place like San Vicente.

We continue our journey, bouncing east along a narrow road that overlooks a wide valley, then descending into a canyon flanked by spectacular badlands—red sandstone on the left and white on the right. Pancho stops the jeep on the narrow strip of land that divides the canyon from the valley. We stand in the wind and gaze across the panorama to the blue mountains on the horizon until the cold finally drives us back into the vehicle. In the sheltered *lecho* at the bottom of the hill, we are soon peeling off our jackets and sweaters and rolling the windows down. By the time we reach temperate Tupiza, we have thawed completely.

We check into the hotel, take showers, and regroup in the airy dining room with picture windows and French doors overlooking the courtyard, where bougainvillea, pansies, and trumpet vines are in full bloom. After ordering lunch, we begin discussing the tasks that lie ahead of us in Tupiza. Roy says that we should pay courtesy calls on the local officials, and Eric wants to take a crack at the judicial archives. Dan and I are eager to return to the COMIBOL shed. Because the Aramayo letter book we found on our previous visit to Tupiza contains only the outgoing letters and telegrams from the Tupiza office, we feel certain that the incoming correspondence is still somewhere in the shed. We'd like to dismantle the shelves and look at every single book until we find all the missing pieces of the puzzle. Roy and Eric want to participate in the search, and good-sport Pamela volunteers to come along; even though she can't read Spanish, she can help sort the books by date.

The waitress brings out two large bottles of beer, five glasses, and a basket of bread. Roy asks for *llajua* to spread on the bread, and we drink a toast to having survived a night in San Vicente. At this point, Pancho returns from eating lunch and gassing up the jeep for his return to Telamayo. After Eric pays him for his time and gasoline, I prevail on him to go over some topographical maps I've been studying in an effort to discover the route Butch and Sundance took from the holdup site to San Vicente. As Pancho is telling me which roads and trails are passable and how long it would take to travel them by mule, a jaundiced, loose-limbed fellow with a black hat and a flowing silk scarf comes into the dining room.

Roy stands up and goes to greet him. "Guillermo! How are you?"

"I'm fine, but what are you doing so far from home?"

When Roy explains our project, Guillermo exclaims, "What a coincidence! I am here doing research on the same subject!"

"Why don't you join us?" Roy gestures toward the table.

"Just let me put my things away." Guillermo enters his room, which opens off the dining room.

Roy returns to the table and says that he met Guillermo some months before at a rock-art symposium in Santa Cruz. "He is now researching Butch and Sundance. Maybe he has found out something useful, and we could join forces."

Guillermo comes out of his room and sits in my chair. He appropriates my glass of beer and teases Roy about working with *gringos*, then mentions his own work with a Miami group making a documentary about Butch and Sundance. "I'm going to an auction at Chajrahuasi tomorrow. They're disposing of the contents of the library, and I plan to buy it all." Then he says that he's gone through the COMIBOL archives and talks about what he has found.

Pancho takes his leave at this point, and I sit down at the table in time to hear Guillermo describe the letter in which Manuel Aramayo complained that the judges in Uyuni were giving the company more trouble than the bandits did.

"How interesting," Dan says in an unusually brusque tone.

What's his problem? The guy may have an irritating high-pitched voice and nervous laugh, but that doesn't justify Dan's rudeness. If

Guillermo is a friend of Roy's, why can't Dan at least pretend to be civil to him?

Eric signals Dan to follow him, then gets up and says to Pamela, "I have to go to the room for a minute." He leaves, and Dan follows him without a word to anybody.

Roy diplomatically changes the subject to rock art as the waitress brings our soup. Five minutes pass, then Roy says, "I'd better go check on Eric and Dan and let them know their soup is getting cold."

Leaving Pamela and me with Guillermo, Roy disappears up the stairs and doesn't return. Meanwhile, I ask Guillermo what he's found in his research.

"I have many documents from the COMIBOL archives," he says.

"From the letter book?"

"I went through everything and took many documents."

"Did you take photocopies or the original documents themselves?"

"I took the originals."

"But those documents are part of the historical record. They should be there for any historian to look at. You can't own history."

"I took them to keep them safe from *gringos* who want to come in here and steal our history."

"If you remove historical documents, you're the one who is stealing." I turn to Pamela and switch into English. "You can stay here with this worm if you want to, but I'm leaving."

The bewildered Pamela, whose lack of Spanish has kept her from following the conversation since Guillermo first sat down, is left sitting at the table with the untouched bowls of soup, the half-drunk glasses of beer, and the man who will forever after be known as "the Worm."

Within moments, she joins me upstairs, where our menfolk are holding a war council.

"The first thing we must do is to establish whether he is telling the truth," says Roy.

"That's a good point," says Dan. "He could have been lying about the archives. He didn't actually say anything that he couldn't have learned from one of our articles, and there are plenty of those floating around in Tupiza."

"Wálter Gutiérrez," I declare, "would never let him walk off with the originals."

We head straight for the COMIBOL office, where we ascertain that Wálter Gutiérrez has left and is now working for the municipal

223

government, and that the current COMIBOL agent, Alfredo Mejía, is out of town. We persuade his wife to open the shed and are relieved to find that it has not been touched since our last visit. "People do not like to go into this building," says Señora Mejía, "because they think it is haunted by ghosts from the Aramayo family."

The Worm may have assumed that the letter book unearthed on our previous trip and now stored in a cabinet is all there is: He might not know about the shed or about the possibility of additional documents waiting to be found. Regardless, he didn't remove any of the documents from the letter book, so he probably fabricated the entire story.

Señora Mejía asks us to wait until morning to begin going through the letter books in the shed, as her husband should have returned by then. In the meantime, Roy and Eric go to the old customs house and call on the district judge, Dr. Dionisio Romero, to advise him of the proposed exhumation in San Vicente. He says that the matter falls under his jurisdiction, and that we will need an order signed by him before we can proceed with the exhumation, but that we may search the judicial archives without filing a *solicitud*.

Dan and I begin looking up old friends. The owner of our hotel tells us that the historian Francisco Salazar has died since our last visit; when we try to visit his daughter Dora, we can't find her house. Gastón Michel, no longer the subprefect, now operates a bar named the "007," but he is indisposed when we call. While Eric and Pamela plow through the judicial archives, Dan and I take Roy to the town hall, just south of the main plaza, to meet Wálter Gutiérrez. After the usual pleasantries, Don Wálter says that he made some inquiries after our previous visit and learned that Butch and Sundance's friend Santiago Hutcheon lived in the building now occupied by the local high school.

Don Wálter shares an office with Carlos Eduardo "Lalo" Mostajo Silva, a young man with straight black hair, classical features, and an interest in history. "In the early 1900s, there were two hotels—the Paris and the Americano—but they closed a long time ago, and the families of the owners no longer live here."

Lalo volunteers to introduce us to the mayor, Aida Moreno de Claros, and Roy says, "Yes, that would be a good idea."

Lalo disappears briefly, then tells us to come back at six o'clock.

In the meantime, Don Wálter has mentioned that Doña Teresa Aramayo, the widow of Fernando Aramayo, is in town for a visit. Don Wálter telephones her on our behalf and learns that she knows nothing about the auction mentioned by the Worm. She offers to accompany us to Chajrahuasi and give us a tour of the house, and we eagerly accept.

We scare up transportation—a jeep belonging to fellow guests at the hotel—and drive to the small adobe home of Doña Teresa's hosts. Dressed in a skirt and sweater, dark stockings, sensible shoes, and a gossamer scarf with metallic highlights, she emerges from the house and climbs into the jeep. "What is it that you are looking for?" she asks.

"We're investigating the 1908 holdup of an Aramayo payroll and the subsequent shootout with the bandits in San Vicente," says Roy. "Do you know anything about it? You probably weren't born yet, but maybe someone mentioned it to you."

"I am ninety years old, well conserved, and very lucid, but I don't have a good sense of the events you described. I know vaguely. I heard something vaguely. There were three or four who died. An Englishman named Smith robbed a shipment of a hundred and fifty thousand *pesos bolivianos* on a train from Uyuni to Pulacayo. They were an Englishman, an American, and the other I don't remember. They had hidden themselves in a cave. The train came from Uyuni with a conductor and some twenty passengers. They had blocked the train with rocks and said, 'Hands up!' Then the shootout began. Afterward, they fled down the mountain on foot to Santa Catalina, Argentina. Three or four were arrested there and taken to Uyuni, and all the money was recovered. But they were such a bother in jail—drinking and causing trouble—that they were released."

She has confused the 1908 holdup with a 1922 robbery by a notorious trio of *gringos* called the Smith gang, but at least their tale had a happy ending.

At Chajrahuasi, the guards defer to Doña Teresa and let us wander through the once-magnificent mansion, which has been broken up into offices and furnished with filing cabinets, metal desks and chairs, and office equipment. Although most of the walls have been painted bureaucratic shades of beige and green, many of the Arts-and-Crafts hammered-metal light fixtures remain, not yet replaced by fluorescent tubes. What is left of the Aramayos' belongings—furniture, paintings, and the like—has been crammed into the old library. We squeeze into the room and find it packed so tightly that we can't examine anything. A built-in bookcase holds a few novels and other books, but we see nothing related to the mine company.

* * *

We run into Dr. Oscar Llano Serpa, a stocky man of about sixty, who says he heard that Butch and Sundance were killed at Eucaliptus during a holdup, but he thinks the story is false. "I used to work in the San Vicente area," he says, "and I saw the grave. There were two tombs side by side within a chain fence, I think. I can't really remember where. A woman from San Vicente went to look at the dead bandits, but unfortunately she has died, and there was no registration of the tomb's location, so it is impossible to be certain of exactly where it is. You might be able to find out from the judicial file. The Aramayo company sent the judges there to carry out the requirements of the Bolivian law, and there are files in the Supreme Court in Sucre."

"My uncle used to work there," says Roy.

"We may have to make a trip to Sucre," says Dan.

"The stolen shipment contained gold and silver coins," says Dr. Llano. "The two *bandoleros* who were killed had come up from Chile—from Antofagasta to Uyuni—and then went south, according to people who knew. The military did not intervene. It was the Bolivian police who killed the pair."

In the evening, we troop over to the mayor's office. Wearing a tailored white suit and sitting behind the big wooden desk in her book-lined office, Aida Moreno de Claros looks like, well, a mayor. But what is she doing in a position of power in rural Bolivia? How did she get elected in a town where so many women seem to be relegated to scut work or wall calendars?

Once we absorb this evidence of progress, we explain our project. The mayor asks a few questions, then wishes us well and sends us on our way.

The air is chilly but not unpleasant as we sit on benches in the plaza and discuss where to eat. Suddenly, the street in front of us fills with children waving blue and white flags and carrying candles in colored-paper holders. They march around the plaza, accompanied by a cacophonous brass band playing Barry Sadler's "Ballad of the Green Beret."

"The long arm of multiculturalism," observes Dan.

Early in the morning, we walk over to COMIBOL. Señor Mejía has not returned, and his wife doesn't know when he'll be back, but she agrees to let us begin working in the shed. Our first task is to locate all

226

the books with dates near November 1908 and within the period covered by Frank Aller's inquiry. Once we have culled these from the rest, we repair to the sunny patio. Each of us takes a book and begins going through it one page at a time. As we make minor discoveries, we shout them out and then keep reading.

"A 1908 order for cement!" yells Eric. "So the tombstone *could* be that old."

"Here's a proposal to install a telegraph line between Tupiza and Quechisla," I announce, "and it's dated *after* the holdup. The reason that Butch and Sundance didn't cut the telegraph wire is that it wasn't there yet."

"On November ninth, they paid fifteen *bolivianos* to the messenger who brought the news of the shootout from San Vicente to Tupiza," says Eric. "And on the sixteenth, they paid the traveling expenses of the examining magistrate and a notary for an inquest in San Vicente into the deaths of the robbers and—are you ready?—two hundred and fifty *bolivianos* for a Doctor Eguía to conduct an autopsy on the cadavers! If we can find the autopsy report, it could be a gold mine."

Our euphoria fades ten minutes later when Eric finds a November 24 entry showing that Doctor Eduardo Eguía had returned the sum of 150 *bolivianos* to the company because his trip to San Vicente had not taken place.

"But if he didn't go," asks Pamela, "why didn't he return *all* the money they gave him?"

"Maybe he went but didn't perform the autopsy," suggests Roy.

One more mystery to solve.

By now, we are filthy and ravenous. We wash our hands and faces and head for the nearest restaurant. While waiting for the food to be prepared, I decide to run out and buy some lotion for my hands, which are chapped from the dry air. As I am leaving the restaurant, I bump into Dora Salazar.

"The market is too far away," she says after I've explained my mission. "Come on back to my place. I'll give you some hand cream."

We have passed her house several times without recognizing it, because she has remodeled it since the death of her father. The odds-and-ends shop is gone, replaced by a formal salon with antique furniture and carved wooden doors. To reach her bathroom, we pass through the courtyard, which contains several birdcages. "I have to lock up my doves when I go out," says Dora, "to protect them from my cats."

Dora has a menagerie to rival Michael Jackson's private zoo: In addition to the doves and five cats downstairs, she has a partridge, an eagle, a turtle, and a monkey upstairs, and a dog on her roof.

While smearing the heavy pink cream on my hands, I ask whether she still has one of our articles, because we gave away our last copy in San Vicente and need to have more copies made for the local officials we are courting.

"No," she says, "I am sorry to confess that I lent all the articles to a man who is here doing similar research, and now he won't return them."

"By any chance," I ask, "is his name Guillermo?"

"How did you know?"

After I describe our run-in with the Worm, she says, "You cannot imagine how it upsets me to hear this. I thought he was honorable, but I shouldn't have trusted him." With obvious embarrassment, she reveals that he has borrowed $200 and refuses to repay her.

After lunch, Dan hits the jackpot: He finds the book containing all the incoming correspondence, including a message Carlos Peró scrawled in pencil on two pieces of notepaper shortly after the holdup. We drop what we are doing and gather around. Dan's hands shake as he unpins the small, lined pages and begins to read aloud in Spanish. He stumbles through a couple of sentences, then hands the note to Roy.

"Here," says Dan. "You can do it a lot faster and better."

We sit entranced while Roy reads us the note.

November 4, 1908

Mr. Rozo

At 9:30 in the morning, we encountered two well-armed Yankees, who awaited us with their faces covered by bandannas and their rifles ready, and they made us dismount and open the baggage, from which they took only the cash shipment. They also took from us a dark brown mule ("Aramayo"), which is known to the stable hands in Tupiza, with a new hemp rope.

The two Yankees are tall; one [is] thin and the other—who carried a good pair of Hertz binoculars—[is] heavyset.

They clearly came from Tupiza, where they must have been waiting for my departure to make their strike, because from the beginning they did not ask me for anything other than the cash shipment.

Please have a messenger hasten to Don Manuel E. Aramayo at once with this note, so that measures to capture them can be taken immediately.

They must have slept in Salo, because from a certain place as we ascended the hill, we saw two silhouettes—who were undoubtedly they—in the distant gap. Don Manuel should not send any more cash shipments without an armed guard, because it is clear that the Yankees in Tupiza are there with the expectation of assaulting whatever shipment the company makes. Andrés Gutiérrez is carrying this note and is charged with delivering it to you as soon as possible.

Carlos Peró

The place in which the Yankees awaited us was on the descent on this side of the heights of Salo, almost at the foot of the hill, at Huaca Huañusca.

"Yankees!" says Dan. "He said nothing about any Chileans."
Roy reads the handwritten message on the piece of paper to which the note was pinned:

Salo

Dear Don Manuel:

Immediately upon my return here, the attached came from Don Carlos, so explicit that it needs no further comment from me.

Those suspects did not sleep in Salo, but I can't give any additional information.

It is 6:30, as the messenger leaves.

Sincerely,
M. Roberts

"This would have been Malcom Roberts," I explain, "an Aramayo official who told a mining engineer named Victor Hampton about the holdup in the 1920s, when Hampton was working in San Vicente."

Another note from Roberts, sent to Tupiza three hours after the first one, said he had just learned that "two individuals were seen approaching here and shortly thereafter disappearing. (They were on foot.) It occurred to us that perhaps the suspects who robbed the cash shipment waited for nightfall to pass between here and there . . . although perhaps one should not assume that the thieves" would remain in the area for twelve hours after the robbery. "Various people have gone out and around here to see whether there are any strangers. Last night, no one was seen and no one slept here other than [Carlos Peró's party]."

When Roy turns the page and discovers a long letter written by Carlos Peró—who had continued on the trail toward Quechisla and stopped for the night at Cotani—I want to jump up and yell like a cheerleader, but I don't want to miss a single word. In the letter, Peró told the Aramayo officials in Tupiza everything he could remember about the holdup and the bandits:

My dear sirs:

The purpose of this letter is to confirm the contents of the [note] I wrote quickly to the attention of Mr. Rozo, the Salo manager, to have passed on without delay to Tupiza, advising that on the descent of Huaca Huañusca, on the rugged, bottom part, we were surprised by two Yankees, whose faces were covered with bandannas and whose rifles were cocked and ready to fire at our slightest suspicious movement. In a very pleasant manner, they ordered my servant Gil González and my son Mariano to dismount, having found me following them on foot, and immediately ordered us to hand over the money we were carrying, to which I answered that they could search us and take whatever they wanted, as we were hardly in a position to offer any resistance. One of them quickly began to search our saddlebags and, not finding what he was looking for, demanded that we unload our baggage, specifying that they were not interested in our personal money nor in any articles that belonged to us, but only in the money that we were carrying for the company. They knew that I spoke English, in which language they asked me if we were not carrying eighty thousand *bolivianos*, to which I replied that the sum was not quite as large as they believed. And when I saw that there was no point in hiding anything, a search of the baggage having begun, I informed them that it was only fifteen thousand.

What I said caused great anguish, momentarily silencing the bandit nearest us. As soon as they saw the package containing the cash, which was beside another very similar package, the bandit conducting the search took it and passed it to his companion without bothering with the other package nor searching any more of the baggage, which shows that they had clear knowledge of the package with the cash. Then they demanded that I give them our servant's mule—the dark brown named "Aramayo," with the Quechisla brand—which is known by all our stable hands in Tupiza. We had to unsaddle the mule and hand it over along with a brand new hemp rope. Keeping their eyes on us and their rifles ready, they departed with the mule. The search was done at the foot of the hill, where a type of natural caves are, so they went deeper into the ravine and undoubtedly continued spying on us from below, while they refitted their baggage. It is quite possible that there were more bandits hidden, because when one of our pack animals broke away from the trail on the descent, our servant noted various animals hidden in the ravine.

The two Yankees wore new, dark-red, thin-wale corduroy suits with narrow, soft-brimmed hats, the brims turned down in such a way that, with the bandannas tied behind their ears, only their eyes could be seen. One of the bandits, the one who came closest to and talked with me, is thin and of normal stature, and the other, who always maintained a certain distance, is heavyset and taller. Both of them carried new carbines, which appeared to be of the Mauser-type, small calibre and thick barrel, rather like—or perhaps the same as—the type Carlos Schmidt has. But they were completely new, which is to say, they had never been used. The bandits also carried Colt revolvers, and I believe they also had very small Browning revolvers outside their cartridge belts, which were filled with rifle ammunition.

Certainly these bandits had been in Tupiza for some time, studying our company's habits and preparing their strike with total coolness and knowledge, and counting on the cooperation of their confederates to gather additional information. Moreover, they undoubtedly planned their retreat carefully; otherwise,

231

they would not have left us with our animals or they would have killed us in order to avoid accusations or to gain time.

"This has all the hallmarks of a job by Butch and Sundance," observes Dan. "And they spoke to him in English."
"What does it say next?" I ask. The commentary can wait.
Roy resumes reading.

When we were free, I initially thought of taking the road to Oploca, in order to send a message from there about what had happened, but on second thought I concluded that they might have people posted on that road to stop us from sounding the alarm, and so we continued on the road to Guadalupe with the hope of meeting someone with whom we could send word, and at Abra Negra, where a road cuts off for Almona, we had the luck to encounter Andrés Gutiérrez, a resident of that area and a muleteer in Salo, to whom we gave the two pages scribbled in pencil from my notebook addressed to the manager at Salo, the message I mentioned at the start of this letter.

We left Salo at six in the morning and, from a point at the bottom of the hill, thought we saw two black dots that crossed over the pass on the hill, but because we were a great distance away, we could not distinguish whether the people were on foot or mounted. But undoubtedly those two black dots were the two individuals who were spying on us from afar with the Goertz trihedral binoculars that the taller, heavier bandit carried. The binoculars caught my attention because of their type and small size, and because they appeared to be very new.

It is useless to send any more cash shipments without taking exceptional precautions to avoid scrutiny, or having sufficient armed men to be ready for whatever surprise. It is also possible, given the relative increase in unemployed North Americans in Tupiza and Uyuni, that there are enough of them to assault and seize our company's cash shipments from all sides. Perhaps it would be good to bring up a special detective from Buenos Aires to conduct a surveillance on all of them.

Upon arriving in Cotani, I encountered two North Americans who were carrying only some saddlebags and a woman's saddle, but they were armed with rifles and pistols. They had slept in Cotani last night and were going to sleep in Guadalupe today. They said that they had lost a revolver in Cotani, and because only a boy had been in their room, they were taking the boy, whose name was Faustino Duran, to Tupiza to report him to the police.

The robbery happened at 9:15 this morning.

I am sorry for what happened; it was unavoidable; and I am hopeful that the measures that have been taken as a result of my message from Abra Negra will help in recovering the money and capturing the bandits.

Sincerely,
Carlos Peró

The messenger who is carrying this is Agustín Llave, who left at 6:00 P.M. with instructions to travel all night.

"Note the phrase 'in a very pleasant manner,' " says Dan. "Being pleasant was Butch's trademark. In fact, the whole *modus operandi* is his. Down to avoiding any bloodshed."

"The physical descriptions fit Butch and Sundance," I add. "And nowhere did Peró call them anything but North Americans or Yankees. Whoever said one of the bandits was a Chilean named Madariaga must have invented it."

On November 5, Peró traveled from Cotani to Quechisla. The next day, he wrote another letter to his superiors in Tupiza. Roy reads it to us.

My dear sirs:

This is to confirm my letter from Cotani . . . sent with the messenger Agustín Llave. . . . Lieutenant Alcoreza and his squad came to Cotani yesterday, and I asked him to come here to inform him in detail about what happened with the bandits at Huaca Huañusca. He leaves for [Tupiza] tomorrow at dawn, because I think it is no longer necessary to continue checking other places in search of the bandits, who could have returned by Salo the day before yesterday at 12 noon and passed by Tupiza or its vicinity toward the Argentine border at 3 P.M., more or less, as my note from Abra Negra reached Tupiza at

8:30 P.M., more than enough time for the bandits to get far away and reach safety.

Today, Mr. Roberts came and told us that the two North Americans I encountered on the approach to Cotani apparently have been taken prisoner in Salo. In view of the arms and money they carried and the strange way they traveled, they are very possibly also criminals. Lieutenant Alcoreza did not meet these two North Americans on the Salo road, and . . . he found the boy Faustino Duran, who had been left by the Yankees. . . . As I met these Yankees upon arriving at Cotani at three in the afternoon, and they awakened in Salo, they must have arrived there before Lieutenant Alcoreza left Salo.

I advise you to station a squad of at least six or eight men in Quechisla, as much for the danger here from the constant passing of adventurers on foot and horseback as for reasons of security that have not escaped your attention, and so that we could lend assistance in the vicinity should something occur there. Moreover, we could then exercise effective vigilance over, and take into custody as necessary, all the suspicious individuals who pass by.

"I'm confused," says Eric. "Who was captured in Salo?"

"They were a couple of relatively innocent bystanders named Walters and Murray," replies Dan. "We read about them in the old newspapers."

"Next," I plead.

After running through a few messages of little or no import, Roy comes to a letter written on November 7 by Malcolm Roberts, who had returned to Quechisla. "It's to Captain Justo P. Concha," says Roy.

"He led the patrol that killed Butch and Sundance," says Dan.

We're finally going to learn what happened in San Vicente!

My dear sir:

At 8:30 P.M. I received your valued message addressed to the manager at Chocaya, dated today, who was kind enough to inform me that the cash shipment's assailants had been captured, having been killed after some resistance. Please accept my most effusive congratulations for the brilliant success in capturing the bandits, recovering the cash shipment, and inflicting such an exemplary and merited punishment that it will certainly serve as sufficient warning against the repetition of such bold assaults and will restore public confidence. . . . I profoundly lament the death of the brave soldier in the fulfillment of his noble duty.

As you are situated more or less equally between Uyuni and Tupiza, and I am not finished with the steps that must be followed with the authorities in these cases, I am of the opinion that you should decide where to go, but because our headquarters are in Tupiza, I would personally prefer that you go there, if it would not inconvenience you.

Sending you deep thanks from myself and from Señor Carlos Peró, who endured the assault and who is now at my side,

I remain . . .

M. Roberts

Not again! Won't somebody please tell us exactly what happened in San Vicente?

On November 8, Roberts sent a note to the Aramayo office in Tupiza saying that Carlos Peró was going to San Vicente that day "in order to make arrangements to settle the matter" and that the messenger bringing the note was "going to collect the cash shipment." A November 10 message from Roberts said that Peró had not yet come back from San Vicente. Once he did return, Peró learned that he would have to turn around and go back to San Vicente for a judicial inquest, which was scheduled for November 18. Before departing on this trip, Peró wrote to the Aramayo office in Tupiza and responded to misinformation being circulated as to the identities of the bandits and their confederates. Roy reads the letter.

My dear sirs:

On my return from San Vicente, I received your message of November 8.

The communication, which was said to have been sent privately to our Don Manuel, that the bandits had offered me their services and that they had asked me the day of my return here, is completely false. Moreover, the two bandits truthfully were completely unknown to me, and they had never talked to me in Tupiza. It has been confirmed with the other two Yankees—who look like Austrians, individuals much taller than the two bandits and much heavier—that I told them there was no work for them in the company; also, they were just railroad mechanics, and I had no occasion to tell them when I would be returning, because there was no point.

In reference to your message . . . transmitted to me by telephone from Cotani, this morning I leave with my son Mariano and my servant Gil González to sleep in Tatasi and to be in San Vicente early on the eighteenth to meet with the authorities who are coming from Tupiza.

In reality, it was very unfortunate and inexplicable that Captain Concha did not go to Tupiza, as they had convinced him in San Vicente that he should do, and as he promised to do. Don Aristides Daza had worked on the report until one in the morning and the guide from Tupiza was ready; therefore, it was a surprise for everyone in San Vicente to learn that the captain had risen at dawn and gone to Uyuni without giving any explanation.

I'm returning to you the enclosed letter from Mr. P. McPartland and with it my response, in which you will see that what has been communicated to him is a gross calumny and the work of a troublemaker.

> Sincerely,
> Carlos Peró

No copy of Peró's letter to McPartland is in the letter book, but McPartland's original letter of complaint has survived. McPartland was employed by Butch and Sundance's friend Santiago Hutcheon, who also hauled material and personnel for the Aramayo company, which may explain how McPartland came to be suspected of complicity in the robbery.

Señor Manuel Aramayo, Tupiza
Sir

    I beg to draw your attention to the fact that Charles Peró of Quechisla has been indiscreet enough to express the opinion publicly to several persons that I am one of the individuals concerned in the robbery of certain moneys from him, as I am led to believe that this took place on or about the 4th [of this month]. Please note that I arrived in Potosí on the 3rd . . . with Mr. Hutcheon's Coach and stayed at the Hotel Colon until the 5th . . . , on the face of which you will see that it is impossible to connect me with the matter.

Trusting that you will contradict the said statement, as I do not wish to be talked about all over Bolivia and probably have to leave the country over it. . . .

P. McPartland

If true, the information in this letter might have cleared McPartland of any charge that he participated in the holdup itself, but the fact that he was out of town when the robbery happened does not mean that he couldn't have passed along information about how the company's payrolls were carried or how much the bandits could expect to find. The accounting records show that an 80,000-*boliviano* payroll went to Quechisla the week after the holdup, which means that the bandits *did* have inside information about the payroll but struck a week too soon. Of course, McPartland would have been less likely than an Aramayo employee to know the size of specific cash shipments. If the Aramayo company ever identified the outlaws' confederates, we find no record of it.

Nor do we find any documentation that the Uyuni court returned the recovered cash shipment, but a November 20, 1908, letter from Manuel Aramayo to the company's agent in Uyuni notes "that the subprefect there has 14,300 deposited in its account—while offering to give you 700, which would make up the difference with the 15,000 recovered— and that the 14,300 are to remain in escrow while the matter is being settled. There is no doubt that it would be better for us to have the amount belonging to us, even if in the form of a deposit, and that it would be more secure in our power. The judges, doctor, and so forth, from here went to San Vicente to investigate the event and judge the case, not of the capturers, as they pretend in Uyuni, but the action of the assailants, who died as a result of their armed aggression."

We come across several more documents, but nothing can compare with the letters from Carlos Peró. Dan and I expected to find something in this search, but we never imagined that Peró would have been so observant and articulate.

Since our first visit to Tupiza, half the shopowners in town have bought photocopiers. The instrument of torture we had to rely on last time has gone to the electronic junkyard in the sky, and the machine we are using now is fast and good at its job. While the machine whirs and clicks, we review what we have learned. Hearing it for the first time in English—in our excitement over the discovery, we neglected to translate the letters for her—Pamela understands why we've been whooping.

"Well," says Dan, "we now know nearly everything there is to know about the holdup."

"We also know that the Aramayo officials were mad at Captain Concha for going to Uyuni," I say, "although that hardly justifies their yanking his reward. After all, Malcom Roberts told the captain that he should decide where to go."

"But," says Eric, "we still don't know exactly what happened in San Vicente. Do you think that Doctor Eguía, who was supposed to perform the autopsy, could have written anything about the case?"

The local hospital is named for Eguía, but his papers are in the School of Fine Arts. Located on the corner of the main plaza, the blue-and-white mansion was erected in 1858 for a diplomat, and the property stretched to the river. Later, Dr. Eguía bought the building and lived there. His papers, including bound copies of his letters, remain in the library; we look through them but find nothing about San Vicente or the Aramayo bandits.

Afterward, Dan and I accompany Roy to Lalo's nineteenth-century home. As we listen to the sad guitar of Alfredo Domínguez, Lalo serves us *chuflays*—a Bolivian specialty made of 7UP, *singani*, lemons, and ice. In the morning, while Roy and Dan finish the fruitless search of the judicial archives, I stay in bed. Too many *chuflays*. I have just dozed off when someone knocks at the door.

"Who is it?" I yell in English and Spanish.

"When will you be going out?" answers the maid.

"Never."

"But I need to come in."

"Not today. We'll make the beds ourselves."

"But—"

"Go away."

I have just dozed off again when there is another knock at the door. "What is it now?"

"I just need to come in for a moment, *señora*." This time, the intruder is a man.

"I'm sick. Please leave me alone."

The footsteps retreat down the hall, and at last I am free to escape into sleep. Minutes later, however, I jolt awake with the knowledge that I have about two seconds to reach the bathroom. I leap out of bed naked and my eyes meet those of a man perched on a ladder outside our scantily curtained window, from whose frame he is hanging a flag in honor of a local holiday. So *that's* why they wanted to get into the room!

Meanwhile, Dan goes to the military office that sells topographical maps. As he is waiting to learn whether they have the maps he has requested, he overhears the Worm talking to a clerk in the next room. The more Dan thinks about the Worm's behavior, the madder he gets. When the Worm comes out to pay the cashier before collecting his purchases, Dan erupts, denouncing him as a charlatan, a liar, and a thief.

"Okay, yes," says the Worm, laughing skittishly, "I lied about taking the documents. I was just trying to impress you."

"You have also been taking money from a friend of ours and refusing to pay it back."

The Worm pulls a fat wad of *bolivianos* out of his pocket and offers to give Dan what he owes Dora, but Dan tells him to repay her directly. "And if you don't repay her immediately, I'll beat your brains out."

Once his map transaction is complete, the Worm hastily departs and heads straight for Dora's house. He repays the $200, then marches into the office of the district judge—who is a friend of his—to lodge a formal complaint against Dan for threatening him.

We still need the judge's signature on the exhumation order, so Dan has no choice but to attend a hearing and try to smooth over the incident as best he can. With Roy along as his representative, he goes to the judge's chambers. The Worm whines for a while about how beastly Dan was, and Dan quotes a Chinese proverb about making big problems into small problems and making small problems disappear. He goes on to say that he was perhaps guilty of being *demasiado caballero*—too much the gentleman—in defending the honor of the women of Tupiza. The judge apparently buys Dan's argument, because the ruling begins with a quotation of the Chinese proverb. As a sop to the Worm, the judge requires Dan to sign a formal apology, which is read on television.

The viewing audience may be perplexed to learn that one person they've never heard of is sorry he insulted another person they've never heard of, but those of us with personal interests in the case welcome the news. I am glad that Dan will not be going to jail. Eric is relieved that the project won't be scuttled because of the incident. Pamela is pleased that she and Eric are now free to catch an all-night bus to Potosí, where she can visit colonial churches instead of rooting around in dusty archives and making do with cold showers or none at all.

By morning, I am well enough to travel and we set off for Salo in a borrowed Land Rover. Now that we have Carlos Peró's letter as a guide, we hope to find someone who can lead us to the holdup site on Huaca Huañusca, which is Quechua for "Dead Cow." "It probably got its name from the fact that a cow died there once," says Roy. Within half an hour, we are bouncing north on the Salo River *lecho*. Dodging hares and sharp rocks, we roar past a boy wearing a Batman backpack and carrying firewood on a bicycle.

In Salo, we approach one of the women who operate the roadside eateries that cater to buses like the one Eric and Pamela caught last night. "Is there anyone around here who could guide us to Huaca Huañusca?" asks Roy.

The woman points to an old man wearing baggy pants, two jackets, rubber-soled shoes, a Coca-Cola hat, and a scarf. "Juan Valdivieso," she says. "He knows every *tola* bush and cactus in the area."

When Roy reads him Carlos Peró's description of the place where the holdup occurred, Señor Valdivieso immediately recognizes it. A traveling charcoal vendor whose route takes him over the same trail Peró followed, Señor Valdivieso lives in nearby La Torre and has seven children, the youngest of whom is twenty-two. He readily agrees to lead the way and directs us past small fields of wheat, beans, potatoes, onions, and corn and up the same road Dan and I took last time. But instead of turning away from the trail, as our previous guide said it did, the road crosses the trail numerous times.

Along the way up the cactus-studded hill, Señor Valdivieso answers our questions about traveling in the region. "A *llama* can go about twenty kilometers a day. A burro can go thirty kilometers, and a mule or a horse can go thirty-five or forty kilometers a day. It takes two days to travel from La Torre to Chorolque with four burros carrying charcoal.''

So Butch and Sundance could have ridden twenty-four miles on their mules that day—or even more if they kept traveling after nightfall.

"Where do you get charcoal around here?" asks Dan.

"We chop down *churqui* in an area south of Salo, cut up the branches, and burn the pieces underground.''

Churqui was also used for telegraph poles. Although the wires have been removed, many of the poles are still standing and serve as landmarks that help us keep track of Carlos Peró's route, which generally parallels the road but sometimes detours around a hill or into a gully. As we climb onto a scrubby ridge, Roy spots a huge pile of rocks on the hillside. Once we reach the top, he insists that we pull over. "It is an *apacheta,* no?"

"*Sí, sí,*" says Señor Valdivieso. "The trail was here before the Spaniards came, but the *apacheta* was built about thirty years ago, at the same time they built the road."

Roy explains to us that travelers add rocks to the *apacheta* to appease the gods and ensure safe journeys. He clearly enjoys finding evidence that cultural traditions are being preserved, connecting the past he studies with the present he lives in. While he climbs onto the *apacheta* and soaks up its spiritual magic, Dan and I stroll beyond the rocks to a twisted telegraph pole and try to imagine Carlos Peró trudging up the hill, his teenaged son and servant riding ahead of him. The trail is littered with feathers. "From partridges,'' says Señor Valdivieso. "Lots of partridges here. The foxes and eagles hunt them."

"How much farther is it to Huaca Huañusca?" asks Dan.

"We're already there. The whole mountain is Huaca Huañusca. The rugged part described in the letter is up ahead a few kilometers.''

While walking back to the jeep, which is parked in the hollow of a long ridge that looks like the spine of a cow with bony haunches running off to the sides, I grasp what our guide meant: The name reflects the hill's shape, not its history. Once back on the road, we pass a mine, then stop at a place called Gringo Huañusca. The terrain is not particularly rugged, but the name is highly suggestive. Could this place— which does not resemble a dead *gringo*—be named after the *gringos* who held up the Aramayo payroll and then died?

"No," says Señor Valdivieso. "They say that two *gringos* lived here and quarreled. One *gringo* killed his companion and then left."

"When did this happen?"

"I couldn't say. It was before I was born, which was in 1926."

Not far beyond Gringo Huañusca, we begin our descent into a huge ravine. The terrain is definitely more rugged, but our guide insists that we are not there yet. Finally, beside a rock painted with the words *Abra Guadalupe,* he says, "Now we walk."

After climbing out of the jeep, Roy checks his altimeter and says, "It's thirty-eight hundred meters. That's nearly twelve thousand feet."

The dusty trail slopes gradually downward into a series of hillocks and gullies. Roy and Señor Valdivieso, who have spent most of their lives at high altitudes, race along the convoluted trail. Dan is a runner and would have no trouble keeping up with them. My bout with pneumonia has left me with a mild case of asthma, however, and I would probably have difficulty with all of this up-and-down even at sea level. At this altitude, I can't walk twenty steps without feeling as though someone were sitting on my chest and squeezing every last molecule of air out of my lungs. Dan stays with me, but I know he is eager to see the holdup site.

Onward I struggle, hoping each hill will be the last. The small gullies are surreal—full of twisted trees with spreading branches, prickly eared cacti, and huge clumps of bright-green *yareta*. In an especially appealing gully, where erosion has eaten into the asphalt hillside and left shady overhangs, I tell Dan to go on without me. I sit beside a trickling stream, take a copy of one of Carlos Peró's letters out of my pack, and begin translating his words into English. I can almost see Butch and Sundance—their hats pulled low and their bandannas over their faces— waiting for their victims in any one of these gullies.

After ten minutes, I feel rested enough to continue. The first hill isn't too bad, but the second one leaves me suffering. Determined to see the exact spot where the confrontation occurred, I forge onward a few steps at a time and at last reach the bend in the road where Butch and Sundance pulled their final job. Everything is just as Carlos Peró described it: the broken rocks that lean on each other to form "a type of" caves; the ravine from which the bandits could "continue spying" on their victims after the holdup; and the proximity to trails leading east, west, north, and south—an array of options that complicated the posses' search.

In the other gullies we've passed through, the bandits would have been visible to the first person to crest each hill, but here they could have remained hidden behind an outcrop until all three victims had come into view heading east—with the sun in their eyes. This is the perfect place for what turned out to be an imperfect crime. After all his careful planning, Butch had every reason to experience the "great anguish" Carlos Peró noted when he informed the bandits that their prize was not the 80,000 *bolivianos* they had anticipated but a measly 15,000—a difference equivalent to nearly $400,000 today. As if that wasn't bad enough, the pair wouldn't live long enough to spend more than a few *centavos*.

To follow up Dr. Oscar Llano Serpa's tip that the Bolivian supreme court's archives contain judicial files related to the Aramayo holdup, we detour to Sucre via Potosí on our way home. After a long taxi ride over dusty roads from Potosí, we at last reach a paved highway and begin descending into Sucre. Halfway down, the driver stops the car and gets out to wipe off the dust with a rag. Finally, he is satisfied, and we proceed to a fine hotel on the main plaza. When the driver opens the trunk, the bellboy takes one look at its contents and runs back into the hotel. He returns momentarily with a feather duster and cleans off our bags before carrying them inside.

Having gone to a lot of trouble to reach Sucre, we feel entitled to find nothing less than a copy of the report sent to Frank Aller in Chile. Instead, we find a couple of newspaper articles about the Aramayo holdup and the San Vicente shootout in the National Archives. The supreme court has no judicial file on the case, and a visit with Doctora Carmen Rua at the Sucre University yields nothing new. "After reading about Butch Cassidy in a newspaper," she says, "we searched all the archives in the city and found nothing. Perhaps you might find something in the archives of the prefecture in Potosí."

"We did," says Dan. "It wasn't enough."

Ordinarily, I'd be dispirited, but the thrill of seeing the holdup site and knowing exactly what happened there, thanks to Carlos Peró, will carry me through more dead ends than this.

Before returning to La Paz, we decide to play at being tourists for a while. An unshaven, voluble man in a yellow sweater, a yellow cap, and a yellow taxi carts us around to museums, churches, and historical sites, then asks whether we would like to see the municipal cemetery. "We are very proud of it. It is the most beautiful cemetery in all of Bolivia. The monuments and mausoleums, they are works of art."

"Why not?"

The taxi driver did not exaggerate. Miniature palaces flank some of the shaded pathways in the terraced cemetery. Elsewhere, elaborately sculpted tombstones sit in landscaped plots. Only the modern niches, stacked to unseemly heights, mar the beauty of the site. For the first time, I feel at home in a place where the living and the dead commune.

As we walk toward the exit, we notice two workmen in overalls hammering on chisels to clear away the concrete at the entrance of a niche ten or fifteen yards to our left. Once the niche is open, the men lay aside their tools and begin pulling a wooden coffin out. One man supports the foot of the coffin on his shoulders while the other man tries to position himself under the head of the coffin, then loses his grip on it. The coffin crashes to the ground, splintering the dark wood and filling the air with dust.

"Let's get out of here," says Dan.

"Not yet," I say. "If we're really going to dig up Butch and Sundance, I want to know what we're letting ourselves in for."

I begin walking toward the rubble, then stop when one of the workmen finishes prying away the remainder of the lid and reaches down into the broken coffin. He takes hold of a piece of dirty red cloth, a dress perhaps, and rips it in half lengthwise. Once the cloth is out of the way, he reaches into the coffin again and begins snapping off ribs as if they were dry branches and chucking them into a paper bag held open by his coworker. The men might just as easily be cleaning up a yard, bagging weeds and dead wood to be carted away and burned.

"I've seen enough."

We barely make it back to the hotel before I throw up.

12 · THE MAN IN THE CASA RODANTE

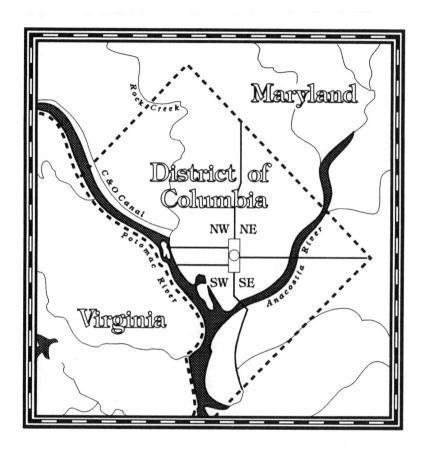

WE return to the States and find our answering machine asizzle with a message from Roger McCord, a New York magazine-publishing consultant, who says that he has the Bolivian judicial records we've been looking for. He and his then-wife Carolyn took the file from the archives in Tupiza in 1972, during a journey around South

America in a 1½-ton pickup with a camper on it. He's the man the Salazars and others saw in the *casa rodante*!

"I caught you on 'Unsolved Mysteries,' " he says when Dan telephones him. "Then I ran a computer search and found the article you guys wrote for *Américas* magazine, and the editor shared your number with me. I thought that maybe we could get together and compare notes, because you obviously have some facts, although I must tell you that you are wrong about the date of the shootout. It happened on the sixth, not the seventh, of November 1908."

"Are you sure?" says Dan. "We found several documents that specifically said the shootout took place on the seventh."

"Trust me. It happened on the evening of the sixth, but they didn't notify anyone until the next day."

The *mañana* factor.

"I assume you went to San Vicente," says Dan. "Did you find the grave?"

"We spent a couple of days there and met everyone in town, but there's nothing in the cemetery, and no one knew anything about the shootout or where the grave was."

"Did you talk to Froilán Risso?"

"I couldn't say without looking at my notes, but the name doesn't ring a bell, and anyway, as I said, we literally met everybody in San Vicente, and nobody knew a goddamned thing."

If nobody knew anything in 1972, either Risso fibbed to us or he was he out of town during Roger's visit. For the moment, however, any reservations we have about Risso's reliability or about Roger's taking the file—he *did* the thing that we were so furious at the Worm for pretending to have done—are outweighed by the prospect of finding out exactly what happened in San Vicente. Dan invites Roger to spend a weekend with us.

He accepts the invitation, then postpones the visit several times. I feel like a kid waiting for Christmas, but Dan is exasperatingly patient. "We'll see the file when we see it."

"But what if he changes his mind about showing it to us?"

"He won't. We have the other pieces of the puzzle. He's as eager to see the Aramayo papers and the diplomatic correspondence as we are to see the judicial file."

Finally, at eleven-thirty one warm night in early autumn, Roger parks his behemoth 1979 Lincoln Town Car in front of our house and rings the doorbell. Nearly four years have passed since we first heard about the man in the *casa rodante,* and here he is in the flesh: a square-shouldered man with a ruddy complexion and blue eyes.

"Oh, you have a cat!" He drops to his knees and pets Rio, who raises her haunches to get the full benefit of his attention.

"We named her Rio," says Dan, "after a cat who rode in a basket beside an Italian stunt driver from Rio de Janeiro to New York in a Studebaker in the late 1920s. Along the way, the driver performed a stunt called the 'Leap of Death' to raise money. The Pan American Highway didn't exist yet, so they took mule trails through the Andes. At one point, they had to make do with refined pork fat instead of motor oil, and three of their four mechanics died from malaria or accidents or something. In Colombia, they got held up by bandits who took everything of value—including the Italian's clothing—but they left Rio and her basket, and she made it all the way to New York."

"During our South American trip," says Roger, "Carolyn and I picked up three abandoned kittens in a campground near Bariloche, and they traveled with us the rest of the way. Carolyn still has Fatsy-Patsy, our dark-grey shorthair. She's eighteen years old now and has the softest fur. She went into heat in southwestern Bolivia and wandered off for three days, but she came back unsullied after failing to find any other cats in the desert. She's really tough, killed a fox once. Pookie Bear had broad shoulders and tiger stripes. He was fearless, but he died about four years ago. Wickie, our longhaired grey beauty, just died recently. God, I miss them."

"When Boca died," I say, "I didn't think I could stand it, but Rio moved right in and took over. I hate to admit it, but now it's almost as though Boca never existed. Isn't that terrible?"

"Tell us about your trip," Dan says as he opens a bottle of Chilean red. "When and where did you go?"

We sit at the table for a midnight snack.

"Well," says Roger, "we left at the beginning of February in 1972 and didn't come home until June of 1974. Basically, we drove down to Tierra del Fuego and back in a customized International Harvester thirteen-ten four-by-four truck with an eight-foot Alaskan camper. We called the rig 'Old Overkill.' The whole purpose of the trip was pissing up a rope, you know, to find out who I am and who and what I want to be. I never had a childhood. I mean, other people can look at childhood, growing up, and think it's rugged. Well, I didn't have that problem. I was supporting my mother and two sisters. I was doing what had to be done, working, going to school, and going to college. Then Carolyn and I got together in 1965, and we spent five years pursuing the commercial grail. We worked our asses off and saved all our money for the trip, which wound up costing us a hundred and twenty-five thousand dollars."

He pauses long enough to eat a cracker and a chunk of *pecorino*, then resumes his story. "The night we left on our odyssey, we were so exhausted from stowing all our gear in the camper that we stopped at practically the first motel outside of town."

I hope he isn't going to give us a day-by-day account of their travels. I'm tempted to say something like "Let's have a look at that judicial file," but that would be rude and probably counterproductive. All I can do is try to steer the conversation in a direction that will hasten the moment I've been waiting for. "How did you become interested in Butch and Sundance?"

"I've always loved the American West," says Roger, leaning back in his chair. "The Grand Canyon was my thing. It went back to when I was a youngster, and I had rheumatic fever, tonsillitis, and scarlet fever on top of each other, and I was looking at a View-Master of the Grand Canyon and Utah and Zion National Park, all that kind of wonderful, beautiful stuff. Then on my first vacation in the Marine Corps, I was covering the West at eleven hundred miles a day, sucking in everything like a sponge. I've driven two million miles in my life. I've visited the Grand Canyon seventy times. And whenever I felt a 'damp, drizzly November in my soul,' it was high time to go out west and put the cowboy boots on and hike down into the Grand Canyon." The words roll out of him at a smooth, low pitch. "And I've always read a lot. I read Zane Grey when I was sick, and packed into every book that Zane Grey wrote are stories he heard around campfires. Much of what he's written is based on fact."

"Where did you grow up?" asks Dan.

"I didn't." Roger throws back his head and laughs, his lower jaw moving up and down as if he were biting the air. "I was born at Central Park West and Seventy-second Street. When I was in college, I lived in Jackson Heights, but I don't think I spent five nights a year at home, because I was going to school at Fordham University in the Bronx and working in midtown—I was the head copyboy for twenty-two writers at *Time*—had two part-time jobs, went to every Broadway show, every ballet, every opera. My job was to get the broadest possible education, so I majored in philosophy, theology, American civilization, history, English, you name it. I guess I carried thirty-two credits a semester."

"That's quite a load," I say. "When did you begin researching Butch and Sundance?"

"We'd seen the movie, which fascinated us, and Butch and Sundance were of special interest to me because I'm in love with Utah. When you go on vacation out west, you run into these wonderful stories and find these wonderful books about wonderful people and times. In any case, here I was, planning the trip of my dreams, outfitting Old Overkill, having lunch and dinner with friends, and saying goodbye, and I got together with James T. Crow, who was editor in chief of *Road & Track* at the time, and Jim says, 'Rog, when you're down there, why don't you follow the trail of Butch and Sundance?' And I say, 'Sure, why not?' "

"So Butch and Sundance weren't the reason for your trip," says Dan, "but you knew beforehand that you would be doing some research along the way."

"I don't know how serious I was about it when we left home, but by the time we got to Bolivia, we were terrifically excited about trying to find out what became of them. It came down to being a way of looking at the country, the way by which we would meet every kind of person, every level of person."

"Exactly," I say. "You see so much more when you travel with a purpose."

"In La Paz, we searched out old diligence drivers, especially those over the age of eighty-four, because they would have been adults when the shootout happened, but we also talked to people in their seventies and eighties. The sadness, of course, is that when we came back about a year and a half later, on our way home, many of these people were dead. You do the best you can, but it's like reading a book: You learn something, then you go out and learn more things, and when you reread the book, you learn even more. By the time we came back to talk to some of these people, we'd have been able to ask some really smart questions, but they had died."

"What did you find out in La Paz?" I ask.

"We visited COMIBOL and went through some of their records without finding anything, but they could not have been nicer. They took us to Tres Cruces in their own vehicle and brought a translator for us. We met some old-timers, including an eighty-four-year-old who had worked at Concordia at the time James D. Horan says that Butch and Sundance were there. Quite frankly, I'm not too sure that either one of them worked for Percy Seibert. I think Butch visited Concordia, but I don't think he was on the payroll."

"Then where did the letters come from?" I ask. "The one Butch wrote from Santa Cruz to 'the Boys at Concordia' and the one he wrote from Tres Cruces to Clement Glass in La Paz about Concordia business? If Butch wasn't working there, how did those letters wind up in Seibert's scrapbook?"

"He may have *been* there," says Roger, "but I don't think he was *working*."

"Do you think Seibert made it all up?" asks Dan, yawning. Three o'clock is way past his bedtime. Roger, however, shows no sign of wearing down, and I won't be able to sleep until I've seen the judicial file.

"It's nice to say, 'Butch Cassidy worked for me,' " says Roger, "but Butch didn't work for him. Neither Butch nor Sundance did. There wasn't anything for them to do. I found no evidence of their having worked there, and I inferred from the old-timers that that part of Seibert's story wasn't true."

"But Seibert wasn't the only person to place them at Concordia," I say. "Roy Letson wrote to Charles Kelly about having hired Sundance to break mules for railroad construction work in Oruro. And Letson was the man who brought Sundance to Concordia, according to Seibert."

"I'd have to see more solid evidence," says Roger, "before I'd discount the word of someone who had actually been there at the time."

"Where did you go next?" Dan calls from the kitchen. He is making coffee.

"We went all over, but our first real success on this project was at the National Archives in Sucre, where the curator, Gunnar Mendoza, brought out all these old magazines and newspapers for us, and we found that there actually was a robbery and that the outlaws were killed. And then we went to Potosí and found a couple of newspaper articles there. From there, we drove straight on down to Cotagaita and then cut over to Quechisla and Atocha and then San Vicente. I liked the way we came in through a dry wash and then the bowl at the top and then downhill into another bowl where the town was."

"When was this?" I pick at the crumbs of cheese on the platter.

"We actually went to San Vicente twice," says Roger. "The first time was in 1972, on our way south. The second time was on our way home, when we drove up through Antofagasta and Calama and San Pedro de Atacama and then came into Bolivia via Laguna Verde and Quetena and on over to San Vicente."

"Did you do any research on Butch and Sundance in Chile?" asks Dan.

"We spent a week in Antofagasta and Calama but didn't find anything."

"We've given up on Chile," I say.

"So what happened when you got to San Vicente?" Dan asks.

"I've got some pictures here somewhere," says Roger. "They're just contact sheets, but they should give you an idea of what it was like."

He hands me a sheaf of black-and-white contact sheets, each of which holds twelve 2¼-inch-square images of exquisite quality. Roger gives the credit to his Hasselblad camera, but he studied with Ansel Adams and surely graduated at the top of the class.

"We arrived on the third day of their three-day fiesta in October," he says. "I can look up the exact date later."

"Good," says Dan. "I'm curious about which San Vicente the town is named after, and knowing when the fiesta is would help me figure out which Saint Vincent it was—a matter of crucial importance to us completists." He passes the coffee cups around and sits down in the chair beside me to look at the pictures.

"Anyway, we got there, met everybody, talked with the gal who owned most of the town at that time. We were told that no one was there who had continuously lived in San Vicente."

"What did the town look like?"

"It was about a third as big as it is now, judging from the picture in your *Américas* article. The area around the cemetery was wide open for several hundreds of yards. None of the houses that are below it now were there back then."

"The new mine-company construction hadn't been built yet," says Dan.

"How many people were living there at that time?" I ask.

"Oh, Jesus, a few hundred. There were horns blaring and drums banging, and everybody was basically pretty shit-faced when we arrived. We had had a lot of experience with fiestas, and you expect that. They don't mean any harm when they turn your vehicle over and shove a gasoline-soaked rag down your gas pipe and light it, which I saw happen in Sorata, near La Paz. Needless to say, we took the precaution of driving out of San Vicente to sleep at night."

"What happened at the cemetery?"

"Well, we were at the fiesta, and at a certain point everybody decided they were going to go help us, to take us up to the cemetery, and off we went. There were only three graves that had any substance to them. All the rest were nothing but sticks, and the whole place was overgrown with weeds, and nobody knew shit from Shinola."

Leafing through Roger's contact sheets, I spy a shot of the grave we're planning to exhume. The surface of the cemetery was a lot lower then, so the monument looks a lot taller, but it's the same one. The cross was still there, and affixed to the U bolts were two old-fashioned padlocks. A rush of adrenaline leaves me speechless, so I grab Dan's arm and point to the picture.

"That's it!" he says. "That's the one Risso showed us."

What is that man in the foreground pointing at? It's the plaque! The image is too small to read with the naked eye. Using a loupe, I can see the fibers in the man's tweed jacket and count the blades of grass at the base of the marker, but I can't make out more than a couple of unconnected letters on the plaque.

"What do you remember about this grave?" Dan asks, handing Roger the contact sheet. "Do you recall what the plaque said or anything about who was buried there?"

Roger props his reading glasses on his nose and studies the photograph briefly, then gives it back to me. "I don't remember what it said, but if it was anything relevant, I would have noticed. I mean, we were there looking for Butch and Sundance, and we knew all their aliases, so if there was any connection, we would have spotted it."

"Is there any chance that it was too worn to read?"

"I guess that's possible. I just don't remember."

Hunched over the loupe, I stare at the photo until my eyes ache. If the plaque was illegible in 1972, Butch and Sundance could be in the grave. But if Roger and Carolyn were able to read the plaque, the grave almost certainly contains some poor soul who had nothing to do with the outlaws.

252

"This is confidential," I say, looking at Dan. He nods and I continue, "We are working with some scientists who are planning to dig up this grave in a couple of months, so we really need to know what is on that plaque. Could we get an enlargement of this shot?"

"Unfortunately, I don't have the negative. All my black-and-white negatives are in storage in Texas in a climate-controlled lab belonging to Rob Muir, who is a friend of mine, but they're not organized, and I can't ask Rob to go through all that stuff when he is busy trying to make a living. So I'll either have to look for it when I go down there or wait until he has the time."

"Well," I say, "whatever you can do will be appreciated, because there's no point in our digging up the grave if it couldn't possibly contain the bandits."

"I'm curious," says Dan, "about why you didn't do anything with the judicial file."

"Basically," says Roger, "it's because when we came back to New York, we couldn't find anyone who was interested in the truth. It's the curse of Butch Cassidy. We spent a fortune solving this mystery, but Robert Stack, at the end of the 'Unsolved Mysteries' show, gets up there and says, 'I guess the mystery will never be solved,' and everybody is happy to leave it at that. In 1974, we presented the concept of an article about the Outlaw Trail to the National Geographic Society, and then they turned around and hired Robert Redford to do it. We just couldn't get anything going in any forum." Roger launches into a tale of betrayal and bad luck.

I know I should be more concerned about his plight, but I can't seem to concentrate on anything but the fact that a battered briefcase in this very room contains the answers to all my questions about San Vicente. Unfortunately, Dan's eyelids are drooping. I might as well accept the fact that Christmas is still many hours away: The wrappings won't come off the judicial file until we've taken some time out to sleep. What a nuisance! Before giving up, I ask one last question: "What caused you to begin working on Butch and Sundance again?"

"Carolyn and I were divorced, and then she and our son moved to Texas, and I was moving out of my house into an apartment. As I was packing to move, I was sorting through boxes in the garage and pulling out books like Charles Kelly's *Outlaw Trail,* and it brought me back to a happier time. It was part of a rebirth, a renaissance of myself, coming back to balancing myself. The research is something that I cared about, and it is also unfinished business. And maybe there's a sense of my mortality going on and that something should be done with this.''

''It's a shame you had to go through all that turmoil,'' I say, ''but I'm glad that it had at least one silver lining.''

Dan is struggling to keep his eyes open as first light begins to glow outside the windows, and the newspaper bangs against the front door.

''I find my research more worthwhile,'' says Roger, ''more meaningful. The importance of Butch and Sundance goes beyond just the detective work. I actually do believe that Butch and Sundance were social revolutionaries. American historians may be doing the politically correct thing by finally taking a look at women and blacks and Indians, but they still don't put it all together. The popular revolt, across the board, has never really been put in perspective. I've never thought that historians covered the West properly, because the fun stuff—the cowboys, the gunmen, and vigilantism—was always disapproved, so we never got the facts. Talking about robber barons doesn't begin to explain the incredible explosion of wealth during the lifetimes of Butch and Sundance. When you look at a guy like Wyatt Earp, while some people say he is a great westerner to admire, he was just a businessman, a ruthless businessman. He killed people. In the Johnson County war, you had good people doing bad things and bad people doing good things. You had ranchers killing people, hiring Tom Horn to kill people, to shoot people. They thought that that was okay. Carnegie would drive people out of business and hire some of the people he drove out of business but destroy some of them, as well. And it's okay to do that. In every goddamned cattle town you can think of, or every town everywhere, rampant, driving capitalistic greed was causing people to destroy each other and sometimes to shoot each other. You didn't have stand-up gunfights. That was too honest. You killed people. The military and the state militia were always being used against the people, against the workers in the Homestead rebellion, the Pullman strike, the Molly Maguires, the this, the that. And the Pinkertons played a big part in busting more than one union.''

Dan sits upright with a start. He's all in. I'm amazed he has lasted this long.

''Thank God for Teddy Roosevelt,'' Roger is saying. ''As much of a rip-roaring egotist as he was, and with his money behind him, he brought some control, stopped the monopolies, fought for the little people, fought for the West, fought for the truth. And he could be an ass at times, but somehow I'm just inclined to ally him with Butch and Sundance. And I do believe they tried to go straight."

"You should have been their lawyer."

At noon, we gather around the table again and resume the discourse over coffee cake. "You know," says Roger, who is wrapped in a royal-blue velour robe, "on the drive down from New York, I was thinking about something Lula Parker Betenson said to me when I came back and I'd found everything and showed everything to her. She grabbed me on the leg and she said, 'They made six movies about Butch, and we never made a dime. Let's just make some money.' Simple as that. That's the lament of the West: 'You're always ripping us off; you're always exploiting us, taking out the gold, the silver, and you're leaving nothing behind here.' "

"We've always thought Lula was just looking to cash in with that book of hers," Dan remarks. "If Butch had really survived, she would have had a livelier tale to tell."

"Her claim that Butch told her Percy Seibert had deliberately mis-identified the bodies so that his pals could come home without worrying about the Pinkertons proves that she made the whole thing up," I say. "Seibert never saw the bodies, nobody identified them, and nobody spread the story here until the 1930s, when the statute of limitations had long since run out."

"Her son, Mark Betenson, told us that Butch didn't come back," says Roger. "Anyway, I was thinking about what Lula said and about how we ought to raise some money and go back down to South America and really do this project right. It should be possible to raise a million dollars from ten investors and then use the interest on that amount to fund trips down there."

"Who would want to put that much money into research about something so insignificant?" says Dan. "We spend thousands of dollars on our trips and come back up here and write an article for four hundred dollars max."

"None of the big magazines will touch the story," I add. "We have a collection of rejection letters from magazine editors who say that they find the subject fascinating but that it's not right for their readers."

"That's where the promotion comes in. There are all kinds of ways you could promote it. Butch Cassidy is a brand name. He could be tied in with many products. You could run contests with people guessing things like the date of the shootout or what they had for their last meal, or you could do a treasure-hunt kind of thing with bottle caps on soft drinks. You could even do a theme park, you know, like Disney World, only on a smaller scale.''

"If you can pull that off," I say, "more power to you. I don't think anyone but an outlaw historian would really care when the shootout happened or what the bandits ate, but then I don't know anything about promotion.''

"I can't see us doing anything along those lines," says Dan. "We have our hands full digging up the facts and writing them down."

"I'd like to write something someday," says Roger, "but I want to do the promotion first to put together the money to really do the thing properly."

Eventually, we begin edging closer to the subject that has been on my mind ever since I heard Roger's first message on our answering machine. By midafternoon, we have made our way to Tupiza. "How long did you stay there?" asks Dan.

"A week," says Roger, "working on this all the time. Exhausting days.''

"How did you meet Francisco Salazar?" I ask.

"We just poked our heads around and grabbed anybody that was old. We probably found him on the street or in the plaza. I have a picture of him on a park bench. I popped his picture with my long lens from the truck."

"The famous *casa rodante,*" says Dan. "He remembered that. He talked about it when we met him. What did he tell you?"

"He said he knew all about Butch and Sundance, but it was clear that he was talking about things that happened in the twenties. And I don't think he was old enough to have been alive at the time. He was just a nice, charming man, so we listened politely and then went about our business. Meanwhile, we had gone to the judge to find out where the records were kept, and then we went there."

"Where *were* the records kept?"

"In the jail. Where else do you keep your records? It was up the street, with a little gate, and they opened it up for us. Everybody in town was basically coming in the first couple of days helping us, although that slacked off when they saw how much work it was."

256

"You have to be highly motivated to wade through all that old paper."

"Some Mormon kids who stuck with us told us about another old-timer, Darío Morales, who actually knew something about the holdup. We all showed up—Carolyn, three or four Mormons, the old-timer's nephew—and Morales was there with a white handkerchief tied over one of his eyes. He talked about how everybody was disappointed in the *asaltadores norteamericanos*, who went under the names of Smith and Low, something like that. He said that they were well known in town, and that Butch was involved in a lot of social activities and was friends with everybody, especially Santiago Hutcheon."

"He remembered Hutcheon?" asks Dan. "We've been trying to locate Hutcheon's descendants to find out what became of him and whether he passed along any stories about Butch and Sundance."

"I don't know what happened to him," says Roger. "Anyway, Morales corroborated the stuff in the newspaper articles about the maps and notebook that they had. They had planned to do many robberies or had done them, because they had escape routes in the notebook."

"Had he seen the notebook?"

"No, he just remembered people talking about the bandits' maps of Bolivia with routes and separate maps of routes and sections, and that they had a notebook full of information, material, and what he referred to as escape routes."

"He could have read about the notebook in the newspaper."

"Uh-huh, although I'm not sure that matters. Anyway, we had started looking for the records that first day, and then the judge called us back the next day and said that we actually had to make application to do this. So we filed the application and then went right on working."

"Did you have to hire a lawyer?" asks Dan.

"We had to hire a lawyer. We made application and it was approved, and we kept looking in the meantime. Everybody was really nice. The funny thing was that the judge called us into his office to meet an old-timer, and when we got there it was Francisco Salazar. He was very, very nice about it, and he explained to the judge, 'I've already met this young couple, and I may have misinformed them, but I was just trying to help them, and they've come so far to learn something, and I was trying the best I could to remember everything I could from the time, but I never knew.' When we left the judge's office, Salazar joined us and the Mormon kids and helped us go through the records. All the prisoners at the jail were also helping. I remember one fellow standing on a chair, reaching up on top of the bookshelves, and pulling down files—which consisted of sheets of paper sewn together. He'd look at a file and throw it over one shoulder, then he'd look at another file and throw it over the other shoulder. After a while, I began to wonder if the prisoners could read, but I figured it was too late to try to find out. And why bother? We were in the hands of God.''

''What did the place look like?'' I ask. ''Was everything on shelves or in cabinets or what?''

''There were double stacks and rows of double stacks and pathways so you could walk between the stacks, which were generally about waist-high. Against the walls, there were bookshelves on one side and double stacks about ten feet high all along one end wall. And we attacked that part toward the end, after we had done everything else. The first nine to eighteen inches of a stack would cover the period between maybe 1740 and 1760. Then the next eight to fifteen inches would be 1630 to 1640. The next would be 1930 to whatever. But there would be other files from those years in other stacks and all over the place. There were also control sheets. Every year, everything that was put away was listed in a single control file that was sewn together. They listed every case that was there. And early on, as I went through the stacks, I began finding the control files for 1900, 1901, 1902, and so on. Once I found the one for 1908, I was able to read the list and find out that the file we wanted did exist.''

''That would really inspire you to keep looking,'' I say.

''Yeah,'' says Dan, ''by the time we got there, it was in chaos.''

''Were the files still in the jail?'' asks Roger. ''Or had they been moved someplace else?''

''They were in the new judge's office in total disarray.''

''It was in disarray when we found it,'' says Roger, ''but the piles were probably neater. The rat shit, dust, and dirt—it was really a job. Maybe that's how I got allergic to dust.''

''That's how I got pneumonia.''

''How many days were you amongst these records?'' asks Dan.

''Five.''

''Five days?''

''Yeah. Well I was probably lying—like the typical outlaw historian—and it was more like four and a half days.''

''That's five days.''

"So," I ask, "who actually found the right one with the right date on it?"

"Me. You've gotta have the vision. You've gotta have the divining stick. We'd gone through everything, and we'd done that whole wall with ten-foot stacks two deep. We got to the last stack in the last section. It was maybe about a foot and a half high. So I went over, and I picked the whole thing up, and I walked back toward the benches. I handed one pile to one person, another to another, passed them around, and I had a little bit left for me. I had the bottom, bottom, bottom, bottom, bottom of the last pile against the wall of the last pile in the entire bloody goddamn room. And I sat there with it in front of me, and I looked at it."

Roger holds a pile of imaginary documents and examines them one at a time. "*No, this isn't it*, I'd think, and I'd put it down, making a nice neat little stack. Down, down, down. We're watching the time, and it's twelve o'clock, and we've spent days here with these possibly illiterate helpers, and I'm really discouraged. The next file on my lap has a blank, torn cover. I look at it absentmindedly and put it down on the stack without even opening it. I'm talking to myself, saying, *You damn fool, there may be no chance in hell of your finding what you're looking for, but after all this meticulous searching, you can't be bothered to open up one lousy file?* So I reach down and pick it up, put it back in my lap, carefully open the torn page, and there it is: 'In Tupiza, so on and so forth.' Bam!"

"What did you do?"

"Yelled and screamed. Carolyn was with me. Salazar had left by that time. A couple of prisoners were still there and a couple of Mormons."

"Then what did you do?"

"What *did* we do? I guess we went to lunch, talked about it, went out and bought our food, then left the next day for Argentina by a circuitous route."

The subject then shifts to Argentina; Roger wants to see our slides of Cholila. After looking at his perfect photographs, I'm not eager to display my own flawed work, but at this point I'm willing to do just about anything to get a look at that judicial file. Although you'd never know it by his tranquil demeanor, Dan apparently feels the same way, because he has brought out every article we've ever written about Butch and Sundance, along with copies of all the Aramayo papers and diplomatic correspondence and translations of the Bolivian and

Argentine newspaper stories. The table has so much paper stacked on it that it looks like an architect's model for a high-rise condominium complex. We give Roger a guided tour through our documents, then Dan suggests that we break for supper.

Supper? How can anyone think of food at a time like this?

At last, twenty-four hours after his arrival, Roger finally shows us the judicial file, which consists of fifty-some faded and chipped pages of onionskin, lined notebook paper, and even graph paper, all numbered and sewn together. Some of the documents are typed, but most are written in florid script similar to that in the Aramayo papers. Roger hands the file over to Dan ceremoniously, as if it were a treaty guaranteeing world peace. After wiping his hands on his jeans to remove any trace of sweat, Dan gingerly opens the file and begins reading aloud: " '*En Tupiza, á horas siete P.M. del día cinco de Noviembre de 1908*—' "

"Could you translate it into English as you go?" asks Roger. "I'm afraid my Spanish is not what it used to be."

Dan begins again. "In Tupiza, at seven P.M. on the fifth of November 1908. . . ." The document turns out to be the first of many about the hapless Ray A. Walters and Frank Harry Murray, the suspects arrested in Salo and reluctantly released by the Tupiza authorities three days after the actual bandits had died in San Vicente.

"Sweets," I interrupt as Dan begins reading the third page on Walters and Murray, "let's cut to the chase. Why don't you flip through there until you come to something about *our* guys? Who gives a damn about Walters and Murray?"

"I do," he says. "I'm a completist, remember? I love it all. I want to read it in the order it was written."

"Grrrrr."

"Actually," says Roger, "I'm getting pretty tired. Why don't we call it a night and start again in the morning?"

When Dan blithely says, "Sure," then hands the judicial file back to Roger, I want to murder them both.

Neither one, however, manages to tear himself away from the table. They begin by comparing notes on the Eucaliptus holdups and soon move to a discussion of contemporary outlaw historians. "They make me sad," says Roger. "They've wasted all of their good contacts— who are probably dead now—in trying to sustain things that were false. They haven't used their investigative sense to ferret out all the interesting stuff that was there. And that's a tragedy.''

"At some point," says Dan, "they get so far down the road that they can't turn back. Plus, there's a virus that makes otherwise reasonable people want to prove that their heroes didn't die.''

"It's hard enough to nail down the truth about characters who were constantly changing their aliases and telling lies to cover their tracks," says Roger, "but when you've got researchers running around accepting old-timer tales at face value and printing them without any documentation, you wind up with a real mess.''

"That," I say, "is what makes outlaw history the most aptly named discipline in the world.''

"Could I take another look at Carlos Peró's letters?'' asks Roger.

As he browses through them, with Dan translating, I seize the opportunity to ask, "While you're looking at that, do you mind if I take another peek at the judicial file?''

What can he say?

I skip Walters and Murray altogether and skim the documents concerning the jurisdictional dispute, which dragged on into March 1909. A November 7 letter to the Aramayo office in Tupiza quoted a note from Captain Concha to the administrator of the Aramayo branch nearest San Vicente: "I am communicating with you to expeditiously notify Tupiza, as well as Uyuni, that the robbers of the cash shipment have been taken. Having resisted with gunfire, they were killed, as was a soldier, of which I am advising you promptly, hoping that you will consult the general administrator as to what he thinks proper. Meanwhile, I await your orders here.''

Nothing new there. Two other letters went out from San Vicente that day. The one from Cantonal Agent Aristides Daza to the district attorney in Tupiza added little more than that the shootout had taken place at eight o'clock and that the cash shipment had been recovered. A letter from the corregidor (roughly equivalent to a mayor), Cleto Bellot, to the subprefect in Tupiza provides more details:

> This is to inform you that yesterday, at 3 P.M., a force from Uyuni commanded by Captain Justo P. Concha arrived in this vice canton with the aim of pursuing the robbers of Aramayo, Francke and Company's cash shipment.
> The presumed robbers arrived here at about 7 P.M. Having

been advised [of this fact], those in charge of the pursuit, in the company of the undersigned, presented themselves at the lodging of the men in order to identify them. We were fired upon, which caused a battle to be joined between the pursued and the pursuers, resulting in three dead—one soldier from the Uyuni column, Victor Torres, and the two foreigners, the alleged robbers.

I hasten to inform you of these events, so that you can proceed accordingly, and in regard for my duty. I will perform the tasks in the manner you direct. Awaiting your instructions, I remain your attentive and faithful servant.

Five days later, Bellot wrote to advise the examining magistrate in Tupiza "that the commission from Uyuni, composed of Captain Justo P. Concha, the police inspector Timoteo Rios, one soldier, and the Aramayo clerk, took the report, all the goods recovered from the presumed robbers, including money, carbines, revolvers, etcetera, and the inventory. [They were supposed to go] to Tupiza, pursuant to the agreement we made. But this commission, violating that agreement, marched off to Uyuni, according to reports I have about the matter."

In a November 8, 1908, memorandum to Tupiza's examining magistrate, the district attorney set in motion the proceedings detailed in this file: "An inquest should be held regarding the criminal acts that occurred in the San Vicente vice canton yesterday, the seventh, between the robbers, whose names are unknown, and the force belonging to the security police of the Porco province. As there are three dead individuals, according to the official, Sr. Daza, a legal medical autopsy should be performed on the cadavers at a designated day and time."

The next day, the examining magistrate, Dr. Hector Solares, issued an order that "Dr. Eduardo Eguía and medic Julio Reyes perform autopsies on the bodies of the robbers and the soldier, who were killed in the vice canton of San Vicente." This might explain why Dr. Eguía returned only 150 of the 250 *bolivianos* to the Aramayo company: The remainder could have been for the medic, who might have gone to San Vicente for the inquest without Dr. Eguía. But the file contains no report or testimony from Julio Reyes.

The memorandum confirming the witnesses' identification of the outlaws does not specify whether an autopsy was performed or not.

Written in black ink on graph paper and signed by the witnesses, the magistrate, and the cantonal agent, the document establishes that the men killed in San Vicente were the bandits who stole the Aramayo payroll on November 4, 1908.

> In San Vicente, at nine A.M. on the twentieth of November, 1908. Established in the village of San Vicente, provincial Examining Magistrate Dr. Hector A. Solares, District Attorney Dr. Nestor S. Jordán, and the undersigned clerk of the court proceeded with the identification of the cadavers killed in the village of San Vicente. Proceeding as follows, they received the sworn testimony of Carlos Peró, Gil Gonzáles, and Mariano Peró, a minor for whom a guardian was named for this proceeding, the appointment falling to Delfín Rivera. They said that they recognized the cadavers on sight as the same as those who stole the fifteen-thousand-*boliviano* remittance they were carrying to Quechisla; that from their size and constitution they were certain to be the same persons who carried out the assault; that for the sake of uncovering the truth, they had not a shred of doubt between the robbers and the victims who were on view.

The magistrate interviewed Carlos Peró, who briefly described the robbery and his efforts to notify his employers, and then addressed the matter at hand: "Today, having had to identify the exhumed cadavers here, despite having seen no more than the robbers' eyes and the corresponding parts of their faces at the time of the robbery, I recognized both of them, without any sort of doubt, as well as the hats they wore, with the exception of their clothing, which is different from what they wore at Huaca Huañusca. The mule recovered by the Uyuni commission that captured the robbers is the same one that was taken from me at the scene of the robbery."

This last statement puzzles me, because weeks after the holdup, the mule was still in Uyuni—a fact repeatedly and bitterly lamented by the Aramayo officials in Tupiza. Unless Peró had gone to Uyuni, how could he be certain about the mule's identity? Perhaps he simply relied on its description.

The first eyewitness interviewed by the Tupiza authorities was Remigio Sánchez, who had brought the corregidor's initial message to Tupiza. Sánchez, a miner from the San Vicente area, testified as follows:

> On the sixth of this November, at about three-thirty in the afternoon, a commission from Uyuni, composed of a captain, a police inspector, and two soldiers, all armed, arrived in San Vicente. Later, at six-thirty, two mounted gringos came from the east, one on a dark brown mule and the other on a solid black mule. They went to the corregidor's house to ask him for lodging. He referred them to Bonifacio Casasola and noticed that each one was armed with a rifle and a revolver. They told the corregidor that they came from La Quiaca and were going to Santa Catalina. After this, the corregidor left and went to notify the commission. The police inspector, with two soldiers and the corregidor, immediately came to look and find out who the men were. Once they had passed through to the patio and were about four steps from the door of the room, one of the gringos—the smaller one—appeared and fired one shot and then another from his revolver at the soldier, who ran screaming to the house of Julian Saínz, where he died in moments.

The smaller one? Butch *did* kill somebody, after all. So much for his image as a gentleman. But the witness said that the house belonged to Bonifacio Casasola, which conforms with what Froilán Risso told us. Risso must know what he's talking about. The testimony continued:

> After this, the corregidor began to round up people and, among others, I came. We arrived at the place of the event and found the captain, the police inspector, and the other soldier, plus the servant, in the door to the street. They immediately posted us to watch the roof and the back of the house, because the captain feared that they might make a hole in the walls and escape, as they were no longer firing. We remained all night until, at dawn, the captain ordered the owner of the house to go inside, because they would do nothing to him as the owner. The captain entered with a soldier, and then all of us entered and found the smaller gringo stretched out on the floor, dead, with one bullet

wound in the temple and another in the arm. The taller one was hugging a large ceramic jug that was in the room. He was dead, also, with a bullet wound in the forehead and several in the arm.

This description supports the claim that Butch put Sundance out of his misery and then shot himself. Funny, but all this time I've thought that the suicide story sprang from some sort of chauvinism, an unwillingness to believe that the legendary Butch Cassidy and the Sundance Kid, who had outrun all those North American posses, could be brought down by a Bolivian posse. But why was Sundance hugging that jug? Was he trying to protect himself from Butch? Could Butch have blamed him for the now-complete failure of their final holdup? First they stole the 15,000-*boliviano* shipment instead of the 80,000 one, and then they were caught. That's enough to annoy anyone, let alone a careful planner like Butch. As I recall, during our first visit to San Vicente Risso mentioned something about the *gringos* arguing over whether to spend the night there or to eat and push on. Something tells me, however, that the question of whether Sundance's death was murder or a mercy killing will never be answered.

The witness Sánchez continued, saying that the cantonal "agent was called immediately and he made an examination of everything, finding a homespun cotton package stitched up with bills inside it, eighty pounds in the pocket of the tallest and forty-six pounds in the pocket of the other one. This is what I was told, but I didn't see it. They also took from the pocket of the tall one a handful of one-*boliviano* bills and some nickel coins. Upon finishing this operation, we went to lunch. In the afternoon, after Delfín Rivera identified them, we interred them."

Nothing like a little time out for *fricasé de llama* in the middle of a busy day.

"The tall gringo," said Sánchez, "was dressed in a light-brown cashmere suit, a grey hat, red gaiters, a belt with about twenty-eight bullets, a gold watch, a dagger (so I was told), and a silk handkerchief. The smaller one wore a yellow suit, apparently cashmere, red gaiters, a grey hat. He had a silver watch, a blue silk handkerchief, a cartridge belt with about thirty bullets. The pair also had bullets in all their pockets. Both were unshaven blonds, with somewhat turned-up noses, the small one a bit ugly and the large one good-looking."

The words *blond* and *turned-up noses* cover a lot of territory in South

America: They apply to anyone whose hair isn't black and whose nose doesn't turn down. Butch and Sundance fit well within those bounds and conformed with Sánchez's assessment of their looks. His testimony also contradicts the popular notion that the bandits were down to their last two bullets when they chose death over surrender.

Knowing that Corregidor Cleto Bellot spoke with the bandits and was present when the shooting began, I can't veil my excitement as I begin reading his testimony. Immersed in the file, I have forgotten that Dan and Roger exist, but they sense that I have found something special, and Dan says, "What is it, kiddo? Read it out loud."

"In English," adds Roger.

Rats! Why couldn't they have toddled off to bed? Reminding myself not to be selfish, and backing up often to straighten out the syntax in my translation, I slog through the document.

> On the sixth, I was at the mining job I have nearby. From there, I came here at about six in the evening. As I was unsaddling my animal, Inspector Rios appeared, greeted me, and withdrew. At that point, I saw the captain in the street. After this, I went into my house to eat. Afterwards, I went to the lodging of the commission to find out what their mission was. There I met two soldiers and a servant of Manuel Barran, with whom I remained until seven at night, their having explained to me that they came in pursuit of the cash shipment stolen from Aramayo, Francke and Company. As none of the chiefs of the commission appeared, and as they were in bed, I withdrew. . . .

> When I reached the door of my [home], two mounted men arrived and stopped at Casasola's door. I went to see them, and they asked me for a hotel or inn, to which I responded that there wasn't one. Addressing Casasola, I told him to give them lodging and that they were going to buy fodder from him. They then went through the street door to the interior, where he showed them an unoccupied room, and the two foreigners unsaddled their animals and gave them fodder. After tending to their beasts and leaving their saddles and two rifles outside, they went into the room, where we began to chat. They asked me which was the road to Santa Catalina and said that they came from La Quiaca, to which I told them that as they had

been in La Quiaca, they could have gone from there, as it is closer. Afterwards, they asked me about the road to Uyuni and Oruro. They then told me that they wanted to buy beer and sardines, which I sent Casasola to buy with money that the taller one gave him.

"Beer and sardines," says Dan. "What a pathetic last supper."

I then withdrew and went to the lodging of the commission and advised them of the arrival of the two foreigners. The inspector ordered that they load their rifles, loading his own as well, and told me to accompany them. The inspector, the two soldiers, and I came to the foreigners' lodging and entered the patio. The soldier Victor Torres went ahead, approaching the room of the guests, and from the door he was shot once with a revolver, wounding him, to which he responded with a rifle shot. The other soldier also fired two shots. Meanwhile, the inspector fired and left, running. The soldier Torres now fell wounded to the floor, dropped his rifle, and hastily retreated. I left then and the other soldier afterwards. But he entered his lodging and got more ammunition. He posted himself at the door to the street and fired from there. At this point, the inspector appeared and also began firing.

I then withdrew to my house, and Captain Concha appeared on the corner, asking for help and that he be given men. I immediately went and gathered some men, whom we stationed around the house. It should be mentioned that, while rounding up the men, I heard three screams of desperation. After the guards were posted, no more shots were heard, except that the inspector fired one shot at about midnight.

At about six in the morning, we were able to enter the room and found the two foreigners dead, one in the doorway and the other behind the door on a bench. We then removed the bodies and took an inventory of everything they had, placing all of it in my custody, in a locked rawhide trunk, which I turned over to the captain. Once this was done, we proceeded to carry out all the formalities, and I wrote messages to the authorities in Tupiza, sending these, the money, and everything inventoried with Captain Concha, who asked me for a wagon, which I gave him, for the trip to Tupiza. This would have been at about ten at night. I went to sleep thinking that said captain would head for Tupiza. The next day, I found out that he had gone to Uyuni, taking with him the documents, money, and everything inventoried. Among other things, we found a packet of bills in homespun cloth, which was unravelling a bit.

"In other words," says Dan, "Captain Concha's role in the famous gun battle was to round up the locals and stand watch. And then he took off with all the loot and left the Aramayos to battle the Uyuni court to get their property back. No wonder they canceled his reward."

While taking the testimony of Cantonal Agent Aristides Daza, the magistrate mentioned that "a post-mortem examination" of the bandits had been performed that day in conjunction with the inquest. Daza then described the aftermath of the shootout.

As there were no local judges in this vice canton, and by governmental requirement, I arranged to meet at six A.M. on the seventh at the site of the events, with Corregidor Cleto Bellot and Captain Concha, who requested my assistance in the attached letter. Upon performing this duty, I found a body in the threshold of Bonifacio Casasola's house with a revolver that appeared to have been fired. Presently, I focused on the other individual, who was on a bench, having used an earthen jug as a shield. Finding him dead, I had to take away his weapon in the presence of the witnesses who were there. Next, I proceeded to remove the bodies, beginning with the first one, who was in the doorway. In his pockets were money, personal effects, and some pounds, as described in the inventory. In the second one's saddlebags was an unaddressed packet of bills wrapped in two unraveling pieces of cloth, which is where the sum mentioned in the inventory was carried. I immediately deposited everything with the corregidor, who at my request [turned it over to] the members of the commission—Captain Concha and Uyuni Police Inspector Rios—who said that, obeying the orders of the competent authority of this vice canton, they would present themselves before the higher authorities of Tupiza for the process of the law, taking with them for said purpose the appropriate official notification for the examining magistrate, including the written records of the proceedings.

Daza concluded his testimony by saying that Concha and Rios took everything to Uyuni instead of going to Tupiza as they had promised.

Following a series of increasingly combative telegrams between the Uyuni and Tupiza judges are three heavily water-stained onionskin pages on which the San Vicente officials listed the items found in the dead bandits' possession.

Inventory taken of money and personal effects found in the baggage and on the persons of those who were the presumed robbers of the cash shipment of the firm Aramayo, Francke and Company. In the presence of the corregidor of the vice canton, the cantonal agent (acting as parish magistrate), the captain in charge of the commission, the police inspector, the witnesses (all of whom signed below), and the undersigned clerk of the court, the inventory proceeded as follows:

Enrique B. Hutcheon (presumably his name):
- One leather purse, containing a paper on which the address of a post office box in La Paz was indicated
- One six-shot Colt revolver, with holster and belt with thirty cartridges
- One silver pocket-watch, with silver chain
- One notebook, with several notations
- Ditto
- Sixteen pounds sterling
- Two half-pounds sterling
- One silver coin with a value of five cents
- One unusable pocket mirror
- Two removable buttons
- One metal comb
- Seven inscribed cards (Enrique B. Hutcheon)
- Ditto (Edward Graydon)
- One linen handkerchief
- One black pencil

<u>Other Individual:</u>

- One watch of 18-karat gold, number 93,220, without crystal
- One leather and metal lasso
- Bills from various banks of the nation in denominations of one

Ninety-one *bolivianos* and fifty cents	Bs.	91.50
Nickel coins (one *boliviano* and fifteen cents)		1.15
Silver coins *(bolivianos* of forty cents)		.40
Total: (Ninety-three *bolivianos* and five cents)	Bs.	93.05

- One nickel penknife
- One English dictionary
- Two linen handkerchiefs
- One ordinary pocket mirror
- Nine removable shirt buttons
- Two cuff links
- Eight small wooden or bone buttons
- One waterproof cloak
- One hundred twenty-one Winchester cartridges
- One modified Winchester carbine (new)

<u>in their baggage:</u>

- One sackcloth saddle-blanket
- One cotton blanket
- One Bolivian poncho
- One plain English saddle
- One pair of iron spurs
- One triangular file (in the saddlebags)
- One pair of leather saddlebags
- Two unusable silk handkerchiefs
- One pair of chamois gloves
- One pair of wool socks
- One used towel
- One map of Bolivia
- Eighty-eight pounds sterling (£88)

- Seven hundred one-*boliviano* bills   Bs.   700
- Thirteen thousand, seven hundred *bolivianos* in bills of various denominations   <u>13,700</u>
- Total *bolivianos* = Fourteen thousand, four hundred   Bs.   14,400
- Nineteen modified Mauser cartridges
- One used bridle
- One saddle skin
- One cinch
- One hundred thirty Mauser and Winchester cartridges
- Thirteen Colt revolver cartridges
- One Argentine-model Mauser carbine with its sheath
- One pair of binoculars
- Three cotton handkerchiefs
- One saddle blanket
- One set of reins
- One whip
- Two mules (which are said to be the company's)

The inventory is dated November 7, 1908, and signed by Corregidor Cleto Bellot, Captain Justo P. Concha, J. Saínz, Braulio Munzon, Police Inspector Timoteo Rios, Bonifacio Casasola, Cantonal Agent Aristides Daza, and Clerk-Witness Gustavo Gutiérrez.

"If one of the bandits was Enrique Hutcheon," says Dan, "why did the death certificate sent to Frank Aller in Chile say *ningun nombre*?"

"Neither of them was Enrique Hutcheon," Roger replies.

"Santiago Hutcheon had a cousin named Adam," says Dan, "but I don't recall seeing anything about an Enrique Hutcheon. Do you suppose Butch was trying out a new alias?"

"No," says Roger. "Enrique Hutcheon was a real person, and he was still alive after the shootout, according to the newspapers."

"A witness named Sánchez," I say, "said the tall *gringo* had a gold watch, and the short one had a silver watch, which means Butch was the one they mistook for Enrique Hutcheon."

"What do you suppose Sundance was doing with an English dictionary?" asks Dan.

"I don't know," says Roger, "but check out the last two items on the list of things found on Sundance's body."

"He had his rifle and more than a hundred cartridges!"

"So all the stories about the rifles being outside where Butch and Sundance couldn't reach them are nonsense."

"Why is only one saddle listed?" asks Dan. "Butch and Sundance wouldn't ride bareback on mule while fleeing a posse."

"And Cleto Bellot spoke of the *two* of them unsaddling their mounts," I add.

"The list maker might have been careless," says Dan.

"Or the saddle could have vanished before the list was made," says Roger.

"Did you notice that the bandits had no changes of clothing with them?"

"Maybe they divvied the clothing up among the gravediggers in lieu of paying them."

As we study the list and try to draw clues to the bandits' identities from the objects they carried, I am struck by the fact that two men with only one pair of socks between them would have so many handkerchiefs. The shorter bandit had one in his pocket, the taller bandit had two, and five were in the saddlebags. "Do you think this could have anything to do with Sundance's sinus problems?" I ask, referring to the Pinkerton's description of him as suffering from catarrh.

"Could be," says Dan, "but that's pretty slippery evidence to base an identification on."

As if the inventory and the eyewitnesses' statements had not already answered nearly every question raised by the Aramayo papers, the judicial file contains a bonus: a surprise witness with startling news about where the bandits were between the holdup and the shootout, as well as information linking them to Butch and Sundance. Interviewed in Tupiza one week after the inquest was held in San Vicente, a laborer named Juan Félix Erazo, who lived in the town of Estarca, told this story:

> About a month ago Mr. Graydon introduced me to a tall, blond, mustachioed, plump foreigner, whose name I don't remember. At that time, we drank a few glasses of beer in Estarca in the home of Fortunato Valencia. They told me that they came from Esmoraca and brought another foreigner, shorter than the other, and the three of them passed through Tomahuaico. . . . On the

sixth of November, I was in Cucho when, at seven in the morning, two gringos arrived. One was the same one Graydon introduced to me in Estarca; the other I don't remember having met. When I saw them in Tiburcio Bolívar's house, I went there, and they were at the door with their two saddled mules, one solid black and the other dark brown. Both carried revolvers and rifles on their saddles, but instead of revolvers, there apparently were pistols conveniently placed in their belts and many bullets, which were also displayed in their belts. I asked them where they were going, and they responded that they were going to inspect or study the wagon trail to San Vicente. I advised them to take a guide, then excused myself and left them. They went at seven-thirty in the morning.

[Bolívar] assured me that they had slept the previous night at the home of Narcisa, the widow of Burgos. Sunday night, the eighth of November, I learned that two gringos had been killed in San Vicente because they had stolen a cash shipment from Señor Peró. With the reports I have had from San Vicente, by the animals, weapons, and date upon which they left Cucho, I am convinced that they are exactly the same.

If only the judicial authorities had interviewed Edward Graydon, Fortunato Valencia, Tiburcio Bolívar, or Narcisa Burgos! Nonetheless, Erazo's testimony supports a 1913 *Wide World Magazine* article that we found early in our search but dismissed as fiction, because its author—a British engineer named A. G. Francis—had mistaken the Sundance Kid for Kid Curry and reported that the Aramayo bandits had ridden south toward Argentina before making a U-turn and heading north to San Vicente, which seemed to us like an unprofessional waste of time.

"We'll definitely have to reevaluate A. G. Francis's tale," says Dan.

"My thoughts exactly," I say, "but did you notice that the district attorney and the examining magistrate are two of the officials who dragged their feet in the Aller investigation?"

"Refresh my memory," says Roger.

"Frank Aller," says Dan, "was the U.S. vice-consul in Antofagasta who sparked an investigation about the shootout after hearing that men called Maxwell and Brown or Boyd died in it. Aller said a judge needed a death certificate to settle Sundance's estate in Chile, but the local officials in Bolivia wouldn't cooperate—until the foreign minister and prefect leaned on them."

"You know what?" I say. "The Uyuni officials never did produce their records, which means that the report sent to Aller was drawn from this file. So we no longer have any reason, aside from curiosity about Sundance's estate, to look for the Aller report. It can stay hidden away on its archival shelf in Antofagasta or Santiago or wherever until it crumbles to dust."

Sated at last, we lean back in our chairs and listen to the chirping of the crickets.

13 · THE BONEYARD

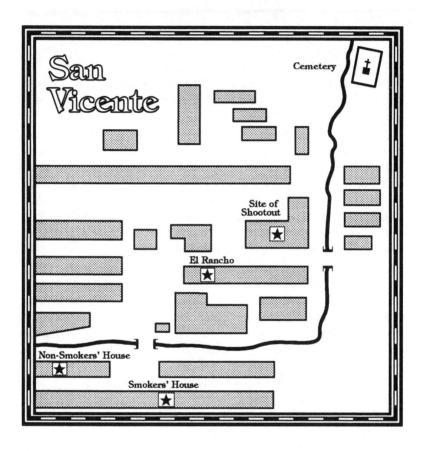

"I DIDN'T sleep real well last night," says Clyde on a sunny morning in La Paz. He gazes out the window at the *Paceños* trotting effortlessly up the steep streets. "Of course, when you're sixty-three years old, you feel lousy even at sea level."

"The best thing for *soroche* is lots of *coca* tea," counsels Dan, pouring himself another cup of the pale-green infusion, "and don't eat much for a couple of days."

"No," I say, "food makes you feel better. Just don't eat anything greasy."

"Try to take a nap if you can," Eric tosses in.

"Well," says Clyde's pal Burney McClurkan, an Arkansas archaeologist who has come along to help with the digging, "let's have it. What are our prospects?"

"It's a crapshoot," says Dan.

"Isn't it always?" Burney has thinning hair and an Abe Lincoln beard. "I have dug more graves with nothing in them than not. People always have stories."

"A couple of years ago," says Clyde, lighting a Camel, "I went down to exhume an American human-rights worker who had been imprisoned on a penal island off the coast of Panama and died there under very suspicious circumstances more than thirty years ago. With the change in the regime, it finally became possible to investigate what had happened to him, but I had some apprehensions about being able to locate the guy in the little graveyard where they buried prisoners. Probably hundreds of people had died there over the years, and finding a particular grave is often a big job when there are no markers or records and the graveyard hasn't been well tended. But they told me, 'Oh no, there's no problem,' because they had two witnesses who were there when he was buried, and they knew exactly which grave he was in. This would be a snap: We'd go over there, find the grave, do the exhumation, and get out, all in one day."

"And you believed 'em?" Burney shakes his head.

"We flew over in a rickety airplane, and I knew I was in trouble when we walked down to the graveyard with our witnesses, who turned out to be a couple of old convicts, and one immediately went toward one end of the cemetery, and the other went in the other direction, and they pointed at different graves. They were both wrong. We spent the whole day trying to find this fellow and didn't succeed. Then it started raining, and we couldn't get off the island. The worst thing was that I hadn't brought a change of clothes because it was supposed to be a one-day deal. I spent three miserable, muddy days in the penal colony for nothing."

"Sounds like good training for San Vicente," says Dan.

"I'd feel a lot more confident," says Eric, between sips of *café con leche*, "if Roger McCord had found his negatives and enlarged that shot of the grave so we could see what, if anything, the plaque said."

"Unfortunately," Dan replies, "Froilán Risso is the only game in town. We either dig up the grave he identified or forget the whole thing."

Roy Querejazu Lewis, just in from Cochabamba, comes over to the table to meet the rest of the team. "I'm sorry," he says to Burney, "but I didn't quite catch your name."

"McClurkan," says Burney, "but you can call me 'Old Fart' if you want."

Thrown by either Burney's Arkansas accent or his earthy humor, Roy hesitates before mumbling, "Glad to meet you."

"Think I'll go down the street," says Clyde, "and buy some booze."

That night, Dan and I have supper with Francisco and Ross Mery Vega and their two-year-old daughter, Natalia. Francisco still works for COMIBOL and has opened a small auto-parts store, as well. "You may have trouble in San Vicente," he says. "The road might be blocked, because the miners are on strike again."

"What are they after?" asks Dan.

"They're upset about the possibility of a joint venture between COM-IBOL and a foreign company. If the mines were no longer run by the state, many workers would be laid off, and the union would lose control."

"The miners are right to be apprehensive," I say. "A private company wouldn't subsidize the industry the way the government has. The company would go out of business if it spent more on mining the ore than the ore was worth."

"Ironically," says Francisco, "San Vicente is one of the few profitable mines, so the state would continue to run it. Nonetheless, the discontent is widespread. You should check in with the authorities in Tupiza and perhaps arrange for a police escort to San Vicente."

"Do you think you'll come back to Bolivia after the project is over?" asks Ross Mery.

"The score is three to zero," says Dan. "It's your turn to come see us."

"We'd like to visit the United States someday," says Francisco, "but we are thinking of buying a house, which would make travel difficult anytime soon."

"In that case," I reply, "we'll just have to come back here."

Morning finds us once more on the *ferrobus*, rolling south over the *altiplano*. "Could you all put together some descriptions of Butch and Sundance?" Clyde asks Dan and me. "Including any injuries or scars they might have had, the locations and types of wounds they suffered during the shootout, what kind of clothes they were wearing when they died, and so forth."

Using Pinkerton reports about Butch and Sundance, Carlos Peró's descriptions of the men who held him up, and the inquest testimony about the slain bandits, we come up with two charts:

	BUTCH CASSIDY	SHORTER ROBBER	SHORTER CORPSE
AGE IN 1908	42		
HEIGHT	5'8" to 5'9"	tall	shorter of the two
WEIGHT	165–170 lbs.	thin	
BUILD	medium	normal stature	
HAIR	light or flaxen, with sandy moustache		blond (*rubio*), unshaven
EYES	blue or grey-blue, deep-set		
NOSE	see pictures		somewhat turned-up
COMPLEXION	light		
IDENTIFYING MARKS	2 cut scars on back of head; small red scar under left eye; red mark on left side of back; small brown mole on calf		one bullet wound in temple and one in arm (no mention of exit wounds)

MISCELLANEOUS	outgoing; amiable; polite; literate; quick movements; good shot; experienced rider and cowboy	polite; spoke English; carried a Colt revolver; wore a new dark-red, thin-wale corduroy suit, a narrow, soft-brimmed hat, and a bandanna tied behind his ears	a bit ugly; had a six-shot Colt revolver; body found stretched out on floor near door; wore a yellow cashmere suit, red gaiters, a grey hat, a blue silk handker-chief; cartridge belt had about 30 bullets

	THE SUNDANCE KID	TALLER ROBBER	TALLER CORPSE
AGE IN 1908	41		
HEIGHT	5′9″ to 6′	tall	tall
WEIGHT	165–190 lbs.	heavyset	heavyset
BUILD	raw-boned and rather slim; progressively heavier in photos		
HAIR	worn in a pompa-dour; light-brown, brown, dark, or black (reportedly dyed sometimes): moustache black, brown, light-brown, sandy, brown with reddish tinge, or reddish brown		blond (*rubio*), unshaven, moustache
EYES	blue, grey, black, brown		

NOSE	rather long; Grecian		somewhat turned-up
COMPLEXION	medium		
IDENTIFYING MARKS	perhaps treated for an unspecified pistol wound in 1901 or 1902		one bullet wound in forehead and several in arm (no mention of exit wounds)
MISCELLANEOUS	shy and quiet; stood erect but carried head down; small feet; perhaps bowlegged; walked with feet far apart and turned in; held arms straight by his sides, with finger closed and thumbs sticking straight out; had stomach trouble and bad catarrh; excellent marksman; skilled cowboy and rider	did not speak; carried binoculars and a Colt revolver; wore a new dark-red, thin-wale corduroy suit, a narrow, soft-brimmed hat, and a bandanna tied behind his ears	good-looking; had a modified Winchester rifle; body found on bench behind door, hugging a large ceramic jug, still holding his "weapon"; wore a lightbrown cashmere suit, a grey hat, red gaiters, a silk hankie; cartridge belt had about 28 bullets

As Dan and I finish collating the information, Eric stops by our seats and says, "It's important to keep our findings under wraps until we know what we have and can verify it in the lab. If we find mummified remains that clearly belong to Butch and Sundance, don't shout 'Eureka!' In fact, don't even smile."

In Tupiza, we learn that the Worm has recently left town without paying his hotel bill, that our old friend Gastón Michel is now the mayor, that Alfredo Mejía is no longer the local COMIBOL agent, and that the vehicles we have planned to lease are unavailable. While Eric scouts around for transportation, Roy visits the COMIBOL office. Mejía's successor says that we shouldn't go to San Vicente because the miners plan to block the roads. We dismiss the notion of canceling the trip, but we don't want to risk an escalation of tensions by traveling with a police escort. Ever practical, Roy purchases a five-liter bottle of *singani* to use as a peace offering for the miners.

Meanwhile, although the heating element in our shower is broken, I decide to take advantage of my last opportunity to be clean. Cold showers are unpleasant even in temperate climates, but wandering the Andes has taught me that the key to survival is to stand outside the icy torrent and keep the various parts of my body as dry as possible until I am ready to wash them. I lean forward to wet my hair and then step back, careful to let the water drip onto the floor rather than down my neck. I suds my hair, step forward to rinse it, lather my body, and plunge into the sleet just long enough to remove the soap from my skin. I then turn off the water with one hand, grab the towel with the other, and wrap myself up as tightly as possible, all the while jumping up and down and chanting, "Yikes, yikes, yikes."

By the time I have toweled off, Dan has come back with the news that Eric has hired a Toyota land cruiser and an antique Land Rover and is busy stocking them with cases of bottled water and toilet paper, two essentials for Andean travel. Dan has picked up twenty-five *empanadas* for the journey. Lalo Mostajo, the industrious mayoral aide we met on our last visit, will come along to help with the digging and the community relations. The COMIBOL agent, having failed to persuade Roy of the potential danger from the strikers, will accompany us also.

Dan and I wind up in the Toyota with Clyde, Burney, Roy, Lalo, and a driver named Hector. Eric and the rest of the team ride in the Land Rover, whose driver—like so many others we've encountered in South America—is nicknamed Pancho. The Toyota purrs along, but the Land Rover, which has a dirty gas line and numerous other problems, conks out repeatedly. We use the stops to stretch our legs, relieve ourselves behind the nearest boulders, and photograph the rugged landscape.

"Is this your first visit to Bolivia?" Roy asks Clyde.

"No," says Clyde, smoke curling from his nostrils as he speaks. "A couple of years ago, we exhumed some kids at a prison farm called Granja de los Espejos near Santa Cruz. The people running the place were taking in prisoners, including minors, and simply keeping them. Even when their terms were completed, very often they didn't leave. Many of them were apparently worked to death or shot or killed."

"How did you find out about it?" asks Lalo.

"Amnesty International called us in. It was pretty shocking. Some of the Argentine team members came up, and we did an exhumation in an isolated graveyard where they'd been burying some of these prisoners. We found fourteen-, fifteen-, sixteen-year-old kids who had been shot to death."

"I remember reading something about that," says Roy. "It was horrible."

"You know," says Clyde, "murder is the most terrible of all crimes, and we have to deal with it in my work all the time. We have to cope with, for example, the reality of serial killers and the obscene motives for murder—sex, money, property—but the grossest motive of all, I think, is the political killing, the killing by a state. It's particularly obscene, because in any civilized society we expect the state to protect us, and we give our trust to our government or state or tribe or whatever political entity. When the tribe or the state or the government turns killer, we're completely helpless. That's the cruelest betrayal of all."

The clattering of pebbles in the wheel wells is the only response.

"Earlier this year," says Clyde, "I was in northern Chile looking for some of Pinochet's victims who had been dumped into abandoned mine shafts that were then sealed with dynamite. We went down into this two-thousand-foot shaft on a pretty scary combination of hoists, ladders, and ropes, and we found these tiny pieces of bodies mixed in with the rocky debris at the bottom. The region is so dry that some of the soft tissue was mummified. We were able to get a print off one of the pieces, which turned out to match the thumbprint of a doctor who had disappeared right after President Allende was overthrown by the army."

I now understand why Clyde is taking time out to dig up our outlaws: Unlike most people he exhumes, Butch and Sundance weren't helpless victims of tyrants or sadists. And Clyde doesn't view the dead with the trepidation that most of us do. In fact, while examining their remains closely and listening to the stories they tell, he establishes a kind of intimacy with them. "Bones make good witnesses," he says. "They may speak softly, but they don't lie, and they never forget."

Hector slows the Toyota to let a herd of goats spill over the edge of the road and down the cactus-prickly hillside, and the conversation turns to the inquest file that Roger and Carolyn McCord found in Tupiza. "I'm glad we have the information," says Roy, "but I don't

282

understand how they were able to take the original records from the judicial archives."

"Roger told us," says Dan, "that the judge said they could have the file."

"Maybe some money changed hands," suggests Clyde.

"Or maybe they just walked off with it," I say. "In the pamphlet Francisco Salazar gave us when we first came to Tupiza, he described their visit and said that Roger told him he was Butch Cassidy's grandson. Salazar said that they searched for a judicial file but found nothing. He specifically wrote that the McCords had 'returned all the papers' and had concluded that the file did not exist. But the pamphlet also said that Carlos Peró headed up the posse, so Salazar could have been mistaken about Roger and the file. We can speculate all we want, but we'll probably never know what really happened."

In the late afternoon, the Land Rover sputters to yet another halt.

"Good," says Burney, "I'm overdue for a pit stop."

The lack of cover on the ridge presents no problem for the men, who simply turn their backs to me, but I must hike quite a distance to find even the scant privacy offered by a clump of *ichu* grass. When I return, Pancho and Hector are bent over the Land Rover's engine, tinkering with the gas line while everyone else mills around. As the sun slides down behind the rolling horizon, Clyde pulls a bottle of Wild Turkey from his canvas knapsack and passes it around to warm us up. Twenty minutes later, the Land Rover still shows no signs of life, and we decide that the Toyota will press on to San Vicente. Hector will drop us off, then return for the occupants of the defunct vehicle. Clyde wants to stay behind—go down with the ship, so to speak—but Burney dissuades him. We leave the Wild Turkey with our stranded colleagues and hurtle on through the night.

Having encountered not a single miner, let alone a roadblock, we eventually reach San Vicente. Hector deposits us at the *rancho*, where the *dueña* serves us a small meal and several pots of *coca* tea, which we spike with *singani*. Meanwhile, Pancho has managed to start the Land Rover; the rest of the team arrives within half an hour. They waste no time in catching up with us in the *singani* department, and we soon stagger off to our quarters.

The COMIBOL agent has located two vacant houses for us, and we divide up in the only civilized way possible: smokers and nonsmokers.

Dan and I find ourselves in the same house we shared with Eric, Pamela, and Roy on our last visit to San Vicente. The only apparent changes are that the light fixture has been removed from the bathroom ceiling and the fixture in our bedroom is broken. Dan and I undress in the dark, zip our sleeping bags together, and snuggle up extra close to stop our teeth from chattering. I'd hate to sleep alone here: Summer in San Vicente feels like winter in Wyoming, without the snow.

In the smokers' house, Burney goes to bed, but Clyde, Roy, and Lalo continue drinking for a while. Clyde talks about organizing a forensic team to search for the disappeared in Argentina. "At the beginning, I wasn't sure the project would work, because the students had no experience. When we uncovered the first body, one of the women on the team burst into tears and left, and the others dispersed. "I thought, *Well, that's it. Nothing can be done here*. Half an hour later, she came back and asked where to find the kettle to make coffee. I knew then that it would work." His eyes brimming, Clyde says, "I never manage to tell that story without crying."

By three o'clock, a quarter of the *singani* has been consumed, and the men head for bed. Breathing heavily from the altitude, Clyde has difficulty removing his boots and trousers and putting on his pajamas, but he eventually succeeds and sits on his bed, which is between Roy's and Burney's.

Thank goodness, thinks Roy, *now we can get some sleep.*

Clyde lights a cigarette.

"Goddamn it," says Burney, "I have to start working in three and a half hours. Put that thing out and lay down."

"I'm all right," mutters Clyde.

Fearing that Clyde will fall asleep and start a fire, Roy fights to stay awake. When he sees an inch of ash hanging from the end of the cigarette, he hands an ashtray to Clyde, who puts the cigarette out. And then lights another one.

"You stupid son of a bitch," yells Burney. "You're gonna burn the goddamn house down and kill us all. Put that cigarette out and go to sleep. If you can't sleep, I'll tell you a story." Burney and Clyde have known each other so long, they interact like the odd couple—except both of them are Oscars. That leaves Roy to play Felix.

"This is the last one," Clyde promises. Within minutes, he is asleep, still holding the lighted cigarette. Roy rises quietly, picks up the ashtray, and is pulling the cigarette out of Clyde's fingers when Clyde wakes up with a start. It is four o'clock and Roy doesn't think he can last through another cigarette, but Clyde slides down into his bed and begins snoring heavily.

In the morning, we sit at a long wooden table in the *rancho* and drink *coca* tea from white cups decorated with royal-blue peacocks. Most of the tables are empty because the strikers have gone to La Paz to present their case, which means I can cross being-stoned-to-death-by-an-angry-mob off my list of things to worry about. That boosts fear-of-freezing to the top.

Plumes of frosted breath chuff in our wake as we trudge uphill to the cemetery, where the corregidor, the cantonal agent, the town judge, and other local officials have gathered for the groundbreaking ceremony. Aside from the ritual spilling of *singani* and dropping of *coca* leaves and cigarettes, we might just as easily be turning the first spade of earth for a shopping center. Prayers are offered up to the earth goddess Pachamama and to the souls of the *bandoleros*. "Please forgive us," Judge Prudencio Bolívar Mamani implores them in Quechua, "if what we are doing is wrong. We promise to bring your bones back to be reburied, and we will not hurt you."

Once Pachamama has been appeased and the outlaws' spirits have been placated, Eric and Burney confer with Clyde about how to proceed. Bulky slabs and headstones sit on the plots east and west of our target, and in the four months since our last visit, a baby's grave—a small mound of mud with a wooden cross—has appeared in the previously open space north of the tombstone. This leaves only the area to the south, a space less than two feet wide by four feet long, available for digging. Eric and Burney establish the perimeter of the hole, then call in laborers with picks and shovels to remove the top layer of dirt.

While my housemates are occupied in the cemetery, I return to our quarters for a chilly sponge bath. Not only am I still covered with dust from the jeep ride, but I have started my period. What a time to be the only woman in a house with minimal privacy and primitive facilities! Water is now available for only an hour a day, so the COMIBOL housekeeper has rigged up a hose from the sink's spigot into the bathtub. When the water is turned on at the source, the tub fills up with a brownish liquid that can be dipped out as needed for flushing the toilet. Nobody has explained any of this to us, however, so I fiddle with the faucet in search of something cleaner than the scum-coated contents of the tub. In the end, I give up and turn to the moist paper towelettes my mother forced on me as I was packing. They do a creditable job, and I vow never to doubt her wisdom again.

Meanwhile, Clyde has decided to leave the digging to Eric and Burney and take a nap. After finding the smokers' house locked, he knocks on our door. "Man," he says as I let him in, "it's cold out there."

"You don't know what cold is," I reply, fastening the snaps on my down vest, "until you put on a frozen brassiere."

After I leave for the cemetery, Clyde falls asleep on Eric's bed but is soon awakened by the sound of running water. He gets up and discovers that the bathtub has overflowed (because I inadvertantly left the tap open too wide). As water streams across the linoleum and into our bedroom, Clyde rescues our bags from the floor and puts them onto the bed. In the process, he notices a plastic bagful of medicine for everything from dysentery to pneumonia. (Ever since a Chilean pharmacist insisted that I could take penicillin even though I was allergic to it, I have traveled with my own drugstore in a bag.) Still suffering the effects of last night's debauchery—bad-bit by the Wild Turkey bird, as Burney puts it—Clyde begins browsing through my drugstore in search of a remedy. He prescribes a Demerol for himself and settles down to sleep off his aches and pains.

Back at the cemetery, Eric and Burney have uncovered the remains of a broken concrete slab, a couple of tin cans, and the wire frames of several old wreaths. The wind has been blowing hard all morning, and the temperature seems to drop by one degree for each bucketful of dirt removed from the grave. Although most of the townspeople (with the notable exception of Froilán Risso) turned out for the ceremony, the crowd steadily dwindles. Three *cholas* planted on ringside slabs remain, passing the hours knitting like Madame Defarge in triplicate and muttering about the evil spirits we are unleashing, as evidenced by the icy wind.

In the afternoon, a small group of men and women comes to the cemetery to protest our trespassing in the realm of the dead. When we refuse to halt the exhumation, they promise to return in force. A mass demonstration never materializes, but Roy meets with the delegation and attempts to persuade them that our motives are pure and that the wind is coincidental. They remain adamant that we must stop.

"Okay," says Roy, "so be it. But when I return to La Paz, I must report to the Ministry of Justice and explain why the project was not carried out. I will need to tell the officials who was responsible." He then asks for the names of the protesters, who back down immediately, the main antagonist leading the retreat.

At the end of the day, all we have to show for our trouble are a neat rectangular hole—two feet wide, forty inches long, and twenty inches deep—and sunburns all around; the air may be arctic, but the sun is tropical.

In the morning, we tie bandannas around our heads to protect our ears from the sun. Burney and Eric set to work, and as the hole deepens, more and more of the monument becomes visible. The small block we have been thinking of as the tombstone turns out to be the uppermost of three blocks stacked with the largest on the bottom, ending at a depth of forty-one inches beneath the surface of the ground. The cement poured for the neighboring slabs has flowed into our grave site, narrowing the width of the hole to eighteen inches. This is definitely not a job for a claustrophobe. The wind has not abated, and those of us with nothing to do but watch and wait occupy ourselves with seeking the most efficacious tombs for sheltering behind. When we break for lunch, my nose feels frostbitten.

By midafternoon, the hole is so deep that the diggers need a ladder. Once Eric has climbed down into the pit, Roy lifts the ladder out to give him as much room as possible. The work continues, overseen by a scrawny black-and-white dog sitting on the cemetery wall. Nearby, children playing anthropologist scoop soil from graves and carry it around in toy buckets made from tin cans and string.

"Intrusive bone," calls Eric.

"When there is a limited amount of consecrated ground," explains Clyde, "new graves are made on top of old graves. And in the course of digging the new graves, bones from the old graves are disturbed and commingled." He examines the femur and says, "Aside from being way too small for our guys, this bone has a flattened shape, which is often seen in indigenous people in mountainous areas. Very well adapted to climbing."

"The Plastic Age bottoms out at six feet," says Eric.

"What?" Dan frowns.

"Below six feet," says Burney, "all the litter is biodegradable."

Dressed in a fleece-lined denim jacket with frayed cuffs over a wool sweater and corduroy trousers, and wearing yellow flannel gloves and his signature green canvas hat, Clyde perches on the concrete slab to the west of the hole and examines various intrusive bones—part of a scapula, a rib, a heel bone, several vertebrae, and a skull—as they emerge. "This cranium is so fragmented," he says, "that it's hard to tell what we've got. The hole in the back of the skull below the ear might be an exit wound, or it might not."

"We're at what we feel confident was the ground surface at the time Butch and Sundance were buried," says Burney.

"If they're down there," says Clyde.

"We've probably got another two feet," says Burney, "before we find what we're looking for."

After placing the intrusive material into a blue plastic bag and lighting his umpteenth cigarette of the day, Clyde says, "Call me when you get some serious bones," then shambles off to the smokers' house for a nap.

At dusk, we assemble in the *rancho* to warm ourselves with *coca* tea and watery french-fry soup—the specialty of the house—followed by twice-boiled rice and half-ounce portions of mystery meat.

"Next time we come up here," says Clyde, "we bring provisions."

"Next time we come up here," Burney responds, "I'm getting an excuse from my mama."

Later, I dream about a big bowl of fettucine with garlic, butter, and Parmesan cheese, then wake up to find myself gnawing on my sleeping bag. In the morning, my jeans are snug—proof positive that I can gain weight merely by thinking about food.

To make matters worse, we have depleted our water supply by washing our hair with water warmed up in a tin can on top of our space heater, and the daily flow from the hose has stopped altogether. Without water, we can no longer flush the toilet at will and must rely on the COMIBOL housekeeper to come in at midday with a bucket of her own water to flush away the accumulated waste. Perhaps it's just as well that we're underfed.

After *coca* tea and stale bread on the third morning of the dig, Roy asks how optimistic Clyde is about finding the bandits.

"It doesn't matter whether you feel optimistic or pessimistic," Clyde responds. "It's what's there that counts."

Up in the cemetery, the wind continues at gale force. Only Eric, scrabbling away in the hole, escapes its gelid touch. At a depth of about seven and a half feet, his trowel finally hits the top of a coffin, and we gather around expectantly.

"Bad sign," mutters Dan. "Nobody would've wasted a coffin on bandits."

A man who has lived in San Vicente most of his life remarks that, as *bandoleros,* Butch and Sundance would have been buried vertically. "Back then, poor people were buried in shallow holes piled with dirt. People with more possibilities were interred in niches. We have been using coffins here only since 1976. Before that, people were simply wrapped in blankets. When I first came here, the cemetery was almost abandoned. This grave you are digging up was one of the few that was here then."

Eric sends up a few threads, a piece of cloth, and a button, then yells, "He's buried facedown!"

"They bury prisoners facedown as a sign of disrespect," says Clyde. "Well, well."

"The top of the coffin has collapsed," says Eric, "so I am hauling out pieces of wood."

Lalo, who is wearing a modified Montana Peak hat, hauls the dark shards of wood up in a bucket made from a plastic jug.

"Correction," Eric calls out, "the body is not facedown. The skull had just flopped over, but the individual was buried with his head pointing downhill."

Although we have cordoned the area off with red plastic tape, like a police line, people keep crawling under the tape for a closer look. When Eric brushes the dirt away to reveal a jawbone with three gold teeth glinting in the sunlight, the crowd surges forward. Worried that the excavation will collapse, Roy asks them to move back. (Within an hour, the town buzzes with the news of a *gringo* plot to steal gold teeth from the cemetery.)

"Take that mandible out real gentle-like," Clyde tells Eric, "and let's see what it looks like."

Eric places the jawbone in the plastic bucket.

"Man!" says Clyde, retrieving the prize. "Okay, we have a male mandible.'' Cigarette in hand, he examines the bone. "He is in the age range of the two fellows we're looking for, based on the dental wear that I see. And this is high-quality dental work. This is not curbside dentistry. So whoever this is could have afforded good dental care and probably took good care of his teeth.''

The cemetery fills up with spectators again as Clyde sits by the grave, studies his bone list, and yells instructions down to Eric. "Let's see, you owe me nine right ribs and five left ribs, and the lower part of the sternum is missing.''

Eric sends up several pieces of cloth, four ribs, a scapula, and a humerus. Roy hauls up the bucket by its long string handle and passes it to Clyde.

"Okay, you owe me four more left ribs.''

"You just ask for it, Clyde,'' says Roy.

"You can't get better service at Wendy's,'' adds Dan.

"Now,'' says Clyde, "you owe me six ribs on the right and five thoracic vertebrae.''

The right scapula comes up.

"I need another humerus, if you got one.''

"Coming up. Bucket!''

Eric continues sending up bones until he reaches the bottom of the coffin, slightly more than eight feet below the ground's surface.

His cigarette firmly wedged between his fingers, Clyde pounds the top of the cranium and shakes the contents, which look like ordinary potting soil, into a plastic bag. "Screen this for me, Roy,'' he says, "and save any non-dirt. We might be looking for some metal fragments from a bullet.''

Panting from the altitude and sniffling from the dust and the cold air, Eric emerges from the grave. The color of his jacket has changed from maroon to terra-cotta. "The head was pushed into the neck, maybe by the coffin falling,'' he says.

I have been bracing myself for the disappointment that has seemed inevitable, in view of what Roger has told us, but even though the mottled brown skull looks too long and narrow to belong to Butch, we can't rule out Sundance. The forehead is shattered between the eye sockets, which Clyde says is consistent with the damage from a gunshot wound at close range, and which tallies with the witnesses' testimony about the taller of the two slain bandits.

Fearful that the monument might fall into the hole and crush the diggers, we truss it up with a green rope attached to a heavy concrete tomb to the north. A laborer removes some of the dirt under the monument, and Eric goes back into the hole to retrieve the pelvis and legs.

"Wait'll you see this," he calls, then passes up a long femur with dark fibrous material hanging from it. For the first time since the dig began, a wave of revulsion washes over me.

Clyde, however, is delighted. "Aha!" he says with relish. "Now this is the kind of stuff we're looking for. He's a big guy."

Once Eric has removed everything he can reach, Burney takes a turn in the hole. He digs nine inches below the bottom of the coffin and determines that no second coffin is below it.

The mood at the *rancho* in the evening is decidedly merry, but Dan remains skeptical. "I just can't get past the coffin," he says. "In a place where wood is so scarce, why would they waste any of it on outlaws?"

"Maybe they put them in coffins to keep their evil spirits locked up," I say, "or to preserve the corpses for the inquest. After all, they dug them up two weeks after the shootout so that Peró could identify them."

"Where's the other body?"

"I don't know. It's probably beside this one, and they'll find it tomorrow."

"What about the lack of bullets? Sundance was supposedly shot several times in the arm, but the arm bones seem to be intact, and we don't even know for sure that the wound on his face came from a bullet. Clyde said that the hole was only 'consistent with' a gunshot wound."

Overhearing this last comment, Clyde says, "You misunderstood what I said about the cavity in the sinus area. I am all but certain that this man was shot in the lower forehead, more or less between the eyes."

"Why isn't there any exit wound?" asks Dan.

"The bullet may not have exited," says Clyde. "Unless they have a very high velocity, bullets will often run out of steam before they get to the other side of the skull. Or it may have exited in the lower back of the skull and missed the neck vertebrae. It's hard to tell the trajectory when there's no exit wound."

"Sweets," I say to Dan, "didn't that *Wide World* article mention something about a bullet from Butch's gun being extracted from Sundance's brain?"

"I don't remember." He turns to Clyde and asks, "Could the wound in the forehead have been caused by someone committing suicide?"

"In most of those cases, the people are shot in the temple or upper mouth."

"Butch and Sundance were supposedly buried between or near a German who blew himself up defrosting dynamite on his stove and a Swede who shot himself getting off a horse," says Dan. "Could this skeleton be either of them?"

"This was definitely not death by dynamite, unless it was from a flying object rather than the explosion," says Clyde, "but the falling-off-the-horse fatality is a possibility."

On the fourth day of the dig, Clyde lays the skeleton out on a table in the upper house. "My preliminary measurements of the arm bones indicate that the decedent's height was seventy-one inches, plus or minus three inches, which means he was five foot eight to six foot two. From the cylindrical shape of the femur, we can safely say that the skeleton is that of a foreigner. An indigenous femur would have a flatter shape, providing more surface area for the attachment of the muscles that help to raise the thigh, which is useful for climbing. It's a functional adaptation. The configuration of the skull is also pretty definitely Caucasoid. As for trauma, we've got an area of massive fragmentation and fracturing here." Although we still have found no bullets, Clyde notes copper stains near the right eye socket and possible metal fragments in the skull. "I haven't had a chance to closely examine the arm bones for bullet wounds, but the elbow appears to have been sheared off, and there are copper stains there."

In addition to the remains, Eric and Burney have found several items that may aid in the identification. These include a small buckle, a removable button of the type listed in the inventory of the slain bandits' possessions, and the soles of a pair of small boots. The boots are intriguing because Sundance's feet were unusually small for someone of his height, which was comparable to that of the individual in the grave.

Everything seems to match up with what we know about Sundance, so I don't share Dan's pessimism about our find. But where *is* Butch?

This morning, Burney and Eric have dug into the east, west, and south walls of the grave and found undisturbed "virgin soil," which means that a body buried next to our skeleton would have gone into a separate hole. That leaves only the north end as a possible resting site for the other inhabitant of a joint grave.

"Doesn't it seem odd," says Dan, "that they would dig a long trench for two coffins rather than stack them on top of each other or lay them out side by side?"

Although Dan feels uncomfortable about being so negative in view of everyone else's optimism, Eric assures him that every scientific team needs a skeptic.

Burney suggests moving the baby's grave so that we can get at the area where Butch might be, but Clyde says, "Only as a last resort."

The baby's father has said he thinks it would be all right, but when he speaks to his wife, she says, "*¡No, absolutamente no!*"

And who can blame her?

In the end, we hire a couple of miners to burrow beneath the baby's grave and shore up the earth with timbers, as if building a mine tunnel. Eric crawls through the passage and finds another coffin, which is smashed and full of intrusive bones, including two extra skulls. Clyde says one of them belonged to a female Indian who might have been shot but was definitely not one of our guys.

At the far end of the grave, Eric finds the top of a cranium with what appear to be entrance and exit wounds in the temples, which jibes with witnesses' descriptions of the shorter bandit's condition. Unfortunately, even if we knew for certain that this was part of the second bandit's skull, we might not have enough of it to establish his identity.

Meanwhile, a bureaucratic crisis has been brewing. Although Clyde needs to take the skulls, shoulder blades, arm and leg bones, pelvis, all of the vertebrae, and a couple of ribs back to his lab for accurate measurements and various tests, a clerical error in the letter from the Ministry of Justice has left us with authorization to remove only the skulls. As a result, we must barter with the San Vicente officials for permission to take the other necessary bones. After we contribute $500 to be used for the local school and church and promise to badger the U.S. embassy to get computers for the school, the officials grant our request.

Clyde oversees the reburial of the intrusive bones in a wooden box lined with black cloth and blessed with *coca* leaves and *singani*. He then leaves the unneeded bones from our skeleton with Judge Bolívar, and packs the rest of the skeleton and two other skulls in cardboard boxes for the trip to Tupiza, where another bone battle awaits.

After all our fantasies about hot showers, Dan and I are assigned the same hotel room we had before, the one with the icy shower. When we object, the *dueño* says, "It's okay now. We fixed it."

Unfortunately, the repairman didn't know when to quit: The water is scalding. We wind up standing outside of the stream and ducking into it briefly, just as we do with cold showers. Moreover, the drain is sluggish, so we must jump around to keep from poaching our toes and must sacrifice one of our threadbare towels to sop up the water that overflows the doorsill and pools beside the bed.

Mayor Gastón Michel wants Tupiza's forensic expert to meet with Clyde to inventory and photograph the bones. The mayor also says that he cannot authorize us to take the bones without the approval of the city council. Because most of the team members must leave on the Sunday-morning *ferrobus* to make their Tuesday-morning planes, a special session of the council is called for seven o'clock Saturday evening.

In the meantime, while I spend the day in Tupiza with Dora Salazar, Roy and Dan take the team on a day-trip to Huaca Huañusca to see the holdup site. When seven arrives, the guys have not returned. At seven-thirty, Lalo comes to the hotel to find out where they are. I tell him that surely they will be back at any moment. Justly peeved at being stood up, the city council disperses to various social events at eight o'clock. Half an hour later, the team finally arrives and finds the town hall deserted. They go to the "007" bar, but Gastón has just left. Although Lalo isn't home, they eventually find him in the plaza; he tracks down Gastón, the mayoral official, and the legal assessor. (Tupiza is small enough that sooner or later you can find anyone.)

"A thousand apologies," says Roy, and Clyde and Eric express similar remorse.

The mayoral official is friendly, but the legal assessor presses Gastón not to give up the bones; the meeting quickly turns acrimonious. Like municipal governments everywhere, Tupiza's city council regularly takes time from its own internal struggles to war with the mayor. Besides, elections loom and everyone is jockeying for advantage. No one wants to stick his neck out for some bone-crazy *norteamericanos*.

Clyde comes back to the hotel to report the legal wrangling. "If you have any influence with the mayor," he says to us, "now is the time to use it."

Dan and I walk over to the town hall and slip into seats near the door as Gastón is saying, "How do we know that you will return the bones? How will you get them back to us? What guarantees do we have? Let's not forget the matter of that *gringo* who stole a judicial file." Looking at Lalo, Gastón says, "When was that? 1970? 1980?"

Lalo turns red. He has obviously spilled the beans about Roger McCord and the inquest file. We were wrong to take Lalo's loyalty to us for granted. After all, he works for the city, so he is bound to put Tupiza's interests ahead of ours. Unfortunately, even though we had nothing to do with the removal of the file and do not condone it, our project may be destroyed by the resultant distrust of *gringos*.

Upon noticing Dan and me in the back of the room, Gastón smiles and waves.

"You cannot take the bones without the city council's permission," the legal assessor declares. "You must follow the process of the law."

"That is impossible," says Eric. "If we are not on that *ferrobus* to La Paz tomorrow, we will miss our plane on Tuesday. Dr. Snow is a very important scientist who has taken the time and trouble to come here without any pay whatsoever, and he is scheduled to leave the United States for Iraq on Friday. He simply must leave here tomorrow morning. He needs to take the bones to his laboratory to study them, but he will send them back as soon as he has finished his investigation. You'll have them in six months."

Sensing that the officials are less concerned about either the bones or Clyde's schedule than about asserting their own authority, Roy tries the same tactic he used so successfully in San Vicente: He asks for everyone's name for his report to the government officials in La Paz.

Gastón leaps to his feet and says, "No one threatens me. If you threaten me, the whole town will rise up."

"I don't mean to offend you," Roy replies, "but the Ministry of Justice supports this project, and they won't be pleased if it cannot be completed."

"You needn't be so aggressive," Gastón says soothingly. "We can work something out, but you must understand my position. I cannot simply disregard my duties."

"You have your duties," says Roy, "and we have ours, but there is no reason that we cannot work together."

"*Bueno*, I will consider the matter and let you know my decision later tonight." Roy and Eric leave, but Dan and I—at the mayor's request—remain.

"We are sorry for the difficulties," says Dan. "Everyone on the team is tired and frustrated because of the arduous nature of the exhumation, the altitude, and the lack of sleep."

"But what is your connection with this group?" asks Gastón.

Hoping to act as a conciliator, Dan tries to distance us from the scientific wing of the team. "We are the historians," he says. "Clyde and Eric approached us last year, and we agreed to help with the project. Despite the tension and angry words, all of the people on the team are honorable and will stand by their word."

"We view this project as beneficial to Tupiza," I interject, "because of the potential for tourism. The region is beautiful, but tourists don't know about it. They get on the train in La Paz or Oruro or Uyuni and ride straight through to the Argentine border. Once they learn about Tupiza, as a result of this project, they will get off the train and spend money on hotels and restaurants and taxis, which will help the local economy."

"We've seen it happen in Uyuni," says Dan. "When we first went there in the 1970s, the only tourists we saw were changing trains and getting out of town as soon as possible. We wrote a blurb about the Laguna Colorada for the *South American Handbook,* and in the years since, Uyuni has become a mecca for tourists. Don Jesús Rosas has doubled the size of his hotel to take care of the increase in business, and there are four or five companies running tours to the *laguna* and other places that used to be impossible to reach."

"Butch and Sundance came here to steal," I say. "It would be poetic justice if they wound up, all these years later, bringing prosperity to the very region they tried to rob."

"*Bueno*," says Gastón, "I need to discuss this matter further with my advisers. Where can I find you half an hour from now?"

"Perhaps the mayor is looking for a bribe," says Lalo.

"I don't think so," says Roy. "He hasn't given any indication to me that money comes into it at all. Has he said anything like that to you?"

"No," says Lalo.

"I don't see what the problem is," says Eric. His hands are battered from the dig. Sitting exhausted and dispirited at the end of the table, he stares into his beer as a half-eaten slice of pizza congeals on his plate.

"The mayor is acting within his authority," replies Clyde. "A team of Bolivians would never be able to march into an Oklahoma cemetery and march out with boxes of bones as easily as we have here in Bolivia."

"The bones are not out of Bolivia yet," says Eric.

"Considering all the different officials who have jurisdiction," says Dan, "not to mention the rivalries between the various political factions, I think we're doing remarkably well."

I spot Gastón and the mayoral official peering through the glass door and wave them into the brightly lit restaurant. They sit at a separate table with Dan, Roy, and Lalo and order *coca* tea. Everyone waits for Gastón to announce his decision: May we take the bones or not?

"We need to meet with the city council tomorrow morning," he says.

This sounds ominous.

"But it should be routine," he adds matter-of-factly.

"I suppose I could stay for the meeting," offers Roy, "and then somehow get to La Paz with the bones in time for them to go on the airplane with Clyde."

Gastón still hasn't said what he intends to recommend or what he expects the council to do. Instead, he and Roy discuss train and bus schedules and the availability of long-distance taxis.

Finally, Gastón turns to Dan and asks, "Are you religious?"

"*Jubilado,*" says Dan, using Argentine slang for the word *retired,* then instantly realizes that it was the wrong answer. The question was serious. Luckily, Gastón doesn't understand the *argentinismo,* and Dan gets another chance. "*Sí, sí,*" he says this time. "*Católico.*"

"*Bueno,*" says Gastón, "then you are a man of your word. Do you give your word that the bones will be returned?"

"*¡Absolutamente!*"

"It's a deal," says Gastón, his hand shooting across the table to shake with Dan.

Clyde is told that the matter has been resolved, but he is already on the *ferrobus* before he learns that the bones are to remain in Tupiza until after the city council meets. As the head of the team, he has no intention of letting the bones out of his sight. "Hand me my bag," he says to Burney. "I'm staying with Roy."

Burney and Eric protest, but Clyde is resolute. Within minutes, the train pulls out; we have no choice but to leave Clyde and Roy to their fate.

The meeting lasts three hours. The council agrees to let Clyde and Roy take the bones on condition that the president of the council—the mayor's cousin and sometime political rival Carlos Michel—accompany them to La Paz, that they obtain permission from the Bolivian Congress to take the bones out of the country, and that the U.S. embassy issue an official promise that the bones will be returned within six months. Knowing full well that the Bolivian Congress won't have time to consider the matter before Clyde's plane leaves, Roy and Clyde agree to the terms.

Once the meeting ends, they ask the city council to lunch, and four or five members accept the invitation. A friendly waiter hands out cards with calendars on one side and pictures on the other. When Clyde, who has received a pastoral scene with daisies, sees Roy's shot of a bare-breasted woman, he snatches the card from Roy's hand and gives Roy the one with the daisies.

After lunch, a taxi driver agrees to take the three men to La Paz but says he'll need time to prepare his car.

"What's wrong with it?" asks Roy.

"Nothing. It's a new car. It just needs to be made ready for such a long journey."

At five o'clock, the driver shows up in a Ford Cortina that was new twenty years ago. They set off with the cardboard boxes full of bones stowed in the trunk. The elderly Carlos Michel entertains the group by singing songs and reciting his poetry all the way to Cotagaita, where they stop for a beer. Clyde invites the driver to join them. As he hobbles into the bar, they notice that his left leg is wooden from the knee down.

They soon resume the journey, but a problem with the generator prevents the engine and the lights from being on at the same time. The driver manages for a while with the light provided by the full moon. Then, about halfway to Potosí, he stops the car in an Indian village, where roadside coffee stands have been set up. He takes a flashlight and paces up and down the road until he finds a length of wire, which he cuts with a butcher knife borrowed from a café and uses to fix the generator. During the two hours' wait while the driver makes the repair, Carlos Michel remarks, "It will be impossible to get congressional approval anytime soon." Once the car has been fixed, he sits in the front seat with the driver.

In the backseat, Clyde and Roy pass the time drinking *singani* and talking. Upon learning that Roy's wife is Argentine, Clyde says, "I've heard that to have an Argentine woman as a mistress is heaven but to have one as a wife is hell."

Roy laughs, then asks what plans Clyde has for the future.

"I'd like to live another hundred years."

"In that case, you'd better give up cigarettes and have a checkup."

"What for? I know what the doctor will say: 'Give up smoking.' "

At two in the morning, when they pull into Potosí with an all-but-empty tank, the gas stations are closed. As the men sit there wondering what to do, they notice two drunks knocking on the door to what turns out to be an after-hours source of liquor and gasoline. The driver siphons gas from a barrel and hits the road again.

Roy suggests that he and the other passengers take turns spelling the driver.

"That's okay," says the driver, "I've got my *coca* to keep me awake."

They pass *llama* caravans and a few vehicles, including an oncoming truck that misses them by a fraction of an inch as they round a curve. Half a mile later, they come equally close to hitting a bus. By dawn, they have reached the *altiplano*, where the driver stops. As Roy, Clyde, and Señor Michel stand watching in the freezing air, the driver jacks up the car and removes the tire, the wheel, and the wheel casing. He proceeds to repack the contents of the casing and rearranges the deteriorating brake lining. Clyde is certain that the man will never manage to put the wheel back together with only one wrench and a battered pair of pliers, but he succeeds. They are once again under way.

During a break for lunch in Oruro, Roy calls Eric in La Paz to report that they expect to reach the hotel at five o'clock.

They arrive an hour late and find Burney at the door of the hotel. "You have to go straight to the consulate," he says. "They're holding it open for you."

"Forget it," says Clyde. "We've been on the road for twenty-five hours. At least let us take a shower."

"Sorry."

Burney joins them in the car for the plunge back into La Paz's horrific rush hour. In a churning traffic circle, the car dies again. To the wail of angry horns, they push the car out of the way and onto the sidewalk. When the driver opens the hood, teenagers leaning out of the window above dump paint onto Burney to distract him so that their confederates below can pick his pockets. Fortunately, Clyde realizes what is happening and yells a few obscenities. The kids run away empty-handed.

The men retrieve the bones from the trunk and hail a cab, which fights traffic all the way to the consulate. Amid throngs of smartly dressed people with Christmas packages, the paint-spattered Burney and the three filthy travelers carry their shabby cardboard boxes up the block and into the consulate, where an official notarizes their signatures on the document Eric has prepared.

Living and working in Bolivia, the official ought to know his way around Latin American names, but he insists on calling Roy "Mister Lewis" instead of "Señor Querejazu." Roy eventually gives up on correcting the man, who has remained behind a sheet of bulletproof glass throughout the transaction.

"What's with the window?" Roy asks Clyde. "Is this guy for sale?"

After repacking the bones into wooden boxes, Clyde catches an hour and a half of sleep before the trip to the airport. Once the plane lifts off, he sinks back into his seat with a glass of Wild Turkey and drinks a silent toast to Butch and Sundance: *Gotcha*.

14 · NEXT OF KIN

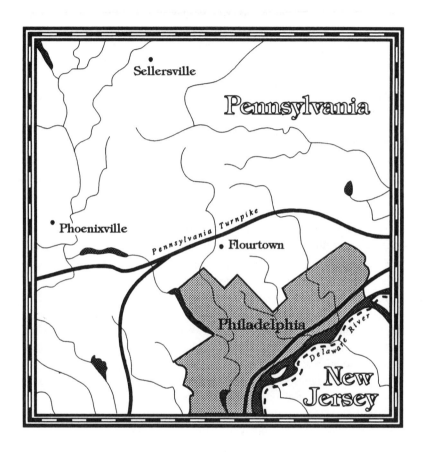

SUNDANCE was "a mean, low cur," according to his Cholila neighbor John Gardiner. Lula Parker Betenson called him "a killer" with "a quick, mean temper." Argentine policeman Milton Roberts considered him "not so much a bad character as a cold-blooded one." At Concordia, Clement Rolla Glass thought him "sullen," and Percy Seibert found him "almost taciturn" and "morose." Pinkerton infor-

301

mant Charles Ayers reported that he was "very quiet," and muleteer Roy Letson wrote that he "kept very much to himself most of the time." Charles Kelly, however, described him as "pleasant, friendly, and cool in any emergency," and British engineer A. G. Francis found him "a most amiable and cheerful companion, possessed of a very equable temper." Canadian cowboy Frederick Ings called him "a thoroughly likeable fellow" and "a general favourite with everyone."

Until now, I have viewed Sundance as little more than Butch's shadowy sidekick. Unlike the uniformly glowing descriptions of the gregarious Butch, reports on Sundance vary so much that he seems downright manic-depressive—charismatic one day and broody the next. Thinking that his relatives might shed light on his character, I tag along with Eric to the home of Sundance's great-great-nephew Paul Ernst in Sellersville, Pennsylvania. In addition to learning whether the family has information about Sundance's injuries, illnesses, or other physical conditions that might help Clyde identify the skeleton from San Vicente, Eric wants to find a relative whose DNA is suitable for comparison with the skeleton's DNA. I am eager to meet Paul's wife, Donna, who has corresponded with us for years. As the family historian, she is writing a book about Sundance.

Cruising north on I-95 on a rainy winter day several weeks after the exhumation, Eric and I discuss the preliminary findings of the scientists Clyde has recruited to help him analyze the remains and the other material from the grave. Oklahoma's state medical examiner, Dr. Fred Jordan, who examined X-rays of the skeleton, noted a metal fragment with cortical thickening around it in the left tibia and concluded that the individual had an old injury, most likely from a gunshot, in his lower leg. Sundance sought medical treatment for an unspecified pistol wound he got in "the extreme West," according to the Pinkertons, so we need to ask Paul and Donna Ernst whether they've been able to discover where the wound was. Eric also wants to ask them about Sundance's teeth. According to Dr. Paul Goaz, an oral-radiology professor at Baylor, the San Vicente skeleton was missing the incisor to the right of his two front teeth.

After X-rays of the skull revealed a few tiny metal fragments embedded in the cranial vault, supporting Clyde's belief that a gunshot wound in the lower forehead was the cause of death, he gave the skull to Dr. Lewis Sadler, who pioneered a technique in which digitized photographs of people are superimposed over video images of skulls to see whether they match at certain critical points. In his laboratory at the Department of Biomedical Visualization at the University of Illinois at Chicago, Sadler placed tissue-depth markers on the San Vicente skull to show what the outline of the head would have been when the skull had flesh on it. He then aligned a video image of the skull with a photograph of the Sundance Kid. The orbits of the eyes fell into place, and the contour of the skull matched. Eric witnessed the procedure and telephoned us to say, "We've got him!"

But Clyde is concerned about the hole. The upper part of the nose, the inside of the orbits, and the lower portion of the forehead were shattered by the bullet. The margin of error in an identification based on a skull-face superimposition increases from about 5 percent to 15 percent when such important parts of the facial bones are missing. And to make matters worse, Sadler and some of the other scientists have been talking to the press.

"Did somebody forget to tell those guys to keep their mouths shut until the testing is complete," I ask, "or are they just hard of listening?"

"It all started with Burney," says Eric. "He told his wife, who told a friend, who told a reporter, who naturally wanted to interview Burney, who told the guy everything about the dig and what we found. He even said that Clyde was ninety-five to ninety-seven percent certain we had Sundance. How Burney came up with those figures, I don't know. And this was *before* the tests began."

The Associated Press picked up the story from the *Arkansas Democrat-Gazette*, and articles soon appeared in newspapers across the country. Clyde got forty-six press calls within a matter of days. Dan and I have been besieged by reporters from Australia to Italy and practically everywhere in between. We have tried to straighten out the historical errors while telling the reporters that we're not qualified to discuss the scientific aspects of the story, even if we were at liberty to do so. The scientists, however, seem to be virtually lining up for press conferences. Although Sadler told the *Chicago Sun-Times* that his tests were inconclusive, Goaz revealed to the *Dallas Morning News* that Sadler had told him he was "convinced" that we had Sundance. Goaz went on to discuss the gunshot wound in the leg, and he described in detail his own findings about the condition of the skeleton's teeth and mentioned having extracted and sent a tooth to a laboratory for DNA analysis.

After winding through unmarked roads in a rural area north of Philadelphia, Eric and I at last reach the Ernsts' hilltop neocolonial house with bosky views on every side. Donna greets us at the front door and leads us to the combination family room and kitchen at the back of the house. There we meet Paul, who is built like Sundance and bears an uncanny facial resemblance to him, as well. "Pleased to meet you," he says softly.

Donna, who has curly brown hair and a broad smile, says, "Paul is like all of the men in our family. They're really shy until you get to know them, and then you can't shut them up."

During our four-hour visit, Paul says little more than hello and goodbye and "I hear you guys really had to rough it in San Vicente." The conflicting reports on Sundance finally make sense: He was bashful, not sullen. Once you got to know him, he was charming, but strangers never saw beyond his reticence.

Donna isn't the least bit shy. "One of the reasons I decided to write my book was that I could see how uncomfortable Paul was with all the distortions about Sundance that were being published. People were just writing any old thing, and then other writers were coming along and copying it. You've got to be very careful what you write."

"I know what you mean," I reply. "I hate seeing errors we made in our early articles being repeated and mutated. We're watching the legend grow and change before our very eyes as a result of our own mistakes."

"It's like the children's game Telephone," says Donna, "where you sit in a circle and whisper something to the person next to you, and by the time it comes around to the beginning, the message is unrecognizable."

"Exactly," I agree. "After one reporter mentioned that Clyde had brought back some hair and cloth, others began saying that the scientists hoped to compare DNA from the bones with DNA from the hair and cloth!"

Eric chortles, then says, "One of the things we need to do today is to figure out whether any of Sundance's living relatives would make suitable subjects for our DNA comparisons. We need someone from an unbroken female line."

"Sundance's sister Emma and brother Elwood never married," says Donna, "so they left no descendants. His brother Harvey had three children, but two of them died young. The third child, William Henry Longabaugh, was Paul's grandfather. Grandpop had two children who survived: Florence, Paul's mom, who died in 1980, and Bill, who is still living."

"Unfortunately," Eric explains, "we can't use any of Harvey's descendants, because the DNA would have come from the wives. There are two types of DNA—nuclear and mitochondrial—but the current state of the technology limits us to using mitochondrial DNA, which is passed through the maternal line. Sundance and his siblings would have had their mother's mitochondrial DNA, but only his sisters could pass it on to their children."

"What about his sister Samanna?" I ask. "Didn't she have kids?"

"Three daughters and two sons," Donna replies. "The girls died young, two of them in infancy. The sons married and had children, but the only one we know is Bill Hallman, whose father was Samanna's son Furman 'Bud' Hallman."

"No," says Eric, "he won't do. We'll have to go back up the line to the sisters of Sundance's mother or grandmother and see whether any of their descendants followed an unbroken maternal line."

Donna, who is an amateur genealogist, brings out her charts of the family tree but is unable to locate a suitable descendant from Sundance's mother's sisters and has no information about his maternal grandmother's siblings. "It's frustrating," says Donna, "because Grandpop could have given me all of this information, I'm sure, but he was so closemouthed about the family. Even though he knew I was into genealogy and history because of my own family's stories, he always told us that he had no living relatives. Then, shortly before he died in 1976, he was talking to his son—Paul's Uncle Bill—and said, 'I had an uncle who was like Jesse James and died in South America.' When Uncle Bill asked him for details, Grandpop said that it wasn't anybody's business and that Uncle Bill should forget about it. Grandpop repeated the story later, but he was senile by then, so Uncle Bill thought he was imagining things.

"We didn't know anything about it until later that year, after the *National Geographic* printed Robert Redford's article about the Outlaw Trail. The article gave Sundance's real name as Harry A. Longabaugh. Uncle Bill was at a church supper, and a friend called him 'Sundance.' Uncle Bill had no idea what she was talking about or who the Sundance Kid was until she explained what she'd read. Suddenly, the things Grandpop had said made sense. Uncle Bill borrowed a copy of the magazine and called us. I wrote to the *National Geographic*, and they put me in touch with Kerry Ross Boren, who was the researcher for the article. He confirmed that Sundance was Grandpop's uncle, and I was able to use the genealogical information to track down some of Samanna's descendants.''

"Did they know about Sundance before you contacted them?''

"The younger generation, the ones our age, hadn't been told and didn't want to know,'' says Donna, ''but Samanna's grandson Bill Hallman eventually admitted that he knew. He has the ledger in which Samanna noted the dates when she received letters from Sundance.''

"Why were they so reluctant to acknowledge the connection?'' I ask. "You'd think they would be curious.''

"They're ashamed of being related to an outlaw.''

"But no one would hold them responsible for his actions.''

"I know,'' says Donna. "We don't condone what he did and we don't agree with making a folk hero out of him, but he's part of history and part of our family, so we find him interesting. The Hallmans don't see it that way. They're extremely religious, and that may have something to do with it. In fact, when Ed Kirby's book on Sundance came out, we were upset about his claiming that Hiram BeBee was Sundance, but the Hallmans were upset about his writing that Samanna and Emma 'loved music and dances,' because dancing is against their religion.''

"If they think dancing is a sin,'' I say, "imagine what they must think of bank robberies and payroll heists.''

"The whole family was embarrassed about it,'' says Donna. "That's why Grandpop didn't like to talk about his relatives. As much as it frustrates me that he died without telling us what he knew, I can understand it. If your uncle was a bank robber, you wouldn't talk about it a lot. Sundance's sister Emma even went so far as to change the spelling of her name to Longabough with an *o* and included a note in her will saying that she didn't know whether her brother Harry was living or dead, but that he was to receive nothing from her estate.''

"When did she write the will?'' I ask.

"In 1918.''

"So ten years after the shootout,'' I say, "Sundance's family didn't know what had become of him. When did Samanna receive her last letter from him?''

"I don't remember the exact date,'' says Donna, "but it was shortly after the shootout. He could have mailed it and then died while the letter was on the boat to the United States.''

"I take it," says Eric, "that you believe Butch and Sundance died in South America."

"Either that or they're down on the corner, having a drink with Elvis."

"That's a possibility we've overlooked. I know Dan will want to check it out right away."

"To answer your question," Donna says to Eric, "if Sundance didn't die, why would he suddenly stop writing to his family?"

Over lunch, we discuss the calls and letters all of us have received since news of the exhumation broke. "We've had a few genuine tips," I remark, "but most of the people who say they have new information turn out to be loons."

"That's for sure," says Donna. "And some of the reporters are just as bad. They'll print anything without bothering to find out what the facts are."

"Except for *Der Spiegel,* which called us a historian-couple, nobody seems able to cope with the fact that Dan and I are a team. *The New York Times* identified him as 'a historian' and me as 'his wife'—which makes them half right—but at least they acknowledged my existence. My favorite reporter was the guy who called our house looking for Dan and wanted to know whether he was involved in the Butch Cassidy project. I said, 'Both of us are involved in it, and I can answer any questions you might have,' whereupon the reporter asked, 'Do you have a number where I could reach Dan?' "

Eventually, Eric steers the conversation around to the information Clyde needs for identifying the San Vicente skeleton. "The Pinkertons said Sundance sought treatment for a gunshot wound. Do you know where the wound was?"

Donna thinks for a moment, then says, "Well, Samanna's family was told that he had been shot in the leg."

"Do you know which leg it was?" asks Eric.

"I think it was the left one," says Donna. She turns to Paul and asks, "Do you remember?"

He shakes his head.

"The skeleton we brought back from Bolivia has an old gunshot wound in the lower left leg," says Eric. "It is also missing some teeth, including one that our dental expert thinks may have been missing since birth. Do you have any information about Sundance's teeth?"

"Not from the family," says Donna, "but there was a memo in the

Pinkerton archives that talks about them." She disappears up the stairs, then comes back with a copy of a report in which William A. Pinkerton mentions an interview with Lillie Davis, who married Wild Bunch member Will Carver. Lillie said that bordello operator "Fanny Porter [knew] Harry Longabaugh. He used to have a gold tooth in front, left side. But he had it taken out, and a white one placed in its stead."

"Unfortunately," says Eric, "the skeleton's missing front tooth was on the right."

"Is that *his* right," asks Donna, "or the right side as you face him?"

"His right, but that's a good point. The woman who talked to the Pinkertons might have meant the left as she was facing him. That would be his right."

"Let's see whether his teeth show in the pictures." Donna leads us to the far end of the room, where built-in shelves crammed with books about western history flank a huge brick fireplace. The Fort Worth Five photo and a WANTED poster hang on the wall above a Victorian lamp; a tintype of Sundance at age four with his father, Josiah Longabaugh, stands on the bookcase near pictures of Sundance's sisters, brothers, and mother. Not a single mouth is open.

I sit on the maroon sofa and study the tintype, and Eric sits on the floor leafing through the Pinkerton documents, while Donna retrieves copies of four photographs Sundance sent home from Patagonia. Three of them are sections of the photograph in which he, Butch, Etta, and several others are lined up in front of the Cholila cabin—the photograph given to us by the Jones family. The fourth picture was taken behind the cabin. Sundance and Butch are seated in chairs, and Etta stands between them, a starched white apron over her dress, her springer spaniel at her feet, a kettle in her hand. A tea party. The bandit trio as respectable ranchers.

"May I have a copy of this picture?"

"I'll give you a copy of my copy," says Donna, sitting down beside me, "but Bill Hallman has the originals of all four pictures, which he's threatened to burn before he dies."

"Maybe we could break into his house while he's at church," I say, "and liberate them."

By the time this mystery is settled, I'll be a full-fledged outlaw. I've already learned how to lie with a straight face when anybody asks me about the project. I even equivocate with my sister Leah, who usually knows all my secrets; she wouldn't leak the story on purpose, but her sister-in-law's sister-in-law writes for *The New York Times,* so whenever Leah asks whether we found Butch and Sundance, I tell her that the tests will take months and months to complete.

Because the second grave was destroyed, Eric and Burney did not find any of the occupants' teeth, hair, or other traditional sources of DNA. As a result, Clyde has warned us, the scientists may be unable to identify the partial skull that bears wounds consistent with those allegedly suffered by the shorter bandit. Using an experimental method, Chris Boles, a molecular biologist at Brandeis University, grinds up a bit of the skull and succeeds in extracting DNA from the powdered bone. Dan and I are disappointed when Eric tells us that it does not match the DNA in hair samples from Butch's relatives, but Clyde says that the test does not eliminate Butch, because the DNA from the skull might have come from someone who touched it after it came out of the earth. Moreover, we have no way of knowing whether the partial skull—which includes the top of the cranium but no facial bones— actually belonged to one of the bandits killed in the 1908 shootout. Later, Clyde determines that the skull is non-Caucasoid, which means that it definitely did not come from one of the Aramayo bandits.

Although Chris has extracted DNA from the tooth sent to him by dental expert Paul Goaz, there is nothing to compare the DNA with yet. Unless we can find a relative from an unbroken maternal line, our only hope is that geneticists will succeed in developing what Chris refers to as a Y-probe—a means of tracing DNA through the paternal line with a male equivalent of mitochondrial DNA.

Meanwhile, Froilán Risso holds court in San Vicente with a stream of Bolivian and foreign correspondents. He uses a stone to diagram the battle in the dirt for Isabel Vincent of Toronto's *Globe and Mail* and pumps his arms as if shooting a rifle while telling Gary Marx of the *Chicago Tribune* that " 'the soldiers had Butch and Sundance surrounded, and everybody was firing their guns. The noise was incredible. . . . The soldiers killed Butch and Sundance and buried them here. My father saw the burial. That's the truth.' "

The truth differs when Risso talks to a reporter from *La Razón* of La Paz: Butch and Sundance " 'killed each other as night began to fall' and their bodies, without coffins, were flung into an open grave in the cemetery, and 'dirt was thrown on them.' " The reporter notes that

Risso is "glorying in a prodigious memory probably combined with a grand imagination."

To Douglas Farah of *The Washington Post,* Risso solemnly explains how his father told him that people would someday come looking for the *gringos* and dictated what his son should tell the visitors and where he should say the *bandoleros* were buried. When Farah asks why he didn't tell anyone about it until Dan and I showed up, Risso says, " 'No one ever asked me. Why did *you* take so long to get here?' "

Also finding himself in the limelight after the exhumation is Judge Prudencio Bolívar Mamani, who has custody of the parts of the skeleton that Clyde did not need to examine further. " 'These are relics that can bring us many things,' " Bolívar tells Farah. " 'Who comes to San Vicente now? We are far away from everything. But these bones could bring us things from the outside.' " To Marx, Bolívar says, " 'For us, the bones of the famous bandits are a treasure. They will put us on the map. People will come from all over the world to see them.' " He tells Isabel Vincent, " 'We'll be rich.' "

He informs Farah that many residents are unsatisfied with our written promise to return the bones. " 'Whether you like it or not, they are our citizens because they died here.' " Bolívar says that the workers fear being exploited. " 'These bones belong to us, and no one else should be able to make a profit from them.' " He complains to Vincent that " 'the *gringos* will use our village for books and films that will not bring us any financial benefit. This will not end in silence. They owe us the cadavers.' "

Local officials wrote to the U.S. embassy in La Paz and demanded compensation for the bones but have received no reply. Bolívar tells Vincent that the U.S. government should construct a proper tomb for the bandits. " 'Maybe they could install a glass display case for the bones. Or build a museum.' "

Both Risso and Bolívar dismiss the notion that the skeleton might turn out to be anyone other than Butch or Sundance or that the bandits died anywhere other than San Vicente.

But while Risso enjoys his celebrity and Bolívar contemplates an influx of tourists, other residents of San Vicente fret over the exhumation. Several have sought medical attention for chest pains, and Justino Rejas, who took part in some of the digging, tells Marx, " 'I couldn't sleep because of what I did with the *gringos.* I was really scared. People should be allowed to continue being dead.' "

Marx finds the body of a black kitten hanging from the cemetery gate, and everyone is still talking about the wind. " 'The wind started to whistle, bit by bit, as soon as the first pickaxe fell,' " Bolívar says to Farah. " 'It was strong, as it never is [at that time of year], and it got bitterly cold.' "

A miner tells Farah, " 'We are all angry because of people coming in here to take the bones. . . . The wind did not stop for a week. It was because the *bandoleros* knew someone was stealing their gold.' "

Bolívar, who has hidden the bones for fear someone will take them, tells *La Razón*'s reporter that " 'if the miners had been here, they would not have allowed the exhumation, much less the removal of the bones to the United States, because they are considered relics.' "

Eric telephones us to say that he has received new information about the San Vicente exhumation purportedly conducted in 1966 by Bolivian president René Barrientos, Polish-Argentine doctor Samuel Tornapolski, and U.S. mining engineer William F. Hutchens. Upon hearing about the recent San Vicente exhumation, outlaw historian Kerry Ross Boren sent Eric a copy of Hutchens's 1972 notarized statement (a document we learned about from author Bruce Chatwin and obtained from outlaw historian Jim Dullenty). Boren also sent fragments of an alleged exchange of correspondence between Tornapolski and Barrientos in 1966. From his cell at the Utah State Prison, where he is serving five years to life for the 1983 beating death of his second wife, Boren asserted that he obtained this correspondence independently of Hutchens's affidavit, had the letters translated into English, then lost the Spanish originals. Also lost, said Boren, were photographs taken in the San Vicente cemetery. One shot supposedly showed Barrientos and Tornapolski standing next to the partly mummified remains of a Swede.

Eric forwards copies of the material, which we read skeptically because Boren subscribes to some of the more outlandish theories about what became of Butch, Sundance, and Etta. He says, for example, that after fighting alongside Augusto Sandino in Nicaragua and Pancho Villa in Mexico, Sundance taught Lawrence of Arabia "how to derail trains to rob arms shipments," then became "a great devotee of Omar Khayyám," and later worked at a Mexican ranch owned by William Randolph Hearst. We are not surprised to discover that several aspects of the Tornapolski-Barrientos correspondence cast doubt upon its authenticity. Tornapolski's July 24, 1966, letter, for example, is addressed to Barrientos at the Palacio Presidio, although the president's house is the Palacio Quemado, and Barrientos was not the president at that time.

After Clyde reads the partial "preliminary report" accompanying the letter, he tells us that it was written "by someone who had a passing familiarity with some forensic terms, but who couldn't quite put them all together. It is written so as to make it sound scientific, but it's not."

Some of Tornapolski's findings, which concluded that neither skeleton was that of a North American bandit, are simply preposterous. Failing to find a gun or a gun belt in the first coffin, for example, the doctor deduced that there "was no evidence that the person was ever a gun carrier," but common sense dictates that a bandit would have been stripped of his gun, holster, and other valuables before burial.

The finding that the second skeleton was European was wrapped in mumbo jumbo: "His elongated skull . . . is not common to the native population. Neither the Spanish nor the Indian characteristics of build or bone structure apply in the case. Moreover, the characteristics of skull curvature and location of the mandibular arrangement indicate, in my opinion, a strictly European origin for this man." Whoever penned Tornapolski's preliminary report was apparently unaware that Spain is in Europe. And his medical expertise was as limited as his knowledge of geography: The report stated that "core samples removed from the skull indicate some deterioration indicative of a disease, possibly typhus," but typhus doesn't damage bone tissue.

Although Tornapolski's preliminary report seems certain to be a fake, we cannot rule out the possibility that an international trio— a Bolivian, a Polish-Argentine, and an American—did conduct an exhumation in 1966. Hutchens's description of the cemetery and the time they spent traveling to San Vicente from Santa Cruz rule out such an expedition to the San Vicente we went to, but Bolivia has at least four other San Vicentes. The only one that Barrientos's team could have reached in a matter of hours is about three hundred miles west of Santa Cruz in Cochabamba's Mizque province. Few Bolivians even today have heard of any of the country's San Vicentes, so it would be natural for Barrientos, as a *Cochabambino,* to assume that the Mizque San Vicente was the only one.

At Eric's request, Roy Querejazu travels from his home in Cochabamba to the Mizque San Vicente and interviews several longtime residents. No one has heard of a visit by President Barrientos or of any North American outlaws who might have been buried there. Roy tours the run-down cemetery, which is located—as is customary in the Andes—outside the village, not attached to a church, as Hutchens alleged. Roy also notes that this San Vicente sits at a relatively low altitude, where the *llamas* and *alpacas* mentioned by Hutchens are simply not found.

We appear to have run into a hoax upon a hoax: Not only is the Tornapolski report a fake, but Hutchens's affidavit seems to be unraveling, as well. Proving that something *didn't* happen, however, is always more difficult than proving that it did. Hutchens has died, and his family knows nothing about his participation in any exhumation. After reaching dead ends with Hutchens and Barrientos, Dan decides to renew his search for Tornapolski.

In his affidavit, Hutchens mentioned that Tornapolski was a colonel on the staff of General Bór, who led the Warsaw Uprising in 1944. According to Hutchens, more than four hundred thousand Poles, including General Bór's entire staff, moved to Argentina after World War II. Following this lead, Dan telephones Jan Karski, a professor of Polish history at Georgetown University and a veteran of the Warsaw Uprising. Karski calls the Tornapolski story "utter nonsense" and says that he has never heard of "four hundred thousand Poles going to Argentina or Bolivia—or anywhere else, for that matter. All of General Bór's staff, including General Bór himself, went into German prison camps. Tornapolski is not even a Polish name!" The professor, who has never heard of Butch or Sundance either, concludes emphatically that "the subject is not worth wasting *one minute* of your time."

Having already wasted millions of minutes on the subject, Dan is not deterred; he just looks for another Polish historian. Zbigniew Kantorosinski, of the Library of Congress's European Division, agrees that Tornapolski isn't a Polish name, but says that "it might be Tarnopolski—derived from Tarnów (a town near Warsaw) and Polski (Polish) and meaning 'a Pole from Tarnów.' " Kantorosinski fetches the 1964 edition of the Buenos Aires telephone directory and reads from it: "Here he is, Tarnopolsky, Samuel. A medical doctor."

The doctor is also listed in the most recent edition at the library.

Using the number supplied by Kantorosinski, Dan places a call to Buenos Aires that evening. The telephone rings interminably.

Finally a man answers.

"Doctor Tarnopolsky?" asks Dan.

"*Sí, sí. ¿Quién habla?*" Who is speaking?

Dan relates the tangled tale—North American outlaws, Hutchens,

Barrientos, San Vicente—as simply and quickly as possible, lest the man at the southern end of the telephone think he is talking to a prankster and hang up.

"I have no explanation as to how my name got mixed up in this," Tarnopolsky says. "I did travel to Bolivia quite a bit in those years, but only as a professor of medicine, specializing in rheumatology." He has no knowledge of the dig in San Vicente, nor of William F. Hutchens. "This whole thing sounds like a fable," he says. "I had absolutely nothing to do in any way with any Barrientos government. *Nada, nada, nada.*"

Tarnopolsky mentions that he has written several medical volumes, including a textbook on rheumatism and a survey of medical quackery in Argentina, as well as a couple of novels. Perhaps, he surmises, Hutchens saw one of his books and appropriated his name.

However he was recruited, Dr. Tarnopolsky is the sole survivor of a trip that never was.

On a breezy spring morning, the San Vicente veterans convene at the Oklahoma state medical examiner's office, where Clyde plans to review the results of the scientific tests with some of the experts who performed them. In a conference room with a gallery of human skulls staring from built-in glass shelves, Dan chats with Eric while archaeologists Roy Querejazu and Burney McClurkan introduce themselves to podiatrist Henry Asin, microscopist Skip Palenik, and molecular biologist Chris Boles. Marveling at how many serious people have been roped into helping us solve our little mystery, I feel like Tom Sawyer watching the whitewash dry on Aunt Polly's fence. But then, as Clyde says, "Scientists have to have fun once in a while. We're up to our knees in tragedy."

While we await the arrival of our dental expert, Paul Goaz, Baylor professor emeritus of oral radiology, Clyde shows Dan and me around the building. We walk past empty offices and through the beige-walled X-ray lab, its cumbersome equipment suspended over stainless-steel tables—no need for padding or sheets in this place. "Let's see what we've got in here," says Clyde, opening an unmarked door.

As soon as I cross the threshold and feel the refrigerated air on my cheeks, I realize that this is the morgue. The room is small, with a low ceiling and three slabs, two of which are occupied. A naked woman who appears to be in her thirties is laid out on the left. Her skin looks waxy, her shoulder-length auburn hair unreal, wig-like. There isn't a mark on her—not one that I can see anyway.

"Possible homicide," says Clyde, reading the paperwork.

The middle slab is empty, but the one on the right contains a blackened heap that looks like a shriveled Labrador retriever. "Arson victim," says Clyde, leading the way out of the room.

"That was a person?" I reconsider my wish to be cremated after death.

Once Paul Goaz has arrived, Clyde lights a cigarette and begins the meeting with an explanation of a chart drawn on the chalkboard at the front of the room:

	SV1	GERMAN	SWEDE	BUTCH	SUNDANCE
SEX					
RACE					
AGE					
STATURE					
HANDED-NESS					
HAIR					
PHOTO SUPER-IMPOSITION					
DENTAL					
GAIT					
ANTE-MORTEM TRAUMA					
PERI-MORTEM TRAUMA					
PERSONAL EFFECTS					

"Now," says Clyde, "SV One stands for the skeleton we found in San Vicente. We can fill in the things we know about that individual and then compare them with what we know about Butch and

Sundance. But they were not the only *gringos* in the cemetery; they were said to be buried between a German who blew himself up defrosting dynamite on his stove and a Swede who shot himself accidentally while getting off a horse. So we must consider the German and Swede as possibilities, even though we know almost nothing about them. Determining whether a skeleton belongs to a particular individual is a process of elimination. You have to take everything you know about the individual and use that as the standard against which to judge the remains. You look at the age, the size, the sex, and so on. If anything fails to match, you don't have him. But as long as the remains are consistent with what you know about the individual, you have a possible match. If you can get mitochondrial DNA out of the remains and match it with the right kind of relative's DNA, then you can be certain of the identity of the deceased. Failing that, you're dealing with probabilities. The more information and consistencies you have, the more confident you can be that you have a match."

Clyde picks up a piece of chalk and fills in the sex and race categories as "male" and "white," respectively, for each of the five individuals.

"A microscopic examination of a cross-section of a long bone can narrow the age down to within three or four years," says Clyde. "Right now, all we can say is that he was somewhere between thirty and forty-five." He writes "30–45" in the age category for SV1, question marks for the German and the Swede, "42" for Butch, and "41" for Sundance.

SV1's height is listed as "68–72 inches" compared with "68–69 inches" for Butch, "69–72 inches" for Sundance, and question marks for the German and the Swede.

"I'm fairly certain that San Vicente One was right-handed," says Clyde, "but what about Butch and Sundance?"

"Photographs show them wearing their holsters on their right sides," I say.

"Okay." Clyde fills in the chart accordingly, then asks, "What about the hair?"

Skip Palenik, a soft-spoken, dark-haired man with a midwestern accent, says, "Most of it was pretty badly deteriorated, but I was able to find regions where there was a lot of the hair structure left. There was enough structure maintained that if he had had a lot of pigment in the hair, it would still be present. So we can say with a reasonable degree of certainty that whoever that hair originated from would have what we call sandy or light-brown hair."

As cigarette smoke curls lazily around his head, Clyde writes "light brown" on the chart under SV1, Butch, and Sundance. "Unfortunately, we're dealing with a Swede and a German," he says, before inserting question marks in their columns. "It's too bad they're not an Italian and a Greek."

Next, Clyde describes the skull-face-superimposition procedure performed by Lew Sadler and says, "If you compare a complete skull with photographs of faces, you'll get a match with five percent of the general population. With San Vicente One, we don't have a complete skull, so we can expect it to match with ten to twenty percent of the population. In other words, if you get a match with a complete skull, there's about a ninety-five percent chance that the skull and the photo belong to the same person. But because the San Vicente One skull is incomplete, the fact that it matches the photo of Sundance gives us about an eighty-five percent chance that the skull is Sundance's. Now, that's pretty good, but I wouldn't want to have to go to a court of law and swear on it."

"Not with that much damage to the facial bones," says Burney.

"Now," says Clyde, "what about the teeth?"

Paul Goaz, a tall man in his late sixties, says that the crowns were swaged, or preformed, a process used until after 1906, when a Chicago dentist perfected a means of casting crowns, which required less gold than swaged crowns did. "As far as maybe ruling out the German and the Swede," says Goaz, "gold-foil restorations of this nature probably had to have been inserted in Chicago or the Chicago area at about the turn of the century, plus or minus about ten years."

"Could they have been made in Europe?" asks Dan.

"I suppose they might have been done there, but I was trained in Chicago, and they think all the best dental techniques started in Chicago."

"Could you tell anything from the fillings?" asks Clyde.

"The pulps of many of the teeth had been devitalized with a process used between 1830 and 1910."

Ouch! Root canals *before* Novocain!

"Two molars on the upper right have very primitive tin fillings," continues Goaz, "which were unlikely to have been done in the United States, because the proportion of tin was three times as high as the average proportion of tin used in amalgams here during that period. Considering the high quality of the majority of the dental work, he

317

probably got the tin fillings in a place, such as rural Bolivia, where perhaps nothing better was available. His upper-right lateral incisor was missing, which may have been a congenital deformity. He may have had a false tooth or a crown inserted there at one time."

"That conforms with a description of Sundance provided by a Texas prostitute," says Clyde, "for whatever that's worth. One thing we do know: He certainly had a rich dentist." Clyde fills in the chart with question marks for the German, the Swede, and Butch, and with the word *consistent* for Sundance, then shifts the discussion to how SV1's gait compares with Sundance's peculiar way of walking.

In November 1901, a Pinkerton agent wrote that Sundance walked erect, with his feet far apart, and was somewhat bowlegged. Unnamed hospital officials who treated him in May 1902, however, told the Pinkertons that he was not bowlegged, but that his feet were small and turned in as he walked. According to a June 29, 1903, wire story about Sundance, "he was bow-legged almost to deformity, his legs being unusually far apart. This fact, together with a shambling, straddling walk, gave him among his associates the sobriquet of 'The Straddler.' It is said that the peculiar foot traces left by him furnished the officers the first definite clue as to the identity of the Belle Fourche bank robbers."

After determining that the leather soles Eric found in the grave with SV1 came from a size 6E pair of top-quality handmade boots with wooden pegs, Clyde gave the remnants of the boots, along with SV1's foot and leg bones, to podiatrist Henry Asin. A wiry man with silver hair, Asin says, "I tried to recreate what his gait was like and what his stance was. He wasn't bowlegged, because the femur was pretty normal, but the tibia shows a bowing, and the fibula, which is also bowed, indicates that he was probably knock-kneed and flat-footed, so that he did assume a somewhat straddle-type gait as he walked. But I could almost determine that he had a real severe callus under the second toe, mainly because he was born with a short first metatarsal bone, which is a condition called Morton's syndrome, and that shifts the weight over to the center of the foot."

"Is that a common problem?" asks Eric.

"I've never seen any actual statistics on it, but I would imagine that less than five percent of the population have this problem, and it is congenital and often times is familial."

"According to Sundance's relatives," says Clyde, "several members of the family have similar problems with their feet." He writes "consistent" for Sundance and draws question marks for the other contenders in the gait category.

"A piece of the insole was removed." Asin continues, miming the action with the stiff leather insole: "He took a knife and slit it down the center and ripped out the center portion to float the area so that he wouldn't have so much pressure on it. Obviously, this particular foot was very painful for him."

"Okay," says Clyde, "that brings us to the evidence of trauma suffered by San Vicente One before his death and around the time of his death. The ante-mortem trauma is an old bullet wound to the left tibia, and we know from the Pinkertons and Sundance's family that he suffered such a wound. The peri-mortem trauma is consistent with a wound caused by a low-velocity bullet entering the lower forehead, more or less between the eyes. The bone in that portion of the face is so delicate that it just shatters. This wound is consistent with reports that the taller bandit was shot in the forehead. However, there are no bullet fragments and no exit wound. That does not rule out a gunshot wound to the forehead as the cause of death, if the bullet didn't penetrate very far or if it exited at the base of the skull."

"Could the wound have been caused by anything else?" asks Roy.

"It could have been caused by the German's dynamite accident if he got hit by a flying object," says Clyde, "but not if it blew him up. The wound could have been caused by vultures if the Swede lay out on the plains for a while, but then you'd expect to find marks made by the vultures pecking at him, and we don't have any peck marks here." Half an inch of ash falls off Clyde's cigarette. Again, the German and the Swede receive question marks, and Sundance is deemed "consistent." Clyde gives Butch a question mark for the ante-mortem trauma and an "inconsistent" for the peri-mortem trauma.

"Clyde," I ask, "what about the elbow that appeared to be sheared off?"

"After looking at it in good light and examining it in detail, I determined that it was a post-mortem phenomenon involving erosion. In other words, the trauma occurred after he died."

We now turn to the personal effects found with the skeleton. These include remnants of clothing, bits of glass, a small buckle, and a removable button of the type listed in the inventory of the slain bandits' possessions. "The jacket," says Skip Palenik, "was made of finely woven wool with a silk lining dyed a deep green that was so dark it looks black. What is unusual about this is that the basic fibers at the turn of the century were wool, cotton, and flax. We need to ask the experts at the Smithsonian how silk fits in here."

After chipping away the dirt with a tiny probe in his Chicago lab, Palenik determined that the buckle was brass with black enamel and contained fiber residue identified as cotton. The words *Paris, solid,* and *TW&W* were engraved on it.

"Paris," says Clyde, igniting a new cigarette, "was the brand name of an American company that made suspenders and other men's accessories around the turn of the century. We should send the buckle to the Smithsonian to see if they can identify exactly what it came from."

"What is obscure to us," says Palenik, "might be obvious to a clothing person." He concludes his presentation by discussing fragments of glass that were found on the right side of the skull near the temple and eye socket. "The glass had two original surfaces," he says. "It was flat, like a windowpane, but was not a modern glass. It had been ground and polished and was pretty thin, about two millimeters. It was definitely not optical or glassware, but it was unusually thin for window glass."

"Could it have been a window over the face in a coffin?" asks Roy. "Bolivian coffins sometimes have glass panes for viewing the deceased before burial."

"Perhaps," Palenik replies.

Clyde returns to the chalkboard and completes the chart (see facing page). "So what do we have?" he asks. "We've got a skeleton that is strongly consistent with what we know about Sundance and inconsistent with Butch, but we know nothing about the German and the Swede, so they can't be excluded."

He retrieves several photographs from a file. "In the last few days, we've gotten some very interesting information that throws another wild card into this deck. Just the other night, we were in contact with Mr. Roger McCord, who was down in San Vicente in 1973 and took some pictures of the monument." Clyde hands out copies of a blown-up version of Roger's photograph of the tombstone in San Vicente. On the plaque are the words *Hier Ruhet aus von jahre langer Arbeit Gustav Zimmer.*

	SVI	GERMAN	SWEDE	BUTCH	SUNDANCE
SEX	male	male	male	male	male
RACE	white	white	white	white	white
AGE	30–45	?	?	42	41
STATURE	68″–72″	?	?	68″–69″	69″–72″
HANDED-NESS	right	?	?	right	right
HAIR	lt. brown	?	?	lt. brown	lt. brown
PHOTO SUPER-IMPOSITION	skull	?	?	doesn't match	matches
DENTAL	missing lateral incisor	?	?	?	consistent
GAIT	abnormal	?	?	?	consistent
ANTE-MORTEM TRAUMA	gunshot in tibia	?	?	?	consistent
PERI-MORTEM TRAUMA	shattered forehead	?	?	inconsistent	consistent
PERSONAL EFFECTS	button, buckle	? ?	? ?	consistent ?	consistent ?

Having received a warning call from Roger, Dan and I are prepared for the news about Herr Zimmer—but not for the sight of Froilán Risso leaning over the shoulder of the man who is pointing at the plaque. Although Risso's tiny dark face was unrecognizable in the contact sheet, his identity is unmistakable in this huge image. But Roger told us he didn't meet Froilán Risso, and Risso said he knew nothing about a man in a *casa rodante*. Obviously, they were mistaken. Did Risso get his information from his father or from the McCords?

As I ponder these questions and the scientists hunch over the photos and try to read the epitaph, Clyde writes an English translation on the chalkboard: " 'Here rests, after long years of work,' " he says, "and then this gentleman's sleeve is partially obscuring the lower part."

Hoots erupt from the team.

"But we can see one word: *Zimmer*," says Clyde, "a common surname in Germany."

Judging from the parts that are visible, the first name is Gustav.

"The epitaph speaks of long years of work," says Clyde, "which makes me think of a person perhaps beyond the upper age limit here. If we find out, for example, that Gustav Zimmer was fifty-five, sixty years old, he's out the window."

"How many Zimmers do you think there are in Germany?" asks Dan.

"How many Zimmers are there in Bolivia?" Chris Boles chimes in. "That's the question."

"In the Tupiza phone book," says Dan.

"Just keep thinking, Clyde," says Burney. "That's what you're good at."

Clyde takes a deep drag on his Camel and says, "It ain't over till it's over."

"You know," I say, "the fact that there's no date on the plaque could mean that the monument was erected sometime after the burial. Maybe his family came over from Germany and didn't know the exact site of his grave and inadvertently put the tombstone over his next-door neighbor, who happened to be Sundance."

Dan rolls his eyes, but I'm not the only one grasping at straws.

"There was a jumbled matrix above San Vicente One," says Burney, "so Zimmer could have been buried above our skeleton."

"Could people digging a later grave have dug up Zimmer and jumbled him?" asks Roy.

"Actually," says Burney, "I don't think so. I'm pretty sure San Vicente One pertains to the tombstone. If there had been a subsequent interment, we would have noticed it."

"Okay," says Clyde. "Do we have Gustav Zimmer, or do we have the Sundance Kid? To find the answer, we'll have to turn to DNA."

"The partial sequences," says Chris Boles, "do not match the Parker DNA with either the putative Butch Cassidy skull or the tooth from San Vicente One. So far, we haven't been able to find a Sundance relative descended through the maternal line, and until we either do that or develop a Y-probe, we won't be able to confirm or eliminate Sundance as a candidate for San Vicente One."

"In other words," says Clyde, "we don't have Butch, and if we can't link the DNA with Sundance, we've got to go back to San Vicente for some more digging."

"What are the chances that a Y-probe will be developed soon?" asks Eric.

"There's only one expert that I know of," says Chris. "It's a long shot. I'll call around to see if anyone else has anything cooking. Even then, reasonably quickly means a couple of months. The fastest way would be to exhume Sundance's brother Harvey, whose mitochondrial DNA would be the same as Sundance's. Usually, you need an order from a court or a medical examiner based on the petition of relatives. You can contract with the cemetery to do it for four or five hundred dollars, but first you have to find the grave. He would probably be in a deteriorated metal casket. You might have to put him in a new casket. The problem is that embalming affects DNA, and from 1880 on, nearly everyone was embalmed except the poor."

"What would be the bones of choice?" asks Clyde.

"Teeth are the least contaminated by embalming," says Chris. "The second choice would be a section of a femur. Before we go to all the trouble of digging Harvey up, we should find out if he had false teeth. In any event, rather than pull a few teeth, it would be better to bring out the entire body and keep it out for two weeks or so. But the easiest thing would be to get a sample from a living relative from Sundance's mother's line. If you want me to, I can find a professional genealogist to locate one for us."

"Well," says Clyde, "it's worth a shot."

"If the genealogist can't find a suitable relative," says Chris, "then we'll exhume Harvey."

"We could also try to get a German genealogist to track Zimmer down," says Clyde. "If we had a picture of Zimmer to compare with the skull, we might be able to exclude him. Or if we found out that he died at the age of seventy, that would rule him out."

Dan and Roy volunteer to look for information about Zimmer.

"We also need to think about returning the bones," says Eric.

"Before I let go of them," says Clyde, "I'll need to take a section of a long bone for an osteon count."

"I'd like to have one more intact tooth and a section of a long bone," says Chris.

"Can we get our deadline extended?" asks Clyde, who will be tied up with projects in Iraq, Ethiopia, and Guatemala in the coming weeks. "Could the Bolivian government handle the return of the bones for us?"

"We could ask Fernando González at the Bolivian embassy," says Eric.

"Well," says Clyde, "we've done a pretty good job so far. Out of two billion people, we've narrowed it down to Sundance or Zimmer."

"You guys kept talking about Froilán Risso," says Roger McCord, when we next speak to him, "but I didn't recognize the name. It wasn't until I found my negative and went through my notebooks that I realized who he was. He was the number-two guy we were talking with. Calixto Risso was number one."

"Froilán Risso told us that his father's name was Calixto Risso," I say, "but that he died in 1957."

"Well," says Roger, "the Calixto Risso that I was talking to may have been Froilán Risso's brother or cousin or something, but the name in my notebook is definitely Calixto Risso. He was the older and shorter of the two, the one with his finger pointing to Zimmer. And right over his left shoulder is Froilán, who didn't really know diddly-squat."

"But he was a quick study," observes Dan.

"Risso had so many details that were accurate," I say. "If he didn't really hear them from his father, they had to be planted by someone, and apparently it was you!"

"Everything he knows, he learned from Carolyn and me and you two and whoever the hell else has been down there. You know, he's met a lot of people."

Despite diligent efforts, we have been unable to trace Butch and Sundance's friend James "Santiago" Hutcheon: The owner of perhaps the most successful transportation company in Bolivia in the early 1900s seems to have vanished into the thin air of the *altiplano*. Then one day, long after we have given up hope of ever finding any of his descendants, the telephone rings, and the caller says, "My name is Nancy Hutcheon. If you're still interested in Santiago Hutcheon, I might be able to help you. He was my husband's grandfather."

An ad we placed in a Scottish magazine four years ago has finally made its way from cousins in Scotland to Hutcheon's youngest son, one of two surviving children, in California. Through phone calls and correspondence with Nancy and her father-in-law, Ian L. Hutcheon, our questions about Santiago Hutcheon's origins and fate are answered.

Born in 1882 near Dyce, Scotland, James Kirton Hutcheon went to Bolivia as a stable-boy. Around the turn of the century, he began hauling freight for railroad-construction companies, then expanded his operations to include passenger service. Although he was only twenty-four or twenty-five when he met Butch and Sundance, he was already quite prosperous. He had married Frances "Fanny" Miller, a Pennsylvania native who had come to Bolivia as governess, and they had started a family that would eventually include nine children.

The Hutcheons traveled often to visit relatives in Edinburgh, and Santiago died there unexpectedly in 1924. He was forty-two—the same age at which Butch had died. Fanny Hutcheon returned to the States with her brood and bought a dairy farm in New York. The cows caught tuberculosis, however, and the family went broke. Eldest son Jimmie, who had done a spot of mining in Bolivia, headed for the gold mines of California. One by one, the rest of the children followed him.

Although he knows nothing about Butch and Sundance and remembers little of his father, Ian identifies Adam Hutcheon as the son of Santiago's uncle John Hutcheon. According to Scottish cousins, Enrique Hutcheon (whose cards were found on Butch's body) was Santiago's half brother. Ian says that Fanny Hutcheon kept a diary and may have mentioned the outlaws in it, but he doesn't know what became of it. When he sends us photographs of his wiry, pipe-smoking father in Scotland and Bolivia, Butch and Sundance's friend finally steps out of the shadows to become real for us. And who knows? Maybe someday we'll track down Fanny's diary and find out what she thought of the company her husband kept.

In the weeks after the Oklahoma gathering, Clyde and Eric send local officials in Tupiza and San Vicente requests for a three-month extension of the deadline for returning the bones. Dan learns that all the early 1900s records from the German embassy in La Paz were sent home to Germany, only to be destroyed by bombs during World War II. An osteon count narrows the age range of SV1 to between thirty-seven and forty-five, and Chris Boles obtains a hair from the nape of Bill Longabaugh's neck in case a Y-probe is developed.

In the meantime, Pennsylvania genealogist Susan Koelble finds a Kentucky man, O. Frazelle Edwards, who is the elderly great-great-grandson of Sundance's grandmother's sister. Chris compares Edwards's DNA with the San Vicente skeleton's DNA and finds a small but significant mismatch. Because of the possibility that an unrecorded adoption somewhere along the way might have broken the genetic connection to Sundance, Clyde decides to dig up Sundance's brother Harvey and have Chris check his DNA against that of Edwards and the skeleton.

On a bright fall morning, nearly a year after the San Vicente exhumation, Dan and I meet Clyde, the Ernsts, and "Uncle Bill" Longabaugh in the Zion Cemetery near Flourtown, Pennsylvania. Evergreens and yellow-leafed maples border the long, narrow cemetery. At one end sits an old stone church. Near the other end, a waterproof canopy stands among headstones labeled Buchanan, Gilbert, Shoemaker, and Longabaugh. Beneath the canopy, beside a table of doughnuts and coffee for the gravediggers and onlookers, a brand-new vault—which looks like a spray-painted silver deep-freeze—awaits the remains of Harvey Longabaugh.

The first problem is to locate him. The Longabaugh family plot contains not only Harvey and his wife, Katherine, but also two of their three children and an infant grandson, who was Uncle Bill's brother. The children's graves are the only ones marked with tombstones, and no cemetery records are available to guide us. "This is like looking for a fish in a river," says Uncle Bill, "but I think he's on the left side."

"The other possibility is to the right of the kids," says funeral director Charles Murray. "But in a crypt, at least, the male is always to the left. It's an unwritten law of cemeteries."

Billy, a short man in blue overalls and a red Budweiser cap, pushes a seven-foot iron probe into the ground to find the casket.

"The standard casket today is thirty inches wide," says Clyde, who is halfway through his first pack of Camels for the day. "Earlier, they were narrower."

Uncle Bill is certain that his grandmother is buried in a concrete vault, so if Billy hits concrete, we have the wrong grave. But the probe hits wood, and Billy ascertains where the edge of the grave is. He then uses a pickax to cut a line in the sod, then switches to a spade for the digging. He throws clumps of sod, which look like Jolly-Green-Giant scalps, onto sheets of plywood lying next to the grave site.

"Don't go no farther down," says senior gravedigger Ray, who is dressed in jeans and a black-and-white wool jacket. "Let's get this clean here." He takes another spade and rearranges the dirt on the plywood to make room for additional soil from the grave.

As he digs through a foot of dark topsoil to the underlying ocher clay mixed with stones, Billy chatters happily.

"Let's get working here," says Ray. "We've got a lot of digging to do."

"Come on, Billy," says Murray. "Let's go."

The wind rises, à la San Vicente, and the sky clouds over. The mound of dirt grows, as does the heap of Clyde's discarded cigarette butts.

"Hold it," yells Murray. "You hit a bone."

"No," says Ray, "it's a stone."

Clyde examines the dirt pile to make certain no bones have been accidentally tossed there. At a depth of about five feet, Billy's shovel strikes something hard.

"If it's a wooden casket," says Murray, "we'll see blackened wood."

"Damn!" says Ray. "Did you hit his feet?"

"I hit something."

"Is it metal?"

"It's a piece of slate."

"It could be the top of the grave," says Murray. "They sometimes lined the grave with brick and put slate on top."

"Brick graves were popular years ago," says Ray, "for six-foot graves. As the casket deteriorates, it sinks to the six-foot level."

At last, Billy finds the top of the wooden coffin.

"Bell out the hole," Murray instructs.

Ray widens the hole with a pike, while Billy takes a coffee-and-cheroot break and Murray tidies up the dirt pile. The wind rattles the branches and swirls dead leaves from the ground.

"I didn't know you owned any old clothes," Uncle Bill says to the ordinarily natty Murray. Before Murray can reply, Uncle Bill loses his footing and sprawls across the grave sideways.

"Don't fall in," says Murray. "Ray will want double."

"We've already got enough Longabaughs in this cemetery," says Clyde, helping Uncle Bill to his feet.

Paul and Donna rush to his side.

"I'm all right," says Uncle Bill. He dusts himself off and plants his hands in the pockets of his bulky jacket.

"The wood is either cherry or walnut," Ray calls from the hole.

He uses a spade bar to square the hole so that the new vault will fit in.

"If I'd known it would be deep, with no complications, I'd have brought the backhoe," says Murray. "In these old cemeteries, we like to dig by hand."

"I think I heard a wild turkey," says Billy, looking at a grove of maples.

"Don't worry about any Wild Turkey," Ray jokes. "Worry about the dirt. Dig."

"Look," Uncle Bill says to Clyde, "when you get a few bones out, take what you need and put the others in the vault, then drop it in on top of whatever is left down there. Is that okay?"

"It's okay by me," Clyde replies.

The top of the casket has collapsed, and the bones have sunk to the bottom. Ray removes a femur from one end, then moves to the other end and clears the dirt away from the skull.

"I remember him," says Uncle Bill, his blue eyes misting. "He was a nice old guy."

"How old were you when he died?" asks Paul.

"Seven and a half." Uncle Bill blows his nose on a white cotton handkerchief. "But they lived with us for a year and a half."

Armed with a whisk broom, a trowel, and a newly lighted Camel, Clyde climbs down into the grave and pulls the jawbone away from the skull. He brushes off the bone and scrapes it clean with a pointed stick. "This is the intact mandible."

"Oh, my God," says Donna. "Did you see that?"

I'd just as soon not look at any more corpses, but skeletons no longer unsettle me. And I've grown quite fond of cemeteries.

"Clyde," says Uncle Bill, "if you want to, take the whole jawbone instead of pulling a few teeth."

"Can you tell the sex?" asks Murray.

"I'd rather not say just yet."

"How about the age?"

328

"The teeth are rather well worn," says Clyde.

Billy points to the sky, where two turkey buzzards spiral upward through the wintry air, and says, "I told you."

"I'm glad we did it," says Uncle Bill. "I wasn't sure how I would feel about it, but it was the right thing to do."

Months pass without any word from Chris Boles. The acidity of the soil has destroyed the DNA in the first tooth he pulls from Harvey's mandible. Chris repeats the process on a second tooth without success. After failing to obtain any genetic material from seven teeth, he finally manages to extract a usable sample of DNA from a ground-up portion of the jawbone. He then sets about comparing it with DNA from the San Vicente skeleton and the man in Kentucky.

Meanwhile, our genealogist pops up in an article in a Pennsylvania newspaper, *The Intelligencer,* which says that "Koelble used her skills to help solve the puzzle of the Sundance Kid's final resting place by verifying that human bones found in Bolivia, South America, were really those of the American outlaw."

Donna sends us a copy of the article with a note saying, "Nothing like taking all the credit and then being wrong!"

Koelble later claims she was misquoted. But whatever Koelble did or didn't say, Chris's DNA comparison will eventually reveal that Harvey is related to the man from Kentucky but not to the skeleton from San Vicente.

Apparently, we've dug up Gustav Zimmer.

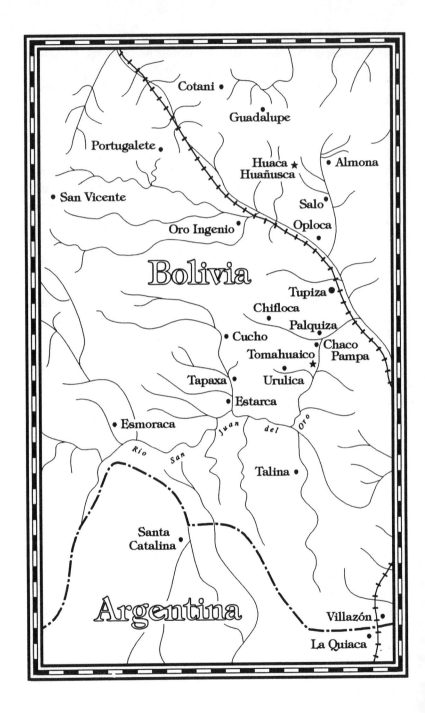

15 · DUST TO DUST

As Butch and Sundance made their way to San Vicente, paleontologist Earl Douglass was roaming their old haunts near Brown's Park, where Colorado meets Utah and Wyoming. A few months after the bandits died, the scientist finally found what he was looking for: the fossilized skeletal remains of dinosaurs swept onto a sandbar by floodwaters 145 million years ago, buried in tons of sand and gravel, sealed with mud and volcanic ash, then gradually brought back to the earth's surface by the forces of erosion and geologic upheaval.

We pass Douglass's dinosaur quarry, now a national monument, on the road to the small homestead where Josie Bassett Morris lived for fifty years, until her death in 1964. Josie's father gave Butch his first job in Brown's Park; her younger sister, Ann Bassett, fed Butch and Elzy Lay when they were in hiding after a couple of holdups; and Josie was said by some outlaw historians to have seen her pal Butch in 1924. Although she had been married several times, Josie lived alone here without electricity or indoor plumbing in a log cabin on a narrow strip of land wedged between Split Mountain and Cub Creek. She spent her days tending her fruit orchard, field crops, vegetable garden, and livestock. Two box canyons with fences across the mouths served as her corrals. Josie hauled water in buckets from a spring to the lean-to kitchen she had added to the cabin, which was heated by a wood-burning stove and a stone fireplace.

Fearing that the changes required to make the rickety cabin safe for tourists would destroy its historical integrity, National Park Service employees merely erected a freestanding roof to shelter the building from rain and snow, then nailed slats of wood across the doors and windows. Vines now scale the walls; insects and rodents burrow through the wood; mold and fungus attack the peeling wallpaper.

Josie's cabin and small outbuildings are unmistakably North American (in their day, the windows went up and down), but the scenery could just as easily be found along the Chubut River in Argentina or the Salo River in Bolivia. However exotic they may have found their neighbors, the language, or the *llamas*, Butch and Sundance must have felt at home on the South American range. We have come full circle—working backward from the end of the bandits' career to the beginning, only to find ourselves in the same landscape.

Our first visit to the bandits' home base has been prompted by the nineteenth annual rendezvous of the National Association for Outlaw and Lawman History. After two days of lectures and slide shows in Vernal, Utah, we pile into a fleet of vehicles for a tour of Brown's Park. Dan and I occupy the backseat of a beige Buick, one of the many rental cars that Paul and Donna Ernst have battered on the Outlaw Trail. The caravan glides north through Ashley National Forest and past the Flaming Gorge reservoir, then turns east onto a dirt road and descends into a wide, grassy valley.

At the old Jarvie ranch on the bank of the Green River, we stop for a picnic lunch. John Jarvie's general store, built of railroad ties in 1881, was the center of trade in Brown's Park when Butch worked on the Bassett ranch. Between holdups, he and other members of the Wild Bunch often hid out in an underground storage room, called a dugout, fifteen or twenty yards from the store. After touring the store, which has been refurbished and stocked with everything from iron skillets to Sunday bonnets, we duck into the dugout. Beyond an entryway, where Mason jars on wooden shelves line the walls, is a low-ceilinged room of perhaps twelve feet by eight feet. Wooden furniture, kitchen utensils, kerosene lanterns, and other quotidian articles lend a certain coziness to the windowless room, but it is as stuffy as a tomb.

A few miles away stands the one-room Lodore schoolhouse, where the children of Brown's Park learned to read and write, and where cowboys and ranch families gathered for monthly dances and other festivities. Today, accompanied by area residents Dawn DeJournette at the piano and Doris Burton on the spoons, old-timers in cowboy hats and jeans swing their partners on the sawdust-covered floor. In the schoolyard, outlaw aficionados in Old West regalia test their marksmanship by shooting at balloons tied to sagebrush. The gunmen raise puffs of prairie dust, but the targets are safe from just about everyone except retired sheriff Arden Stewart, whose aim is keen enough to annihilate an entire gang of balloons.

After a visit to the Bassett family cemetery, where Josie and Ann slumber beneath the weeds, we drive across a swinging bridge and thread our way through the enchanted, red-walled Crouse Canyon, then find ourselves slipping, sliding, and finally stuck on the increasingly muddy incline that leads to a shortcut back to Vernal. Dan and Paul scout the road ahead and come back covered with mud and the news that we'll never make it. We reluctantly turn around and take the long way back. I make a mental note to remember this place the next time I find myself smugly cursing some back road in South America.

The evening's entertainment is a barbecue with rope twirlers and western poets in the tradition of Arthur Chapman, who broke the news of the San Vicente shootout in his 1930 *Elks Magazine* article after making a name for himself with the oft-quoted doggerel, "Out Where the West Begins." Most of the poets are old-timers, echoes from an era that was already dying when Butch and Sundance left the Rockies for the last time. While we sit at picnic tables and sip lemonade, retired cowpuncher Allan Brewer—whose ten-gallon hat is nearly as tall as he is—puffs up his chest like a bullfrog and croaks into the microphone:

I was shootin' some pool and drinkin' some booze,
  When I see a man with some beautiful alligator shoes,
I passed him my bottle and as we sat there,
  I swore to my maker I'd get me a pair.
So I took me a trip into the everglades,
  I couldn't much swim and it's too deep to wade.
I found me a 'gator along about my size,
  I made a good sneak, I'd take him by surprise.
I jumped on his back with my arms round his neck,
  My spurs in his flanks and I rode him, by heck. . . .
We was both of us dinked but I was on top,
  The 'gator was docile and I had the drop. . . .
And I could imagine how I'm gonna prance
  When I'm wearin' them shoes to the next country dance. . . .
But my victory was short lived, my dreams was uprooted,
  I rolled him on his back and found him barefooted.

The new deadline for returning the bones has come and gone. Although we have dug up Harvey by this time, Chris Boles is still struggling to extract DNA from the teeth. Clyde doesn't expect a favorable result and has begun talking about going back to Bolivia. The historical evidence has convinced him that Butch and Sundance are buried in San Vicente, but he won't be satisfied until he obtains scientific proof.

Perhaps with ground-penetrating radar equipment, he says, we could locate a grave containing two Caucasoid skeletons. The other members of the team don't share his enthusiasm about returning to San Vicente, but Roy Querejazu gamely travels to southern Bolivia to ascertain the prospects for another exhumation. Angry that the bones have not been returned as promised, the local officials give Roy a chilly reception. He recommends that we give up the notion of further digging and return the remains as soon as possible.

Dan and I agree with him; we have been agitating for months to have the bones put back where they came from. More time passes while Eric asks the Bolivian embassy to serve as an intermediary for returning the remains. Eventually, after the embassy turns down Eric's request, Roy, Dan, and I are elected for the job.

Clyde wraps the large bones in foam and puts the small pieces—including the teeth, the finger and toe bones, the soles of the boots, and the other artifacts—into plastic containers. He packs the lot with Styrofoam popcorn in two cardboard boxes and sends them to us via Federal Express. To avoid any unpleasant surprises when we turn the remains over to the local officials in Bolivia, Dan decides to check the contents of the boxes to make certain that nothing is missing. He accidentally breaks the lid from one of the small containers and has trouble finding a suitable replacement in our recycled-plastics bin. He neglects to mention any of this to me, and I come downstairs to see Gustav Zimmer's skull sitting on the dining-room table beside a container topped with a lid bearing the name of a local deli, Sutton Place Gourmet.

When a tooth arrives by FedEx from a Texas laboratory while we are packing for our flight to Bolivia, Dan dubs our mission "DeadEx."

"Did the airline make you fill out any special forms for transporting human remains?" I ask on the way to the airport.

"I didn't inquire," Dan replies. "I was afraid there might be a bureaucratic hassle, and I'd already bought the tickets. I figure we'll just check them through and hope for the best."

"What happens when they X-ray the boxes and see the skull?"

"I hadn't thought of that."

"What if the drug-sniffing dogs in Miami get hold of them while we're changing planes?"

"They'll have a nice game of fetch."

"Should we say anything when we check in, or just take our chances?"

"Let's take our chances. I have all kinds of documents from the Bolivian government I can pull out if necessary."

At the ticket counter, the clerk picks up the boxes and asks, "Any perishables in here?"

"No," says Dan.

The boxes go onto the conveyor belt and disappear into the bowels of the airport.

We change planes without incident in Miami and arrive in La Paz to find that our grisly cargo has survived whatever encounters it may have had with X-ray machines and police dogs during its long journey south. In fact, our luggage is the first to come off the plane.

A customs inspector gives our bags a cursory search, then asks, "What's in the boxes?"

"Human bones," Dan replies.

"*¿Huesos humanos?*" the inspector repeats, disbelieving.

"*Correcto,*" says Dan. "They're from a scientific project."

"We'll have to open the boxes."

"Okay."

"Wait here."

The inspector goes into an office and returns with a kitchen knife whose serrated blade is too dull to penetrate the layers of packing tape Dan has wrapped around the boxes. I hand over my junior Swiss army knife, and presently one of the lids is free. Just as the inspector lifts it, someone farts nearby.

The inspector's eyes widen in alarm. "Is that smell coming from the bones?"

"No, he's been dead for eighty years."

The inspector begins to remove the skull, then looks around the crowded room and thinks better of it. He closes the lid and summons his supervisor, who asks whether we have any authorization papers. Dan produces several documents, and the supervisor looks them over.

"You'll have to wait."

The inspector sets our boxes behind the counter and begins going through the luggage of other passengers. While Dan and I stand in a corner, porters in many-zippered overalls scurry about, and the entire planeload of passengers shuffles through customs. Finally, after Dan endorses a photocopied set of documents with his name and passport number, the supervisor permits us to take the boxes and go.

The *ferrobus* no longer operates out of La Paz, so we must pick it up in Oruro. This gives us a chance to see our old buddy Francisco Vega Avila, who now lives in Oruro with his wife, Ross Mery, daughter Natalia, and a new baby, Nazareth. Francisco has quit the auto-parts business but still works for COMIBOL. He invites the three of us to supper, and Ross Mery prepares *sajta de pollo* (a spicy chicken stew) with potato pancakes. Afterward, Roy and Dan watch a soccer game on television with Francisco and a friend of his, while Ross Mery and I play with the mischievous, button-eyed Natalia.

Dan and I have given Natalia a stuffed panda bear, and she brings it to the train station in the morning to see us off. Standing with her parents on the platform, she clutches her panda with one chubby hand and waves goodbye with the other. I feel sad at not knowing when we'll see Francisco and his family again. In the process of tracking Butch and Sundance, we've made a lot of friendships that are difficult to sustain over such great distances and time lapses, and once the bones have been returned, our business in Bolivia will be finished. It's been too long since we've seen our Argentine friends; we'll have to go there next time we can scrape together some traveling money. And then there's the rest of the world to see.

As I settle into my seat, Roy is describing his most recent trip to southern Bolivia. "When I arrived in Tupiza, the city-council president and the mayor—who is no longer Gastón Michel, by the way—were in La Paz, and the acting mayor was opposed to another exhumation. The word around town was that the *gringos* had betrayed Tupiza. Because Lalo went to San Vicente with us, he was accused of collaborating with the enemy. He lost his job with the change of administrations and has been out of work for months. Gastón Michel was also suspected of having sold out to us."

"That's a bad rap if I've ever heard one," says Dan.

"I had to wait a week for the officials to return from La Paz," Roy continues, "so I used the time to meet people and make some allies, including the subprefect, Raúl Castro, and Félix Chalar Miranda, a lawyer who owns a television station. Both of them felt that the project would be good for the local economy, and they lobbied the acting mayor for it, but he wasn't moved. While I was waiting for the real mayor, Raúl and Félix went with me to San Vicente."

"What was that like?" asks Dan.

"The residents in the *pueblo civico* were friendly. They said that another exhumation was okay with them. All they wanted in exchange was some cement so they could build a little community office, and they asked us to persuade COMIBOL to connect them to the electricity and potable water. Félix said he would help them put together a budget and talk to COMIBOL."

"What about the miners?" I ask. "Did you talk to them?"

"We met with the union chiefs. They were complaining about the *gringos* stealing their treasures. Prudencio Bolívar, the chap we left the bones with, was particularly aggressive. He said that we weren't respecting their dead. At that point, Raúl said, 'You're the one who is showing the bones to reporters and getting your picture in the paper.' Bolívar denied it, said that he was just a repository for the remains. Raúl told him, 'Then you should take better care of them.' There were some tense moments."

"So the miners said no to another exhumation?" asks Dan.

"At first, the union leaders demanded that we build them a racquet-ball court. Then they said that they would have to have a meeting to let the miners vote on whether to approve the project. Later, they sent a letter saying they had decided to oppose any further exhumations in the cemetery. In the meantime, I met with the mayor and the city-council president in Tupiza. One of them, a man named Mario Mariscal, was very strict."

"In what way?" I ask.

"He didn't seem pleased, and he thought we were making money off it."

Dan and I laugh. Our obsession has practically bankrupted us, and we've refinanced our house more than once. Sometimes I think that we've gone off the deep end, like Richard Dreyfuss's character in *Close Encounters of the Third Kind*: The highlight of each day is the arrival of our "Butch mail"; the history of the world divides at 1908 (*Before* the Shootout and *After* the Shootout); and the universe revolves around a time and place that no longer exist.

"You know," says Roy, "the people down here don't seem to

realize that whether the bones are Butch and Sundance's or not doesn't affect the region's role in their story. They don't have to have a tomb to attract attention."

"In some ways," I say, "Gustav Zimmer is a blessing. At least Tupiza and San Vicente won't fight over who gets to display his bones in a glass case. We'll have an easier time putting them back into the ground."

"I don't think we should take them to San Vicente ourselves," says Roy. "There is no telling what might happen to us there."

"I agree," says Dan. "We should leave them with the Tupiza city council and hire someone to take them back to San Vicente for re-burial."

"But what if they don't do it?" I want to be certain that Zimmer's bones are returned to what was supposed to have been his final resting place.

"They'll bury the remains if we pay the expenses," says Roy. "And it won't anger the miners if somebody from the region brings them back. If we showed up six months after the second deadline, the miners would probably be extremely hostile."

"I suppose you're right," I say, "but how are the Tupiza officials going to react if we just dump the bones in their laps?"

"They inserted themselves into this when they made us get their permission to take the bones out of Tupiza," says Roy.

"They can hardly object to getting them back," says Dan.

"What about our missing the deadline?" I ask.

"The worst they can do is impose some kind of fine on us," says Dan.

"Or put us in jail," says Roy.

Hmmm.

"How will the news of Gustav Zimmer be received in the United States?" asks Roy.

"I doubt that anybody but outlaw historians will pay attention to it," says Dan. "A few of them might seize on the exhumation's failure, because they can't refute the historical evidence."

"Even a positive DNA match probably wouldn't convince some of those guys that their heroes died in Bolivia," I add.

"That's true," says Dan. "We've unmasked the two leading impostors, exposed a double hoax, and documented that two *gringos* using Butch and Sundance's known aliases were killed in San Vicente, but the diehards either ignore the evidence or invent ludicrous theories to explain away the obvious.''

"All we've ever wanted was to satisfy our own curiosity,'' I say, "and we've done that. Nothing else matters.''

The *ferrobus* roars south, passing the Salar de Uyuni, Roy's Incan church, the sand dunes, sharp-peaked Chorolque, Atocha's hillside cemetery, the Sleeping Monk, and all the other landmarks. We've taken this ride so many times, I'm beginning to feel like a commuter.

When we arrive in Tupiza, the hotel is full of teenagers celebrating a friend's fifteenth birthday. The only room available is the one the Worm was staying in when we first met him. Roy opts to spend the night at the hotel's nearby annex, although the plumbing is broken there and he'll be without water. We reluctantly check into the Worm's old room.

The birthday party jangles on until five o'clock, and I am bleary-eyed three hours later in the shower. After turning off the water, I notice what look like several rubber bands near the drain. I put on my glasses for a better look and immediately let out a shriek.

"What's wrong?'' calls Dan.

"You're not going to believe this.''

"What?''

"The floor in here is covered with worms!''

In an airy room on the second floor of the Casa de Cultura, we meet with Mayor Boris Poklepovic, President Mario Mariscal, three members of the city council, and Lalo Mostajo. When the mayor hands the running of the meeting over to Don Mario—who exhibited the greatest antipathy for our project during Roy's visit—we fear the worst.

"We are holding a hearing for Señor Roy Querejazu,'' says Don Mario, "in the matter of the scientific and historical investigation into the deaths of two North American *bandoleros* in San Vicente, and the exhumation of their presumed remains from the cemetery in that town, which is under the jurisdiction of Tupiza. We are ready for your report.''

Roy explains the various tests conducted on the remains and describes the meeting in Oklahoma, which took place nearly a year ago. "Although all the signs seemed to point toward the skeleton's being that of the Sundance Kid,'' says Roy, "the discovery of a photograph of the monument taken in 1972, when it still bore a plaque with the name of Gustav Zimmer on it, has cast doubt on that conclusion.

The preliminary results of the DNA testing were negative, but we are continuing to explore other possible tests, so the final report has not been written. We shall, of course, send a copy of the report to Tupiza. Until then, the bones and other material from the grave should probably remain in Tupiza."

"Do you plan to conduct further exhumations?" asks Don Mario.

"Clyde Snow is still interested in the possibility, but the miners' union vehemently opposes it, and they have prohibited our team from any more work in the cemetery."

"The union can't prohibit anything," says Don Mario. "They have no legal standing. Tupiza can give you permission to continue. This could be a great advantage for Tupiza. There is much interest in the *bandoleros* in the United States and in Latin America. Therefore, we will grant the permission to continue."

Evidently, we won't be going to jail.

"The question of another exhumation would have to be explored with Dr. Snow," says Roy. "I don't know what his schedule is, but he has been very busy in Bosnia. On another matter, Dan and Anne have spoken with Sundance's family. They have no objection to his remains' being returned to Bolivia, but they do not want him to be put on display. Obviously, if the skeleton is not Sundance's, there is no reason to display it. In any case, the remains should be reburied in San Vicente. Until then, they need to be kept in a safe place because there are several gold crowns and gold fillings in the teeth."

"The remains must be returned to San Vicente," says Don Mario. "They should not be exhibited in a museum."

"The San Vicente *campesinos*, they have no interest in this foreigner," says one of the councilmen. "They would probably steal the gold. We must ensure that the remains are buried."

Another councilman proposes that two members of the council take the bones to San Vicente and oversee their burial, and that we pay the cost of the expedition. Roy asks them to prepare a budget for the trip.

As part of our effort to persuade the *Tupizeños* that Butch and Sundance can bring economic benefits to the region, Dan has looked into the requirements for participation in the Sister City program. He gives the city council the application forms and says, "You might want to request Telluride, Colorado, as a sister city, because it was the site of Butch Cassidy's first bank robbery and the Tupiza region was the site of his last holdup. Also, with their mountain settings and historical roles as mining centers, Telluride and Tupiza have a lot in common.''

The council members need no convincing. In the months since Roy last met with them, they have clearly become interested in capitalizing on the bandits. According to many Bolivians, criminals in this life do good deeds in the next life; all those offerings the *San Vicenteños* left on what they thought was Butch and Sundance's grave must be paying off.

After obtaining permission to make a statement for the record, Lalo says that he received nothing—no monetary or other benefit—from the exhumation team, and that he accompanied us to San Vicente solely in his official capacity as a city employee.

"That is correct," says Roy. Dan and I nod our agreement.

"I also think that we should open the boxes," says Lalo, "and examine the bones to be certain that nothing is missing."

Not wishing to offend the council members' sensitivities, we have avoided suggesting that they look at the remains, but we are delighted with the opportunity to establish that we have brought everything back. If anything goes missing later, nobody can blame it on us. Watching a councilman pull the mandible and maxilla from the nearest box—its purple-and-orange Federal Express label still affixed—I feel that our mission has finally been fulfilled. Now all that remains is to tie up a few loose ends in our research and say goodbye to our Tupiza friends.

Dan is knocking on Gastón Michel's door when a man on a bicycle wheels up to the curb. "You don't want to see him," says the man. "He was responsible for letting those *gringos* take our bones out of the country. He sold us out."

"Is that a fact?" says Roy.

Dan keeps knocking.

"Where are you from, anyway?" asks the man, who reeks of beer. "I know you're not from around here."

"Where do you think we're from?" I ask.

"You two are French," he says, pointing at Roy and me. "Your friend is Uruguayan. Am I right?"

"Maybe," says Roy, with a barely perceptible smile.

"They promised to return the bones, but they didn't." He struggles to keep his bicycle upright. "Do you believe that Butch Cassidy was ever in this region?"

"Could be," says Roy, "but I don't know much about it."

Gastón isn't home. Later, we run into him on the street, and he beams at the news of the bones' return. Now, maybe he and Lalo will be let out of the purgatory we *gringos* condemned them to by holding on to the bones far longer than we had said we would.

"I spoke to an old historian," says Gastón, "who told me that men of bad character would have been buried standing."

"If that is true," replies Dan, "subsequent burials undoubtedly have disturbed the remains, which means that there is no way to find them."

"The cemetery changes often," says Gastón. "They resell the burial grounds and dig up the old graves."

"Another exhumation would probably be a waste of time," I say. "The documents are good enough for me."

"A Bolivian fellow has also been researching Butch Cassidy," says Gastón. "A real scoundrel. I've had several run-ins with him. Maybe you know him. His name is Guillermo."

"We call him the Worm."

Gastón laughs and says, "He was back here recently going through the judicial files."

If the Worm still has larceny on his mind, he's too late for the inquest file: Roger has already beaten him to it. But a friend of Roy's has discovered that all the issues of *El Chorolque* that contain articles about Butch and Sundance's last holdup and the San Vicente shootout are now missing from the National Archives in Sucre. And heaven help the Aramayo records. Dora Salazar tells us that the Worm has been going through them, too.

As a result of her experience with him, she has hung a sign saying NO MONEY LENT on her wall. She has given her partridge to Gastón but still has most of her menagerie, including five cats. "I like them a lot," she says. "One of them was bothering my doves, so I took him to some property I own in the country, but he came back here. I don't know how he found his way."

Dan tells Dora about our meeting with the city council and describes Roger's photo of the grave we exhumed in San Vicente.

"This man Zimmer stole the payroll?" she asks.

"No," I say. "He had nothing to do with the holdup. Froilán Risso just identified the wrong grave."

"We know from the judicial inquest file found by Roger McCord that the *bandoleros* were buried in the San Vicente cemetery,'' adds Roy.

"But my father went with him to look through the judicial files, and they didn't find anything."

"Roger and his wife found the file after your father left, and they took it with them. They planned to write something about it, but they never did."

"Then he wasn't Butch Cassidy's grandson?" She sounds disappointed.

Our final task is to finish retracing the bandits' escape route. We've been to the holdup site, and we've followed the last leg of Butch and Sundance's journey into San Vicente. But we haven't yet seen all the countryside in between. Roy suggests that we visit Félix Chalar Miranda, the lawyer who went to San Vicente with him. Félix is filming a documentary about Butch and Sundance, with a couple of Peace Corps volunteers in the title roles, and might be able to help us find the route.

Félix's television station is closed for the evening, but he lives next door. A boy answers our knock and says that Félix is out.

"Are you sure?" asks Roy. He knows not to take no for an answer.

The boy disappears, and presently a pregnant woman comes to the door. Félix is napping, she says, but she will wake him up. A stocky man with a black mustache, grey chin-whiskers, and aviator glasses finally appears, dressed in a blue jogging suit. He yawns, then spots Roy and comes to life. We invite him out for a drink, and on the way to the bar he peppers us with questions about Butch and Sundance.

"How accurate was the movie?"

"Let's put it this way," says Dan, "it captured the spirit of the legend. As far as the facts go, the movie more or less followed what was known at the time, except that it skipped over the period when Butch and Sundance tried to go straight, when they were living with Etta Place on their ranch in Cholila."

"The movie also had the bandits robbing lots of Bolivian banks," I say, "but we found evidence of their participation in only four robberies during the eight years they spent in South America."

"What about the shootout?" asks Félix. "The place Froilán Risso showed Roy and Raúl and me in San Vicente was very small, but the movie showed them in a big plaza."

"In a documentary about the making of the movie," I say, "George Roy Hill, the director, mentioned that he had used a bigger space for cinematic reasons. Ironically, he said that the number of soldiers seemed excessive to him but that he was following what the historians had said. Unfortunately, the historians were wrong."

"Butch killed Victor Torres immediately," says Dan, "and Captain Concha's contribution to the battle seems to have been limited to rounding up locals to stand guard outside the hut. That means Butch and Sundance were up against the other soldier and the Uyuni police inspector. In other words, it was two against two."

"And contrary to the legend," I say, "they didn't leave all of their rifles and ammunition in the patio. Sundance had a rifle with him, and both he and Butch had enough bullets to kill every resident of San Vicente several times over."

Near the plaza, we bump into Willy Alfaro, a local folksinger who is composing the music for Félix's documentary. We invite Willy to supper later and commandeer a back room in a restaurant. After we demolish a *parillada*—an assortment of steaks, ribs, organs, and sausages grilled on braziers beside the table—Willy takes up his guitar and plays the documentary's haunting instrumental theme. "I don't have enough information to write any words," he explains.

"We can fix that." I whip out a notebook and set down in my ungrammatical Spanish a narrative of Butch and Sundance's activities in the area, including the names of the people they met, the places they visited, and the highlights of the holdup and the shootout. Nothing beats a song for spreading a legend, so the lyrics ought to contain a fact or two. And even though our research is nearly done, Félix has obviously caught the outlaw-history bug and will go on digging for information after we leave. He can fill in the gaps for Willy—and for us, too.

A versatile tenor who looks like a diminutive Jay Silverheels with wavy hair, Willy sings everything from tangos to calypsos: One minute he is Carlos Gardel; the next, Harry Belafonte. He searches for a song that everyone knows the words to, and we wind up singing "*La Cucaracha*," after which we agree to leave the music to Willy.

A ten-year-old shoeshine boy opens the door in the middle of a song and comes into the room looking for customers. Félix shoos him out, but Willy stops strumming his guitar and calls the boy back. "Go get a sack and take these leftovers home to your mother."

344

The boy returns with a plastic bag and empties every grill and plate in the room. When he departs, not so much as a wilted leaf of lettuce remains.

Butch and Sundance would have liked Willy.

Early in our research, we came across a May 1913 *Wide World Magazine* article by a British engineer, A. G. Francis, who claimed to have spent much of the time between August and November 1908 with the two North Americans who held up the Aramayo payroll and then died in San Vicente. Because he mistook the Sundance Kid for Harvey "Kid Curry" Logan and claimed that the bandits had taken an escape route that seemed illogical to us, we dismissed the article, as did William A. Pinkerton, who called a colleague's attention to the article and wrote, "I believe the whole story to be a fake."

Since reading the inquest file, however, we have reevaluated Francis's story, because one of the witnesses confirmed that the bandits had followed the route Francis described. In 1908, Francis was supervising the transportation of a gold dredge from Verdugo, a village about fifteen miles south of Tupiza, to Esmoraca, at the source of the San Juan del Oro River.

> The country thereabouts is very rough and uncivilized, inhabited principally by Indians with extremely primitive ideas. Roads, as we understand the term in England, are unknown, and consequently the work of transporting a large quantity of heavy and bulky machinery and constructional ironwork was a slow and arduous task, attended by many difficulties and occasionally not a little danger. The work was done by means of heavy two-wheeled carts, drawn by six, nine, or twelve mules, and owing to hard work, poor pay, and the hardships inseparable from the life, the *carreros,* or carters, were recruited from a very low class of humanity. My crowd of about thirty men were made up of Argentine and Chilian criminals of varying degrees and Bolivian half-castes. . . .
>
> One evening during the month of August 1908, I was enjoying a solitary meal, when a loud outcry on the part of my dogs announced the arrival of visitors. Going to the door of my house I was in time to greet two riders, who, from their saddles and general appearance, I judged to be Americans.

This opinion was confirmed when one of the new-comers, a burly, pleasant-looking man with a moustache, said cheerily: "How do? We have seen Teddy"—my friend—"in town, and he told us you wouldn't object to having us stop here awhile to rest our animals."

"Get your saddles off, boys," I said, "and come right in."

I then called my boy to attend to the newcomers' animals, and after seeing that this was done I rejoined my visitors. The big fellow . . . informed me that his name was Frank Smith, and the other, a rather slightly built man of middle height, with a fair beard and moustache and eyes like gimlets, was George Low. . . . They had been in the stock business together, and later on intended to proceed to the Argentine.

During the next two or three days, while the men were busy loading the carts for the next journey, Smith and Low proved very pleasant and amusing companions, and I was therefore not at all sorry when, as we were about to start on our trip to Esmoraca, they offered to accompany me.

For the following few weeks the transport work went on as usual, Smith remaining with me and Low spending a good part of his time in visits to Tupiza. At the time I had no idea that he had any other motive in this but that of enjoyment. . . .

Of course, it was impossible to live for any period with these men in such intimate companionship without becoming aware that they were somewhat out of the ordinary run of men to be met with, even in Bolivia, although no suspicion of the real truth had so far crossed my mind. Then, one night at Verdugo, an incident occurred which gave me an insight into the character of Smith. . . .

Francis described an altercation between Smith—who was actually Sundance—and one of the Chilean carters. Sundance wanted to stick around and have it out with the man, but Francis urged him to drop the matter and give the Chilean time to cool off.

I pointed out that if anybody was killed an inquiry would result in Tupiza, and that this would probably interfere with the transport work, which we were very anxious to get finished before the rainy season came on. This—and possibly the reflection that an inquiry in Tupiza would upset his own plans—decided him, and he rode away at daybreak, while the *carreros* were still under their blankets. . . .

Starting on our next trip, [Butch] went ahead with the carts, while [Sundance] remained with me to settle a few outstanding matters.

We were delayed longer than we anticipated, so that it was late in the afternoon of the following day before we set off to catch up the men. Overtaken by a mist on the pampa, we were forced to make the best of our way to the Argentine Custom House, in order to obtain food and shelter. On our arrival, however, we found that their supply of forage was very small, and consequently, on leaving early next morning, we wended our way to the frontier *pueblo* of Santa Catalina, in order to obtain a square feed for our animals. The Comisario . . . of Santa Catalina was a friend of mine, and in addition to his official duties kept a store, so we decided to fill our requirements at his establishment.

On our arrival we found that my friend had two other visitors, the Comisarios of Cordoba and Jujuy, two important towns in the Argentine Republic. . . . The whole party settled down to the enjoyment of several *aperitivos* together, and later on, when breakfast was announced, [Sundance] and myself were invited to join our new friends at this repast. At breakfast we became quite a merry party, and on the conclusion of the meal we amused ourselves for some time by various trials of strength. It was while one of these was in progress that I saw [Sundance] suddenly break away from the two Comisarios and disappear through the door. A moment later I heard his horse gallop past.

Although ignorant of the cause of this sudden departure, I lost no time in following his lead, and mounting my animal, standing ready in the *patio*, I clattered away in pursuit. On overtaking [Sundance], which he only allowed me to do on seeing that I was unaccompanied, he explained that the men had tried to take away his revolver, and he did not allow anyone to do that. Some time afterwards he further enlightened me by saying that he thought that the Cordoba man had recognized him and wished to disarm him in an apparently friendly way.

On leaving the village a mile or two behind we quitted the road, and for the next four or five hours climbed up one side and scrambled and slid down the other of some of the most rocky, rugged, and barren mountains possible to conceive—habitation or vegetation there was none—until we finally reached the camp about eleven o'clock at night.

On our return to Verdugo, [Sundance] paid a few days' visit to Tupiza, and on his return had a long private conversation with [Butch], following which the latter rode off to town, and [Sundance] and I went down the river to take up our quarters at Tomahuaico, distant about [three miles] from Verdugo. There we remained until, some five days later, [Butch] returned. The following day [he] requested me to lend him my big grey horse and rode away with [Sundance] back to town.

Francis next saw Butch and Sundance about sixteen hours after Carlos Peró and his party had been relieved of the Aramayo remittance at Huaca Huañusca.

I was sleeping in a hammock slung between two posts on the veranda at Tomahuaico, when about one o'clock I was awakened by the barking of my dogs, and, looking towards the road, dimly discerned two horsemen approaching, one leading a spare animal. I called out, "*Quiénes son?*" (Who are you?), and [Butch's] voice answered: "Don't you know your old horse in the dark, kid?"

I immediately tumbled out and helped them to unsaddle. [Butch] appeared to be sick, and after taking his gear into my room immediately turned in. [Sundance] and I, however, went into the dining-room, and he made a very fair meal on whatever I could find, during which he entertained me with an account of their latest exploit.

When they first arrived in Tupiza from the north of Bolivia, he told me, their intention was to hold up the National Bank there. However, a few days after their arrival the [Abaroa] cavalry regiment arrived to take up their quarters in town, and as this regiment was in barracks in the same square as the Bank, and only a stone's throw from it, they decided that it was too dangerous for the moment to attempt this proceeding, and that it would be necessary to await the regiment's removal to another part of the country. It was then that they looked about for an out-of-the-way retreat in which to pass the time, and came out to me at Verdugo. Their funds getting low, however, and no signs of the departure of the regiment being apparent, they had to alter their plans.

During their many visits to Tupiza they made unobtrusive inquiries, and learnt that it was the custom for Messrs. Aramayo, Francke and Cia. to send the pay-money for their employés at the smelter and neighboring mines . . . once every month by means of pack-mules escorted by two or three *arrieros*. After completing their inquiries they went over and made their final arrangements for carrying out a "hold-up," and then quietly returned and waited for the next remittance to be sent.

After watching the departure of the escort on the morning in question, and singling out one of the pack-mules possessed by the party for capture later on, they returned to the [Hotel Internacional] and left almost at once. . . . Taking a much shorter and rougher track over the mountains, they reached the spot already selected by them for the scene of the "hold-up" some time in advance of the pay escort.

Francis briefly described the robbery and then turned to Butch and Sundance's subsequent actions.

After watching the party well out of sight, the two bandits mounted their animals and, leading the mule they had taken from the escort, made their way across the mountains to a desolate spot, where they decided to wait until nightfall before pursuing their journey to Tomahuaico. As soon as darkness came on they resumed their march, and finally descended into the valley of the Río San Juan, about [three miles] below the house in which I was quartered, having encountered not a soul since the departure of the escort.

After giving me these particulars, [Sundance] joined his partner in my room, and I returned to my hammock to pass the rest of the night. I thought deeply over the story I had just heard, and did not at all care for the position in which I found myself, practically the accessory of a couple of brigands. I did not see what I could do to alter matters, however; any attempt to give the men away would undoubtedly have cost me my life, and that very quickly.

We were all astir shortly after daybreak, and nothing having yet been heard in the neighborhood regarding the affair, everything went on as usual. At about ten A.M., the two bandits and the writer being seated on the veranda, we received our first tidings from Tupiza by the arrival of an acquaintance on a spent horse, who exclaimed as he dismounted: "You had better get out of this, boys; they are saddling up a hundred men to come after you."

After he had refreshed himself with a drink, the new-comer told us that the news of the "hold-up" had reached Tupiza the previous evening, and that parties of soldiers, accompanied by Indian trackers, had been out all night searching for traces of the outlaws. He had heard just before leaving Tupiza that tracks had been found, and had seen the soldiers mustering in the Plaza, on which he had secured the best horse he could obtain and galloped all the way to Tomahuaico to warn the two friends. After telling us that the soldiers could not be very far distant, he again mounted and rode away.

When he had gone [Sundance] turned to me. "You might tell that boy of yours to get breakfast ready quickly, will you, kid?" he said. "I suppose we had better be moving."

[Sundance] and [Butch] then began to get their riding gear ready, deciding to take with them the mule they had stolen the previous day, but leaving their pack behind. They displayed no nervousness or hurry in their proceedings, and when breakfast was ready, we disposed of the meal in very good spirits and with considerable appetite.

"Say, kid," said [Sundance], suddenly turning to me, "you had better saddle up and come with us."

Needless to say, that was the last thing I wished to do, but argument was useless. Evidently, [Sundance] wanted to make certain of my silence. I accordingly saddled up, and shortly after the three of us started up the river at a gentle trot, [Butch] leading the stolen mule and [Sundance] and myself following behind.

"Suppose the soldiers arrive," said I, "what are you going to do about it?"

"Why, we'll just sit down behind a rock and get to work," replied [Sundance], calmly.

Reflecting upon my position, I felt it to be a very unenviable one, as, should the soldiers catch us, I should certainly stand a very good chance of suffering the same fate as my companions, although entirely innocent of any complicity in their crimes. However, no other course being open to me, I decided to put as good a face on the matter as possible, and trust to my good luck to pull me through.

Presently I asked a question. "Where are you going to—the Argentine?"

"No," replied [Sundance], "we can't go there. We want you to guide us . . . to Estarca. We are going to make for Uyuni and the north again. Once we get there we know a place to lie low in until this affair blows over."

"I think you're foolish," I answered.

"Oh, they won't get us," said [Sundance], confidently.

Shortly after this we turned off the main bed of the river into the narrow and winding canyon leading to the small Indian *pueblo* of Estarca, having seen nothing of our pursuers. Now, for the first time, I felt that I had a fair chance of escape should we be overtaken, as this canyon turns and twists to such an extent that the track is not visible for more than about a hundred yards at one time throughout its length, very frequent fordings of the river being necessary, with inaccessible heights on either side.

Late in the afternoon we drew near the village, and I was then instructed to ride ahead, make inquiries as to whether all was safe, and should such be the case return to the river road, when they would enter the village. I did so, and finding that no news of the "hold-up" had been received, returned and awaited the arrival of the two bandits.

Engaging a room, which I had occupied on many previous visits, we made our arrangements for the night, the two partners occupying a bed in the corner, and I a mattress placed on the floor immediately opposite the door.

"Good night, kid," said [Sundance]. "I wish we could celebrate to-night, but in the circumstances it won't do."

I fell asleep very soon, and did not wake until roused by the daylight, when I went into the village to make inquiries and purchase provisions. Finding that everything was quiet, I returned to the house, and shortly afterwards we left the village on our journey towards Uyuni.

About eight o'clock that morning, after learning all the particulars I could give them regarding the road they wished to follow, [Sundance] and [Butch] suddenly pulled up their animals, and the former held out his hand.

"Well, good-bye, kid," he said. "You don't want to come any further with us. If you meet those soldiers, tell them you passed us on the road to the Argentine."

Exchanging farewells, I turned my horse and rode towards Tomahuaico, catching the last glimpse I ever had of the bandits alive as they rounded a bend in the valley.

The following day an Indian passing Tomahuaico informed me that two white men had been killed the previous evening at San Vicente. . . . His descriptions of these men tallying with that of the robbers, I saddled up at once and rode to San Vicente, learning on the way further details which convinced me that it was indeed my late companions who had come to their untimely end.

After describing what he had learned about the shootout, Francis expressed sympathy for the men who had involved him in this adventure:

I must confess that it was with a feeling very much akin to grief that I wended my way homeward. [Sundance] told me once that he had made several attempts to settle down to a law-abiding life, but these attempts had always been frustrated by emissaries of the police and detective agencies getting on his track, and thus forcing him to return to the road. He claimed that he had never hurt or killed a man except in self-defence, and had never stolen from the poor, but only from rich corporations well able to support his "requisitions."

If Butch and Sundance felt persecuted, they had reason to: Two years after their deaths, William A. Pinkerton wrote of his continuing hopes "to apprehend these people" in the United States or to "get them killed" in South America. Although Butch and Sundance were beyond the Pinkertons' reach, at least one innocent bystander was snared in the manhunt that never officially ended. On May 3, 1913, the La Paz police arrested a forty-three-year-old itinerant carpenter named Francis Lowe, who matched a Pinkerton circular's description of "George" Parker, alias Butch Cassidy and Jim Lowe. Francis Lowe protested that he was not a bank robber, but the Bolivians were all set to deport him when U.S. Chargé d'Affaires Charles Strangeland intervened. After making extensive inquiries, wrote Strangeland, "I became convinced that Mr. Lowe was not the man sought by the Pinkerton Detective Agency. My conviction was confirmed by assertions made by certain Englishmen and others here that a man known as George Parker (whom the La Paz police were seeking) had been killed in one of the provinces two or three years ago while resisting address, and that the charge against Mr. Lowe must be one of mistaken identity." Once the chief of police was persuaded that his real quarry was dead, the hapless carpenter—who had spent his birthday in the La Paz jail—was released. Apparently, no one bothered to advise the Pinkertons that they could call off the search.

Our final goal is to travel the route Butch and Sundance followed from the outskirts of Tupiza to Tomahuaico and from there to Estarca and Cucho, but we can't find anyone who knows where Tomahuaico is, nor can we locate it on our maps. Félix suggests that we go first to Estarca and get directions from there. Rounding up transportation, however, proves difficult. Pancho's Land Rover is in the garage, and Hector's Toyota is already booked. Roy asks Manuel Mitru, the *dueño* of our hotel, if anyone else might be able to cart us over the bandits' escape route, but he can't think of anyone.

Having seen that Butch and Sundance are good for business, the Mitru family is preparing to set up a tourist agency in the hotel and run tours of the local Outlaw Trail. "You know," Don Manuel says, "I thought you were going to be arrested, so I didn't officially register you until after the city council meeting. I'm glad everything worked out okay."

When the day of our trip dawns, we are still without mobility. While I wait for Félix in the dining room, Roy and Dan go out to look for a taxi. The few cars on the street are either unavailable or unfit for a trip over the rough roads that lie ahead of us. Roy and Dan eventually give up and come back to the hotel, where Félix and I are having breakfast. Félix suggests that we try to find a taxi at the train station.

"We already looked there," says Roy, "but we can try again."

As we stroll toward the station, Dan and Félix chat about the Smith gang and other outlaws sometimes confused with Butch and Sundance in these parts.

"They don't have the proper sense of urgency about finding a vehicle," Roy says to me.

"If we don't leave almost immediately," I agree, "we won't make it back before nightfall."

There are still no cabs at the train station, but we run into Willy Alfaro, who tells us that his neighbor, Fermín Ortega, has a jeep and is an excellent driver. Don Fermín obviously had other plans, but our objective intrigues him. After the usual negotiations and delays for refueling and battery charging, we set off at half past ten, with Willy Alfaro singing to us from Don Fermín's cassette player.

The route to Estarca runs past fields of sugarcane and through lumpy clay hills streaked white and bristling with cacti. Beyond a low pass, a murrey ridge rises, and spined *churqui* bushes sprout from a dry canyon. Red rocks lie like heaps of broken bricks alongside the gravel road. A hawk lifts off from a bush and flaps by my window. We pass two *campesinas* wrangling a couple dozen goats. The hills turn amber, then green with willows and flowering shrubs. The jeep climbs a precipitous road through a narrow canyon of red conglomerate. Condors coast between huge rock formations thrust up like stalagmites in a vast cave turned inside out.

"This is Palquiza," says Don Fermín as we pass a few adobe huts with roofs of mud and grass, tile, or tin. A white chapel stands near a soccer field and a small, walled cemetery.

"What do people around here do for a living?" asks Dan.

"They mine antimony and gold," replies Don Fermín.

Following adobe walls crowned with thorns to keep out vermin of both the two- and four-legged variety, we leave Palquiza and drop through another pass into the wide San Juan del Oro Valley, where a child rides a burro across a strip of cracked mud that looks like a rustic tile floor. Among the blades of red rock upended by earthquakes, sprout willows, foxtails, and *retama,* a yellow-flowered bush whose leaves are used in tea to calm the nerves and induce sleep.

"It is considered better than *coca* for the dead," says Roy. "Mourners mix the *retama* with other flowers in cemetery wreaths."

"Chaco Pampa," says Félix as we pull into a town where schoolchildren in snappy white coats march, like an army of miniature lab assistants, past a big cottonwood tree. The twin-towered church has a metal roof, but the steep roofs of the houses are made of cane, mud, and grass and bordered with thin ceramic tiles. "These roofs used to be infested with *vinchucas,* which carry Chagas disease," says Félix, "but it is under control now."

"It was terrible," agrees Don Fermín. "The disease destroys the nerves before it kills."

Beyond Chaco Pampa, on a road paralleling the San Juan del Oro River, we wind through hills banded salmon, umber, topaz, and tan. Across the river, a jagged layer of red rock tops the steep iron-colored cliff face. Driving through hills now white and rippled with shady crevices, we encounter the remains of several small landslides. Where chunks of the road have fallen away, the jeep climbs over the scree. The land dries out until the only plants are thorn scrub, cacti, and *yareta. Llamas* with pink-tasseled ears lounge around a dried-up pond. Feral cattle sprawl in the road; at our approach, the calves get up and wobble off, but the adults stay put like horned logs, forcing Don Fermín to drive around them. He stops the jeep at a wide spot in the road, beside a hill where rusty slabs of rock protrude through the meager vegetation. Roy measures the altitude at 3,830 meters, or 12,566 feet.

We turn away from the river, and a flock of yellow parakeets blows by. A train of burros, followed by a woman and three children, clops along the road. With the snowcapped Lípez Mountains on the western horizon, we descend scrubby hills purpled with wildflowers and pause on the lip of a three-thousand-foot drop-off. We can't see them, but Estarca and Cucho are in the valley below, Estarca to the left and Cucho to the right, nine or ten miles apart.

"Go slow and carefully," Roy says to Don Fermín as we head down a seemingly endless series of switchbacks on the rocky road. The foxtails in the valley flash in the sunlight.

"What is the name of that blue flower?" I ask.

"Don't distract the driver," commands Roy. "Watch out for that curve!"

Something must be wrong with me: I've lost my fear of falling.

Although I wouldn't want to meet anything wider than a motorcycle in oncoming traffic, I'm not particularly worried about this road. Don Fermín seems to have complete control of the jeep, and all that *paja brava* on the slope looks deceptively soft.

My ears pop.

"That was a tough descent," says Don Fermín.

"Yes," says Roy, "but you still need to be cautious. We are not all the way down yet."

Pigeons roost on tall cacti, and parakeets dart among the nameless blue wildflowers. Fifty goats flee down the hillside near Tapaxa, which huddles on a spit of land above the *lecho*.

"The corn was killed by frost," says Don Fermín, pointing toward the dead stalks propped together like tepees in small, rock-fenced fields.

Seven sheep bunch up near a grove of willows on the *lecho*, where we stop to shed our jackets. Roy measures the altitude at 2,170 meters, or 7,120 feet, and Félix says, "I used to hunt *vizcachas* around here."

Don Fermín removes the Willy Alfaro tape and switches to a brass band for the brief ride to Estarca, which is strung along a shelf with yellow trees between the hills and the riverbed.

In his testimony to the judicial authorities in November 1908, Juan Félix Erazo said that about a month before the Aramayo holdup, Edward Graydon had introduced him to the taller bandit at the home of Fortunato Valencia in Estarca. Erazo was in Cucho on the morning of the sixth of November and saw the bandits talking to Tiburcio Bolívar, who later told Erazo that the *gringos* had spent the night at the home of Narcisa Burgos. These individuals, therefore, were among the last to see Butch and Sundance alive. Perhaps in the wake of the shootout, they tried to recall everything they could about their encounters with the doomed *bandoleros*.

Hoping to find family stories handed down through the generations, we ask around for anyone related to Erazo, Valencia, Bolívar, or Burgos.

"A family named Burgos owns three houses here in Estarca," someone tells us, "but they live in Tupiza."

We have already spoken with two members of the Burgos family in Tupiza and ascertained that they know nothing about the bandits' activities in Estarca.

Nobody recognizes the other names. We then ask whether anyone knows where Tomahuaico is located.

"There's no such place," says a middle-aged woman in a skirt and sweater.

Other residents recall hearing of Tomahuaico but cannot direct us to it.

Finally, an old man with a battered fedora and a mouthful of *coca* leaves says, "Tomahuaico is south of Chaco Pampa and north of the Urulica ravine."

"How long would it take to travel from here to Tomahuaico by mule?"

"Four hours through Urulica, but you can't take that route in a vehicle."

"How about the *lecho*?" asks Roy. "Is it possible to drive on the *lecho* around the mountain and up the San Juan del Oro Valley to Tomahuaico?"

"No, *señor*," says the old man. His teeth are worn to nubs. "Before, yes. Now, no. The way is blocked."

"How old is Estarca?" asks Dan.

"It was built by the Spaniards," says the old man. "The town was famous for making shoes with wooden nails."

"Do you still make them?" asks Félix.

"No, *señor*. Not any more."

"Why do you want to know?" asks a young man who stinks of *singani*. His shirttail is half in and half out of his dirty khaki slacks, and his zipper is undone.

Félix ignores him. "Did the chapel exist in 1908?"

"Yes," says the drunk. "Why do you ask?"

Another man says, "The old chapel was destroyed. This one is newer."

"That's right," says the drunk.

"To me," says Roy, "the bell tower looks old, but the chapel looks new."

"Exactly," says the drunk.

"I was born in 1928," says an *anciano* "and the church has been here all my life. It has not changed."

"Hasn't changed," says the drunk. "But why do you ask these questions?"

"Nobody is talking to you," Félix says to him, "so quit interfering and leave us alone to continue our conversation in peace."

"I'm *from* here," the drunk replies. "I know this place."

"I'm *not* from here," says Félix, "and I know more than you do."

We withdraw to the cool interior of the local *boliche* and lunch on hard bread, tinned meat, papaya soda, and beer. The *boliche* sells a bit of everything—crackers, canned goods, razor blades, batteries, notebooks, yarn. The wares are piled on the floor and laid out on rickety shelves along the back wall. A wooden case on the counter is stuffed with candy and shampoo. Purple tins of alcohol and white blocks of salt are stacked on one of the built-in adobe benches.

Noticing that the benches are like those mentioned in the inquest file, I look around at the windowless whitewashed walls, the wooden door, the vaulted ceiling, and the uneven dirt floor and realize that this room fits the description of the one in San Vicente where the bandits died. I feel cold, anxious, sad. Butch and Sundance may live on in legend, but Robert LeRoy Parker and Harry Longabaugh are dead. For the first time, their deaths seem real, not just pieces of the puzzle we play with.

Before I can tell Dan what I'm thinking, we are attacked by a swarm of biting flies. They dive for our faces, and we flail at them wildly. My arms are soon covered with welts.

The road to Cucho is used so seldom that bushes grow in the middle of it. Eventually, we lose the track and cut across country down onto the *lecho*. Don Fermín drives through a few puddles near Estarca, and then the riverbed dries up completely. The mud is puckered, peeling, and chipped. Dust blows across the sharp rocks. Sunlight glints off cactus spines in the folds of copper-colored mountains. As we approach Cucho, I want to call across the years: Take this trail or that one, but don't go to San Vicente. And yet, if Butch and Sundance had taken a different road, if they hadn't disappeared into unmarked graves, we would never have set off on the path that began in Cholila and has led us to this forgotten corner of the world.

The river narrows, we round the curve, and there sits Cucho—a few adobe huts and a chapel at the foot of a hill studded with cacti.

"This used to be a busy village," says Félix, "with lots of traffic from all the mines in the area. It had hotels, bars, the works, but almost everyone has left or died."

Five families remain in Cucho. "Tiburcio Bolívar was the brother of my husband's father," says an ageless woman wearing a black sweater and skirt under a black poncho fastened with two safety pins. She invites us into her one-room house, which is furnished with a bed, a table, three chairs, a bench, two shelves, a radio, a large earthen jar, and scores of flies. "My mother might have known something about the *bandoleros*, but she is dead."

"Is this where Tiburcio Bolívar lived?" asks Roy.

"No, he lived up the way. This house used to be a hotel. It was larger then, but it was hit by a flood and later rebuilt."

"Where is San Vicente from here?" I ask.

"There used to be a trail over there."

The prow of a red butte points northwest toward the place where Butch and Sundance met their fate.

Don Fermín takes us in the opposite direction, over furrowed hills that look as if they had been raked by giants, then through the uninhabited Carbonera ravine, where a rufous curtain of rock pierced by an enormous hole stands perpendicular to the road. At length, we find ourselves back in Chaco Pampa and heading south toward Tomahuaico.

"What does *Tomahuaico* mean?" I ask.

"I don't know," says Roy. "It's probably a Quechua word."

"*Toma* is from the Spanish for 'take,' " says Don Fermín, "and *huaico* is Quechua for 'ravine.' Together, they mean 'a place where water is diverted for irrigation.' "

The sun is setting as we roar south in search of Butch and Sundance's last home. Don Fermín seems unable to decide which of the many ravines is the correct one. Finally, we cross an irrigation ditch.

"This must be it!" says Roy, pointing up the ravine, whose pale sandstone walls gleam like ghosts in the last rays of the day. The sky beyond is lavender.

"I don't know," Don Fermín replies and continues driving south. Five minutes later, the road widens out and joins the *lecho*. "I guess it was that ravine back there, after all."

As we recross the irrigation ditch, the sun's afterglow fades. In the jeep's headlights, a building is visible halfway up the hill, but we're too late for exploring. We'll have to come back. To be so near the end of the trail and then be forced to wait is maddening.

In the morning, barking dogs hector us to the city limits. We retrace our path to the irrigation ditch, then Don Fermín drives up into the wide gravel ravine. On a ledge with a splendid view of the San Juan del Oro River sits an old house with a stone roof and a paved veranda.

"The construction looks colonial," says Roy. "Note the roof."

"This would have made a perfect place for Francis's hammock," I say.

"The door is fastened with a wire," says Dan, untwisting it.

We enter the hut, which has a vaulted ceiling like the one at the *boliche* in Estarca. Hay is piled at one end of the room. At the other end, a picture of the Virgin Mary hangs over a small niche, which contains several scraps of paper, an old-fashioned key, a dirty rag, a rope lanyard, a button, a bolt, and a photo of a soldier. We reverently carry these relics out into the sunlight, lay them on a boulder, and photograph them from every conceivable angle. Although the papers date from the 1960s and 1970s, the soldier's portrait looks much older. Moreover, we *feel* the presence of Butch and Sundance. I envision them sitting on the veranda, calmly eating breakfast after hearing that soldiers were headed this way.

The magic lasts until we meet Pedro Castro, who lives across the ravine. "This isn't Tomahuaico," he says. "It's Quenchamali."

The place has nothing to do with Butch and Sundance.

"*Quenchamali* is Quechua for 'bad luck,' " says Don Fermín.

"That house belongs to my cousin," says Señor Castro, pointing to the hut we have just burgled. He is fifty-two and walks with the aid of a bamboo cane. "Tomahuaico is the next *quebrada*. There used to be a town there, but it was destroyed by a flood."

Roy persuades him to come with us to the site; we want to be sure we've got the right ravine before we turn our imaginations loose again. As we jostle onto the gravel edge of the *lecho,* Señor Castro says, "The Spaniards who came looking for gold, they built the town with lots of white houses, but everything was carried off by the flood fifteen or twenty years ago."

Just beyond the spot where we turned around last night, the sheer walls of the Quebrada Tomahuaico rise from a broad, sandy slope. Below an irrigation ditch, an expanse of tall grass marks the place where the white houses used to stand and where Butch and Sundance spent their penultimate night. Cottonwoods border the riverbed behind a dike built with eight tons of stones hauled down from the upper reaches of Tomahuaico and topped with *churqui* thorns.

"How long would it take to travel from here to Estarca by mule?" asks Dan.

"If you go up the Urulica ravine," says Señor Castro, "you will reach Estarca in one day. The nearest town is Monte, on the other side of the river, but there are no boats, so you can't get across during the rainy season."

"What if you absolutely must go there?" I ask.

"You just wait for the dry season, that's all."

"What do you remember about Tomahuaico?" asks Dan.

"When I was young, we always came here for *carnaval*," says Señor Castro. "The houses were abandoned but full of artifacts. Then the river washed them all away."

"What a shame that nothing is left," says Roy. "Now we'll never know what it was really like."

This isn't the first blank wall we've hit while tracking Butch and Sundance, but for once I don't mind. The truth is hard enough to recognize when it unfolds before your eyes, let alone when it happened long ago in an alien land. Standing with Dan in the shade of the cottonwoods, gazing across the wind-ruffled grass toward the heights of Tomahuaico, I smile: How fitting to arrive at the end of our journey into the past and find the place gone, vanished into memory and beyond.

SOME SOURCES

S O M E of the material is organized geographically, rather than chronologically. The contemporary events took place between January 1986 and August 1993. The Bolivian exhumation occurred in December 1991. A complete bibliography listing the thousands of interviews, letters, and publications that served as resources for this book would be longer than the book itself. This list of publications and archival materials, therefore, is merely a sampler.

Information about Butch and Sundance's backgrounds and early careers was drawn primarily from Pearl Baker, *The Wild Bunch at Robbers Roost* (New York, 1971); Lula Parker Betenson, *Butch Cassidy My Brother* (Provo, Utah, 1975); Donna Ernst, *Sundance, My Uncle* (College Station, Texas, 1993); Mary Garman, "Harry Longabaugh, the Sundance Kid, the Early Years," *Bits and Pieces* (Newcastle, Wyoming, 1977); High River Pioneers, *Leaves from the Medicine Tree* (Lethbridge, Alberta, 1960); Charles Kelly, *The Outlaw Trail* (Salt Lake City, Utah, 1938); the Papers of Charles Kelly (1889–1971) at the University of Utah Libraries in Salt Lake City, Utah; Vicky Kelly, "Butch and the Kid," *Glenbow* magazine of the Glenbow Institute (Calgary, November 1970); Edward M. Kirby, *The Rise and Fall of the Sundance Kid* (Iola, Wisconsin, 1983); Larry Pointer, *In Search of Butch Cassidy* (Norman, Oklahoma, 1977); and Matt Warner, *The Last of the Bandit Riders* (New York, 1940).

Descriptions of turn-of-the-century South America came chiefly from Enrique Agullo Bastias, *Antofagasta: la ciudad heróica* (Antofagasta, 1979); James Bryce, *South America: Observations and Impressions* (New York, 1912); Pierre Denis, *The Argentine Republic: Its Development and Progress* (London, 1922); Juan Panades Vargas and others, *Antofagasta: Una historia en imágenes* (Antofagasta, 1979); James R. Scobie, *Buenos Aires: Plaza to Suburb, 1870–1910* (New York, 1974); J. B. Thacher, "Patagonia" (November 1897), "Some Geographic Features of Southern Patagonia" (February 1900), and "The Indian Tribes of Southern Patagonia" (January 1901), *National Geographic*; Ricardo

Vallmitjana, *Bariloche, My Home* (Buenos Aires, 1989); and Bailey Willis, *Northern Patagonia* (New York, 1914).

Information about the bandits' activities in South America came from numerous sources, including Hiram Bingham, *Across South America* (Boston, 1911); Arthur Chapman, " 'Butch' Cassidy," *The Elks Magazine* (April 1930); Bruce Chatwin, *In Patagonia* (New York, 1977); the COMIBOL Archives in Tupiza, Bolivia; *Expediente de los Sucesos del 6 y 7 de 1908 en San Vicente, Sud Chichas, Bolivia, Archivo del Juez Instructor, Juzgado de Instrucciones, Tupiza, Bolivia*, collection of Roger McCord; A. G. Francis, "The End of An Outlaw," *The Wide World Magazine* (May 1913); the writing of James D. Horan, especially *The Authentic American West—The Outlaws* (New York, 1977) and (with Paul Sann) *Pictorial History of the Wild West* (New York, 1954); the Pinkerton Detective Agency's Archives, now located in Van Nuys, California; the files of the Policía del Territorio Nacional de Chubut; Hugo Pratt, *"Patagonia, La Ultima Pista," Cuadernos de Fierro*; Osvaldo Topcic, *"¿Butch Cassidy Cabecilla del Robo? Asalto al Banco de Tarapacá," Todo es Historia*; the U.S. National Archives, Record Group 84, "Bolivia Post Files" and "Chile Post Files" (Washington, D.C.); and Glyn Williams, *"Butch Cassidy y Sundance Kid a Llwyd ap Iwan," Ffenics* (Summer 1972).

Of the hundreds of newspapers, magazines, and journals that reported Butch and Sundance's crimes, their deaths or survival, and the aftermath of the San Vicente exhumation, the following periodicals were particularly useful; the *Buenos Aires Herald, La Prensa, La Nación, El Clarín,* and *Caras y Caretas* (Buenos Aires); *El Antártico* (Río Gallegos); *El Mercurio* (Antofagasta); *El Chorolque* (Tupiza); *La Prensa* (Oruro); *La Mañana* (Sucre); *The Wide World Magazine* (London); *The Globe and Mail* (Toronto); the *Chicago Tribune*; *The Denver Post*; the *Daily Yellowstone Journal*; the *New York Sunday Mirror Magazine*; the *Ozona Kicker*; *True West*; *Old West*; the *NOLA Quarterly*; *The Washington Post*; and the *WOLA Journal*.

Dan and I have written a number of articles that discuss particular aspects of our research in detail. Overviews of the bandits' last years can be found in "The Aramayo Mule," *South American Explorer*, February 1988, and "Running Down a Legend" or *"En Busca de una Leyenda," Américas*, vol. 42, no. 6, 1990–91. Etta's background and fate are addressed in "Etta Place: Wild Bunch Mystery Lady," *English Westerner's Society Tally Sheet*, Spring 1993. The results of the forensic testing are described in "Grave Doubts," *South American Explorer*, June 1993.

363

The Argentine holdups are discussed in "Wild Bunch Holdup in Argentina," *NOLA Quarterly*, Winter 1987–88; *"Muchas Cuentas y Pocos Datos,"* *Feed Back*, May 1989; "The Wild Bunch in South America: Escape from Mercedes," *WOLA Journal*, Spring-Summer 1991; "The Wild Bunch in South America: Closing in on the Bank Robbers," *WOLA Journal*, Fall-Winter 1991; "The Wild Bunch in South America: Merry Christmas from the Pinkertons," *WOLA Journal*, Winter-Spring 1992; "The Wild Bunch in South America: A Maze of Entanglements," *WOLA Journal*, Fall 1992; "Leaving Cholila," *True West*, January 1996; and "Wild Bunch Neighbors on Argentine Hotseat: Revelations from Long-Lost Chubut Police File," *WOLA Journal*, Spring 1996.

The evidence that Butch and Sundance died in Bolivia is laid out in "Showdown at San Vicente," *True West*, February 1993; *"Butch Cassidy en Bolivia: Su Vida y Su Muerte,"* *Opinión* (Cochabamba, Bolivia), February 6, 1992; "Did Butch and Sundance Die in Bolivia?" *Bolivian Studies*, vol. IV, no. 1, 1993; *"¿Murieron Butch Cassidy y Sundance Kid en Bolivia?"* *Opinión* (Cochabamba, Bolivia), March 10, 1994; "Truly Western: Gnawing Questions," *True West*, April 1994; and "Death in the Andes: The Last Days of Butch Cassidy and the Sundance Kid," *Wild West*, forthcoming.

William T. Phillips's claim to be Butch Cassidy is debunked in "The Many Deaths of Butch Cassidy," *Pacific Northwest*, July 1987; "Where Lies Butch Cassidy?" *Old West*, Fall 1991; and "Letters to the Editor: No Closer than Spokane Map Room," *WOLA Journal*, Winter-Spring 1995. The Barrientos-expedition hoax is exposed in "Skulduggery: Three Men and a Shovel," *True West*, December 1993.

ACKNOWLEDGMENTS

SPECIAL thanks go to Dan Buck, who led me into the adventure and stayed by my side all the way; to Francisco Vega Avila, who opened the door to our discoveries in Bolivia; to Roy Querejazu Lewis, our guardian angel, who kept us from going over many a cliff; to Celia Beloso, Raúl Cea, Marcelo Gavirati, Francisco Juárez, Osvaldo Topcic, and Ricardo Vallmitjana, who helped us sift the facts from the fables in Argentina; to Donna and Paul Ernst, who welcomed us into Sundance's family; to Roger McCord, who shared the judicial inquest file with us; to Larry Pointer, who lent us the research files from his book *In Search of Butch Cassidy*; to Jim Dullenty and Ed Kirby, who steered us through the mazey world of outlaw history; to Clyde Snow, who made the exhumations happen; to Jesús Rosas Zúniga, who kept the hot showers and the *singani* flowing; to Froilán Risso, who helped the legend grow; to Félix Chalar Miranda, Fabiola Mitru de Sánchez, and Beatriz Michel Torres, who took up where we left off; to Tom Walsh and Mariano Goñi, who untangled our translations; and to Mary Cadette, Ann Wright Dye, Lavinia Edmunds, and Dorothy A. Meadows, who improved the manuscript with insightful suggestions. Thanks also to my editors, Pete Wolverton and Bill Thomas; my agent, Nina Graybill; and the hundreds of others who contributed to this project:

IN ARGENTINA—Melania Acevedo, Yolanda Acheritobehere de Cea, Griselda Bonansea de Daher, Ana Marie Braun, Armando Braun, Miguel Calderón, Inés Cea, Edmundo Cornejo Tello, Carlos Chiaraviglio, Simón Daher, Victoria Demarchi de Goñi, Patricia Fierro, Alejandro Godoy, Luz Goñi, Santos Goñi, Ronald Hansen, Enrique Himschoot, Carol Jones, Edith Jones, Matthew Henry Jones, Cristina Juárez, Erika Kerwitz, Catherine Kennard, George Kennard, Julio Luqui Lagleyze, Henry Maples, Cecile Meadows, Ricardo Moura, Rodríguez Muñoz, Sara Josefina Newbery, Douglas C. Norman, Gloria Padros de Henning, Juan Carlos Ocampo, José Pedro Pico, Justo Piernes, Tegai Roberts, José Romero, Luis Ruiz and family, Hans Schultz, Aladín Sepúlveda, Alberto Sheffield, Oscar Sheffield, Samuel Tarnopolsky,

Paul Truitt, Jorge Vallerini, Michael Weaver, Elspeth Whewell, Roger Whewell, Luisa Zuberbuhler, the American Chamber of Commerce in Argentina, the *Buenos Aires Herald,* Casa Pardo, the Instituto Geográfico Militar, Lloyds Bank, the Museo Histórico Regional in Gaiman, and the Museo de la Patagonia Francisco P. Moreno in Bariloche.

IN BOLIVIA—Alfonso Aguirre, Xavier Albó, Willy Alfaro, Alberto Andre, Dionisio Aparicio, Teresa Aramayo, Hector Arandia, Isabel Arce, Roberto Arce, Pedro Barbery Arzabe, Josep Barnadas, Humberto Bernal, Isaura de Bolívar, Prudencio Bolívar Mamani, Abon Borda, Hector Burgos, Juan Cabrera, Pedro Castro, Raúl Castro, Guillermo Clavijo, Rosemary Clavijo, Jennie Cosio de Mejía, Alfonso Crespo, Jorge Crespo Velasco, Carmen Diaz de Poklepovic, Antonio Eguino, Laura Escobardi de Querejazu, Jorge Eyzaguirre Durán, Anastacio Flores, Fernando González Quintanilla, Javier Gisbert, Wálter Gutiérrez (in Telamayo), Wálter Gutiérrez (in Tupiza), Werner Guttentag, Jaime Guzmán Balza, Gloria Hall, Alberto Jara, Leon Kirmayer, Dorothy Lewis de Querejazu, Rodolfo Lisarazu Pantoja, Oscar Llano Serpa, Víctor Maldonado Guzmán, Guillermo Manning Trigo, Mario Mariscal, Froilán Martínez, Peter McFarren, Alfredo Mejía, Jaime Méndez, Wilson Mendieta Pacheco, Gunnar Mendoza, Samuel Mendoza, Carlos Michel, Gastón Michel Alfaro, Manuel Mitru, Adolfo Monje Palacios, Aida Moreno de Claros, Carlos Eduardo Mostajo Silva, Juan Mogro Mogro, Mario Montaño Aragón, Antonia Nina, Ciprián Nina, Javier Nuñez de Arco, Alberto Oño, Fermín Ortega, Armando Pagano, Roger Pando Viamontt, Marta Paredes, Antonio Paredes-Candia, David M. Pereira Herrera, Fernando Peró Diez Canseco, Boris Poklepovic, Wálter Porcel, María Olga Querejazu de Achá, Jorge Querejazu Calvo, Roberto Querejazu Calvo, Stewart Redwood, Toribio Risso, Dionisio Romero, Carmen Rua, Dora Salazar Burgos, Francisco Salazar Tejerina, K. Schwenn, Juan Siles Guevara, José E. del Solar, Oscar Soria, Pedro Susz, Verónica Tellería, Marcelo Thórrez López, Felipe Tredinnick, Elvira Ukra, Edgar A. Valda Martínez, Juan Valdivieso, Angel Vargas, Aquiles Jorge Vargas, Joaquín Vargas, Pancho Vargas, Ross Mery Vega, Luis Velasco Crespo, Iris Villegas, Augusto Wáyar Fernández, Amigos del Libro, the Archivo del Ministerio de Relaciones Exteriores y Culto, the Archivo Histórico de La Paz, the Archivo Histórico de Potosí, the Banda Espectacular de Poopó, the Biblioteca de la Universidad de San Andrés, the Biblioteca del Congreso, the Biblioteca Municipal in La Paz, the Biblioteca Municipal in Oruro, the Biblioteca

Municipal in Tupiza, the Biblioteca Municipal in Uyuni, the Casa de Cultura in Tupiza, the Consejo Nacional Autónomo de Cine, the Corporación Minera de Bolivia, the Embajada de la República Federal de Alemania, the Fuerzas Armadas de Bolivia, Gisbert y Cia., the Junta Municipal of Tupiza, the Ministerio de Interior, *La Opinión* in Cochabamba, and the U.S. embassy.

IN CANADA—Alan Boras, Lynn Bullock, Simon Evans, Simon Graus, Douglas Minor, Lindsay Moir, Roanne Mokhtar, Gordon Muir, Bob Oberg, Ron Ostrum, Colin Rickards, Gord Tolton, Isabel Vincent, Vicky Kelly Williams, George F. W. Young, the Calgary Police Service Museum Society, the Environment Canada Parks Service, the Friends of the Mounted Police Museum in Regina, the Glenbow Institute in Calgary, the High River Historical Society, and the National Archives.

IN CHILE—Bernardino Bravo Lira, Patricia Cerda, Félix Colque, Horacio Chávez Zambrano, Germana Fernández, Juan Figueroa, José Antonio González Pizarro, Jorge Lyons Meléndez, Ximena Morena, Felicindo Muñoz, Victoria Roepke, Ricardo Valenzuela, Gisela Von Muhlenbrock Michaelis, the Antofagasta (Chile) and Bolivia Railway P.L.C. in Antofagasta, the Archivo Nacional, *El Mercurio* in Antofagasta, and the U.S. embassy.

IN THE UNITED KINGDOM—Barry Ackroyd, Peter Ayers, Andrew Barnard, Mike Bell, Jeff Burton, Anne Cafferky, Mandy Chang, Bruce Chatwin, Andy Doonan, David Dugan, Nigel Gallop, Stuart Hodsell, Jim McGowne, Rose Mitchell, Roy O'Dell, Claire Sawford, Steve Standen, Tom Wanless, Stephen Yates, Bertram Rota Ltd. Booksellers, the English Westerners' Society, the Public Record Office, the Royal School of Mines, and Windfall Films in ENGLAND, Sheena Aradale, Ian Brown, Elizabeth Cameron, James Dempster, E. Duncan, Maurice Fleming, Ian Keillar, James McGowne, Diane Morgan, David Reid, Alistair Smith, Leslie Smith, Mary Snowie, David Stevenson, David Toulmin, the *Aberdeen Evening Express*, the *Aberdeen Leopard*, the *Aberdeen Press Journal, The Scots Magazine*, and the University of Aberdeen's Centre for Scottish Studies in SCOTLAND; and P. W. Davies, Len Howell, Mrs. Non Jenkins, Mrs. S. H. Lloyd, Catrin Morris, Glyn Williams, the County Council Education Department in Mold, and the National Library of Wales in WALES.

IN THE UNITED STATES—Joe Allen, Caroline Aller, James C. Aller, Ruth Aller, William Aller, Kathyrn Allison, Nyal Anderson, Charles Arnade, Frank Arnall, Brent Ashworth, Henry Asin, Ronald

Bachman, Johanna Baker, Pearl Baker, Shirley Baker, Richard Baker, Bates, Gerard Béhague, Alfred Bingham, Bill Bixler, Elizabeth Blake, Joe Blake, Joy Bland, Peter Blodgett, Alexis Boles, Chris Boles, Hank Bowers, Jean Brainerd, Carl Breihan, Allan Brewer, Cindy Brown, James Burns, Doris Burton, Dan Callan, Andrea Camp, Charlie Camp, Leslie Campbell, Richard Canada, Fred Caploe, Barbara Carlson, Bill Casaday, Sey Chassler, Bob Chatten, Geniece Childress, Sandra Childress, Emmett Chisum, Patricia Churray, Eldon Clark, Lawrence Clayton, Charles Coffin, Melvin Cohen, Burt Collins, Dick Collins, Glen Cook, John Byrne Cooke, Constance Cooper, John Coyne, Gregory Craig, Joanne Kingsbery Craig, Don Crane, Bart Cravella, Gart Crowdus, Ken Cummins, Clifford Cutler, Marsha Lea Daggett, Fred Dahlinger Jr., Eliseo Da Rosa, Cynthia Davidson, Kathryn Derry, Peter DeShazo, Elliott Dickler, Bill Doty, Warwick Downing, Mary Duffeck, Bill Duncan, Gareth Dunleavy, Lisa Dunn, Margaret Dvorken, Phillip Earl, O. Frazelle Edwards, Barbara Ekker, Rafael Elias, Catherine Engel, Douglas Farah, Paul Fees, John Ferguson, Jane Fish, Scott Forslund, Craig Fouts, Cynthia Fox, Edward Fox, Kristine Fredriksson, Samuel Freeman, Eduardo Gamarra, Pilar Garffer, Mary Garman, Sam Gary, Eleanor Gehres, Florean Geiger, Jay Gibson, Charlene Gilbert, Paul Goaz, William Goldman, Stella Graham, Wayne Graham, Howard Greager, Don Green, Judy Green, Michael Green, Nonie Green, Paolo Greer, Gene Gressley, Jeanne Griffiths, Milton Gustafson, Bruce Haase, E. A. Haine, George Waverly Hall, Maxine Halprin, Carl Hansen, Robert Hardison, W. P. Hardison, Chan Harris, Dane Hartgrove, Bob Hartman, Peter Hassrick, Richard Boyd Hauck, David Hays, Cathy Healy, Ed Healy, Robert Healy, Kitty Bowe Hearty, Ruth Heitfeld, Harry Hellerstein, Cathy Henderson, Douglas Henderson, Denise Hibary, Emmett Hoctor, Colette Hodge, Lilian Holesovsky, Brian Horan, Gary Horan, Charles Hoyt, M. S. Huber, Mrs. Lester Hunt, Jocelyn Hutchens, Ian D. Hutcheon, Ian L. Hutcheon, Nancy Hutcheon, John Inslee, Deborah Jakubs, Kenneth Jessen, John Joerschke, Richard Johnston, Kathyrn Jones, Kristine Jones, Thomas Jones, William H. Jones, Zbigniew Kantorosinski, Kathy Karpan, Howard Karno, Jan Karski, Mike Kelsey, Harold Kelshaw Jr., Scott Kennett, Jesse Cole Kenworth, Jeannie Kihm, John Kline, Susan Koelble, George Kopp, Kristine Krueger, Thomas Kyle, Bruce Lamb, John Lamb, Harold Lasiter, Linda Lebsack, Jeff Legg, Solomon Lieb, Michael Lieberman, Florence Lind, Rebecca Lintz, Robert Litjens, Michael Lofaro, William Lofstrom, Barbara Loken, Bill Longabaugh, James Blair Lovell, John Lovett, Leila Lowry, Nancy Lyon, James Mack, Bill Mackin, Steve Marsters, Gary Marx, A. D. Mastrogiuseppe, Arthur Matz, Patricia Maus, Sam Maynes, Helene McAllister, Carolyn McBryde, Burney McClurkan, Loren McIntyre, Cynthia McKee, Norman McKee, Kevin McKelvey, John McLaughlin, Faith McMenemy, Louise McReynolds, Ralph Mecham, Rebecca Read Medrano, Raymond Merrick, Leon Metz, Rick Miller, Joe Mode, Don Montague, Linda Moore, Alan Moorehead, William Morgan, Frank Morn, Doug Morris, Emil Moschella, Martin Murphy, Charles Murray, Patti Myers, Ann Nelson, Ernesto Newbery, Thomas Newbery, Conrad Newman, Donna Nielson, Peggy Noonan, Dick North, Kathy Oakes, Thomas O'Brien Jr., Kathleen Ochs, Stan Oliner, Lee Olson, George O'Neill, R. Orozco, Stanley Pahr, Skip Palenik, Chuck Parsons, Ricardo Pastor, Richard Patterson, Allesen Peck, Debbie Pepper, Florencia Peró Urquidi, Patricia C. Petty, J. S. Pierce III, Doris Platts, Billy Posey, Barclay Prindle, Dermot Putgavie, Dirk Raat, Richard Rattenbury, Marvin Rennert, David Hall Rhys, Jim Rich, Joseph Richey, William Ritcher, Wright Rix, Tim Rogan, Kate Roth, Duke Ryan, Lewis Sadler, Annamarie Sandecki, Kristin Sandefur, Ann Schmidt, Dick Schmidt, Judy Schmidt, Robert Schmidt, Beth Schneider, Jim Schroeder, Pat Schroeder, Blanche Schroer, William Seegmiller, James Sherman, Cristie Silva, Julio Silva, Alan Simpson, Peter Simpson, Richard Slatta, Duane Smith, Gladys Soto, Arthur Soule, Lisa Stevens, John Stewart, Rick Stewart, N. S. Stirman, Simon D. Strauss, Eleanor Sweaney, Nina Taylor, Barry Tharp, Debbie Tharp, Linda Thatcher, Letitia Thompson, Dan Thrapp, Sammy Tise, Gary Topping, Gary Ubelaker, Paul Vanderwood, Lance Vanzant, Claudia Vargas-Sherwood, Warren Vinson, Greg Vistica, Beth Walker, Larry Walker, Stephanie Walker, Barbara Walton, Gary Warner, Joyce Warner, Mary Watt, Jenny Watts, Jerry Weddle, Terry West, Theodore Willis, Allen Woll, Mitchell Yockelson, Nanci Young, Sally Zanjani, David Zeigler, the Academy Foundation of the National Film Information Service, the American Antiquarian Society, the American Bankers Association, *Américas,* the Amon Carter Museum, the Angelo State University's Porter Henderson Library, ASARCO, Asman Custom Photo Service, *Bolivian Studies,* Browning, the Buffalo Bill Historical Center, the California State Archives, the Chico (Texas) Library, the Circus World Museum, the Colorado Historical Society, the Colorado School of Mines, Colt Manufacturing Company, Columbia University's Butler Library, Cosgrove/Meurer Productions, CPP/Pinkerton, the Crockett County (Texas) Historical Society, the Delaware Bureau of Archives and Records Management, the Denver and Rio Grande Western Railroad Company, the Denver Public Library's Western History Department, the Descendants of David Crockett, *The Elks Magazine,* the Embassy of Bolivia, the Embassy of Chile, the Fayette County (Texas) Historical Society, the Federal Bureau of Investigation, the Fort Worth Public Library, the *Forth Worth Star-Telegram,* the Historical Society of Delaware, the Historical Society of Michigan, The Huntington Library, the International Association of Chiefs of Police, the Johnson County (Wyoming) Library, the Knox County (Tennesee) Public Library System's McLung Historical Collection, the Latin American Paper Money Society, the Lenawee County (Michigan) Historical Society, the Library of Congress, the National Archives and Records Administration, the National Association for Outlaw and Lawman History, the National Cowboy Hall of Fame & Western Heritage Center, the National Geographic Society, the Nebraska Historical Society, the Nevada Historical Society, the New York Public Library, the Nita Stewart Haley Memorial Library, *Nova*/WGBH, the Oklahoma Office of the Chief Medical Examiner, the Outlaw Trail History Association & Center, the *Ozona* (Texas) *Stockman, Pacific Northwest, RPCV Writers & Readers,* Rocky Mountain House, the St. Louis County (Minnesota) Historical Society, the San Angelo (Texas) Historical Society, the San Miguel County (Colorado) Historical Society, the Smithsonian Institution National Museum of American History, the South American Explorers Club, the Steamboat Springs (Colorado) *Pilot,* the Telluride (Colorado) Chamber Resort Association, the Texas State Library, Texas Tech University's Southwest Collection, Tiffany & Co., Twentieth Century–Fox Film Corporation, the University of California at Los Angeles Library, the University of Colorado's Norlin Library, the University of Oklahoma Library's Western History Collections, the University of Texas (Austin) General Libraries and Humanities Research Center, the University of Utah's Marriott Library, the University of Wyoming's American Heritage Center and International Archive of Economic Geography, the USDA Forest Service Office of Public Affairs, the U.S. Postal Inspector, the Utah State Historical Society, the Western Outlaw-Lawman History Association, Western Publications, the Wyoming Secretary of State, the Wyoming State Archives, and the Yale University Library.

IN OTHER COUNTRIES—Kevin Healey in AUSTRALIA; Jane Ellen Stevens in BALI; Elizabeth Nyers in BELGIUM; Gino Bauman in COSTA RICA; Juan German-Ribon in FRANCE; Detlef Knappe in GERMANY; D.O. Luanaigh, Kathleen Lydon, Eileen Malloy, the National Library of Ireland, and the U.S. embassy in IRELAND; and Robert Eaton and the U.S. embassy in PARAGUAY.

INDEX

Numbers in bold refer to maps.

Abaroa Regiment, 134, 137, 145, 164, 348–349
Abra Negra, **220**, 232, 233
Acevedo, Melania, 3–6, 9
Acheritobehere de Cea, Yolanda, 5–7
Alaska, 108–109, 114, 206
Alberta, **18**, 31
Albornoz, Francisco, 69
Albuquerque, New Mexico, 108
Alcoreza, Lieutenant, 166, 233–234
Alfaro, Willy, 344–345, 354, 356
Aller, Frank, 80, 127–129, 134, 137–139, 182–183, 187, 189, 191, 195–196, 198–199, 243, 271, 273–274
Aller inquiry, 127–129, 137–139, 183, 227, 273
Aller report, 129, 134, 139, 169, 182, 187, 189, 243, 271, 274
Allsop, Santiago, 69–70
Alma, New Mexico, **18**, 33
Almona, Bolivia, 149, **220**, 232, **330**
altiplano, 88–91, 99, 135, 141, 143–144, 193, 212, 221, 278, 299, 324
    animals, 90, 93–94, 141, 148, 150–151, 173–177, 213, 221, 240–241, 299
    vegetation, 90, 141, 148, 150–151, 156, 173–177, 213, 240
American Bankers Association, 43
Américas, 246, 251
Amnesty International, 282
ancianos, 158, 200
Anderson, Nyal, 133
Andes Mountains, ix, xii, 1, 3, 11, 40, 53, 59, 70, 74, 76, 82, 88, 93, 106, 109, 111, 116, 144, 150, 180, 247, 281, 313
Antártico, El, 67–68, 363
Antofagasta, Chile, 79–80, **87**, 88, 127–129, 164, 168, **172**, 173, 177–196, 226, 251, 273–274, 362
    cemetery, 189–190
    conservador y archivero, 182, 184
    early 1900s, 79, 88, 179–180, 189–190, 192
    immigrants, 179–180, 182, 189–190
    jail, 87, 182
    juzgado, 184, 187–189, 192
    newspaper, (see *El Mercurio*)
    train to Oruro, 88–91
Antueno, Julio O. de, 12, 63
ap Iwan, Llwyd, 43–44, 51, 59–60, 210
Aramayo, Avelino, 166
Aramayo, Félix Avelino, 149, 161
Aramayo, Fernando, 224
Aramayo, Francke y Compañía, 101, 134, 138, 140, 147, 155, 159, 161–163, 166, 168, 195, 222, 225–226, 229–232, 235–238, 261–263, 266, 268–269, 349
Aramayo, José Avelino, 158
Aramayo, Liborio, 168
Aramayo, Manuel E., 166, 168, 222, 229, 235–237
Aramayo, Teresa, 224–225
Aramayo family, 149, 158, 162, 168, 195, 224–225
Aramayo holdup, 101–102, 131, 133–135, 138, 148–149, 155, 159–160, 162–164, 166–167, 171, 193, 211, 225, 227–233, 235, 237–238, 240–

Aramayo holdup (*cont.*)
    243, 250, 263, 265–266, 273,
    342–345, 348–351, 356
  bandits, 131–135, 138, 143, 147,
    149, 152, 155, 159–160, 163–
    168, 182, 193, 210–212, 214–
    215, 222, 225–226, 228–236,
    238, 241–243, 253, 261–263,
    269–270, 272–273, 278–280,
    309, 345, 351
  escape route, 166–167, 222, 230–
    231, 233–234, 241, 257, 272–
    273, 343, 345, 349–361
  inside information, 229–231, 236–
    237
  mule, 102–103, 107, 134, 149, 152,
    163–164, 166, 168, 228, 231,
    263, 271, 349–350
  posses, 131, 133–135, 149, 151,
    159–160, 162, 164–167, 212,
    230, 233–234, 242, 261, 264–
    267, 350, 352
  reward, 166, 168–169, 238, 268
Aramayo papers, 149–150, 154–155,
    159–164, 166–167, 169, 182,
    221–224, 227–237, 246, 259–
    261, 272, 342
Arandia, Hector, 216–217
Arce, Isabel and Roberto, 139–140
Argentina, **viii**, x–xii, **1**, 2–17, 19, 37,
    39–61, **62**, 63–86, **87**, 94, 101,
    106, 109, 113, 119, 121, **154**,
    166, 170, **172**, 208, 225, 233,
    259, 273, 284, 296, 313–314,
    330, 331, 346–347, 351–352,
    362
  desaparecidos, 48, 207–208, 284
  early 1900s, 37, 46–48, 77
  immigrants, 6, 10, 46, 50–52, 59–
    60
Arizona, 12, **18**, 33, 108–109, 115,
    117, 120, 131–132, 206, 209
Arroyo Pescado, **38**, 43–44, 59–60,
    210

Ashworth, Brent, 133
Asin, Henry, 31, 304, 314, 318–319
Atacama Desert, 88, 144–145, 172,
    176–179, 196–197, 207, 282
Atocha, Bolivia, 107–108, **130**, 147–
    148, 150, **154**, 155, 166, 213,
    220, 250, 339
Atuel River, **62**, 84
Ayers, Charles, 302

Baggs, Wyoming, 35, 108
Bahía Blanca, Argentina, 41, 43, 45,
    62
Baja Caracoles, Argentina, 73
Bajo de la Leona, 68, 75
Baldwin, Harry, 114–115
Banco de la Nación (Trelew), 63
Banco de la Nación (Villa Mercedes),
    63, 80–85
Banco de Tarapacá y Argentino
    Limitado, 63, 65–68, 78, 363
Bandit Invincible, 116, 118
Bar U Ranch, 31
Bariloche, Argentina, **1**, 5, 14, 16, **38**,
    49–54, 56–59, **62**, 73, 247, 363
Barran, Manuel, 266
Barrientos, René, 117–118, 214, 311–
    314
Bass, Harry, 31
Bassett, Ann, 113, 120, 331–332
Bassett, Herbert, 22, 331
Bassett, Josie, 22, 202–203, 331–332
Bassett Ranch, 22, 332
Beagle, HMS, 74–75
Beaver, Utah, 20
Beazley, Francisco J., 40, 42
BeBee, Hiram, 109, 122–123, 202,
    205–206, 306
Behere de Cea, Yolanda, 5–7
Belle Fourche, South Dakota, **18**, 32,
    318
Bellot, Cleto, 261–262, 266–268,
    271–272
Bennion, Hiram, (see BeBee, Hiram)

374

Bennion, Marion, 122
Benson, Alexander, 127–129
Benton, Montana, 28–29
Betenson, Lula Parker, 21, 113–114, 123, 201–203, 206, 255, 301, 362
Betenson, Mark, 255
Big Beaver, Saskatchewan, **18**, 32
Bingham, Hiram III, 130–132, 134, 363
Bishop, Arturo, 66–68
Bishop, Ethel, (see Place, Etta)
Black Hills, 27, 29, 115
Blanco River, 1
Blotner, Pamela, 208, 210, 212, 214–216, 218, 221–224, 227, 238, 240, 284
Bluford, John, 25
Boedeker, Hank, 114–115
Boles, Chris, 309, 314, 322–326, 329, 333
Bolívar, Prudencio, 285, 294, 310–311, 337
Bolívar, Tiburcio, 273, 356, 358–359
Bolivia, **viii**, ix–x, 8, 43, 51, **87**, 88–104, 106, 111–113, 116–117, 119, 121, 124–125, 128, **130**, 135–153, **154**, 155–171, **172**, 173–177, 191, 193, 208, 210–219, **220**, 221–244, 247, 249, 251, 257, 270, 273, 275–300, 307, 309–314, 318, 322, 324–325, 329, **330**, 331, 333–361
    air force, 118
    Estado Mayor, 136–137
    ministry of foreign relations, 127–129, 137–139, 273
    ministry of justice, 136, 211, 287, 293, 295
    national archives, 243, 250, 342
    soldiers, 92–93, 102–104, 107, 112–113, 132, 134–138, 149, 152, 161, 164–168, 261, 264, 266–267, 269, 309, 344, 348, 350–352, 360

supreme court, 226, 243
Bolivian embassy, 210–211, 324, 334
Bonansea de Daher, Griselda Irene, 9–10
Boren, Kerry Ross, 117, 201, 305, 311
Borges, Jorge Luis, 44
Boston, Massachusetts, 26, 120
Botaro, Angel M., 41, 63
Boyd, Bill, 123
Boyd, Frank, (see Sundance Kid)
Boyd, Mary, (see Rhodes, Mary Boyd)
Boyd Lejitimo, 193
Bracken, J. W. K., 112
Brady, (see Cassidy, Butch)
Bravo Lira, Bernardino, 185–186
Brewer, Allan, 333
Brown, H. A. "Enrique," (see Sundance Kid)
Brown's Park, **18**, 22, 24, 33, 113, 120, 331–332
Bryce, James, 37, 46–47, 362
Buena Esperanza, Argentina, **62**, 85
Buenos Aires, Argentina, xii, 3, 10, 12, 16, 40–42, 44–50, 56, 59–60, **62**, 64, 67, 78, 81, 84, 94, 117, 121, 130, 134, 173, 208, 232, 313, 362
Buenos Aires Herald, 80, 82–83, 96, 207–208, 363
Buffalo, New York, 37
Bullion, Laura, 36
Burgos, Narcisa de, 273, 356
Burton, Doris, 120, 332
Butch Cassidy and the Sundance Kid, ix–x, 19, 136–137, 249, 343–344
Butte County Bank, 32
Button, Vic, 203

Cabrera, Juan, 148, 150–151, 153, 155, 169
Calafate, Argentina, **62**, 75, 76

Calama, Chile, **87**, 143, **172**, 173,
177–178, 251
Calderón, Miguel, 2–3
Calgary, Alberta, **18**, 31–32
Calgary–Edmonton Railway Com-
pany, 31
caliche, 178
California, **18**, 35, 52, 70, 73, 109,
121, 123–124, 133, 201–206,
209, 325
Canada, **18**, 28–29, 31–32, 39, 124
Capehart, Tom, (see Logan, Harvey)
Capel, George, 120
Capraro, Primo, 5
Caras y Caretas, 64, 82, 363
Carbonera Ravine, 359
Carro family, 15–16
Carver, Will, xi, 33–36, 308
Casa de Cultura, 339
Casa de Moneda, 142–143
casa rodante, 160, 214, 217, 245–
247, 256, 321
Casasola, Bonifacio, 152, 264, 266–
268, 271
Casper, Wyoming, 110
Cassidy, Butch (Robert LeRoy Parker),
ix–xi, 2–4, 7–9, 11–15, 17, 19–
25, 27, 31–37, 39–45, 49–54,
56–60, 63–65, 67, 69–70, 72–75,
77–80, 82–83, 87–88, 90–91,
93–97, 99–117, 119–127, 129,
131–137, 140, 147–148, 150,
153, 155–156, 160, 163–165,
171, 173, 178–180, 182, 184,
189–193, 195, 200–207, 210–
211, 214, 216, 222, 224, 226–
227, 232–234, 236, 241–244,
248–257, 259, 264–266, 271–
272, 278, 280, 282–283, 288–
290, 292–293, 296, 300, 302,
307–311, 313, 315–325, 331–
333, 336–338, 340–345, 347–
350, 352–354, 356, 358–361
alias Brady, 67, 70
alias George Cassidy, 22, 24–25
alias George Low, 257, 346
alias Jim Lowe, 33–34, 101, 353
alias J. P. "Santiago" Maxwell, 93–
95, 99, 101, 127–129, 273
alias George Parker, 43, 353
alias Roy Parker, 21–22
alias James P. "Santiago" Ryan, 6–
8, 11–12, 37, 41–42, 63–64, 69
at Concordia, 93–97, 100–101
burial, 107, 111–112, 128, 139,
149, 152–153, 203, 206–207,
212, 216, 226, 265, 289, 292,
309, 316, 333, 342–343
character, 6–8, 19–23, 25, 51, 57,
78, 96, 99–100, 119–120, 131,
233, 254, 264–265, 279, 302
death reports, 4–5, 7–9, 12, 51,
101, 105–106, 108–113, 123,
128–129, 203, 206, 226
descriptions, 5, 13, 20, 23, 70, 97–
98, 265–266, 278–279, 316, 321
desire to go straight, 5, 34, 96, 255,
343
early life, 20–21
family, 20–21, 23, 113–114, 255
handwriting, 116, 119, 124, 133
health, 11
letters, xi–xii, 11, 23–25, 35, 39,
51, 53, 97–98, 116, 119, 132–
133, 250
North American crimes, 21, 24,
32–35, 49
posthumous sightings, 108–110,
113–115, 122–123, 202–204,
206
prison, 24
shooting horses, 59, 67, 82, 84
South American arrest reports, 64,
87–88
survival stories, 8, 59, 110–112,
114, 116–117, 255
trip to Santa Cruz, 97–98
Cassidy, George, (see Cassidy, Butch)

Cassidy, Hopalong, 207
Cassidy, Mike, 21
Castle Gate, Utah, **18**, 32
Castro, Pedro, 360–361
Castro, Raúl, 336–337
Cea, Manuel José, 5, 7
Cea, Raúl, 5–8
Central America, 7, 109, 276, 311
Cerro Rico, 140, 143
Chaco Pampa, Bolivia, **330**, 355, 357, 359
Chajrahuasi, 149, 161, 222, 225
Chalar Miranda, Félix, 336–337, 343–344, 353–358
Chapman, Arthur, 93, 101–102, 106, 117, 124, 333, 363
Charter, Bert, 112
Chatwin, Bruce, 117, 311, 363
Chávez, Horacio, 184–185
Chiaraviglio, Carlos, 3–4, 6
Chicago, Illinois, 41, 43, 126, 303, 317, 320
Chicago Tribune, 309, 363
Chico River, **62**, 74
Chiguana, Bolivia, **172**, 176
Chile, **viii**, xii, **1**, 3, 5, 8, 12–13, 43, 45, 51, 53, 56, 59, **62**, 64, 76, 79–80, 83–84, **87**, 88–89, 106, 119, 125, 127–128, **172**, 173, 177–179, 185–186, 189, 192, 196, 226, 243, 251, 271, 273, 282
Chocaya, Bolivia, 148, 234
Choele Choel, Argentina, **38**, **62**, 70
Cholila, Argentina, **viii**, xi–xii, **1**, 2– 12, **38**, 40–41, 43, 45, 49–51, 53–54, 57–58, 61, **62**, 63–65, 70, 75, 78–80, 83, 96, 121, 200, 259, 301, 308, 343, 358
    bandits' departure, 5, 7–8, 12–13, 49–50, 59, 63, 78–79, 96
    ranch, xi–xii, 1, 6, 11–13, 40–42, 49, 53–54, 64–65, 119, 308, 343
    Sundance's return, 80

Chorolque, 148, 150, 154, 171, **220**, 339
Chorolque, El, 342, 363
Clarín, El, 363
Christensen, Mart, 114–115
Chubut River, **38**, 41, 59, 61, **62**, 331
Chubut Territory, Argentina, xi, **38**, 40–41, 64, 70
    governor, 6, 8, 63–64
    police, 11–13, 59, 63–64, 68–69, 79
chullpas, 175
Churquipampa, Bolivia, 168
Circle Valley, Utah, 20–21
Circleville, Utah, **18**, 20–21, 112– 113, 203
Clinton, Bill, 207
Clarke, Richard, 78
Club Saloon, 33
Cobija, Chile, 196–197
Cochabamba, Bolivia, **87**, 99, 136, 211, 217, 277, 312
Cochamó, Chile, **1**
Cochamó Pass, 13–14, 45, 53
Colorado, **18**, 21–22, 26–27, 31, 34, 36, 110, 202, 331, 340
Colorado & Southern Railroad, 34
Colque, Félix, 177–178
COMIBOL, 140, 147–149, 151–152, 155–159, 162, 173, 183, 211, 214–216, 218, 221–224, 226, 249, 277, 280–281, 283, 285, 288, 336–337, 363
Comodoro Rivadavia, Argentina, 45, **62**
Compañía Mercantil del Chubut, 59
Concha, Justo P., 135–136, 138, 166– 169, 234, 236, 238, 261–262, 267–269, 271, 344
Concordia Tin Mine, **87**, 93–101, 114, 131–133, 140, 167, 250, 301
Conway, Lenore, 203
Córdoba, Argentina, 347
Cornejo, Eduardo, 83–84

Cortez, Colorado, **18**, 27, 31
Cosio de Mejía, Jennie, 224, 226
Cotagaita, Bolivia, **130**, 149, **154**,
    165, **220**, 250, 298
Cotani, Bolivia, 134, **154**, 164–167,
    171, **220**, 230, 232–234, 236,
    330
Coy Inlet, **62**, 69
Crespo Velasco, Jorge, 210–211
Crockett, John, 56
Crockett County, Texas, 9–10
Crook County, Wyoming, 27, 30
Cucho, Bolivia, 272–273, **330**, 353,
    355–356, 358
Cuello, Francisco, 69
Culbertson, Montana, **18**, 32
Curicó, Chile, 45, **62**
Curie, Marie, 111
Currie, "Flatnose" George, 32–34

Daher, Simón, 4, 7, 9
Daily Yellowstone Journal, 28, 363
Dane, G. Ezra, 107
Darwin, Charles, 74
Davidson, Art, 111, 122
Davis, Eph K., 27–28, 30
Davis, Lillie, 35, 308
Daza, Aristides, 236, 261–262, 268–
    269, 271
Deadwood, South Dakota, **18**, 30
Deer Lodge, Montana, 31
DeJournette, Dawn, 332
Delta, Utah, 108
Denver, Colorado, 97, 109, 121, 206
Desaguadero, Argentina, **62**, 85
Desaguadero River, **62**, 84
DeYoung Studio, 37, 39, 41
Dilly, Tom, 112
Dimaio, Frank, 40–42, 49, 59
diplomatic correspondence, 127–129,
    182, 246, 259
DNA, 302–305, 309, 316, 322–323,
    326, 329, 333, 338, 340
Domínguez, Alfredo, 238

Domínguez, Ventura, 81
Douglass, Earl, 331
Dr. Pierce's Invalids Hotel, 37
Dullenty, Jim, 114, 117, 124, 126,
    133, 201–205, 311
Durán, Faustino, 233–234
Durango, Colorado, 26–27

Earp, Wyatt, 108, 254
Ecuador, **viii**, 88
Edwards, O. Frazelle, 326, 329
Eguía, Eduardo, 227, 237–238, 262
Ekker, Barbara, 203
El Bolsón, Argentina, **1**, 14–17
El Maitén, **1**, **38**, **62**, 69
Elko, Nevada, **18**, 33
Elks Magazine, 101, 106, 333, 363
England, 12, 20, 55, 109, 189, 194,
    345
Erazo, Juan Félix, 272–273, 356
Ernst, Donna, 36, 302, 304–308, 326,
    328–329, 332, 362
Ernst, Paul, 36, 302, 304, 326, 328,
    332–333
Ervin, Frank, 113
Escoriani, Bolivia, 150, 155, **220**
Esmoraca, Bolivia, **154**, 166–167,
    272, **330**, 345–346
Esquel, Argentina, **1**, 10–11, **38**, 52,
    58–59, **62**, 63, 69–70
Estancia de Luna, 84
Estarca, Bolivia, **154**, 166, 272–273,
    330, 351–358, 360
Ester, Henry, 31
Eucaliptus, Bolivia, **87**
    holdups, 99–100, 143, 193, 226, 260
Evans, Robert, 8, 43–45, 60, 65, 69–
    70, 210
exhumations, 210–211, 215, 221,
    224, 239, 276, 282, 286, 296,
    302, 307, 310–313, 326, 334,
    336–342
    Barrientos expedition, 118, 214,
    311–314

Pennsylvania, 323, 326–329
permission, 210–211, 221, 224,
    239, 298, 323
San Vicente, 224, 253, 280, 285–
    293, 296, 302–303, 307, 326,
    338–339, 342

Farah, Douglas, 310–311
Farlow, Ed, 114–115
Federal Bureau of Investigation, 39,
    124
Federal Express, 334, 341
ferrobus, 140–142, 148, 155, 172,
    212–213, 278, 294–295, 298,
    336, 339
Filey, Harry, (see LaPlace, Harry)
First National Bank of Winnemucca, 35
Flourtown, Pennsylvania, **301**, 326
Folsom, New Mexico, **18**, 34
forensic evidence, 291–293, 302–303,
    308–309, 314–325, 329, 333,
    339–340
    meeting with scientists, 314–325
Fort Macleod, Alberta, **18**, 31
Fort Washakie Indian Reservation, 108
Fort Worth, Texas, **18**, 35–36, 43, 56,
    120
Fort Worth Five photo, 35–36, 78,
    206, 308
Fortín Chacabuco, 54–56
Fountain Green, Utah, 109
Fouts, Craig, 133
Francis, A. G., 110–111, 273, 302,
    345–352, 360, 363
Fredonia, Arizona, 109
French, William, 33–34, 110
fronterizas, 44, 106, 121

Gaiman, Argentina, **38**, 60
García, Mr., 80
Gardiner, John, 11–12, 121, 301
Gatico, Chile, **172**, 195–199
Gebhard, Mateo, 44, 121
Gérez, Blanca de, 8

Gibbon, Daniel, 11, 63, 69, 78–80
Gibbon, Mansel, 11, 52
Gibbons, Charley, 52, 112
Gillies, Annie, (see Parker, Annie
    Gillies)
Glass, Clement Rolla, 93–95, 132–
    133, 250, 301
Globe, Arizona, 115
Globe and Mail, 309, 363
Goaz, Paul, 302–303, 309, 314–315,
    317–318
Gobernador Gregores, Argentina, **62**,
    73
Goldfield, Nevada, 109, 111
Goldman, William, x, 20, 119–120
González, Fernando, 210–211, 324
González, Gil, 230–231, 236, 241, 263
González, José Antonio, 190
Gooldy, John F., 120
Gottsche, William, 22
Graham, Stella Seibert, 124–125
Graham, Wayne, 124–125
Grand Central Hotel Saloon, 32
Grand Junction, Colorado, 204
Granja de los Espejos, 281
Gray, Eunice, 120
Gray, William, 195
Graydon, Edward, 269, 272–273, 356
Great Northern Railroad, 31, 36
Green River, 22, 25, 332
Green River, Utah, 207
Green River, Wyoming, 106
Grey, Zane, 248 .
Grice brothers, (see Evans, Robert,
    and Wilson, William)
Gringo Huañusca, 241–242
Guadalupe, Bolivia, **154**, 163–164,
    167, 171, **220**, 232–233, 242,
    330
Güer Aike, Argentina, 68–69
Gutiérrez, Andrés, 229, 232
Gutiérrez, Gustavo, 271
Gutiérrez, Wálter (of Telamayo),
    148–150

Gutiérrez, Wálter (of Tupiza), 149, 159–163, 169, 223–224

H2 Ranch, 31
Hainer, Al, 23–24
Hallman, Bill, 305–306, 308
Hallman, Furman "Bud," 305
Hallman, Oliver, 26
Hallman, Samanna Longabaugh, 26, 37, 41, 305–307
Hamilton, Frank, 32
Hampton, Victor, 107–108, 150, 153, 195, 229
Hanby, Buck, 30–31
Hanks, O. C. "Deaf Charley," 36
Hanksville, Utah, 25, 203
Hanlon, George, (see BeBee, Hiram)
Haward, Lincoln, 63
Hazen, Josiah, 34
Hearst, William Randolph, 311
Hell's Half Acre, 35
Herminius, 37
Herring, Johnny, 106
High River, Alberta, **18**, 31, 362
Hill, George Roy, 344
Hochschild, Mauricio, 140
Hole-in-the-Wall, **18**, 32, 34
Hole-in-the-Wall Gang, ix
Hollywood, California, x, 108, 201, 205
Homestead rebellion, 254
Honda River, 150
Honorius, 42
Horan, James D., 66–67, 82, 93, 97, 101, 107, 117, 201, 250, 363
Horn, Tom, 254
Hornos, Bolivia, 156
Horse Creek, Wyoming, 23
Hotel Argentino, 67, 69
Hotel Avenida, 144, 172
Hotel del Globo, 63
Hotel Europa, 40–42, 48
Huaca Huañusca, **220**, 229–230, 233, 240–243, 263, 294, **330**, 348

Humboldt, Nevada, **18**, 33
Humphreys, Eduardo, 63
Hutchens, William Frank, 117–118, 311–314
Hutcheon, Adam, 271, 325
Hutcheon, Enrique B., 269, 271, 325
Hutcheon, Fanny, 325
Hutcheon, Ian L., 325
Hutcheon, James "Santiago," 99, 101, 131, 160–161, 195, 224, 236, 257, 271, 324–325
Hutcheon, Nancy, 324

Idaho, **18**, 24, 35, 108, 206
Ingersoll, 98–99
Ings, Fred, 31, 302
Ireland, 207, 370
Irvine, Tom, 29

James, Jesse, 20, 29, 108, 206, 305
Jara, Alberto, 214, 218
Jarvie, John, 332
John T. Murphy Cattle Company, 31
Johnnie, Nevada, 109, 203
Johnson, Everett C., 31
Johnson County War, 115, 254
Jones, Carol, 56–57
Jones, Edith, 53–56
Jones, Jarred, 53, 56–57, 59, 64
Jones family, 53–57, 308
Jordan, Fred, 302
Jordán, Nestor S., 263
Juárez, Cristina, 44–45, 51
Juárez, Francisco "Tito," 44–45, 48–51, 53, 64
judicial process, 137–139, 168, 235–237, 261–265, 267–273, 295
autopsy, 227, 238, 262–263, 268
inquest, 168, 226–227, 235, 237, 262–263, 266–268, 272, 278, 282, 291, 295, 342, 345, 358
inventory, 262, 265, 267–272, 292, 294, 319
jurisdictional dispute, 137–139,

167–168, 222, 235–237, 261–
262, 268–269
records, 137–139, 157, 184, 226,
243, 245–246, 248, 253, 256–
270, 272–274, 282–283, 295,
342–343, 345, 358, 363
Jujuy, Argentina, 347

Kansas, **18**, 209
Kantorosinski, Zbigniew, 313
Karski, Jan, 313
Kaycee, Wyoming, 32
Kelly, Charles, 75, 93, 106, 112–117,
123, 201, 250, 253, 302, 362
Kennard, Catherine, 57–59
Kennard, George, 57–59, 82
Kerwitz, Erika, 50–51
Ketchum, "Black Jack," 34
Kid Curry, (see Logan, Harvey)
Killik Aike Springs, 69
Kilpatrick, Ben "Tall Texan," 33, 35–
36, 49
Kirby, Ed, 117, 122–123, 202–203,
205–206, 306, 362
Kirby, Kaki, 202
Kloth, Bill, 203
Koelble, Susan, 326, 329
Kyle, Thomas, 126

La Americana, (see Place, Etta)
La Claire Ranch, 108
La Paz, Bolivia, **87**, 92–95, 116, 118,
121, 127–129, 135–140, 143,
162, 183, 191, **200**, 210–212,
214, 243, 249–250, 252, 269,
275–278, 285, 287, 295–300,
309–310, 325, 335–336, 353
La Quiaca, Argentina, **87**, 130, 132,
136, **154**, 167, 264, 266–267,
330
La Torre, Bolivia, **220**, 240–241
Laguna Colorada, 144, **172**, 176, 296
Laguna Verde, **172**, 173, 176, 251
Lake Argentino, 69, 74–76

Lake Ballivián, 212
Lake Minchin, 212
Lake Nahuel Huapi, 11, 50–51, 55,
70, 78
Lake San Martín, 75
Lake Uru Uru, 141, 212
Lander, Wyoming, 23, 108–109, 114–
115
LaPlace, Harry, 194–195
Las Horquetas, Argentina, 69, 72–73
Las Vegas, Nevada, 109, 181
Lavaisse, Argentina, 85
Lavina, Montana, **18**, 31–32
Lawrence of Arabia, 311
Lay, Maude Davis, 25
Lay, William Ellsworth "Elzy," ix, xi,
22, 24–25, 32–34, 112, 121,
201, 331
LC Ranch, 27
Leeds, Nevada, 112
LeFors, Joe, 35
Leleque Company, 12, 56
Letson, Roy, 93–94, 250, 302
Lezana, Julio, 8
Licancábur volcano, 176–177
Limay River, **38**, **62**, 69
Linden, (see Sundance Kid)
Lípez Mountains, 355
Llano Serpa, Oscar, 226, 243
Llave, Agustín, 165, 233
Llewellyn, Richard, 121
Lodore schoolhouse, 332
Logan, Harvey, 12, 27, 32–33, 35–36,
42–43, 45, 49, 67, 84, 96, 110,
345
alias Kid Curry, 27, 64, 273, 345
alias Tom Capehart, 110
Logan, Lonnie, 32–33
London and River Plate Bank, 42, 48
Longabaugh, Annie Place, 26
Longabaugh, Elwood, 26, 35, 304
Longabaugh, Emma, 26, 37, 41, 304,
306
Longabaugh, Florence, 304

Longabaugh, Harry A., (see Sundance Kid)

Longabaugh, Harry II, (see Sundance Jr.)

Longabaugh, Harry Thayne, (see Sundance Jr.)

Longabaugh, Harvey, 26, 37, 41, 304–305, 323, 326, 328–329, 333

Longabaugh, Josiah, 26, 308

Longabaugh, Katherine, 326

Longabaugh, Samanna, (see Hallman, Samanna Longabaugh)

Longabaugh, William David "Uncle Bill," 304–305, 325–329

Longabaugh, William Henry "Grandpop," 304–306

Longenbaugh family, 26–27, 31

Los Angeles, California, **200**, 205

Lost Soldier Pass, 34

Low, George, (see Cassidy, Butch)

Lowe, Francis, 353

Lowe, Jim, (see Cassidy, Butch)

Mackerrow, Alexander, 67–68

MacWilliams, Mrs., 58

Madariaga, 163–164, 182, 233

Madden, Bill, 27, 31

Magellan, Strait of, **62**, 63, 70, 76

Magor, Janette, 121

Malta, Montana, **18**, 31

Maltese, Corto, 8

Manso River, 13–15, 109

Mañana, La (Sucre), 135, 363

Marion, Oregon, 122

Mariscal, Mario, 337, 339–340

Marshall Ranch, 21

Marston, Otis "Dock," 106

Martínez, Froilán, 170–172

Marx, Gary, 309–311

Mason, Thomas, 128

mate, 15, 55–56, 73

Maxwell, J. P. "Santiago," (see Cassidy, Butch)

McCarty, Tom, 21, 31, 27

McClurkan, Burney, 276–277, 281, 283–288, 291–293, 298–300, 303, 309, 314, 317, 322

McCord, Carolyn, 245–248, 252–253, 257, 259, 282, 321, 324

McCord, Roger, 245–261, 266, 271–273, 277, 282–283, 290, 295, 320–321, 324, 342–343, 363

McCurdy, Elmer, 208–210

McDermott, B. V., 113

McHugh brothers, 31

McPartland, P., 236–237

Meadow Creek, 108

Medicine Bow, Wyoming, 33

Meeks, Bob, 24

Mejía, Alfredo, 224, 226, 280

Mendoza, Argentina, 45, **62**, 84–85

Mendoza, Gunnar, 250

Mendoza Province, Argentina, 82

Mengele, Josef, 207

Mercurio, El, 190–196, 363

Merrick, Ray and Grace, 202, 204

Mexico, **18**, 22, 64, 106, 108–109, 121, 140, 311

Michel Alfaro, Gastón, 157–158, 224, 280, 294–297, 336, 341–342

Michel, Carlos, 298–300

Michigan, 115–116, 123–126

Miles City, Montana, **18**, 21, 27, 29, 32

Millar, Herb, 31

Mizque Province, Bolivia, 312

Moab, Utah, 25, 111

Molly Maguires, 254

Montana, **18**, 21, 27–29, 31–34, 36, 49, 108, 110, 122, 201–202

Montana Peak hats, 54, 289

Monte, Bolivia, 360

Montpelier, Idaho, **18**, 24

Moonlight, Thomas, 30

Morales, Darío, 257

Moreno de Claros, Aida, 224, 226

Mormons, 7, 20, 21, 112, 257

Morris, Josie Bassett, (see Bassett, Josie)

Mostajo, Carlos Eduardo "Lalo," 224, 238, 281–282, 284, 289, 294–297, 336, 339, 341–342
Mount Carmel, Utah, 123
Mount Fitz Roy, **62**, 75
Mount Pleasant, Utah, 109
Mudge, Celia, 115, 123, 125–126
muerte presunta, 184, 189
Mullins, Bob, 111
Munzon, Braulio, 271
Muñoz, Felicindo, 198–199
Murray, Charles, 326–328
Murray, Frank, 134, 165, 229–230, 232–234, 236, 260–261
Musgrave, George, 121
Myers, D. J., 133

N–N Ranch, 27, 32
n.n., (see *ningún nombre*)
Nación, La (Buenos Aires), 64, 363
Nahuel Huapi, Argentina, **38**, 56, 64
National Association for Outlaw and Lawman History, (see NOLA)
National Geographic, 18, 52, 253, 305, 362
Neuquén, Argentina, **38**, 49, 56, **62**, 69–70
Nevada, xi, **18**, 33, 35, 108–109, 111–113, 203
New Jersey, 96, 205, **301**
New Mexico, **18**, 33–34, 64, 108–109
New Mexico Territorial Prison, 34
New Orleans, Louisiana, 36
New York, New York, 10, 24, 26, 37–43, 48, 60, 78, 101, 115, 120, 185, 245, 247–249, 253, 255
New York Daily Mirror, 203
New York Sunday Mirror Magazine, 65, 363
New York Times, 307, 309
Newbery, George, 40, 42, 53–55
Newman, Paul, ix, 20
Niagara Falls, 37
Nicaragua, 7, 311

Nina, Antonia, 173–177
Nina, Ciprián, 173–174, 176
ningún nombre, 48, 182, 271
nitrate industry, 79, 88, 178–180, 192, 197
    desert travelers, 196–197
    oficinas, 179, 197
Nogales, Arizona, 108
Noguchi, Tom, 209
NOLA, 200–205, 332–333, 363
    San Jose rendezvous, 201–204
    Vernal rendezvous, 332–333
Ñorquinco, Argentina, **1**, 11, **38**
North Dakota, **18**, 32
North–West Mounted Police, 31, 54
Nueva Escocia, Argentina, 84–85

O'Day, Tom, 32
O'Grady, Frank, 11–12
O'Neill, George, 39, 190
Oil Creek, Wyoming, 30
Oklahoma, **18**, 208–210, 297, 302, 314–325, 339
Oliveros, Belisario, 82
Ollagüe volcano, 176
Oploca, Bolivia, **154**, 156, 165, **220**, 232, **330**
Oregon, **18**, 109, 122, 180
Oro Ingenio, Bolivia, 156, **220**, **330**
Ortega, Fermín, 354–356, 358–360
Oruro, Bolivia, **87**, 88, 90–91, 93, 99, 101, 128, 133, 141–142, 144, 162, 193, 195, 212, 250, 267, 296, 299, 336
Oswego, Montana, 32
Ozona Kicker, 10, 363

Palenik, Skip, 314, 316, 320
Palquiza, Bolivia, **330**, 354
Pampa Chiviri, 176
Panama, 276
Pando, Roger, 211–212
Parachute, Colorado, **18**, 36
Paraguay, **viii**, 121

383

Parker, Annie Gillies, 20–21, 23, 126
Parker, Bob, (see Cassidy, Butch)
Parker, Dan, 23, 27
Parker, Ellnor, 114
Parker, George, (see Cassidy, Butch)
Parker, Max, 114
Parker, Maximillian, 20, 21, 114
Parker, Robert LeRoy, (see Cassidy, Butch)
Parker, Roy, (see Cassidy, Butch)
Patagonia, x, **1**, 8–9, 11, 18, **38**, 40, 42–43, 50, 52, **62**, 65, 67, 70–71, 73–78, 177, 207, 210, 308, 362–363
  animals, xi–xiii, 1, 3, 6–7, 10–16, 50–53, 55–57, 59–61, 69–78
  immigrants, 6, 10–11, 50–52, 59–60
  Indians, 10–11, 53, 70, 74
  roads, 12–17, 59–60, 70–78
Patiño, Simón I., 140
Paz Zamora, Jaime, 212
Pennsylvania, 26, 36, 41, 80, **301**, 302–308, 325–329
Percivals, 58–59
Perito Moreno, Argentina, **62**, 71–72
Peró, Carlos, 133–135, 160, 163–166, 168, 170–171, 211–212, 228–238, 240–243, 261, 263, 273, 278, 283, 291, 348
  inquest testimony, 263
  letters, 166, 228–237, 240, 242, 261
Peró, Fernando, 211–212
Peró, Mariano, 168, 211, 230, 236, 241, 263
Perry, Bertie, 10, 61
Perry, John "Juan Comodoro," 5, 7–11, 79
Perry Gérez, Florencia, 8–9
Peru, **viii**, 5, 43, 70, **87**, 97, 106, 130
Philadelphia, Pennsylvania, 26, **301**, 303
Phillips, Bob, 126

Phillips, Gertrude Livesay, 115–116, 124
Phillips, Laddie J., 115, 123
Phillips, William J., 126
Phillips, William T., 114–116, 119, 122–126, 202, 205–206
  background, 115–116, 123–124, 126
  claim to be Cassidy, 116, 124
  death, 115, 122–123
  death certificate, 115, 123
  detractors, 123
  handwriting, 116, 119, 124
  resemblance to Butch Cassidy, 116, 119, 126, 206
  trips to Wyoming, 114–116
Phoenixville, Pennsylvania, 26, **301**
Piernes, Justo, 67
Pinkerton, Alan, 39
Pinkerton, Robert, 39, 42
Pinkerton, William, 39, 43, 308, 345, 352
Pinkerton Detective Agency, x, 12, 17, 19, 26, 38–44, 50, 53, 57, 59, 63–66, 80, 84, 87–88, 94, 110–111, 117, 131–132, 182, 194, 200, 254–255, 272, 278, 301–302, 307–308, 318–319, 345, 352–353, 363
Place, Anna Marie, (see Place, Etta)
Place, Annie, (see Longabaugh, Annie Place)
Place, Emily Jane, 120
Place, Enrique, (see Sundance Kid)
Place, Etta, x–xi, 2, 4, 6–8, 11–13, 15, 25, 32, 36–37, 39–46, 49–51, 54, 57, 59–60, 63–64, 67, 69–70, 75, 79–80, 83–84, 88, 97, 106, 110, 120–122, 189–191, 202, 308, 311, 343
  background, x, 39, 44, 64, 120–122
  candidates, x, 36, 120–122
  descriptions, x, 5, 12–13, 41
  fate, x, 44, 88, 97, 120–122

384

name, x, 12
Place, Harry A., (see Sundance Kid)
Pleasant Valley Coal Company, 32
Pointer, Larry, 116–117, 124, 205, 362
Poklepovic, Boris, 339
Porco Province, Bolivia, 137, 139, 262
Porter, Fanny, 35–36, 308, 318
Portland, Oregon, 109
Portugalete, Bolivia, **130**, 150, 155, **220**, **330**
posesión efectiva, 184, 189
Potosí, Bolivia, **87**, 127, **130**, 136–143, 146–147, 162, 170, 237, 240, 243, 250, 298–299
Powers, Orlando W., 34
Pratt, Hugo, 8, 363
Prensa, La (Buenos Aires), 64–65, 80–84, 134, 363
Prensa, La (Oruro), 133–134
Preston, Douglas, 34–35
Price, Utah, 108, 113
Prindle, Barclay, 203
pueblo civico, 1.1, 218, 337
Puerto Deseado, Argentina, **62**, 68
Puerto Madryn, Argentina, 10, **38**, 40, 42, 60–61, 64
Puerto Montt, Chile, xii, **1**, **62**
Puerto Natales, Chile, **62**, 76–77
Puerto Suárez, Bolivia, 98
Pulacayo, Bolivia, 144, 146, 225
Pullman strike, 254
Punta Arenas, Chile, **62**, 69–70
Punteney, Walt, 32

Quechisla, Bolivia, **130**, 134–135, 144, 147–150, **154**, 155, 160, 162, 164–166, 193, 215, **220**, 227, 230–231, 233–234, 236–237, 250, 263
Quenchamali Ravine, 360
Querejazu Lewis, Roy, 211–218, 221–230, 232–235, 238–242, 277, 280–282, 284–290, 294–300,

312–314, 319–320, 322–323, 334, 336–343, 353–357, 359–361
Quinto River, 85

Ralston, Wilmer, 26
Rawlins, Wyoming, 109
Rawson, Argentina, **38**, 41–42, 49, 60–61, **62**, 64
Razón, La (La Paz), 309, 311
Red Lodge, Montana, 32
Redford, Robert, ix, 253, 305
Regan, Jim, 114, 123
Rejas, Justino, 310
Reyes, Julio, 262
Rhodes, Mary Boyd, 116, 123
Ricca, Carlos, 81
Rickard, Tex, 121
Río Gallegos, Argentina, 43–45, 62–70, 75–78, 82, 363
Río Gallegos holdup, 43–45, 63–70, 76, 82
   bandits, 43, 64–70, 75, 77–78
   escape route, 68–69, 75, 77
   posses, 68–69, 75–78
Río Mulato, Bolivia, **130**, 141
Río Negro Territory, Argentina, **38**, 67–69
Río Pico, Argentina, 8, **38**, 44
Río Turbio, Argentina, **62**, 76–77
Río Villegas, Argentina, **1**, 13–14, 16
Rios, Timoteo, 135–136, 145, 262, 266–269, 271
Risso, Calixto, 217, 324
Risso, Froilán, 151–153, 210, 214, 216–218, 246, 252, 264–265, 277, 286, 309–310, 321, 324, 342–343
Risso, Toribio, 218
Rivera, Delfín, 263, 265
Robbers' Roost, **18**, 25, 32, 52, 105, 362
Roberts, Malcom, 107, 164–165, 195, 229, 234–235, 238

Roberts, Milton, 12, 43, 63–64, 301
Roberts, Tegai, 60
Rock Springs, Wyoming, **18**, 22, 34, 108
Rockville, Utah, 109
Rogers, Will, 37
Romero, Dionisio, 224
Roosevelt, Teddy, 37, 254
Rosas Zúniga, Jesús, 144, 146, 148, 172–173, 296
Rua, Carmen, 243
Ryan, Sheriff James, 27, 29, 30
Ryan, James P. "Santiago," (see Cassidy, Butch)

Sadler, Lewis, 126, 302–303, 317
Saint–Exupéry, Antoine de, 78
Saínz, Julian, 264, 271
Salado River, **62**, 84, 121
Salar de Uyuni, **87**, **130**, 173–174, 212, 339
Salazar, Francisco, 159–160, 224, 246, 256–257, 259, 283
Salazar Burgos, Dora, 159–160, 224, 227–228, 239, 246, 294, 342, 356
Salo, Bolivia, **130**, 133–135, 144, 149, 151, **154**, 155–157, 159, 163–165, 167, 170, 195, **220**, 229–230, 232–234, 240–241, 260, **330**
Salo River, 170, **220**, 240, 331
Salt Lake City, Utah, 24, 108, 111, 133, 206
salteñas, 135, 173
San Andrés University, 135
San Antonio, Texas, **18**, 35–36
San Francisco, California, 35, 64, 79–80, 108–109
San Jose, California, **200**, 201
San Juan, Bolivia, **172**, 174–175
San Juan del Oro River, 110, **330**, 345, 349, 354–355, 357, 359
San Julián, Argentina, **62**, 68

San Luis Province, Argentina, 43, 45, 63, 78, 82–83
San Miguel Valley Bank, 21, 31
San Pedro de Atacama, Chile, **172**, 177–178, 251
San Quentin, 123
San Rafael, Argentina, **62**, 85
San Vicente, Bolivia, **viii**, ix, **87**, 101–104, 106–108, 110–112, 116–119, 124, 127–128, **130**, 133–139, 143–144, 147–149, 151–153, **154**, 155–156, 160, 162, 166–169, 175, 182, 193, 195, 210–212, 214–219, 221–222, 224–229, 234–238, 243, 246, 250–253, 260–265, 267, 269, 272–273, **275**, 276–277, 280, 283–295, 302–304, 307, 309–317, 319–320, 322–323, 325–327, 329, **330**, 331, 333–334, 336–345, 352, 358–359
after the exhumation, 309–311, 337
cemetery, ix, 107–108, 139, 149, 151–153, 210, 215–216, 252, 275, 285–291, 293, 311, 339, 342–343
grave, ix, 147, 153, 214–217, 226–227, 246, 252–253, 277, 285–291, 293, 320–322, 339–340, 342
negotiations, 286–287, 293
rancho, 216, 218, 221, 275, 283, 285, 288, 291
San Vicente One, 289–292, 294–295, 298, 300, 302–303, 307, 310, 315–326, 329, 333–342
return of remains, 323–325, 333–342
San Vicente shootout, 19, 102–104, 107, 113, 116–118, 128, 131–139, 143, 147–149, 151–152, 160, 166–169, 182, 193, 195, 212, 216, 225–226, 234–235, 243, 246, 250, 261–265, 267,

272, 275, 278, 309, 333, 342–344, 352
  attempts to confirm, 112, 116–118
  corpses, 112, 132–135, 139, 143, 146–147, 152, 168, 215–216, 226, 255, 262–265, 267–271, 278–280, 290–291, 309–310, 319, 338, 352, 358
  participants, 102–103, 112, 131–138, 145, 149, 152, 160, 166, 168–169, 193, 226, 234–235, 260–266, 268, 271, 273, 309, 344
  rifles, 132, 270–272, 344
Sánchez, Remigio, 263–266, 271
Sandino, Augusto, 311
Sandusky, Michigan, 123, 126
Santa Catalina, Argentina, 136, **154**, 225, 264, 266, **330**, 347
Santa Cruz, Argentina, **62**, 68
Santa Cruz, Bolivia, **87**, 97–98, 132, 138, 222, 250, 281, 312
Santa Cruz Territory, Argentina, 8, 67–68
Santa Rosa, Argentina, **62**, 84, 86
Santiago, Chile, **62**, 182–190, 274
  Archivo Judicial, 183–186
  Archivo Nacional, 182–187
  Registros Conservatorios, 183
Saskatchewan, **18**, 32
Sawtell, Billy, 112
Schroer, Blanche, 123
Scobie, James R., 46–47, 362
Scotland, 11, 189, 325
Seattle, Washington, 108–109
Seibert, Jeanne, 95, 97
Seibert, Percy, 93, 95–97, 100–101, 108, 112, 114, 124–125, 132, 191, 250, 255, 301
  scrapbook, 97, 124, 132–134, 250
Seibert, Stella, (see Graham, Stella Seibert)
Selcer, Richard F., 120
Sellersville, Pennsylvania, **301**, 302
Sepúlveda, Aladín, 3–4, 9

Sepúlveda, Rómulo, 3, 7
shootouts
  Río Pico, 8, 44
  San Vicente, (see San Vicente shootout)
  elsewhere, 5, 106, 121, 201, 226
Siringo, Charles A., 34
Sister City Program, 340
skull-face superimposition, 302–303, 317
Slater, Colorado, 120
Smith, Frank, (see Sundance Kid)
Smith, W., 28–29
Smith Gang, 225, 354
Snow, Clyde, ix, 207–210, 275–278, 281–300, 302–304, 307, 309–310, 312, 314–320, 322–329, 333–334, 340
Solares, Hector A., 262–263
Soldier Prince, 39, 41
solicitudes, 157–158, 186, 189, 191, 224
Solís, Ventura, 8
Solís, Wenceslao, 79
soroche, 135, 275
Sosa, Cipriano, 83
South American Construction Company, 100
South American Explorer, 18, 208
South American Handbook, 296
South Dakota, **18**, 27, 30, 32
Southern Pacific Railroad, 33
Sovén, Argentina, **62**, 85
Spiegel, Der, 307
Spokane, Washington, **18**, 109, 114–116, 123, 125
Spring City, Utah, 109
St. Louis, Missouri, 36, 64, 108
St. Paul, Minnesota, **18**, 27
Stack, Robert, 253
Star Valley, Wyoming, 24
Stewart, Arden, 332
Stover, Eric, 207–208, 210–211, 214–218, 221–224, 227, 234, 238,

Stover, Eric (*cont.*)
    240, 276–277, 280–281, 284–
    287, 289–300, 302–305, 307–
    309, 311–312, 314, 318, 323–
    325, 334
Strangeland, Charles, 353
Sucre, Bolivia, **87**, 135, 226, 243–
    244, 250, 342
Sucre University, 243
Sud Chichas Province, Bolivia, 137–
    138, 167, **220**
Sundance Jr., 121–122
Sundance Kid (Harry A. Longabaugh),
    ix–xi, 2, 4, 7–9, 11–13, 15, 17,
    19, 25–26, 30–37, 39–46, 49–54,
    56–57, 59–60, 63–65, 67, 69–70,
    72–75, 78–80, 84, 88, 90–91,
    93–98, 100–104, 106–114, 116–
    117, 120–125, 127–129, 131–
    132, 134–137, 140, 147–148,
    150, 153, 155–156, 163–165,
    171, 173, 178–180, 182–184,
    189–195, 200–202, 205–207,
    210–211, 216, 222, 224, 226–
    227, 232–234, 236, 241–242,
    244, 248–257, 259, 265–266,
    271–274, 278–280, 282, 288–
    292, 296, 300–311, 315–326,
    329, 331, 333, 336, 338–354,
    356, 358–361
  alias Frank Boyd, 80, 128, 137,
    193, 273
  alias H. A. "Enrique" Brown, 127,
    129, 137, 273
  alias Linden, 67, 70
  alias Kid Longabaugh, 30
  alias Harry A. "Enrique" Place, x,
    6, 8, 11–12, 37, 40, 41, 42, 63,
    69, 79, 194, 195
  alias Frank Smith, 257, 346
  at Concordia, 93–97, 101
  burial, 107–108, 110–111, 128,
    139, 149, 152–153, 206–207,
    212, 216, 226, 265, 289, 292,

    309, 316, 333, 342–343
  character, 7–8, 11–12, 19, 29–31,
    51, 57, 78, 94, 131, 254, 280,
    301–302, 304, 346, 352
  death reports, 5, 8, 51, 101, 106,
    108–113, 116, 128, 206, 226
  descriptions, 5, 12–13, 27, 42, 70,
    97, 122, 265–266, 272, 279–
    280, 308, 316, 318–319, 321
  desire to go straight, 5, 37, 96, 255,
    343, 352
  early life, 26–27, 96
  escapes, 27–32
  estate, 189, 191, 193, 273–274
  family, 36, 64, 80, 121, 302, 304–
    308, 318–319, 323, 326, 328–
    329, 332–333, 340
  health, 11, 37, 41, 272, 302, 307,
    318–319
  in Canada, 28–29, 31–32
  letters, 29–30, 39, 51, 79–80, 306–
    308
  North American crimes, 27–35, 318
  posthumous sightings, 109–110,
    122, 202, 206–207, 311
  prison, 30
  problem with Chilean government,
    80
  return to Cholila, 80
  survival stories, 8, 110, 117, 121,
    123
  trip to Santa Cruz, 97–98
  visits to North America, 39–42, 49,
    64, 75
Sundance, Wyoming, **18**, 27, 29–30
Swartz, John, 35–36
Swisher, James, 31

Table Rock, Wyoming, 35
Tacoma, Washington, 121
Talina, Bolivia, 168, **330**
Tambillo, Bolivia, 167
Tapaxa, Bolivia, **330**, 356
Tarija, Bolivia, **87**, 221

Tarnopolsky, Samuel, 117–118, 311–314

Tatasi, Bolivia, 160, **220**, 236

Telamayo, Bolivia, **130**, 148, 159–160, 162, 169, 211, 213, 215, 218, 222

Telluride, Colorado, **18**, 21, 27, 31, 340–341

Tennessee, 36, 42, 109, 132

Texas, 7, 9–10, **18**, 27, 35–36, 39, 43, 53, 80, 253, 318, 334

Thayne, Anna Marie, 122

Thorp, Jack, 20

Tierra del Fuego, **62**, 73, 247

Tiffany's, 37

Tipton, Wyoming, **18**, 35

Tomahuaico, Bolivia, 272, **330**, 348–350, 352–353, 356–357, 359–361

Tombstone, Arizona, 109

Toodles, 201

Topcic, Osvaldo, 67, 363

Tornapolski, Samuel, (see Tarnopolsky, Samuel)

Torres, Victor, 152, 168, 262, 267, 344

Torres del Paine, **62**, 76

Train Robbers' Syndicate, ix

Trelew, Argentina, 10, **38**, 41

Tres Cruces, Bolivia, 250

Tres Lagos, Argentina, **62**, 75

Trevelín, Argentina, **1**, 58

Tryone, Mary, 122

Tupiza, Bolivia, **87**, 101, 127–128, **130**, 131, 133–135, 137–138, 144, 147, 149–151, 154–170, 172, 195, 212, 217, **220**, 221–240, 245, 256–264, 267–269, 272, 277, 280–283, 294–298, 322, 325, **330**, 336–350, 353, 354, 356

city council, 294–295, 297–298, 336–341

COMIBOL office, 156–159, 162, 221–224, 226–237, 280

district judge, 224, 239, 256–257, 283

hotel, 221–223, 225, 238–239, 281, 294–295, 339, 353

judicial archives, 156–158, 221, 224, 238, 245, 256–259, 283, 342–343

negotiations, 294–298

old customs house, 156, 169, 224

Ukra, Elvira, 174–175

Ultima Esperanza, 69, 76

Union Pacific Railroad, 33–35

United States, ix–x, 4, 8, 10, **18**, 19–37, 39, 42, 45, 49, 52, 54, 63–64, 66, 70, 75, 79, 95–96, 101, 106, 110–111, 113–114, 116–117, 119, 121–122, 127–129, 131, 134, 136, 139–140, 143–144, 186, 189, 200–211, 214, 245, 277, 295, 302–308, 311–329, 331–335, 338, 340, 353

embassies, 116, 118, 293, 298–300, 310

Library of Congress, 18, 88, 134, 313

National Archives, 127–129, 139, 163, 363

"Unsolved Mysteries," 205–206, 246, 253

Uruguay, **viii**, 8, **62**, 106

Urulica Ravine, **330**, 357, 360

Utah, xi, **18**, 20–22, 24–25, 32, 34, 52, 106, 108–109, 111–112, 115, 117, 120, 122–123, 133, 206, 248–249, 311, 331–332

Utah State Penitentiary, 34, 206

Utah State Prison, 122, 311

Uyuni, Bolivia, **87**, 90, 101, 128–129, **130**, 133–139, 143–149, 151, 163–164, 166–168, 172–173, 193, 212–213, 221–222, 225–226, 232, 235–238, 261–264, 267–269, 274, 296, 339, 344, 351–353

Valdés Peninsula, **38**, 60
Valdivieso, Juan, 240–242
Valencia, Fortunato, 272–273, 356
Valenzuela, Ricardo, 186–187
Valier, Montana, 110
Valley of the Moon, 178
Vallmitjana, Ricardo, 51–54, 56, 363
Valparaíso, Chile, **62**, 64, 79, 192
Vargas, Joaquín, 214–215, 362
Vega Avila, Francisco, 147–150, 153,
    211, 277–278, 336
Vega family, 277, 336
Venezuela, **viii**, 106
Verdugo, Bolivia, 345–346, 348–349
Vernal, Utah, 24, 106, 109, 332–333
Vernon, Tom, 202
Villa, Pancho, 109, 311
Villa Mercedes, Argentina, 43–45,
    51, 53, 62–64, 78–80, 82, 84–
    85, 87, 96, 121, 162
Villa Mercedes holdup, 43–45, 51,
    63–64, 80–85, 87, 121, 162
  bandits, 43, 45, 64, 80–86
  escape route, 45, 83–86
  posses, 82–84, 96
Villagrán, Alejandro, 7
Villazón, Bolivia, **87**, **154**, **330**
Vincent, Isabel, 309–310
Voz del Sud, La (Villa Mercedes), 84
VVV Ranch, 27

W. S. Ranch, 33–34
Wagner, Montana, **18**, 36, 49
Walker, Joe, 105–106, 112
Walters, Ray, 134, 165, 229–230,
    232–234, 236, 260–261
Warner, Joyce, 113
Warner, Matt, 21–22, 24–25, 27, 31,
    34, 75, 112–113, 201, 362
Warner, Rosa, 24
Warsaw Uprising, 313

Washington, D.C., 18–20, 127–129,
    200, 208–211, **245**, 246–274,
    334–335
Washington Post, 310, 363
Weaver, Betty, 121, 202
Wells Fargo, 36
Wenberg, Reverend, 101
West Vincent, Pennsylvania, 26
West Virginia, 36
Western Outlaw–Lawman History
    Association, (see WOLA)
Whewell family, 55–56
Wide World Magazine, 65, 273, 292,
    345, 363
Wilcox, Wyoming, **18**, 33
Wild Bunch, ix–x, 12, 18, 24, 27, 33,
    35–36, 39, 44, 49, 63, 107,
    111, 117, 121–122, 127, 179,
    200, 202–203, 205, 207, 308,
    332
Wilson, William, 8, 43–45, 60, 65,
    69–70, 210
Winnemucca, Nevada, xi, **18**, 35
WOLA, 205, 363
Worm, the, 222–225, 228, 239–240,
    246, 280, 339, 342
Wyoming, 2, **18**, 22–24, 27, 30–35,
    37, 106, 108–111, 114, 116,
    123, 207, 284, 331
Wyoming Cattleman's Association,
    111
Wyoming Territorial Prison, 24, 30
Wyoming Writers' Project, 114

Y–probe, 309, 323, 325

Zenteno, Gumersindo, 69
Zimmer, Gustav, 320–324, 329, 334,
    338, 339, 342
Zion Cemetery, 326